Severely and Profoundly
Handicapped
Students

Severely and Profoundly Handicapped Students

Their Nature and Needs

edited by

Peter J. Valletutti, Ed.D.
Professor of Special Education
Coppin State College
and
Assistant Professor of Pediatrics
The Johns Hopkins School of Medicine
Baltimore

and

Bernita M. Sims-Tucker, M.A.
Coordinator of Severely/Profoundly
Handicapped Teacher Training Program
and
Assistant Professor of Special Education
Coppin State College
Baltimore

Baltimore • London

Paul H. Brookes Publishing Co.
Post Office Box 10624
Baltimore, MD 21204

Copyright 1984 by Paul H. Brookes Publishing Co., Inc.
All rights reserved.
Chapter 5, "Severely and Profoundly Language Impaired Students: Developmental Dysphasia," copyright 1984 by Audrey S. Hoffnung.
All rights reserved.

Typeset by Brushwood Graphics, Baltimore, Maryland.
Manufactured in the United States of America by The Maple Press Company, York, Pennsylvania.

Library of Congress Cataloging in Publication Data

Main entry under title:

Severely and profoundly handicapped students.

    Includes index.
    1. Handicapped children—Education—Addresses, essays, lectures. I. Valletutti, Peter J. II. Sims-Tucker, Bernita M., 1950– [DNLM: 1. Mental retardation.
2. Handicapped. 3. Affective disorders. 4. Child development disorders, Pervasive. WS 350.6 S498]
LC4019.S43 1983   371.9   83-7383
ISBN 0-933716-33-8

Contents

Contributors vii
Preface ix
Acknowledgments xi

Chapter 1   Introduction and Overview
            Peter J. Valletutti 1
Chapter 2   Severely and Profoundly Mentally
            Retarded Students
            David P. Wacker and Roger C. Hoffmann 11
Chapter 3   Severely and Profoundly Physically
            Handicapped Students
            Olive Scola Smith 85
Chapter 4   Severely and Profoundly Emotionally
            Disturbed and Autistic Students
            Kate E. Grosman 153
Chapter 5   Severely and Profoundly Language
            Impaired Students: Developmental
            Dysphasia
            Audrey S. Hoffnung 217
Chapter 6   Severely and Profoundly Auditorially/
            Visually Impaired Students: The
            Deaf-Blind Population
            Bernita M. Sims-Tucker and
            Corinne Klein Jensema 269

Index 319

Contributors

Kate E. Grosman, M.Ed.
Assistant Professor in Education
St. Mary's Dominican College
New Orleans, LA 70118

Roger C. Hoffmann, M.A.
Vocational Education Service
Division of Developmental Disabilities
University of Iowa Hospital School
Iowa City, IA 52242

Audrey S. Hoffnung, Ph.D.
CCC–Speech Pathology
Lic. N.Y.S.
Associate Professor
Department of Speech Communication
  and Theatre
St. John's University
Jamaica, NY 11572

Corinne Klein Jensema, Ph.D.
Educational Consultant
Writer and Editor
Silver Spring, MD 20902

Bernita M. Sims-Tucker, M.A.
Coordinator of Severely/Profoundly
  Handicapped Teacher Training
  Program
Assistant Professor of Special Education
Coppin State College
Baltimore, MD 21216

Olive Scola Smith, Ph.D.
Supervisor of Special Education
Camden City Public Schools
Camden, NJ 08101

Peter J. Valletutti, Ed.D.
Professor of Special Education
Coppin State College
Assistant Professor of Pediatrics
The Johns Hopkins School of Medicine
Baltimore, MD 21216

David P. Wacker, Ph.D.
Assistant Professor
Department of Pediatrics
University of Iowa
Iowa City, IA 52242

Preface

It is the purpose of this book to acquaint inservice and preservice professionals and paraprofessionals in education and rehabilitation with the nature and needs of severely and profoundly handicapped students. The efforts of many dedicated individuals over the past decade have brought about a public "consciousness raising" with respect to unserved and underserved low-incidence handicapped populations. Legislation and litigation have reinforced basic individual rights and have led to the development of programs and services to address the needs of persons with serious handicaps. And, although oftentimes reluctantly provided, services have been expanded and programs initiated, and such efforts continue. An advocacy movement continues to grow and its members, encouraged, pursue their goals with vigor. Yet, growth in the knowledge base and the state of the art in the field of services to severely handicapped individuals have not matched public concern and the fervor of advocates. As traditional medical labels are discarded in favor of designations based on degree of disability, adaptive behavior, and functional skills, disorder is invited: To whom, exactly, does this newly minted rubric refer and how are services to be provided?

When we, the volume editors, as teacher educators found ourselves with the awesome task of teaching introductory courses in the characteristics, nature, and needs of severely and profoundly handicapped persons, we became actively and acutely involved in organizing instructional experiences that would illuminate this population of handicapped individuals in a comprehensive and enlightening manner to students at the graduate or undergraduate level entering the field.

Finding that confusion abounded in terminology as well as in other significant dimensions when attempting to discuss severely and profoundly handicapped learners, we sought clarity. We soon grew frustrated by the need to explore and to use in our classrooms resources from a variety of articles and texts. In order to make teaching a course in characteristics more manageable both for professors and for students, we set out to develop a comprehensive introductory text that would clarify and illustrate this heterogeneous population. Toward this end, we contacted experts in the field and asked them to share in writing their keen perspectives and special insights into the subgroups of severely and profoundly handicapped students.

Each chapter of the resulting text focuses on the particular needs and capabilities of one segment of the severely and profoundly handicapped population. It is hoped that the combined wisdom of the several contributors provides a uniform and inclusive understanding of severely and profoundly handicapped individuals so that educational and therapeutic services may be offered that are built upon a substantial theoretical foundation.

Acknowledgments

We acknowledge with appreciation the outstanding chapters provided by our contributors. The quality of their work is a product not only of their scholarship and professional wisdom but of their many years of dedicated service to severely and profoundly handicapped individuals.

It is not possible to include the names of all who have made this book possible. We wish, however, to acknowledge those who have performed a variety of special tasks.

For their professional review of chapters: Lynne Cobb, Dennis Harper, Al Healy, Leta Lee, Marion Madison, Steve Maurer, Dennis Steil, and Angelo Valletutti.

For typing and retyping: Olga Cook, Harriet Grosman, Eleanor Hass, Ruth Petty, and Mary Strawhorn.

For diverse clerical tasks: Evelyn Berman, Beverly J. Gregory, Robin Griner, Vernal Harrell, Linda Holdiness, Shirley Holinsky, Barbara Hudson, Lorraine Richter, and Kayla Tollen.

The photographs that enrich this book were graciously provided by the following agencies and persons: Baltimore Association for Retarded Citizens, Inc.—Agnes Riina; The Children's Guild, Inc., Baltimore—Brenda Bridge and Stanley Mopsik; John F. Kennedy Institute for Handicapped Children—Michael Bender and Redessa Harris; Metropolitan Baltimore Hearing and Speech Agency—Jean Chapman and Holly Fleckenstein; and the Maryland State Department of Education—Deborah Sterrett.

Special thanks also go to those individuals who gave us permission to use their pictures and, in the case of minor children, to those parents who agreed to allow us to publish pictures of their children.

We also acknowledge with love the many severely and profoundly handicapped children who have enriched us and have made our professional lives exciting, challenging, and rewarding. We are especially grateful for those serendipitous occasions with these individuals that have made burnout impossible.

To my beloved late mother-in-law, Julia Breitzer, my late and dearly missed brother-in-law, Caspar Mayrsohn, and my late best friends, Sylvia Lane Miller and Dr. Jack F. Grosman.

PJV

To my late mother, Marie Elizabeth Sims, my beloved husband, Nigel Tucker, my sister, Anita Sims, and my good friend Debra Brown for their support and love.

BST

Severely and Profoundly Handicapped Students

Chapter 1

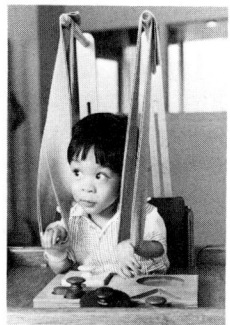

Introduction and Overview

Peter J. Valletutti

History's response to the problem of dealing with severely and profoundly handicapped individuals has ranged from pockets of commitment to widespread indifference and even planned extermination. While, in the distant past, severely and profoundly handicapped persons were more often than not abandoned to the elements and made to fend for themselves, more "enlightened" societies in recent centuries invariably warehoused severely and profoundly handicapped persons in remote and impersonal institutions. In these out-of-sight, out-of-mind receptacles, custodial care was the customary treatment, and the unfortunate "beneficiaries" of such care lived in unrelieved monotony.

While purgatorial institutions and rudimentary treatment abounded through the ages, even into the 20th century in some cases, certain isolated individuals, such as the legendary Itard in France and Anne Sullivan in the United States, dedicated themselves to improving the lives of particular severely/profoundly handicapped persons (i.e., Victor, the wild boy of Aveyron, and Helen Keller), while others endeavored to identify and treat subgroups of this low-incidence yet heterogeneous population, as demonstrated by Leo Kanner's reports from Johns Hopkins Hospital in 1943 on infantile autism. Countless other unrecognized individuals have devoted much of their lives to handicapped individuals and groups in attempts to free them from punitive and unresponsive environments that have turned substantial disabilities and deviations into severe and profound handicaps.

The efforts of the few notwithstanding, indifference to the human needs of severely/profoundly handicapped people, and especially their education, has been a social constant, whether because programs and services do not exist (or have been discontinued or reduced in the name of national defense) or because programs are ill-conceived and executed in half-hearted attempts to conform to federal and state regulations. One has only to visit a residential institution and watch severely/profoundly handicapped adults rocking in their places and staring in self-stimulatory oblivion at an inane television program, or to observe some classrooms and watch glorified babysitters engaging severely/profoundly handicapped students in busywork such as crayoning, cutting, and pasting to be convinced that education for critical functional skills and opportunities for productive diversion are being sorely neglected. Benign neglect is still neglect, and it is still destructive.

A NONCATEGORICAL APPROACH TO LABELING

Perhaps among the diverse reasons for the lack of productive services for the severely/profoundly handicapped population is the confusion about their nature and needs. To many the term *severely/profoundly handicapped* is synonymous with *severely and profoundly mentally retarded*. However, the mentally retarded subgroup of the severely/profoundly handicapped population represents just one of a range of conditions in which severity is the principal diagnostic consideration. The extent of homogeneity of this special education category is a matter of the degree of the handicapping condition and of the severity of impact on the individual's life-functioning, rather than simply being based on traditional medical classifications. Confusion invariably arises when words specifying degree—on a continuum of occurrence from subclinical to profound—are used, because of their subjectivity and the ambiguity of their boundaries. When severity is the key to categorical inclusion and when traditional medical classifications are not allowed to cloud a flexible approach to treatment, the population described necessarily becomes heterogeneous and includes all handicapping conditions that are severely and profoundly debilitating.

This is not to say, however, that the medical label can be ignored in an etiology-be-damned approach. The noncategorical approach to treating severely/profoundly handicapped individuals requires an in-depth understanding both of medical conditions and of severity. In addition, the inextricable relationship between severity and physiological and psychological status must be appreciated if programs are to be created that address the complex and varied needs of persons who require extraordinary and creative educational and therapeutic strategies.

NEEDED: A NEW OUTLOOK

In addition to the need for programs that incorporate a noncategorical approach, there is also a need for new attitudes toward teaching severely and profoundly handicapped persons. While on the surface, it might appear that minimal skills are needed by practitioners who work with students possessing minimal potential, the reality is that the more limited the student's ability, the greater is the professional challenge and need for professional expertise (Umbreit, Karlan, York, & Haring, 1980). In addition, when working with severely/profoundly handicapped students, education necessarily takes place in "asynchronous" classrooms, in which nontraditional "basics" such as mobility training, toilet training, the reduction of self-stimulatory and self-destructive behaviors, and other activities of daily living assume justified prominence in relation to academics. Such an approach is alien and, indeed, anathema to many traditional educators. Thus, efforts must be made to promote greater understanding among educators and the public if programs for severely and profoundly handicapped students are to succeed.

DISCARDING STIGMATIZING LABELS

This book endeavors to serve as a compendium of information about the major subgroups of the severely/profoundly handicapped population. A prerequisite to determining the nature and needs of these individuals is the recognition that they are, first of all, persons—persons who have, among other things, disabling conditions. This perception is not easily accomplished, since the more severe the handicap, the more likely that the observer engages in unidimensional attribution; that is, the label society assigns to the individual becomes all-pervasive, to the point that the individual is regarded as a specimen exemplifying the condition itself. Thus, cerebral palsied children, for example, capture the interest of many because they epitomize a syndrome or condition and exhibit pathological traits. A more human approach, however, mandates that such children be described as persons who have a condition identified as cerebral palsy. Of course, cerebral palsy profoundly shapes a disabled person's life and cannot be viewed as an incidental aspect; at the same time, it is crucial that the *person* not be submerged under the clinician's scrutiny.

An essential programming skill for practitioners is to look first at handicapped persons and at their abilities before exploring the dimensions of their disabilities. Such an appraisal sequence is facilitated if one remembers that disabled persons are also *able* persons, provided one is willing to discard the stigmatizing label. In recognizing their abilities, however, one must look beyond the external signs of behavior and appearance. Severely and profoundly handicapped individuals, for example, may exhibit few standards of "normality"; their bodies may be deformed, their gait peculiar, they may use sign language, use a wheelchair, rely on a white cane, and/or engage in bizarre behavior. The more severe the handicap, the greater likelihood that the observer will focus on the condition and will fear the handicapped individual and grow anxious in his or her presence. The challenge, then, is to fight the largely universal "diagnostic set" and see the total individual. Of course, the disabling elements must eventually be considered, in order that they may be eliminated or minimized, while treating them from a more holistic perspective.

It is the hope of this book that, by equipping human service practitioners with knowledge of the diverse conditions that fall under the generic term, *severely and profoundly handicapped,* practitioners will be able to use this knowledge holistically to develop and apply treatment programs for such individuals. As stated earlier, the dimensions and etiology of a condition cannot be ignored, because they possess direct implications for educational and treatment interventions.

Would-be human service practitioners must be aware, for example, that there are persons who are severely/profoundly handicapped because they are unable to comprehend spoken language sufficiently to be able to make sense of their world; who are unable to acquire spoken language to master their environment; and who, because they cannot internalize language, are unable to grow cognitively. Moreover, practitioners must understand, for example, that athetosis, a form of cerebral palsy, is characterized by involuntary, uncontrollable, writhing movements that increase upon intention, i.e., the movements are exacerbated when the individual attempts to perform a motor task such as speaking and writing. Since much of education involves, or should involve, the performance of motor tasks, teachers of students with athetosis must be aware of this untoward medical condition in order to provide them an educational program designed to meet their needs. Similarly, teachers of deaf/blind students must be acutely aware of the devastating effects of this severe sensory deprivation on a person's ability to acquire knowledge and skills; teachers must also be aware of the specialized techniques appropriate to educating this population. Educators, also, must be sensitive to the fact that communication disorders may be a sign of severe emotional disturbance. For instance, emotional maladjustment may be expressed in elective mutism, in which an individual refuses to speak to adults, despite the fact that he or she is able to speak and does so to stuffed animals, pets, or younger children. While this behavior may outwardly seem to represent a severe language disability, in reality, it manifests a deep-seated, serious problem in interpersonal relations that requires psychotherapeutic intervention. Again, in this case, understanding the etiology of the behavior clarifies the nature and objectives of therapeutic approaches.

MULTIPLE HANDICAPPED PERSONS

Discussing the nature of a handicapping condition is useless unless it aids in professional decision making that builds on an individual's strengths, corrects deficiencies, and modifies the environment in ways that will minimize the effects of a disability. While the learning discrepancies endemic to a particular subgroup of severely/profoundly handicapped persons are substantial in themselves, they are compounded by the fact that many of the conditions represent multiple handicaps. In fact, most handicapping conditions have multiple dimensions. There is no great compensatory "supermechanism" that counterbalances disabilities with abilities; rather, disabilities cluster together in blatant disregard of providential fairness. Therefore, what might not be considered a severe or profound handicap when it occurs singly becomes one when found in combination with another handicap; the two disabilities acting together cause the individual to experience significant problems in adjusting to the demands of surviving in a complex society. This multiplying effect is best exemplified when one views the severe functional handicaps experienced by deaf/blind individuals. While either deafness or blindness occurring in isolation requires programming modifications and is likely to have a serious impact on the affected individual, when both occur together they severely and profoundly interfere with the person's ability to perform fundamental activities of daily living and to provide for his or her basic safety and survival. Each of the single severely/profoundly handicapping conditions described in this book (severely/profoundly mentally retarded, severely/profoundly physically handicapped, severely/profoundly emotionally disturbed, and severely/profoundly language impaired) may occur as components of multiple handicapping conditions. It is thus possible to find individuals with multiple handicap dyads, including severely/profoundly mentally retarded/emotionally disturbed persons; severely/profoundly deaf/mentally retarded persons; and severely/profoundly physically handicapped/emotionally disturbed persons. These disabling conditions may even occur in triune or greater forms, resulting in a severely/profoundly physically handicapped/emotionally disturbed/mentally retarded/deaf/blind and language disordered person.

Multiple handicapped persons require the assistance of exceptional teachers and a host of other human service personnel including physicians who understand the dimensions of each contributory condition as they occur both singly and in interaction. While the multiple handicapped category is a recognized subgroup of the severely/profoundly handicapped population, this book addresses only deaf/blind individuals (Chapter 6). To do otherwise would require a host of chapters to discuss the many variations of multiple handicaps. However, by studying the individual chapters in this book, readers should be able to envision the program and services required by individuals with multiple handicaps.

SEVERELY AND PROFOUNDLY LANGUAGE IMPAIRED PERSONS

While the category of severely and profoundly language impaired is not usually identified as a subgroup of the severely/profoundly handicapped population, a chapter dealing with these individuals is included in this book. Its inclusion is justified if one considers that severely and profoundly language impaired individuals are massively impaired in their abilities to function socially and cognitively. Spoken language, after all, is the most human of all behaviors. Children who are unable to comprehend spoken language may behave like profoundly deaf, severely/profoundly emotionally disturbed, or severely/profoundly mentally retarded individuals. Differential diagnosis is likely to involve an exhaustive search to determine why the individual, failing to respond to oral language, does not respond to any sound, does not have any meaningful utterances, and does not behave in socially expected ways. Children with severe and profound oral expressive deficits that prevent them from expressing their needs, desires, thoughts, and feelings are profoundly handicapped in their ability to interact with others, to learn from experience, and to develop intellectually. The omission, in the past, of the severely and profoundly language impaired subgroup from the severely/profoundly handicapped population stems perhaps, from the fact that, formerly, children with aphasia (or some other medical label) were treated and managed by speech, hearing, and language therapists. Until passage of the Education for All Handicapped Children Act in 1975 (PL 94-142) most moderately to profoundly handicapped individuals, with the notable exception of sensorially handicapped persons, were rejected by the public schools and their education left to other agencies and professions. The public schools' rejection of these individuals reflected a narrow philosophy of education that distinguished education from training and from therapy. Can almost 30 years have passed since William M. Cruickshank (1956) argued against the inclusion of trainable (moderately) handicapped persons in public education? It is interesting that he characterized this newly designated moderately handicapped group as severely impaired. The education of the moderately handicapped has long been a responsibility of public education. Today, educators have not only an ethical but a legal mandate to increasingly accept responsibility for educating severely/profoundly handicapped students, including language disordered students.

INTERDISCIPLINARY APPROACHES

In no other field of special education is the need for interdisciplinary information and cooperation so great as in the severely and profoundly handicapped area. This is true not only because of the historic role other professions have played in the education/rehabilitation of severely/profoundly handicapped populations, but also because these individuals, generally, require multidimensional treatment and education (Beck, 1977). Interdisciplinary communication and cooperation is essential in identifying goals for severely/profoundly handicapped persons and in prescribing treatment priorities, sequences, and strategies, implementation processes, materials, and evaluative procedures. An important first cooperative step involves sharing information and developing a mechanism through which professionals may collectively design appropriate programs for their students. The boundaries between therapy and education become blurred when working with students who are functioning at such low levels that education for them is often what is remedial or therapeutic for less disabled students. For example: Who is to teach the self-care activities of dressing and grooming — the teacher or the occupational therapist? Who then is to teach the self-care activities of feeding and eating — the teacher; the speech, hearing, and language therapist; or the occupational therapist? Are the arm and hand movements of feeding to be left to the occupational therapist? the chewing and swallowing movements to the speech, hearing, and language therapist? and the menu planning to the teacher? In the interest of serving severely/profoundly handicapped individuals, members of each discipline, in a transdisciplinary spirit, must be willing to relinquish certain roles and assume some responsibilities not normally assigned to them. This requires a substantial degree of self-confidence and flexibility. There is never justification for less than complete interdisciplinary cooperation. A situation in which different professions compete for a piece of the action and their piece of the handicapped person is intolerable (Valletutti & Christoplos, 1977). The *total* individual, and this is true for educating nonhandicapped as well as handicapped persons, must be served.

MAINSTREAMING, NORMALIZATION, AND DEINSTITUTIONALIZATION

During the past decade, society and the fields of special education and rehabilitation have been engaged in several sociological experiments. These experiments have emanated from the growing public view that the segregation of handicapped persons, no less than that of cultural minorities, is unjust. Integration of handicapped persons in the classroom and in society in general was the goal mandated in PL 94-142, which further spurred the practices of mainstreaming, normalization, and deinstitutionalization. Placing people in the "least restrictive environment" (as stipulated in PL 94-142), i.e., the most natural environment, became the *rallying cry* for advocates of handicapped persons and champions of civil liberties (Bradley, 1978).

While integrating handicapped persons into public schools and society is an objective that no one could rightly downgrade, it is unfortunate that certain problems were not anticipated and that programs and services have yet to be developed to make the ideal a workable reality. Mildly handicapped students, for example, have been mainstreamed into regular classes without first being prepared to function in these classes either socially or cognitively. Teachers of mainstreamed classes have likewise not been prepared to teach handicapped students and often have displayed the same rejecting and hostile attitudes that their nonhandicapped students have frequently exhibited. In addition, the traditional academic curriculum has neither taken into account the multiple roles that handicapped students will be expected to assume as adults, nor has it provided for the acquisition of skills, knowledge, attitudes, and values to make independent living possible (Valletutti & Bender, 1982). The classroom environment must thus be changed from a competitive to a cooperative milieu in which teachers guide students to help each other grow, both for the good of the individual and the group. Not until some of these issues are faced will the mainstreaming ideal be more than a sociological experiment in which many innocent handicapped youngsters are too often made to suffer emotionally. Ideally, severely/profoundly handicapped students should be mainstreamed as well if one is not allowed the escape hatch of the term *least* restrictive. A restrictive environment, of any kind, given the democratic ideal, should only be operative in extraordinary circumstances. Indeed, there are some severely/profoundly handicapped individuals who are so damaged that they must be restricted to prevent, for example, self-destructive behavior. In cases where it has been possible to mainstream severely/profoundly handicapped students into public schools, a marvelous opportunity has been presented for nonhandicapped peers to experience and interact with fellow human beings whom they might not normally have the opportunity to even meet, and vice versa. Of course, the classroom teacher needs the required extra resources such as a classroom aide and specialized equipment, and nonhandicapped peers as well as teachers must be oriented and prepared for what to many is a traumatic experience.

Many deinstitutionalized severely/profoundly handicapped persons have been successfully mainstreamed into community life, especially when this normalization process has occurred under the jurisdiction and direction of an advisory group such as a chapter of the Association for Retarded Citizens. Other severely and profoundly handicapped persons, namely, the mentally ill, have not been so fortunate. Too many have been physically mainstreamed but are still lonely and isolated in an alien and unresponsive world. For many living in the community in a variety of settings (group care homes and apartments, motels, day care hospitals, halfway houses, and community foster homes), the integration cure has proved more virulent than the disease. Without adequate preparation for their new environment and lacking supportive programs and services in the community, many severely/profoundly emotionally disturbed and, occasionally, severely/profoundly mentally retarded people have been left to their own designs and have become "street people," sleeping on park benches, living out of shopping bags, or living in marginal residential settings with petty criminals, drug addicts, and other outcasts. They are easy targets for assault, robbery, and exploitation because they often carry everything they own with them, lack interpersonal skills, and do not understand the value of money, including their personal possessions.

EDUCATIONAL PROGRAMMING

A key problem in providing educational programs for the severely and profoundly handicapped population is the dramatically different curriculum required. For example, long-term and short-term objectives for this population should *not* be watered down versions of objectives identified for nonhandicapped populations. As stated earlier, an educational program for severely and profoundly handicapped students often includes aspects of human behavior and interaction that are not part of a traditional academic curriculum. To carry out such a program, teachers must operate in unfamiliar areas that were previously the exclusive province of parents or therapists; for instance, in many classrooms for severely/profoundly handicapped children, toilet training is the primary educational objective. Teachers must also familiarize themselves with a range of assistive devices such as wheelchairs, canes, crutches, and walkers, as well as hearing aids, Braille books, voice synthesizers, catheters, braces, standing tables, artificial limbs, and a plethora of other materials and equipment. Behavioral management techniques also assume unusual prominence in classrooms for severely and profoundly handicapped students, as attempts are made to enhance desired behaviors and to eliminate undesirable ones. In addition, the skill of informal diagnosis as the precursor of logical and meaningful instructional programming becomes more acute because formal procedures and tests are often not available. Then, too, the programming puzzle is often confounded by input from therapists and counselors who frequently have conflicting goals, methods, and priorities.

In summary, educational programming for severely/profoundly handicapped youngsters calls upon teachers to learn new ways of assessing; to design instructional programs for skills they have never before taught; to manage behaviors they never dreamed existed; and to organize classrooms in order that students may receive a variety of medical and other therapeutic interventions. The challenge is formidable; the task, though overwhelming, is achievable. Fortunately, many preservice and inservice teachers welcome the challenge, seeing it as an opportunity for creative teaching, while providing the rare chance to provide services to individuals with extraordinary need.

CONCLUSION

This book is written to assist preservice and inservice teachers of severely/profoundly handicapped individuals, as well as other professionals who wish to become knowledgeable advocates for this population. A basic assumption of this volume is that by understanding the nature of severely and profoundly handicapped persons, one can better serve them. At the same time, practitioners must be acquainted with current prevention, treatment, and educational programs in order to evaluate whether such programs complement students' needs and, if necessary, to design better ones. A goal of this book, then, is to contribute to practitioners' understanding of this population as a means to improving programming for them. Toward this end, each of the remaining chapters, except for the chapter on severely/profoundly physically handicapped individuals, covers the following major topics:

Definitions
Incidence
Screening, identification, and diagnosis

Etiology
Classification systems
Symptomatology
Prevention and treatment programs
Educational programs and services

Chapter 3, on severely/profoundly physically handicapped persons is organized differently because of the numerous diverse conditions it explores. Following an introductory section, the chapter discusses various physical anomalies, each according to the following format:

Description
Incidence
Etiology
Treatment

Chapters 2–6 also include study objectives (listed at the beginning of each chapter) as well as discussion questions (featured in each chapter after the references).

Finally, readers are again cautioned to keep the handicapped individual *as a person* uppermost in mind, so that while one may come to understand the relationship between a physical or psychological state and its impact on diagnosis and the provision of programs and services, one may never forget the treasured uniqueness of each individual, regardless of the severity of that individual's handicap.

REFERENCES

Beck, R. Interdisciplinary model: Planning, distribution, and ancillary input to classrooms for the severely/profoundly handicapped. In: E. Sontag, J. Smith, & N. Certo (eds.), *Educational programming for the severely and profoundly handicapped*. Reston, VA: The Council for Exceptional Children, Division on Mental Retardation, 1977.

Bradley, V.J. *Deinstitutionalization of developmentally disabled persons*. Baltimore: University Park Press, 1978.

Cruickshank, W.M. Planning for the severely retarded child. *American Journal of Mental Deficiency*, 1956, *61*, 3–9.

Umbreit, J., Karlan, G., York, R., & Haring, N.G. Preparing teachers of the severely handicapped: Responsibilities and competencies of the teacher trainer. In: P. Cegelka & H. Prehm (eds.), Teacher education and special education. *Journal of Teacher Education*, 1980, *3*, 57–72.

Valletutti, P.J., & Bender, M. *Teaching interpersonal and community living skills*. Baltimore: University Park Press, 1982.

Valletutti, P.J., & Christoplos, F. *Interdisciplinary approaches to human services*. Baltimore: University Park Press, 1977.

Chapter 2

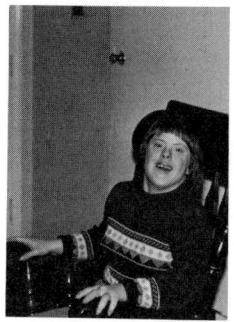

Severely and Profoundly Mentally Retarded Students

David P. Wacker and Roger C. Hoffmann

CHAPTER OBJECTIVES

After reading this chapter, you should be able to:

1. Define *mental retardation* according to the American Association on Mental Deficiency's (AAMD) definition and discuss the dimensions of its three major components.
2. Define *developmental disabilities* and discuss the several criteria of diagnostic inclusion.
3. Discuss the difference between the terms *incidence* and *prevalence* and explain the discrepancy between hypothesized and actual prevalence for the mentally retarded population whose IQ level is below 50.
4. Discuss the nature and importance of prevention in the total rehabilitation process.
5. Identify the classification levels of mental retardation and cite the approximate IQ levels for each of these classifications, according to the Stanford-Binet, Cattell, and Wechsler scales.
6. Discuss the significant biological causes of mental retardation, citing examples for each of the time frames that are traditionally used to characterize biological causes.
7. Identify the symptoms that distinguish severe and profound mental retardation.

8. Discuss the history of institutionalization and of deinstitutionalization and describe the benefits and problems that are associated with community alternatives.
9. Describe traditional and more recent approaches to vocational assessment, citing the problems that occur in each approach.
10. Identify a number of common training strategies that help severely and profoundly mentally retarded persons acquire vocational skills, citing specific skills taught to this population.
11. Describe various approaches to the development of oral and non-oral communication skills.
12. Discuss the nature of self-help skills and describe methods that will stimulate their acquisition.
13. Identify curriculum approaches to educating this population, exploring problems that confound curriculum development.
14. Discuss the nature and scope of social, interpersonal, and community living skills that are often required by this population and describe methods of facilitating their acquisition.
15. Identify frequently occurring inappropriate behaviors and the techniques used for their elimination.

Historically, severely handicapped persons, and particularly severely and profoundly mentally retarded individuals, have been isolated in large, state institutions. Apart from the mainstream of society, these individuals have been, and in many cases continue to be, taught behaviors that are nonfunctional, that is, behaviors that do not increase a person's ability to interact more effectively.

A major goal for the next decade is to provide severely handicapped individuals with skills and environmental situations that facilitate more normalized outcomes (e.g., community living, independent vocational placement, and appropriate social development). To accomplish this goal requires the coordination of many interrelated educational components. For example, public laws such as PL 94-142 (Education for All Handicapped Children Act) must be supported, advocacy groups such as TASH (The Association for the Severely Handicapped) must continue to lobby for community alternatives, and research on both what to teach and how to teach severely handicapped individuals must be undertaken and implemented.

The format of this chapter is derived from two common approaches to describing severely and profoundly mentally retarded persons. The first approach (as discussed in the Definitions and Classifications Systems sections), which might be considered a classification approach, describes these individuals based on standardized assessment measures or descriptive classification systems. Such an approach is useful to the extent that it clarifies membership characteristics and potential etiological or developmental patterns. The second approach (presented within the Educational Programs and Services section), which might be considered a descriptive approach, identifies severely/profoundly mentally retarded persons based on typical behaviors and educational approaches associated with this population. Such descriptions are necessary in order to appreciate the heterogeneous nature of severely and profoundly mentally retarded individuals. A combination of both approaches allows for the presentation of information that both unifies (e.g., intellectual performance) and separates (e.g., social behavior) individuals within the severely/profoundly mentally retarded population.

DEFINITIONS

Mental Retardation

> The term "mental retardation" covers a multitude of sins of omission, commission, and transmission, with the resultant range and complexities of behavior manifestations which make unitary consideration out of the question (Harlow, 1976, p. ix).

Defining the concept of mental retardation is not as simple as one might anticipate. This is especially true when one examines the concept of severe and profound retardation. As components (e.g., intellectual functioning and adaptive behavior) of what is widely accepted as a definition for retardation are addressed, it becomes increasingly apparent that no universal definition exists.

Smith (1971) has characterized individuals classified as mentally retarded in terms of their display of poor aptitude in skill areas that are normally taken for granted and that form the basis for performance on more complex tasks. Such a description, regardless of its accuracy in specific cases, is not comprehensive enough to allow us to place individuals either within or outside the category of mental retardation.

The American Association on Mental Deficiency (AAMD) definition of mental retardation is the most widely used current definition: "Mental retardation refers to significantly subaverage general intellectual functioning existing concurrently with deficits in adaptive behavior and manifested during the developmental period" (Grossman, 1977, p. 5). In other words, the three major components of the AAMD definition of mental retardation are: 1) significant subaverage general intellectual functioning, 2) concurrent deficits in adaptive behavior, and 3) manifestations of components 1 and 2 during the developmental period. A summary of these three components follows.

Intellectual Functioning "Significantly subaverage general intellectual functioning" refers to performance on a standardized individual test of intelligence that is two standard deviations (a measure chosen arbitrarily) below the average or mean. The two most common intelligence tests are the Stanford-Binet Intelligence Scale and the Wechsler Intelligence Scales. Two standard deviations below the mean is an IQ of 68 on the Stanford-Binet or an IQ of 70 on the Wechsler. The two-standard-deviations threshold describes the least severe level of mental retardation (i.e., mild). Each additional standard deviation from the mean indicates more severe classifications of mental retardation (i.e., moderate retardation, three standard deviations from the mean; severe, four standard deviations from the mean; and profound, five standard deviations from the mean). Grossman (1977) cautioned, however, that a finding of low IQ is never by itself sufficient to make a diagnosis of mental retardation. (For more extensive information on IQ and its related concepts, including a description of the test instruments used, the reader is referred to Sattler, 1974.)

Adaptive Behavior Adaptive behavior is defined as the "effectiveness or degree with which the individual meets the standards of personal independence and social responsibility expected of his age and cultural group" (Grossman, 1977, p. 5). Meyers, Nihira, and Zetlin (1979), in an in-depth discussion of the adaptive behavior, identified four dimensions that should be emphasized in distinction between adaptive behavior and IQ: 1) everyday behavior (ability to cope with environment) instead of thought processes; 2) overt behavior (e.g., can or cannot dress independently) instead of "traits"; 3) common or typical behavior, not potential; and, in some cases, 4) socioemotional or maladaptive behavior that only minimally correlates with IQ.

Two common scales for measuring adaptive behavior are the Vineland Social Maturity Scale (Doll, 1969) and the American Association on Mental Deficiency (AAMD) Adaptive Behavior Scale (Nihira, Foster, Shellhaas, & Leland, 1969, 1974). Other adaptive behavior scales include the Cain-Levine Social Competency Scale (Cain, Levine, & Freeman, 1963), the Comprehensive Behavior Checklist (Gardner, 1970), the Adaptive Behavior Checklist (Allen, Cortazzo, & Adams, 1970), and the Balthazar Scales of Adaptive Behavior (Balthazar, 1971).

Meyers et al. (1979) have outlined seven domains of adaptive skills and competence that are common in most scales. These domains include: 1) self-help, 2) physical development, 3) communication skills, 4) cognitive functioning, 5) domestic and occupational activities, 6) self-direction and responsibility, and 7) socialization.

Also to be considered when examining adaptive behavior are the chronological age expectations inherent in the concept. For example, Grossman (1977) has indicated that just as cognitive expectations vary according to different age ranges, deficits in adaptive behavior also vary at different ages. Grossman (1977, p. 13) has identified the following standards in relation to age to be used in defining deficits in adaptive behavior:

1. Infancy and early childhood: a) sensorimotor skills development, b) communication skills (including speech and language), c) self-help skills, and d) socialization (development of ability to interact with others)
2. Childhood and early adolescence: a) application of basic academic skills in daily life, b) application of appropriate reasoning and judgment in mastery of the environment, and c) social skills (participation in group activities and interpersonal relationships)
3. Late adolescence and adult life: vocational and social responsibilities and performances

The Developmental Period In an attempt to separate mental retardation from other disorders of human behavior that might manifest themselves in later years (e.g., accidents resulting in physical or mental impairment), Grossman

(1977) has defined the developmental period as extending from birth to 18 years of age. Thus, an individual must demonstrate significant subaverage intellectual functioning and concurrent deficits in adaptive behavior by age 18 to be classified as "mentally retarded."

Two other classifications have an impact on the concept of severe/profound mental retardation. As pointed out in Chapter 1, the terms *developmentally disabled* and *severely handicapped* have frequently been used interchangeably with mental retardation, and specifically with severe and profound mental retardation. The terms, however, actually describe a larger population of which severe/profound mental retardation is but a part.

Developmental Disabilities

The Developmental Disabilities Assistance and Bill of Rights Act of 1975 (PL 94-103) and the Rehabilitation Act of 1973 (PL 94-112) have been extended and revised under the Rehabilitation Comprehensive Services and Developmental Disabilities Amendments of 1978 (PL 95-602). According to the Developmental Disabilities Act, the term *developmental disability* means a severe, chronic disability of a person that: (a) is attributed to a mental or physical impairment or combination of mental and physical impairments, (b) is manifested before the individual attains age 22, (c) is likely to continue indefinitely, (d) results in substantial functional limitations in at least three areas of major life activities including self-care, receptive and expressive language, learning, mobility, self-direction, capacity for independent living, and economic sufficiency, and (e) reflects the person's need for a combination and sequence of special interdisciplinary or generic care, treatment, or other services that are of life-long or extended duration and are individually planned and coordinated.

The term *developmentally disabled* is a popular generic term used to describe a broad scope of disabilities and may refer to cognitive or psychological impairments, physiological body functions, and categorical labels such as mental retardation.

Severely Handicapped

The basis for the term *severely handicapped* is also strongly tied to federal law. The Rehabilitation Act of 1973 defined a severely handicapped person as an individual with "a severe disability which seriously limits his functional capacity, who will require multiple vocational rehabilitation services, and who is experiencing substantial functional limitations due to a combination of disabilities" (p. 226). This law, which identifies as a priority the provision of services to individuals (severely handicapped) who had been previously excluded from services, defines the population in terms of an individual's employment potential. It also tends to be prescriptive (i.e., service needs) rather than simply defining the population.

More recently, attempts to further refine the term *severely handicapped* have been undertaken in education. Sontag, Smith, and Sailor (1977) have identified severely handicapped individuals as a heterogeneous group with impairments that render them "functionally retarded." According to these authors, "when we speak of the severely and profoundly handicapped, we are referring not simply to the severely mentally retarded but to a population of multihandicapped persons, including the severely emotionally disturbed, the severely health impaired, and so on" (p. 5). The definition makes no attempt to categorize individuals but rather seeks to point out common characteristics that the authors attribute to all severely handicapped persons.

After researching the existing definitions of severe handicap, Baker (1979) has proposed a more general educational definition. She has concluded that a definition of *severely handicapped* should focus on an individual's deficits "[in providing] for his or her own basic life-sustaining and safety needs" (p. 60), whether or not those deficits come from an IQ deficit. (See also discussion under Definitions in Chapter 3.)

INCIDENCE

Practitioners examine incidence in an attempt to attach numerical figures to the concept of mental retardation. According to Marozas, May, and Lehman (1980), the terms *incidence* and *prevalence* are rarely defined in the literature and in some cases are used interchangeably. As a result, confusion has surrounded the presentation of these terms in textbooks on mental retardation and special education. Marozas et al. recommend the use of the Morton and Hebel (1978) definition of *incidence* as: the number of new cases of a condition in a population over a period of time. Robinson and Robinson (1976) have indicated this period is ordinarily a year. *Prevalence,* meanwhile, refers to the number of people in a population who have the condition at a given time.

If one looks at the normal distribution of intelligence and uses an IQ of 70 points (two standard deviations or more below the average or mean) as the indicator of mental retardation, approximately 3% of the United States population would be considered mentally retarded. Robinson and Robinson's (1976) estimate of the number of mentally retarded individuals in the United States is nearly 6.5 million. While a prevalence of 3% is widely accepted, this estimate is based solely on IQ. However, the use of the AAMD definition of mental retardation, in which IQ and adaptive behavior are used concurrently, could well reduce this estimate to 1%.

Dingman and Tarjan (1960), in a classic study of the distribution of low IQs, projected the number of individuals who would be classified as mentally retarded based on the normal distribution of IQ. The authors then compared this projection to an estimate of the actual number of mentally retarded individuals in the United States at various IQ levels. They reported that at measured IQs above 50, the figures showed only minor differences. Below an IQ of 50, however, major differences were found. Robinson and Robinson (1976) have updated Dingman and Tarjan's (1960) figures. According to Robinson and Robinson, a projection calculated from the normal curve would yield 186,692 individuals with IQs between 0 and 50, while their figure for estimated actual prevalence was 524,935. This difference of 338,243 represented a significantly greater number of actual cases of severe and profound retardation than was predicted on the basis of normal distribution of intelligence. Robinson and Robinson (1976) have hypothesized that this excess in group size is due to pathological factors such as major genetic abnormalities or brain injuries.

SCREENING, IDENTIFICATION, AND DIAGNOSIS

As stated, the concept of mental retardation according to the AAMD definition (Grossman, 1977) is based on performance on an intelligence test that is two standard deviations below the mean. Two standard deviations result in a classification of mildly mentally retarded. Each subsequent classification level is one additional standard deviation further away from the mean (see Figure 1). Approximate IQ levels are listed in Table 1 for the Stanford-Binet, Cattell, and Wechsler scales as adapted from Grossman (1977). While the threshold for severe mental retardation is set at an IQ of 35 by the Stanford-Binet Intelligence Scale and at an IQ of 39 by the Wechsler Intelligence Scales, these IQ levels are arbitrary (Grossman, 1977).

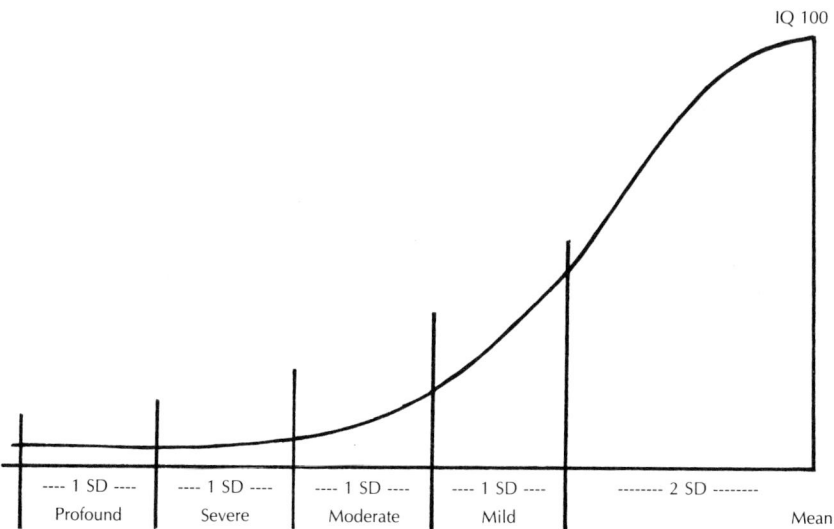

Figure 1. Relationship of AAMD classifications to normal curve of intellectual ability. (SD, standard deviation.).

Table 1. AAMD levels of intellectual functioning

Obtained intelligence quotient: Stanford-Binet and Cattell	Level	Obtained intelligence quotient: Wechsler Scales
19 and below	Profound	24 and below[a]
35–20	Severe	39–25[a]
51–36	Moderate	54–40
67–52	Mild	69–55

Source: Adapted from Grossman (1977, p. 19).
[a]Extrapolated.

Berkson and Landesman-Dwyer (1977) have outlined the problems inherent in attempting to derive a valid IQ measure on individuals at the lower end of the intelligence scale (severe/profound). They indicated that it is difficult, if not impossible, to administer an IQ test to a severely or profoundly mentally retarded individual in a standard manner. In addition, many individuals are classified in the profound range of mental retardation not because of a poor score but because they are found to be "untestable." Berkson and Landesman-Dwyer (1977) have concluded that "testability probably is a major characteristic differentiating individuals at this level..." (p. 428).

As with IQ levels for severely/profoundly mentally retarded persons, the measurement of adaptive behavior at this level presents some major problems. There are no precise tests to measure adaptive behavior for severely/profoundly mentally retarded persons (Berkson & Landesman-Dwyer, 1977; Grossman, 1977). In addition, the historical role of adaptive behavior scales has been to identify areas for training, rather than to serve a predictive function.

Smith, Neisworth, and Greer (1978) have reported that the accuracy of identifying an individual as being in one category of mental retardation as opposed to another is based on "the reliability and validity of the measuring instruments used for the purposes of evaluating mental ability and adaptive behavior" (p. 169). Most measures are questionable, with respect to assessing severe and profound retardation.

ETIOLOGY

In relation to the study of mental retardation, etiology concerns the cause(s) associated with an outcome of retardation. Berlin (1978) outlined two areas of causes of mental retardation: biological and environmental. Within the biological area, Berlin grouped causes in relation to the time frame (before conception, at conception, during gestation, and during labor and delivery) in which the specific cause occurs. Berlin described the second area, environmental, as a controversial area regarding the effects of the environment on mental retardation. This area is supported by family and twin studies.

Within the biological classification, the first major time frame as outlined by Berlin (1978), is "before conception." This subgroup includes the health of the mother (e.g., use of drugs by the mother) and chromosomal disorders (the most common result in offspring being Down's syndrome).

The second major time frame is "at conception," the period when genes of parents unite, sometimes in such a way as to produce genetic disease in the offspring, and a time, also, when maternal use of drugs can be damaging. Multiple pregnancies (more common now with fertility enhancing drugs) increase problems and also can lead to brain damage.

The third major time frame is "during gestation." This area includes effects on the fetus of maternal disease (e.g., mothers with diabetes and serious kidney diseases), toxins (exposure to drugs and chemicals by the pregnant woman), radiation, general nutrition (when a mother's diet does not provide the developing fetus the necessary calories and proteins), and infections (including rubella and syphilis).

The last major time frame within the biological area is "during labor and delivery," the period when the fetus moves from the uterus to the outside world. During this time, when the breathing mechanism is developing, compromised oxygen supplies can result in damage to brain tissue. It is a time, also, when the infant is subjected to disease (such as infections in the birth canal) and trauma.

Berlin's (1978) second area of causes, the environmental area, is more difficult to define than the biological, yet environmental deprivation accounts for a significant portion of those individuals classified as mentally retarded. Environmental influences include cases where there is a sensory or environmental deficit with no evidence of disease or trauma. Usually this area is defined after the fact when no evidence of disease or trauma is found and when environmental factors are assumed.

A second approach to classifying causes is the AAMD (Grossman, 1977) medical classification. That system, while it also separates biological from environmental influences, arranges biological influences by medical category, with a time frame of when specific causes occur as a subclassification of each category. Two examples are: Category—Infections and Intoxicants, Subclassifications—prenatal infection, postnatal cerebral infection; and Category—Trauma or Physical Agent, Subclassifications—prenatal injury, mechanical injury at birth, perinatal hypoxia, postnatal hypoxia, and postnatal injury. Grossman (1977) outlines 10 medical categories, as follows: 1) infections and intoxicants, 2) trauma or physical agent, 3) metabolism or nutrition, 4) gross brain disease (postnatal), 5) unknown prenatal influence, 6) chromosomal abnormality, 7) gestational disorders, 8) post-psychiatric disorders, 9) environmental influences, and 10) other conditions.

CLASSIFICATION SYSTEMS

Classification refers to the sorting of members of a large class (e.g., the mentally retarded population) into more homogeneous groupings (e.g., causes/ subclassifications of mental retardation) (Salvia, 1978). According to Salvia, classification is conducted under the assumption that persons in more homogeneous subdivisions benefit from similar kinds of services.

Smith (1971) has outlined several classification systems, one of the more convenient of which categorizes the known causes of mental retardation according to three major landmark periods within the person's life: the prenatal period, the perinatal period, and the postnatal period. The prenatal period (from conception to labor) includes genetic causes (transmission of a recessive or dominant trait) and environmental (intrauterine) difficulties that may result in a mentally retarded child. The perinatal period covers the interval from labor to birth, during which, for example, various types of brain injury (e.g., anoxia) resulting in mental retardation may occur. The postnatal period (after birth and throughout early childhood) is described by Smith as having two major components: physical and environmental. The physical component covers disease, trauma (e.g., lack of oxygen, blows to the head) and insults (e.g., tumors and poisoning). The environmental component, which accounts for a substantial portion of those individuals labeled as mentally retarded, represents environmental deprivation, usually without any identifiable brain damage.

Other examples of classification systems provided by Smith (1971) include: medical, intellectual, and syndrome classifications. Medical classifications are "classifications by cause" (e.g., Cartwright & Cartwright, 1978). An example of this approach to classification is given in the *AAMD Manual on Terminology* and *Classification in Mental Retardation* (Grossman, 1977), which outlines the 10 medical classifications mentioned earlier in this chapter under Etiology. The intellectual classification scheme uses some measure of intelligence to establish subgroups. This system is described by MacMillan (1977) as "classification by degree." Within the AAMD definition, the use of the terms *mild, moderate, severe,* and *profound* mental retardation is an example of such a classification. Smith (1971) also points to educational labels of mental retardation, i.e., educable, trainable, and custodial (dependent or low-grade), as another example of an intellectual classification, though this system is no longer used.

The last classification system as mentioned above is based upon syndromes (clinical symptoms). For instance, Robinson and Robinson (1976) cited the example of microcephaly (characterized by a small brain and skull) as one argument for the use of syndromes. They pointed out that while microcephaly is readily identifiable, it is not necessarily linked to cause (etiology), since in some cases microcephaly can be traced to hereditary factors while in other cases environmental factors are the cause.

Attempts to group or classify types of mental retardation are hampered by the lack of a universal, precise definition of mental retardation. As a result, the specific needs of various disciplines usually guide the choice of what classification system to use. Between 65% and 75% of people identified as mentally retarded are not able to be classified by cause or etiology.

SYMPTOMATOLOGY

Smith, Neisworth, and Greer (1978) have provided a behavioral description of severe/profound mental retardation according to age levels. According to Smith et al. (1978) the severely mentally retarded preschool child exhibits deficits in motor development, speech, and self-help training as well as in socialization characteristics. The profoundly mentally retarded preschooler typically exhibits gross deficits in all of these areas. The severely mentally retarded school-age child usually exhibits minimal communication skills, has potential for training in basic health habits, and will profit from systematic habit training. The profoundly retarded person, however, will have only limited degrees of success in self-help instruction, although some basic motor development may be evidenced during the school-age years.

As adults, severely mentally retarded persons may be at least partially independent under direct supervision, and they should develop at least minimal self-protection skills. Profoundly mentally retarded adults may develop basic communication capabilities and elementary self-care skills.

The concept of mental retardation is limited in its ability to characterize those individuals it purports to include. The concept of severe/profound mental retardation has even more critical problems establishing boundaries for its population. For example, some severely mentally retarded adults may be completely independent in some activities, even though the above descriptions would not include "complete independence" as a possible skill attainment.

It is, however, problematic at best to attempt to define a heterogeneous population such as severely or profoundly retarded individuals based solely on a behavioral description. As noted earlier, given the difficulty in obtaining a valid IQ measure at the lower end of the intelligence scale (Berkson & Landesman-Dwyer, 1977) and with no precise tests to measure adaptive behaviors (Berkson & Landesman-Dwyer, 1977; Grossman, 1977), individuals will vary significantly in behavioral characteristics in both the severely and profoundly retarded groups. Furthermore, even if valid standardized assessments were available for these individuals, the information provided by these assessments could not be definitive in terms of precisely describing the typical behavior of an individual.

A more extensive description of behaviors and approaches to these behaviors is presented in the Educational Programs and Services section of this chapter, which also discusses current research on successful programs to modify behaviors.

As previously discussed, severely handicapping conditions (e.g., severe or profound mental retardation) do not imply homogeneity in performance. Unless otherwise indicated, no further attempt is made to distinguish between these groups. Instead, the more generic term *severely handicapped*, is used for the remainder of the chapter.

PREVENTION AND TREATMENT PROGRAMS

Prevention

> In the field of mental retardation we have long been accustomed to dealing with situations after the fact. The measures which can be used in prevention are few and the treatments, which are specific, are often still in their early stages (Kugel & Shearer, 1976, p. 374).

Kugel and Shearer (1976) considered the greatest barrier to a truly effective prevention program our inability to "take prevention seriously." They cited, for example, the impact that diet has had on improving phenylketonuria (PKU), but point out that the potential PKU population is a relatively small segment of the mentally retarded population, and that research into both the causes of and preventive measures against other forms of mental retardation is desperately needed.

Jancar and Simon (1980), after outlining what they consider to be the seven most widely practiced and effective preventive measures against mental retardation, go on to discuss the implications of preventive programs, and emphasize the administrative, ethical, moral, social, and economic implications of even the most simple prevention program. They offer the following example:

> In theory, if a programme were instituted to study every pregnancy where the mother is over 35 years of age, it could prove effective in avoiding 30% of Down's syndrome babies being born. This, however, depends on every vulnerable person agreeing to the investigation and subsequently consenting to a therapeutic abortion if the diagnosis is confirmed. Every step is fraught with ifs and buts. Will *all* mothers in this group be known and included? Will *all* agree to investigation? Would those with positive findings consent to a therapeutic abortion? Positive answers to these questions cannot be ensured very easily in a democratic society, although ultimately the cost-effectiveness of the programme will depend on them (p. 12).

In spite of recent strides in the area of genetically caused mental retardation, in many instances these steps have failed to spur a true prevention program; and, in some cases, these advances potentially affect only minor segments of the mentally retarded population. Not until these strides are accepted as an important component of the whole will prevention become an integral aspect of the study of mental retardation.

Readers are referred to Gearheart and Litton (1979) for a discussion of current treatments within a framework of common clinical and genetic syndromes associated with moderately mentally retarded individuals. For a more in-depth look at treatments, readers are referred to Robinson and Robinson (1976).

Institutionalization

> Ever since the Spartans cast their defective children off cliffs, mentally retarded persons have been exiled, shunned, sterilized, and institutionalized. They have been stripped of their dignity, their citizenship, and even their lives. Nowhere have such indignities been more apparent than in institutions for mentally retarded persons (Plotkin & Gill, 1979, p. 637).

In 1969, Butterfield reported that approximately 60% of individuals in institutions were severely mentally retarded persons and that the current trend was toward the admission of increasingly more such persons. In a more recent study, Scheerenberger (1976) reported that severely mentally retarded individuals comprised 72% of the institutionalized population and that this percentage was likely to increase. Eyman and Borthwick's 1980 report indicated that the majority of severely mentally retarded persons reside within institutions. Thus, any discussion of severely mentally retarded individuals must include the topic of institutionalization, despite the widespread advocacy in recent years for de-institutionalization.

History The United States has a history of service to mentally retarded individuals based on the institutional model. Institutional services were begun in the mid-1800's with the idea of habilitation (and, in some cases, "cure") as a goal. This initial optimism, however, was frustrated by the minimal habilitation outcomes that characterized institutional services through the beginning of the 20th century.

The changes in outlook of individuals working with mentally retarded persons have been described by White and Wolfensberger (1969) who assigned time periods to these changes in attitude. Between 1850 and 1880, White and Wolfensberger characterized services as aimed at "making the deviant undeviant." Between 1870 and 1890, the failure of this concept became apparent and the resultant frustration led to what White and Wolfensberger have termed "sheltering the deviant from society." Between 1880 and 1900, White and Wolfensberger noted a reversal of concerns, characterized by "protection of society from the deviant."

In terms of the 20th century, Rosen, Clark, and Kivitz (1976) have stated that the first half of this century was characterized by the sterilization and segregation of mentally retarded persons. During this time the institutional environment as it is now known—marked by large, isolated, and physically separate facilities within a medical "treatment" milieu—emerged. This environment embodied the principle of isolating mentally retarded individuals from society in favor of promoting their interaction with mentally retarded peers.

Society's acceptance of and reliance upon this treatment model was reflected in the phenomenal growth of the institutional system. Rosen et al. (1976) reviewed the early literature describing institutional growth, from the establishment of the first two schools for mentally retarded persons in the United States in 1848 to the estimated 4,000 residents in state and private institutions for mentally retarded individuals by 1888. In their 1969 report, Kugel and Wolfensberger estimated that 230,000 residents resided in more than 150 public institutions for mentally retarded persons.

By the end of the 1960s, however, professionals and advocates began to analyze and question the practices and principles of institutionalization. The pressures of this early criticism have generated a forceful, ongoing deinstitutionalization movement.

Issues in Institutionalization Many of the issues surrounding institutionalization focus upon the austere nature of environmental conditions in institutions for mentally retarded persons (Blatt, 1970; Blatt & Kaplan, 1966; MacAndrew & Edgerton, 1964) and the consequences of these conditions for the individual (Dennis & Sayegh, 1965; Vail, 1967; White & Wolfsensberger, 1969). Investigations in the 1960s and 1970s did reveal deplorable conditions within many—though certainly not all—institutions for mentally retarded persons. Blatt and Kaplan's (1966) brief description of a visit to one institution is still valid in some institutions today:

> In each of the dormitories for severely retarded residents, there is what is euphemistically called a day room or recreation room. The odor in each of these rooms is overpowering.... Floors are sometimes wooden and excretions are rubbed into the cracks, leaving permanent stench. Most day rooms have a series of bleacher benches, on which sit unclad residents, jammed together, without purposeful activity, communication, or any interaction. In each day room is an attendant or two, whose main function seems to be to "stand around" and, on occasion, hose down the floor "driving" excretions into a sewer conveniently located in the center of the room (p. 22).

While the preceding description may be an extreme example, Reuter, Archer, Dunn, and White (1980) have also described inadequate care in a private, intermediate-care residence for severely and profoundly handicapped young children. The residence described was a licensed 24-hour care facility with a full staff of professionals and with a federal demonstration project on site. Although the children were awake 85% to 95% of the time between 7:00 A.M. and 9:00 P.M., they were likely to be in bed for 50% of those waking hours, with no structured activities or adult interaction.

A study by Raynes (1980) also evaluated institutional settings, contrasting care in each of three residential facilities for mentally retarded persons according to the functioning level served. For the severely mentally retarded population, Raynes found that care practices were more institution-oriented (i.e., lining up, rigid time scheduling, and high staff-resident social distance) than resident-oriented. He also found that the less competent residents were less likely to be talked to in a stimulating way and their physical environment was more barren (e.g., lack of closets and lockers in many living quarters, lack of curtains, and no mirrors or trash cans in rest rooms). Underscoring the fewer chances given to severely mentally retarded persons to interact with the normal environment in comparison to higher functioning individuals, Raynes cited three residences for severely mentally retarded persons that had not taken their clients shopping or even on a bus ride during the preceding month.

The deprivation and relatively long periods of inactivity to which many severely mentally retarded persons in institutions are subjected are major problems that must be addressed. DeVellis (1977) has reported that if an individual, because of prolonged inactivity, is no longer motivated to respond to the environment, it may be impossible to teach that individual the requisite skills for interacting effectively with his or her environment. Furthermore, if the environment is unresponsive to the individual, learned helplessness (Seligman, 1975) may result, in which the individual no longer even attempts to interact with or control the environment.

Hayward and Tapp (1966) have reported that the nature of the physical environment itself can affect the type of behavior that occurs. For example, Kaufman (1967) and Eyman, Tarjan, and Cassady (1970) have presented evidence that acquisition of self-help skills and social behaviors can be slowed after admission to an institution. Tizard (1964), for example, moved 16 severely mentally retarded children from a crowded, large institution to a small family-type unit. The children made significantly greater advances in verbal and social development in their new environment than did 16 matched children who remained in the institution. Such studies offer further support to arguments in support of removing mentally retarded persons, including severely mentally retarded individuals, from institutions.

Least Restrictive Alternatives   While the literature has addressed the effects of institutionalization and, more recently, the concept of community alternatives, the United States courts have themselves been mandating action. Judicial action in three institutional court cases is summarized below.

In the case of *Wyatt* v. *Stickney* (1971), the court found that programs of habilitation in the state institution were inadequate. It reasoned that if an individual was institutionalized (and thereby deprived of certain rights) for the sake of habilitation and that habilitation was not occurring, then that individual had been deprived of constitutional rights. In its decision, the court set standards for habilitation, but, more important, it supported the principle that the individual has the right to habilitation in the least restrictive environment. The order decreed that there could not be an admission to an institution unless a prior determination had been made that the placement into an institution was the least restrictive habilitative setting for that individual.

New York State Association for Retarded Citizens v. *Carey* (1973), through a consent decree, called for a reduction of a residential facility from 5,700 to 250 clients or fewer over a 6-year period. To accomplish this, a review panel was formed to develop (among other mandates) a plan for the state to use community alternatives to achieve the court-ordered results.

In *Halderman* v. *Pennhurst State School and Hospital* (1978), the court upheld the constitutional right to habilitation in the least restrictive environment. In addition, the court ordered the closing of the facility in favor of suitable community alternatives, and it affirmed other rights of the individual. While a portion of this case has been ruled on negatively by the United States Supreme Court, many of the principles of the original consent decree are still enforced.

Similar cases that have also had an impact on the concept of least restrictive alternative are two major right-to-education lawsuits. *Pennsylvania Association for Retarded Citizens (PARC)* v. *Commonwealth of Pennsylvania* (1972) sought a ruling that all school-age retarded children, regardless of severity of handicap, be provided a free public education. *Mills* v. *Board of Education of the District of Columbia* (1972) sought a decision for the public education of all handicapped children. Both cases in effect paved the way for The Education for All Handicapped Children Act of 1975 (PL 94-142), which established the public policy of a free public education for *all* handicapped children and youth. These cases and law are important, because without a guaranteed free public education, the meaningfulness of the concept of least restrictive alternative would be limited.

Normalization   Wolfensberger (1972) has defined the normalization principle as, "utilization or means which are as culturally normative as possible, in order to establish and/or maintain personal behaviors and characteristics that are as culturally normative as possible" (p. 28). The principle is based on the premise that many of the differences between mentally retarded and severely mentally retarded individuals and "normal" peers are not the result of any real differences in functioning ability but are caused by our approaches to services for these individuals (e.g., isolating in institutions). The principle holds that we must help to build progressively more normal behaviors as we also make every effort to integrate the individual into his or her natural community.

The issues surrounding institutionalizing a severely mentally retarded person are complex at best. With the more recent recognition of the right to habilitation in an environment that exhibits the least restriction, and with the concept of services that are as "normal" and as much a part of the community as possible gaining momentum, the matter of community alternatives for severely mentally retarded individuals is receiving considerable attention.

Issues in Community Alternatives   The bridge between the philosophies of institutional and community services for severely mentally retarded persons is best presented by Nihira and Nihira (1975). They indicated that while some severely mentally retarded individuals need highly structured supervision (e.g., institutionalization), the majority can function in smaller, less structured, and more normalized settings (including such living situations as group homes, foster homes, and with natural parents).

Ability to Adapt to the Community   While the process of deinstitutionalization has focused on the movement of higher functioning individuals out of institutions, current research suggests that community success is not restricted to higher functioning individuals. In a review of 175 studies of community placement, McCarver and Craig (1974) studied 11 variables, including IQ, as a basis for predicting a mentally retarded individual's success in community placement. They were unable to conclude that any single variable was a reliable predictor of successful community placement. In terms of the IQ variable specifically, a more recent study by Schalock, Harper, and Genung (1981) examined 166 retarded adults in Nebraska. The authors reported that clients who were unsuccessful in community placement were significantly less retarded than those successfully placed. They did, however, indicate that results of applying the IQ variable have been, at best, inconsistent.

Several studies have reported that severely mentally retarded persons are capable of acquiring many of the skills needed for community placement, including: competitive employment, shopping, planning menus, mobility within the community, use of a telephone, and solving functional mathematics and reading problems (Vogelsberg, Williams, & Friedl, 1980). However, only a few empirical studies report the actual attainment of community living skills by severely mentally retarded persons.

Community placement of severely mentally retarded persons may also lead to gains in functioning over performance of those observed in institutional settings. For example, Thompson and Carey (1980) investigated the benefits of a group home placement for eight severe and profound mentally retarded women who had previously been institutionalized. They reported that the women showed improvement in language skills, in ability to perform domestic tasks, and in use of leisure time. In addition, the women's intellectual performance on an IQ test increased significantly. While gains due to living in a more normalized setting could not be separated from the type of programming received in this setting, these results do suggest that community placement of severely mentally retarded persons may be beneficial in the development of many skills.

Ethics of Placement and Cost Intagliata, Wilder, and Cooley (1979) have outlined two traditional assumptions that provide the major rationale for deinstitutionalization and community-based residential alternatives: 1) community alternatives provide the potential for more normalizing influences, and 2) community alternatives may be less costly than institutionalization. The concept of community alternatives providing more normalized services remains strong within the literature today, as demonstrated in the recent work of Thompson and Carey (1980) and Vogelsberg, Williams, and Friedl (1980). The cost advantages of community alternatives, however, remain uncertain. Intagliata et al. (1979) reported that the cost of a resident per year in an institution at that time was $14,630; the cost of a resident in a group home was between $9,255 and $11,000; the cost of family care was $3,131; and the cost for the natural family was $2,108. Other investigations regarding the cost of community placements found these costs to be equivocal. For example, Retish, Hoy, and Boaz (1978) described a community alternative in Iowa that cost about the same as institutional placement within the state.

Still other investigations have found that costs of community alternatives vary according to such factors as staffing and programming. Gage, Fredericks, Baldwin, Moore, and Grove (1978) studied the costs of two halfway houses, one of which used house parents and the other of which used three rotating managers. Costs were found to be less than those associated with institutionalization for the house with house parents, but more for the house with rotating managers. It should also be noted that most studies have indicated costs that are directly related to in-house services and programs, and do not include the cost of related services (e.g., educational services, sheltered employment, and medical care).

While studies have shown, then, that overall costs may be lower in the community than in institutions, the fundamental issue must be ethically based. If costs were to rise dramatically for community services tomorrow, would we then reinstitutionalize mentally retarded persons? In this time of fiscal restraint, relative cost of community services is clearly a factor, but it should not be the overriding determinant. Indeed, the literature shows that deinstitutionalization has occurred and continues despite, in some cases, greater cost.

Maintenance Skills Needed Additional issues surrounding the utilization of community alternatives address the skills needed to remain within the community. Various studies have indicated a positive correlation between successful community adjustment and social behavior (Crawford, Aiello, & Thompson, 1979; Heal, Sigelman, & Switsky, 1974; Schalock et al., 1981) and between community success and acquired work skills (Bell, 1976; McCarver & Craig, 1974; Schalock et al., 1981). However, the presence or absence of maladaptive behavior appears especially important to successful community placement. Crawford et al. (1979) have reported that the occurrence of maladaptive behavior is a better predictor of successful community placement than are other demographic or functional skill characteristics of the clients. In addition, Sutter, Mayeda, and Call (1980) have reported that clients who had relatively high levels of self-help and social skills but who were unsuccessful in community placements frequently also demonstrated maladaptive behavior.

Although maladaptive behavior often interferes with community placement, Schalock et al. (1981) have reported that many clients remain in the community despite the presence of maladaptive behaviors that are similar to those of other clients who are reinstitutionalized. The authors attributed these outcomes (based on a study of 166 deinstitutionalized retarded individuals) to the following five reasons: 1) the behaviors occurred most frequently in the residential or training environments, not in the community, 2) the clients were relatively successful in behavior management programs, 3) each client had an advocate, 4) most clients were receiving services from local mental health centers, and 5) the staff working with the clients were patient and committed to community placement.

Behavior Following Transfer   Another consideration with respect to community placement relates to the effects of changing environments on client's behavior following transfer. For example, Cohen, Conroy, Frazer, Snelbecker, and Spreat (1977) reported that when lower functioning mentally retarded persons were placed into the community, both functional and nonfunctional behaviors increased in frequency, at least temporarily. Coffman and Harris (1980) have reported that environmental changes can cause far-reaching consequences, including disorientation, regression, and emotional distress. The authors related this trauma to the same transitional adjustments experienced by nonretarded individuals in the community (i.e., divorce, release from prison, or cross-cultural adjustments). Relocation, however, may be a positive experience if it improves the physical and social conditions surrounding that client's life and if it is voluntary or desired (Carsrud, Carsrud, Henderson, Alisch, & Fowler, 1979). Carsrud et al. (1979) followed multihandicapped retarded residents from an older, crowded living unit to a modern, uncrowded living unit. They concluded from the study that environmental and social alternatives can provide a wide variety of positive changes within the institutionalized, mentally retarded population.

Availability of Services   The availability of services within the community has also been reported to be a major component for the successful use of community alternatives. Heal et al. (1974) have indicated that the success of placement depends primarily on the quality of community support systems rather than on the characteristics of the subjects themselves.

According to Intagliata, Kraus, and Willer (1980), the deinstitutionalization movement has led to a greater need for community-based services, in that organizations must serve not only noninstitutionalized mentally retarded persons, but previously institutionalized individuals who frequently have different needs. Nihira and Nihira (1975) have cautioned that a more in-depth look at the community may be required prior to placement of severely mentally retarded individuals. In addition, they have suggested that the special needs of severely mentally retarded persons may necessitate community living environments that are substantially different from those of other individuals.

Aided by social conscience, litigation, and in some cases, the argument of lowered cost, deinstitutionalization and the use of community alternatives have become dominant goals for mentally retarded persons, including severely mentally retarded individuals. And though many questions still remain as to how best to accomplish these goals, the advantages for handicapped persons of a least restrictive environment remain. As Bradley (1980) has summarized: "deinstitutionalization is sometimes sold as a way of dramatically improving the therapeutic possibilities for mentally disabled persons. Recent reviews are inconclusive on this point, but this should not suggest that the whole reason for moving people out into the community thereupon vanishes" (p. 85).

Problem of Readmission   A major area of concern regarding deinstitutionalization is that readmissions to institutions have increased more rapidly than community placements (Conroy, 1977). At least two reasons may account for this finding. First, the popular appeal of the deinstitutionalization movement may have resulted in the premature release of many clients without giving proper consideration to adequate community based alternatives (Throne, 1979). Second, it is important to realize that community group homes are frequently only smaller versions of the institutions in which the clients previously resided (Throne, 1979), and as such are not necessarily providing skills for community living. Throne has pointed out the need to scientifically investigate the variables related to de-institutionalization, normalization, and mainstreaming and has cautioned against deceiving ourselves that normalization occurs simply by moving clients from large to small facilities. For example, Birenbaum and Re (1979) investigated the effects of moving young mentally retarded persons from a large isolated state school to a community placement. After 4 years, the clients had not displayed any greater independence within the community environment.

Baroff (1980) has investigated the importance of the size of the institution as it relates to resident care practices in both institutional and community settings. Size was found to make a difference, in that the smaller residential settings (10 or fewer residents) are more responsive to individual needs. Landesman-Dwyer, Sackett, and Kleinman (1980), however, have reported that staff/resident interactions did not vary as a function of size of facility, and, moreover, that the smaller group homes investigated in their study did not afford opportunities for multiple peer social interactions.

The object of deinstitutionalization should not be merely to move clients from one setting to another. Rather, the purposes should be two-fold: 1) to determine those factors that facilitate successful community integration and 2) to determine those behaviors, training practices, and skill levels needed by institutionalized persons to optimize their opportunities for community-based placement.

Prevocational/Vocational Education

The trend toward community placement of institutionalized persons increases the need for training programs that prepare severely mentally retarded persons for adaptation to their new environments (Cuvo, Leaf, & Borakove, 1978). Therefore, programming for severely mentally retarded persons should focus on skills and behaviors that increase independent functioning in real-life settings (Mithaug, Mar, Stewart, & McCalmon, 1980) and that are chronologically age-appropriate and functional (Brown, Branston, Hamre-Nietupski, Pumpian, Certo, & Gruenewald, 1979).

One set of skills that facilitates independent community living is vocational skills. The ability of severely handicapped persons to perform vocational tasks has been documented repeatedly in the literature (e.g., Bellamy, Peterson, & Close, 1975; Crosson, 1969; Gold, 1972, 1976; Hunter & Bellamy, 1976; Irvin & Bellamy, 1977). In fact, the literature indicates that severely handicapped persons can perform highly complex tasks (e.g., Bellamy et al., 1975; Gold, 1972, 1973b;

Karen, Eisner, & Endres, 1974; O'Neill & Bellamy, 1978) previously thought to be beyond their capabilities (Karan, 1977). For example, severely mentally retarded persons have been taught multi-step bicycle brake assemblies (Gold, 1972) and saw-chain assemblies (O'Neill & Bellamy, 1978).

The following subsections describe research that has been conducted on the evaluation, acquisition, and production rates of vocational performance in severely handicapped persons. Problems associated with vocational performance and placement are also discussed, and several model programs or approaches are presented. Many of the procedures described here involve behavior modification techniques, which have been among the most effective means available for training severely handicapped persons (National Center for Law and the Handicapped, Inc., 1980; Revell & Wehman, 1978).

Evaluation Vocational evaluation for mentally retarded persons can be defined as "a comprehensive process involving an interdisciplinary team approach to assessing an individual's vocational potential and training and placement needs" (Brolin, 1976, p. 81). The vocational evaluation of persons below the educable level of mental retardation has been neglected, resulting in a lack of valid and reliable vocational assessment procedures (Quinones, 1978; Rosen, Kivitz, Clark, & Floor, 1980). This lack of appropriate vocational assessments has resulted in: 1) inappropriate training, 2) inappropriate placement, 3) inability to evaluate the effectiveness of vocational training programs, and 4) lack of information regarding amount of training time, number of training trials, and total costs of programming (Quinones, 1978; Revell & Wehman, 1978). In addition, Revell and Wehman (1978) reported that severely mentally retarded persons are part of the severely handicapped population who have not benefited significantly from direct-service delivery by state vocational rehabilitation programs. These authors argued that rehabilitation counselors, as a group, do not have the training to understand and work effectively with severely mentally retarded persons who are frequently nonverbal and have limited receptive language (Wehman, 1976).

A major reason for the failure of traditional assessments to provide appropriate evaluation data is that the assessments are comprised primarily of standardized psychological tests, standardized vocational tests, and interviews. IQ scores have been reported to be of limited use in prediction of vocational performance (Gold, 1973a), and most other standardized tests have not been normed on severely mentally retarded persons. In addition, standardized assessments frequently mask individual differences and capabilities. Standardized vocational tests are also frequently of marginal value because of the restricted work history of severely mentally retarded persons, and interview information is seldom useful because of the frequent expressive communication problems of such persons (Revell & Wehman, 1978).

These concerns about traditional assessment procedures have led researchers and professionals working with severely mentally retarded persons to develop new procedures to evaluate vocational potential, including work samples and observation systems. In addition, while most of these procedures include traditional assessment procedures, they also require situational assessments (Brolin, 1976).

Work samples are vocational tasks that closely simulate actual industrial tasks (Stodden, Casale, & Schwartz, 1977). Stodden et al. reported that the advantages of work samples over traditional assessment procedures include: 1) they assess the same skills as competitive employment, 2) they are less affected by educational level and anxiety, 3) they resemble real work situations, and 4) they afford the opportunity to observe actual work behavior in a controlled setting.

Schreiner (1978) assessed the predictive power of work samples with 127 mentally retarded adults (mean IQ = 60). Schreiner compared work samples with standardized tests (IQ, Wide Range Achievement Test (WRAT), and dexterity measures), subject characteristics (sex, age, and secondary handicaps), and ratings by vocational evaluators (work habits, ability, and independent living skills). In general, subject characteristic data were the poorest predictors of vocational performance, while work samples were the best predictors.

There are at least three major problems connected with work samples (Stodden et al., 1977): 1) many jobs cannot be duplicated, 2) work samples frequently require subjective observation, and 3) there is a lack of standardization with respect to behavioral criteria. For these reasons, other procedures are frequently used, and new procedures must be developed. For example, Mithaug and Mar (1980) noted that career planning usually begins with an assessment of the person's vocational interests, but this can seldom be conducted with severely handicapped persons because of their lack of communication skills. To overcome this problem, Mithaug and Hanawalt (1978) employed a nonverbal method to assess the task preferences of three noncommunicative severely mentally retarded adults. The procedure was to provide the subjects with a tray of objects and then to permit them to work with the object selected (all objects used were concrete examples of the jobs to be performed). Mithaug and Hanawalt (1978) reported that all three subjects consistently selected some objects over others, indicating task preferences. Mithaug and Mar (1980) reported similar findings, but also demonstrated more thoroughly that the selection response did indicate subject preference of some vocational tasks over other tasks.

A final approach to vocational evaluation involves the use of observational tools or checklists. Observational tools and checklists would appear to have many advantages over most other procedures, including economy of time, diversity of information covered, and applicability to standardization and scoring procedures. As a result of these benefits, many checklists and observational systems have been and continue to be developed (see Walls and Werner, 1977, for a listing of 39 checklists containing items related to vocational behavior; and Walls, Werner, Bacon, and Zane, 1977, for a listing of 157 checklists for use with various populations and content areas). The following is a description of one of these checklists developed by Mithaug and his colleagues (Johnson & Mithaug, 1978; Mithaug & Hagmeier, 1978; Mithaug, Hagmeier & Haring, 1977; Mithaug et al.,

1980) that appears to have great potential for use as a vocational assessment procedure with severely mentally retarded persons in sheltered work settings.

Mithaug et al.'s (1977) approach to vocational skill training is based on an approach to educational skill training similar to that reported by Brown, Branston-McClean, Baumgart, Vincent, Falvey, and Schroeder (1979). The method requires that vocational training be based on work standards used by workshop supervisors. In other words, the vocational behavior trained should match the entry level standards required by workshop supervisors. Mithaug and Hagmeier (1978) and Johnson and Mithaug (1978) presented an interview form to various workshop supervisors and asked the supervisors to indicate their entry level requirements for placement into sheltered employment. Mithaug et al. (1980) then used the most frequently identified criteria to develop the Prevocational Assessment and Curriculum Guide (PACG). They reported that there is a strong relationship between the behaviors included within the PACG and actual characteristics of workers in sheltered workshops and that the guide is very useful in determining not only the skills needed for placement but also the training needs of employees (e.g., attendance, independence, and production rate). The PACG system may be the most comprehensive of its kind for use with severely mentally retarded persons in sheltered work settings. Rusch, Schutz, and Agran (1982) utilized a similar approach for determining the entry level skills required in community job settings (food service and janitorial/maid service occupations).

Acquisition A great deal of recent research has been conducted on the variables necessary to acquire vocational behavior by severely mentally retarded persons. Clark, Greenwood, Abramowitz, and Bellamy (1980) described three strategies for the vocational preparation of severely mentally retarded persons. First, skills for employment in sheltered workshops may be taught in both school-based programs (e.g., Lynch, 1979) or in special programs designed to teach workshop skills (e.g., Mithaug et al., 1977). Within either of these programs, training can be conducted not only on acquisition and production of vocational behavior but also on the social behaviors required for continued employment. Second, portable training environments (e.g., Potter, Biacchi, & Richardson, 1977) that simulate several vocational tasks may be used. Third, community-based work environments to teach the behaviors required for a definite job can be conducted (Clark et al., 1980). All three approaches have been used successfully. Very little is known, however, about using portable environments, especially with respect to how they might be used to develop sustained performance and appropriate social behavior (Clark et al., 1980).

Many vocational behaviors have been taught to severely mentally retarded persons, most according to the first strategy described by Clark et al. (1980). In addition, a variety of procedures have been used to teach vocational skills, usually as part of training packages combining many of the following procedures.

Much of the acquisition research with severely mentally retarded persons has focused on attentional skills (Close, Irvin, Prehm, & Taylor, 1978) as a result of the discrimination research conducted by Zeaman and House (1963). Zeaman and House reported that the failure of many retarded persons to quickly learn a task may be due to their inability to select and attend to the relevant dimension(s) of the task. For example, mentally retarded individuals may take longer than nonretarded people to identify which aspects of a task are critical for successful task completion. Based on these findings, it may be important that the relevant dimensions for task completion be identified or emphasized for mentally retarded learners, at least in the initial stages of learning (Fisher & Zeaman, 1973).

Studies derived from Zeaman and House's attention theory have demonstrated that stimulus manipulation procedures do act to direct attention to the relevant dimensions of tasks (e.g., Gold, 1972; Gold & Barclay, 1973b; Irvin & Bellamy, 1977). These procedures frequently entail the use of color-coding or exaggerating cue differences and have been successful in teaching mentally retarded persons complex vocational tasks.

Correction and prompting procedures have also been used frequently as part of the programming of severely mentally retarded persons on vocational tasks. For example, verbal correction (Bellamy et al., 1975; Gold, 1972; Gold & Barclay, 1973a; Irvin & Bellamy, 1977), physical correction (Bellamy et al., 1975; Gold, 1972), and repeated practice or overcorrection (Rusch & Close, 1976) have all been successful. Most commonly, the normal sequence for prompting includes: 1) verbal instruction, 2) modeling plus verbal instruction, and 3) physical guidance plus verbal instruction (Brown, Bellamy, Perlmutter, Sackowitz, & Sontag, 1972; Cuvo et al., 1978). These procedures have been used to teach such diverse vocational performances as bicycle brake assembly (Gold, 1972) and janitorial skills (Cuvo et al., 1978) to severely and moderately retarded persons. Whatever the types of prompting and correction used, direct feedback of errors is almost always more successful than extinction procedures (Close et al., 1978).

Another common training strategy has involved task analysis procedures. Mithaug (1979b) defined task analysis as breaking complex tasks down into their component parts, specifying the required behavior sequences necessary for task completion, using the principles of shaping (systematically reinforcing behaviors that approximate the desired behavior), and chaining (a procedure in which simple responses already acquired by the subject are reinforced to form a sequence of behaviors or a more complex behavior) to develop the appropriate skill. Task analysis is a prevalent feature of studies that involve training vocational behavior, e.g., drill press operation (Crosson, 1969), envelope stuffing (Brown & Pearce, 1970), card assembling (Brown, Jones, Troccolo, Heiser, Bellamy, & Sontag, 1972), bicycle brake assemblies (Gold, 1972; 1976), CAM switch assembly (Bellamy et al., 1975), cable harness assembly (Hunter & Bellamy, 1976), and janitorial skills (Cuvo et al., 1978). The reader interested in conducting task analyses for vocational tasks is referred to Wehman and McLaughlin (1980) for an outline of over 100 task analyses.

Task analysis procedures are advantageous in that they: 1) identify prerequisite responses for completing a task, 2) specify the objectives of training, and

3) specify the sequence of instruction (Cuvo et al., 1978). A potential difficulty with such procedures, however, is that while they provide information on how to train a subject on a particular task, they may not specify how the required skills contribute to what Mithaug (1979b) referred to as "generative responses"; in other words, they do not specify what general skills are necessary for successful vocational performance. As a result, each new task must be systematically trained (Mithaug, 1979b), and little information is provided regarding the skills necessary for most vocational tasks of a given class.

Finally, various reinforcement procedures have also been used to train vocational performance (most training programs use reinforcement to at least some extent). For example, Koop, Martin, Yu, and Suthons (1980) compared the use of social reinforcement versus social-plus-edible reinforcement on the acquisition rates of mentally retarded persons. The results indicated that social-plus-edible reinforcement was more effective for training both simple and complex tasks. Bateman (1975) used a variation of the Premack Principle (using high frequency of preferred behavior to reinforce low frequency behavior) to increase the time spent on less preferred tasks, by making work on preferred tasks contingent upon time spent on less preferred tasks. While reinforcement procedures have been effective in training new vocational behaviors to mentally retarded persons, the greatest impact of these procedures has been on increasing production rates (Kazdin, 1978; Mithaug et al., 1980).

Production Rates Although the ability of severely mentally retarded persons to learn vocational tasks has been documented, vocational success may also depend largely on the maintenance of acceptable production rates for extended time periods following the acquisition of vocational skill (Bellamy, Inman, & Yeates, 1978). This is especially the case in sheltered employment settings where clients are frequently required to assemble, sort, and/or package the same items during every work day. However, production rates can seldom be predicted from acquisition rates (Gold, 1973a; Wehman, Renzaglia, & Schutz, 1977). In other words, the speed at which the person learns a task does not predict the speed at which the task will be produced once learned. Several investigators have reported that severely mentally retarded persons can be trained to complete vocational tasks at industrial standards of speed with low error rates (Bellamy et al., 1975; Spooner & Hendrickson, 1976; Wehman et al., 1977). Therefore, it is important to train a client to criteria on a vocational task before decisions are made with respect to how fast the client will produce (Revell & Wehman, 1978).

Bellamy (1976) reported that there is great variability in production rates among mentally retarded workers. Some of the factors identified as affecting production rates included: 1) type of reinforcement contingency used, 2) supervisor's instructions, 3) distractions in the work area, and 4) modeling from work partners. Martin, Pallotta-Cornick, Johnstone, and Goyos (1980) reported that no one variable or procedure was effective for all clients and that effects observed for any given variable were frequently only temporary.

Reinforcement procedures have been particularly effective in increasing production rates of severely mentally retarded workers (Bellamy, Inman, & Horner, 1978; Schroeder, 1972). For example, Karen et al. (1974) provided severely mentally retarded students with tokens for completing various vocational tasks. In addition, timeout procedures (5 or 10 minutes of isolation) were used to control for disruptive behaviors. Results indicated that both production rate and accuracy of performance increased. Bellamy et al. (1978) taught three severely handicapped adults to assemble a cable harness. The investigators reported that they were able to reduce the time taken to complete the task by implementing a timer contingency, whereby the workers received two pennies rather than one if they completed the task before the timer rang.

Horner, Lahren, Schwartz, O'Neill, and Hunter (1979) compared the effects of differential reinforcement and self-delivery of reward on the production rates of severely handicapped workers. While contingent reinforcement procedures are successful in increasing production rates, they also frequently require great amounts of supervisory time. The alternative may be to develop self-management procedures. For example, Helland, Patuck, and Klein (1976) reported that subjects with low IQs can be taught to deliver their own reinforcers, and that self-reinforcement is as effective as contingent external reinforcement. Horner et al. (1979) replicated these findings, with the exception that they found the self-reinforcement system to be more effective in controlling production rates than external reinforcement.

A final procedure effective in controlling production rates was reported by Martin and Morris (1980). They speculated that low or declining production rates by severely mentally retarded persons may be due to a lack of well-defined "functional work ethic," which they describe as comprising: 1) a work history in which the client is reinforced for working, 2) the knowledge that work is a means of making money, 3) an understanding of the concept of the buying power of money, and 4) additional environmental factors such as peer expectations. To partially test this supposition, Martin and Morris (1980) provided training to severely handicapped workers on the relationship between production output and monetary reward by showing the clients how much money they made for each item produced. Production rates were found to increase following this procedure.

Programs and Approaches to Vocational Instruction Karan (1977) outlined a vocational model being conducted at the Waisman Center on Mental Retardation and Human Development, University of Wisconsin, Madison. The program is composed of three centers and was developed under the suppositions that while competitive employment is a reasonable goal for many severely handicapped persons, it should not be assumed to be immediately appropriate for all handicapped persons; and that, at the same time, it is important for all handicapped people to be placed in the least restrictive environment possible.

The first center, located in a state residential facility, deals with clients formerly thought by society to be too severely limited for vocational services. The purposes of the center are: 1) to prepare severely handicapped people for entry into rehabilitative programs and 2) to assist these people in becoming less dependent on society. The second center, located in a community-based rehabilitation facility, is a sheltered workshop and serves as a transition from institutional residence and employment to community employment. The third center is a short-term program for clients who are not yet ready for competitive employment but whose needs are better met by supervised rather than sheltered employment.

Wehman, Hill, and Koehler (1979) reported on a program called Project Employability, supported by the Virginia Department of Rehabilitative Services. The program is for moderately and severely retarded persons who have not previously displayed employment potential. The program uses on-the-job training procedures by which the trainee is moved from a local activity center into a job opening in the community with gradually reduced supervision. As of 1979, Project Employability had placed 15 clients into job locations. All of these clients were previously unemployed and had been considered unemployable.

Clark et al. (1980) used a CETA (Comprehensive Employment Training Act) program to train and place 10 severely handicapped persons on summer jobs. Each client worked with a nonhandicapped peer as a partner after CETA had defined the jobs. Nine of the 10 placements were successful, and, on a pre/post basis, parents reported improvement in the clients' social and personal behavior.

Mithaug (1979b) and Mithaug and Stewart (1978) described a prevocational training approach called Match-Sort-Assembly (MSA). The MSA approach does not analyze an existing task or focus on training a single set of responses. Instead, it is comprised of a sequence of simple to complex training steps designed to gradually shape increasingly complex levels of performance. The purpose is to teach skills that will generalize across tasks, avoiding the necessity of having to systematically teach every task learned. These goals are consistent with a longitudinal skill sequence described by Williams and Gotts (1977), whereby the client learns generalized and coordinated use of skills. Williams and Gotts (1977) stated that clients should learn: 1) the several skills necessary to complete a task, 2) a single skill required to complete many tasks, and 3) the coordination of several skills in the performance of a variety of different tasks.

A second approach to vocational training that appears promising for severely handicapped persons is the use of picture prompts (Wacker & Berg, in press). Picture prompts facilitate performance by first showing the client a picture of each step of the task to be performed and then training the client to use the pictures to guide his or her performance on the task.

Connis (1979), Sowers, Rusch, Connis and Cummings (1980), and Wacker and Berg (in press) used picture prompts to train mentally retarded clients to become more independent in vocational settings. Sowers et al. (1980) used picture prompts to train three moderately mentally retarded adults to go to and from work break and lunch independently. The clients were taught to respond to clock faces that prompted the clients to leave and return from lunch and work breaks. Wacker and Berg (in press) taught five moderately and severely mentally retarded adolescents to use picture prompts on one or more complex assembly tasks. Following acquisition, three of the clients generalized their use of the picture prompts on novel vocational tasks, resulting in a substantial reduction in training time.

Remaining Problems Several procedures for the evaluation and training of vocational behavior with severely mentally retarded persons have been identified and briefly described here. While impressive gains are being made, at least four major problems continue to confront researchers and professionals. Two of these problems were previously identified, i.e., a lack of generalization of vocational performance across tasks (necessitating that each new task be formally programmed through task analysis or some other procedure) and the lack of appropriate evaluation procedures.

A third problem concerns the ongoing need to eliminate behavior problems. Behavior problems frequently prohibit the placement of severely mentally retarded workers into vocational settings, even when such individuals have acquired the necessary vocational skills and have acceptable production rates (Malgady, Barcher, Davis, & Towner, 1980). Procedures for dealing with inappropriate behavior are reviewed in a later section of this chapter and are therefore not discussed here. However, the reader should be aware that behaviors such as disruptive behavior (Mithaug, 1978), poor grooming, and poor personal hygiene (Karan, 1977; Mithaug et al., 1980) frequently prevent the vocational placement of severely mentally retarded workers.

Little research is available regarding the relationship of adaptive and maladaptive behavior to vocational success (Malgady et al., 1980). To partially address this problem, Malgady et al. (1980) developed the Vocational Adaptation Rating Scale (VARS) to measure the frequency and severity of maladaptive behavior likely to occur in vocational settings. The authors reported that the VARS predicted placements in sheltered workshops better than IQ, age, or sex.

The fourth problem concerns the relative lack of research concerning the community work placement of severely mentally retarded persons (Whitman & Scibak, 1979). Most of the studies previously reviewed were concerned with sheltered employment, rather than competitive or community employment. Although sheltered employment is a positive development, it still falls short of job placement into competitive employment (Mithaug & Haring, 1976; Usdane, 1976; Wehman et al., 1979). There are several reasons for the lack of competitive employment opportunities for severely mentally retarded persons. First, societal and supervisory expectations for severely handicapped persons have traditionally only included sheltered working (Gold, 1973b; Revell & Wehman, 1978; Wehman et al., 1979). Second, there is a lack of clearly defined behavioral outcomes (i.e., the basic responses, skills, and behavioral patterns) for competitive employment (Mithaug, 1979b). Third, because job openings are rare, clients are sometimes placed into work environments without careful attention paid to the suitability of the placement (Wehman et al., 1979). Fourth, sheltered employment is restrictive in that it includes only handicapped workers, limiting the opportunities of severely mentally retarded workers to interact with nonhandicapped workers (Wehman et al., 1979).

Wehman and McLaughlin (1981) presented several factors that should be considered in community job placements. These include: 1) determining the most probable job sites and skills necessary for performance (e.g., Mithaug et al., 1977), 2) noting the subject's work history so that previous failures can be avoided, 3) evaluating the client's current levels of functioning (e.g., Mithaug & Hagmeier, 1978; Walls & Werner, 1977), 4) noting the client's potential living situation and transportation needs, and 5) surveying available community jobs, with food service, grounds keeping, and maintenance jobs given high priority because severely mentally retarded persons have been successful at these jobs (Becker, 1976; Wehman & McLaughlin, 1981).

Communication Training

Communication is a prime requirement for meaningful human interaction, and severely mentally retarded persons often lack significant language skills (Hodges & Deich, 1978; Lloyd, 1976). It has been estimated that 54.9% of all mentally retarded persons manifest some form of speech handicap (President's Commission on Mental Retardation, 1975), with 75% to 80% of people with IQs below 50 having severe speech problems (Garcia & DeHaven, 1974; Reich, 1978).

Although the terms *communication* and *language* are frequently used synonymously, the majority of research with severely mentally retarded persons has focused on communication, not language. For the purposes of this section, communication can be considered a process of exchanging information about objects or events, while language is a structure of linguistic rules used to communicate (Sternberg, Battle, & Hill, 1980). Many investigations support the notion that severely mentally retarded persons are able to learn to communicate effectively. Past researchers, however, argued that for many such persons, communication is not synonymous with language because severely mentally retarded individuals may be incapable of dealing with a formalized, structured language (Sternberg et al., 1980).

There are two major approaches or techniques to foster communication skills with severely mentally retarded persons. The first approach, variously called the developmental or cognitive approach, focuses on the development of specific cognitive skills to effect communication and is based on the hypothesized relationship between cognitive and linguistic development (Bates, Benigni, Bretherton, Camaioni, & Volterra, 1977). In addition, the cognitive/developmental approach emphasizes the need to define and describe the developmental status of the child (Miller, 1978), i.e., the developmental level of the person's comprehension and production skills. According to this approach, differences in the communication performance between mentally retarded persons and nonretarded persons of similar chronological ages occur because of differences between the children's mental/developmental ages. Therefore, at any stage of development, the mentally retarded child is comparable in cognitive and language functioning to that of a chronologically younger child (Inhelder, 1976; Rogers, 1977). In other words, this approach contends that mentally retarded children acquire language in the same sequence as normal children but at a slower rate, and this slower rate is accounted for primarily by the overall slower cognitive development of the child.

Haring and Bricker (1976) suggested that developmental models hold the greatest promise for implementing comprehensive communication approaches with severely handicapped children. They reported that developmental models assume three basic tenets: 1) growth or changes in behavior follow a developmental hierarchy, 2) behavior acquisition moves from simple to complex, and 3) complex behavior results from coordinating or modifying simple component response forms.

The second major approach to communication skills, the behavioral/remedial approach, does not assume that communication skills are necessarily related to developmental level, but rather, contends that many communication skills are subject to, and modifiable by, the same environmental contingencies that affect any other behavior. As a result, behavioral techniques focus on implementing operant conditioning techniques (e.g., positive reinforcement, imitation, and prompting) to develop, establish, and maintain communication behaviors such as verbal imitation, instruction-following, and grammatical and syntactical usage (Jones & Robson, 1979; Whitman & Scibak, 1979). Spradlin (1963, p. 551) noted, "studies of the effect of reinforcement on speech and vocal behavior, though far from conclusive, indicate that vocal language behaviors may be subject to the same reinforcement principles as non-language behavior."

It is beyond the scope of this section to articulate further the differences between these approaches or to discuss their implications for the communication and language training of severely mentally retarded persons (see Jones and Robson, 1979, for a more thorough discussion; Harris, 1975, for a discussion of teaching language skills to nonverbal children; and Chapter 5 of this book). However, it should be noted that the technology for teaching communication skills to severely mentally retarded persons is far from complete and that it is still debatable which behaviors should be taught, how they should be taught, or when intervention should occur. As noted by Bloom and Lakey (1978), the exact nature of what constitutes a language disorder is far from explicit in the literature, especially for mentally retarded individuals.

The remainder of this section focuses on some of the findings of communication research with severely mentally retarded persons. Most of the literature, particularly with respect to oral communication, has analyzed expressive rather than receptive skills (Jones & Robson, 1979; Whitman & Scibak, 1979). Readers should also be aware that a number of complicating and often confounding variables have been found to affect the communication performance of severely mentally retarded persons, i.e., lack of ability to organize perceptual stimuli, limitations in physiological ability to articulate sounds, history of failure in communication training programs, and extent of physical handicaps that may limit expressive nonverbal communication (Michaelis, 1978).

Oral Communication Training As noted by Harris (1975) and Hodges and Deich (1978), programs aimed at developing oral communication skills with mentally retarded persons have had varying degrees of success (e.g., Bricker & Bricker, 1970, 1974; Richardson, 1977; Schiefelbusch, 1967). However, both behavioral and cognitive/developmental approaches have been reported to be successful. Diverse aspects of communication skills, both receptive and productive, have been modified with behavioral procedures (Kazdin, 1978; Reid & Hurlbut, 1977; also see Garcia & DeHaven, 1974, for a review; and Morris, 1976, 1978, for prescriptive training suggestions). For example, Striefel, Bryan, and Aikins (1974) used a combination of reinforcement and fading of physical guidance to develop instruction-following behavior in a profoundly retarded boy, and Striefel and Wetherby (1973) used essentially the same procedures to teach the same skills to three severely mentally retarded children. Whitman, Zakaras, and Chardos (1971) trained severely mentally retarded children to respond to instructions such as "sit down" using physical guidance for compliance and food/praise reinforcers. In addition, generalization to novel instructions was also observed. Many other examples of training instruction-following to severely mentally retarded children are available in the literature (e.g., Frisch & Schumaker, 1974; Kazdin & Erickson, 1975).

Developing instructional control over behavior has been emphasized in the literature for severely mentally retarded persons, particularly by behavioral researchers, because it is one area of receptive communication that can have an immediate, direct effect on behavior (Kazdin, 1978). However, other aspects of communication have also been taught, although infrequently. Baer and Guess (1971) trained generalized understanding between "er" and "est" suffixes (e.g., "bigger" and "biggest") through differential reinforcement procedures. Following training, the subjects were able to generalize their learning to new combinations of adjectives that had not been previously trained. Bricker and Bricker (1974) trained a mentally retarded child in the receptive labeling of different objects by having the child first manipulate the objects.

The development of verbal imitation is considered very important in developing speech skills, particularly by behavioral researchers (Morris, 1978; Simeonsson & Wiegerink, 1974; Whitman & Scibak, 1979). Therefore, much of the research on expressive skills has focused, at least initially, on the development of imitation skills. Training usually begins, especially with subjects who demonstrate no speech, by reinforcing vocal imitations of sounds or words (Garcia, Baer, & Firestone, 1971; Kazdin, 1978). For example, Risley and Wolf (1967) developed functional speech in an echolalic child by reinforcing the child for imitating the name of an object placed before him. The experimenter gradually faded saying the word and taught the child to say the name of the object following the auditory direction "What is this?" Guess, Sailor, Rutherford, and Baer (1968) trained the generative use of a plural morpheme in a severely mentally retarded girl by reinforcing her for correctly imitating verbalizations in response to objects placed before her. Finally, Baer and Guess (1973) taught severely retarded children to say the suffixes "er" and "est," and Garcia, Guess, and Byrnes (1973) developed the expressive use of plural and singular sentences using procedures similar to those reported by Risley and Wolf (1967). The critical features of these approaches have been the use of imitation, fading the experimenter's verbal prompt, and then establishing functional word skills (Wehman & Bates, 1978).

Variations of this procedure have also been used to teach severely mentally retarded and severely handicapped persons vocabulary skills (e.g., Brown et al., 1972; Dorry & Zeaman, 1975), question asking or answering skills (Garcia, 1974; Twardosz & Baer, 1973), and sentence acquisition skills (Stevens-Long & Rasmussen, 1974). The study reported by Garcia (1974) deserves special mention because of the scope of the project. Garcia attempted to establish a conversational speech form in two severely mentally retarded nonverbal persons. The speech form consisted of three different three-word sentences associated with a picture, as well as questions concerning that picture. Using procedures consisting of imitation and fading, both subjects learned the sentences and partially generalized their learning to new stimuli and to a different experimenter.

Non-oral Communication Training Since the early 1970s, there has been a dramatic increase in the use of nonspeech communication systems with persons having essentially normal hearing but severe communication impairments (Fristoe & Lloyd, 1978; Lloyd, 1976). For example, over 10% of the 689 persons responding to a 1975 national survey of speech, hearing, and language service providers for mentally retarded persons indicated that they were using some form of nonspeech communication with their clients (Fristoe & Lloyd, 1978). Using a similar survey, Goodman, Wilson, and Bornstein (1978) received information regarding the communication services of approximately 4,000 clients (the largest diagnostic group being severely mentally retarded persons) residing in 28 states. Based on these results, well over 10,000 mentally retarded persons may be receiving sign language. In addition, 44% of the persons receiving training were 5 years of age or younger, indicating that even very young children are now receiving sign language services.

The remainder of this section provides an overview of nonspeech communication procedures available for use with severely mentally retarded persons. Emphasis is given to sign language training, as it is reported to be the most frequently used non-oral communication system with severely mentally retarded persons (Fristoe & Lloyd, 1978).

1. *Overview of Nonspeech Communication Systems* Although nonspeech communication systems have been used only relatively recently with severely mentally retarded persons, most researchers agree that non-oral communication

modes can and should be used to augment verbal communication (Fristoe & Lloyd, 1979a; Nietupski & Hamre-Nietupski, 1979). The provision of both visual and verbal input simultaneously, referred to as "simultaneous communication" by Kopchick and Lloyd (1976) and Stremel-Campbell, Cantrell, and Halle (1977), is important for two reasons: 1) most people communicate verbally and 2) simultaneous communication may be necessary if an attempt is made to promote speech with a manual system (Nietupski & Hamre-Nietupski, 1979).

While manual sign systems are the most frequently used nonspeech system, several other systems (briefly reviewed later) are available. Since many people automatically assume manual signs are used when reference is made to nonspeech systems, Nietupski and Hamre-Nietupski (1979) have recommended referring to all nonspeech systems, including manual signs, as "auxiliary communication systems." Auxiliary systems are recommended when: 1) a physical impairment such as a cleft palate or fixed motor deficits precludes the development of an adequate vocal response, and 2) the child is both well beyond the age when spontaneous language should appear, and verbal systems have failed to produce significant communication gains (the reader is referred to Vanderheiden & Grilley, 1976, for more information on auxiliary systems).

2. *Manual Signs* As mentioned previously, manual sign systems are the most frequently used auxiliary communication system with severely mentally retarded persons. However, several different manual systems are available for use with this population, including American Sign Language, Signing Exact English I and II, and Signed English (see Fristoe and Lloyd, 1977, 1979b, for an extensive listing of manuals and booklets, and Fristoe and Lloyd, 1978, for a listing of systems used with severely mentally retarded persons).

Goodman et al. (1978) reported that use of a particular system was regionally based, indicating that systematic examination of potential systems was not conducted. Of special interest is that both Goodman et al. (1978) and Fristoe and Lloyd (1978) reported that professionals who responded to their surveys were frequently unfamiliar or confused about the actual system used. For example, Goodman et al. (1978) concluded that many respondents who claimed to be using American Sign Language were actually using American Sign Language signs in an English word order (American Sign Language does not parallel English word order). Fristoe and Lloyd (1978) recorded identical findings.

Manual sign systems have been used successfully as a means of communication with nonverbal handicapped and severely mentally retarded persons who had previously not responded to oral language training (e.g., Berger, 1972; Bonvillian & Nelson, 1978; Bricker, 1972; Fristoe & Lloyd, 1977; Topper, 1975; Zweiban, 1977). One explanation for the success of sign systems with these populations is that many signs are iconic, at least for many of the beginning words (Griffith & Robinson, 1980). To partially test for the validity of this explanation, Griffith and Robinson (1980) tested the impact of iconicity of signs with verbal, moderately and severely mentally retarded persons. They reported that the subjects acquired more sign/word combinations with iconic rather than non-iconic signs.

Other investigators have studied the influence of using sign or simultaneous communication training on the receptive and expressive communication skills of mentally retarded persons. For example, Kohl, Karlan, and Heal (1979) investigated whether simultaneous communication facilitates the acquisition of instruction-following skills with severely mentally retarded children. These authors noted that while acquisition of instruction-following behavior with severely mentally retarded persons has been addressed frequently with verbal instructions (e.g., Striefel et al., 1974; Striefel, Wetherby, & Karlan, 1976), the influence of simultaneously presenting both oral and sign instructions has not been frequently studied. However, Kohl et al. (1979) reported that pairing signs with verbal instructions did facilitate the acquisition of instruction-following behavior with four severely retarded children.

Reich (1978) investigated the influence of pairing gestures with words on the speech of mentally retarded preschool children. As noted by Nietupski and Hamre-Nietupski (1979), there has been some fear by professionals that the use of auxiliary communication modes might inhibit speech, even though several investigators have reported that there is either no evidence to support this fear (Wilbur, 1976) or that an increase or improvement in vocalization occurred following sign programming (Grinnel, Detamore, & Lippke, 1976; Harris-Vanderheiden, Brown, MacKenzie, Reinin, & Scheibel, 1975; Hopper & Helmick, 1977). Reich (1978) taught nine preschool mentally retarded children 24 oral words, 12 with gestures paired with the words and 12 without gestures. He recorded the children's spontaneous use of these words and their imitation of the words. The results indicated that more spontaneous usage of the oral words occurred when the words were trained with gestures, but that no difference in imitated words occurred between the two sets of words.

Bricker (1972) and Janssen and Guess (1978) investigated the training of receptive labeling skills with mentally retarded individuals. Bricker reported that imitative sign training facilitated the development of word-object discriminations when the functional use of an object or a representational movement for each object was taught prior to providing the label (word) for the object. Janssen and Guess (1978) investigated whether the speed of acquiring receptive labeling skills is increased when the function of the object is taught in conjunction with the label. Their results indicated that using the function of an object in addition to the object's label does facilitate receptive labeling skills, but that teaching the function is not necessarily prerequisite to learning the object's label.

3. *Non-sign Systems* Reid and Hurlbut (1977) noted that despite the rapidly accumulating number of investigations on communication skills of mentally retarded persons, the major emphasis of these investigations has been on the development of oral communication skills (see also Snyder, Lovitt, & Smith,

1975, for a review). This has been especially true for auxiliary systems other than manual signs, even though many severely mentally retarded children are unable to learn either oral or sign language (e.g., Murphy, Steele, Gilligan, Yeon, & Spare, 1977). Two alternatives to manual sign communication training are presented here: the use of Premack symbols and the use of communication boards/picture communication systems (see Nietupski & Hamre-Nietupski, 1979, for a review of these systems and the advantages and disadvantages of each).

The emphasis of the Premack system is not on production of a symbol (as in speech or signing) but on recognizing various plastic geometric shapes that differ with respect to size, shape, and color (Hodges & Deich, 1978). Carrier (1974) and Hollis and Carrier (1975) used a variant of the Premack symbol system to teach non-oral communication skills to moderately to profoundly mentally retarded individuals. Hodges and Deich (1978) also used the Premack system with eight moderately to profoundly mentally retarded, nonverbal children. All eight learned the system; of special interest was the finding that the learning rates of the children had no relationship to mental age and IQ.

Murphy et al. (1977) and Reid and Hurlbut (1977) successfully used communication boards to teach communicative skills to severely handicapped individuals. Typically, the communication board approach involves the use of pictures, words, or signs displayed in an ordered fashion on a board in front of the individual. The subject is able to communicate by pointing or gazing at the picture or word displayed (Hagen, Porter, & Brink, 1973; Levett, 1969). Murphy et al. (1977) reported that a picture communication approach was successful in teaching a severely mentally retarded adolescent 13 words after sign communication training had been unsuccessful. Similar findings were reported by Reid and Hurlbut (1977), using a communication board with severely handicapped adults.

Difficulties in Communication Training Obviously, tremendous strides have taken place in the communication programming of severely mentally retarded persons. While many remaining difficulties still exist, some of which are reviewed briefly below, much of what is now routine practice was not considered even a remote possibility a decade ago.

During her review of verbal communication studies with mentally retarded people, Harris (1975) concluded that generalization does not seem to occur spontaneously. Rather, systematic efforts to provide for generalization must occur. This problem is certainly not unique to verbal communication training (e.g., Stokes & Baer, 1977), but does warrant attention. Before one can conclude that any method for promoting communication is effective for the severely mentally retarded population, documentation of the events necessary for generalization of training/treatment gains is necessary. In part, the solution may be to move communication training from the therapy/treatment room into the classrooms and residences of the client (Nietupski, Scheutz, & Ockwood, 1980). In other words, total communication, in which communication becomes a part of everyday living, is a desirable and necessary step. In addition, the variables connected with generalization of performance must be identified and tested (Stokes & Baer, 1977).

Another difficulty confronting communication training is to document the optimal sequence of communication skills training. As noted by Umbreit (1980), there are at least three different ways to sequence instruction: 1) developmental approaches (Bricker, Dennison, & Bricker, 1976), 2) semantic approaches (Miller, 1977), and 3) behavioral-remedial approaches (Guess, Sailor, & Baer, 1977). Whichever method is selected, strategies must be devised to allow professionals to identify skills and tasks that are both functional and age-appropriate for the student (Brown et al., 1979; Falvey, Brown, Lyon, Baumgart, & Schroeder, 1980; Umbreit, 1980).

Self-Help Skills

The term *self-help skills* is ambiguous and can potentially refer to almost any skill or behavior needed for "normalization" (Wolfensberger, 1972) or community placement. In this section, self-help skills refer to: 1) toileting, 2) dressing, 3) grooming, 4) eating, and 5) community-living skills (e.g., pedestrian and public transportation skills, telephone usage, and money usage). Note that while self-help skills and academic skills are treated separately in this chapter, the distinction is artificial. The majority of educational programs for severely mentally retarded persons not only include but emphasize the development of self-help skills (Haring & Bricker, 1976; Wehman & McLaughlin, 1980).

The acquisition and maintenance of self-help skills are especially important for severely mentally retarded persons, because such skills contribute to and, in many cases, are necessary for deinstitutionalization (Adkins & Matson, 1980; Sowers, Rusch, & Hudson, 1979; Wehman & McLaughlin, 1981). Clients who have not acquired these skills also frequently require large amounts of staff time, which can detract from training time in other areas such as in communication, education, and vocational programs (Gruber, Reeser, & Reid, 1979; Whitman & Scibak, 1979). For example, the majority of professional workers in state institutions for mentally retarded persons (contacted in a survey by Gruber et al., 1979) reported that they needed to escort their clients to school because the clients did not have independent pedestrian skills.

The development of self-help skills has been investigated frequently and the literature has reported numerous successes. Behavior modification procedures have been especially successful. The subsections following briefly review some of the findings in this area. The reader is referred to Morris (1978) and Wehman and McLaughlin (1981) for prescriptions and task analyses of these and other self-help skills. In addition, Spellman, DeBriere, Jarboe, Campbell, and Harris (1978) provide a complete description of how to train daily living skills using picture prompts.

Toileting Many successful methods for teaching toileting have used a combination of moisture-sensitive devices attached to the person's underpants and shaping procedures (e.g., Azrin & Foxx, 1971; Foxx & Azrin, 1973b; Mahoney, VanWagenen, & Meyerson, 1971). Mahoney et al. (1971) reported that a self-initiated toileting response is a chain of behaviors, including: walking to the toilet, removing clothes, sitting on the toilet, eliminating, cleaning oneself, and dressing.

The moisture-sensitive device is used to alert both the subject and the experimenters that urination is occurring. This device is sensitive enough that very early detection is possible. The major features of most of these programs involve: 1) frequent fluid intake to increase number of urinations, 2) scheduling toileting frequently (e.g., every half hour), 3) reinforcing dryness and proper elimination, and 4) correcting errors and using timeout to control for accidents.

In addition to being successful, the majority of these programs are also very rapid. For example, Azrin and Foxx (1971) taught nine severely mentally retarded males, who were incontinent 90% of the time, appropriate toileting skills within an average of 6 days. The investigators accomplished this by first increasing the amount of liquids consumed. When accidents occurred, the investigators were alerted by the moisture-sensitive device, and proceeded to require the boys to: 1) undress, 2) shower, 3) dress, and 4) clean the floor and wash clothes. In addition, brief timeout procedures were used.

Dressing Fewer reports of investigations of independent dressing/undressing training procedures are available than for most of the other self-help skills discussed here (except for pedestrian skills), and behavior modification procedures have not been as effective with this behavior (Kazdin, 1978; Whitman & Scibak, 1979). However, several procedures are available (e.g., Colwell, Richards, McCarver, & Ellis, 1973; Martin, Kehoe, Bird, Jensen, & Darbyshire, 1971), involving almost all garments; buttoning skills, zipping skills, and clothes selection (Azrin, Schaeffer, & Wesolowski, 1976; Karen & Maxwell, 1967; Minge & Ball, 1967; Nutter & Reid, 1978). Most of these procedures have entailed the use of task analysis and chaining with various prompting and reinforcement procedures (Morris, 1978; Wehman & Bates, 1978).

An example of a successful, economical procedure for teaching complete dressing and undressing skills was reported by Azrin et al. (1976). They taught the entire sequence of dressing and undressing to seven severely mentally retarded adults who could not dress, even with assistance, by using elaborate manual and verbal prompting. All seven subjects learned these behaviors with no assistance after 2 days of training (training was conducted during only two 2–3-hour sessions).

Grooming Severely handicapped people have been taught a variety of grooming skills, e.g., washing and drying their hands (Karen & Maxwell, 1967; Minge & Ball, 1967; Treffry, Martin, Samels, & Watson, 1970), and brushing their teeth (Horner & Keilitz, 1975). For example, Horner and Keilitz (1975) trained mentally retarded adolescents to brush their teeth using a detailed task analysis comprised of 15 component responses (e.g., wetting the toothbrush and putting toothpaste on the brush).

Token systems have also been used extensively to program grooming skills with severely mentally retarded persons. Tokens are reinforcers such as points or money that can be exchanged for other reinforcers such as food (Kazdin, 1978). For example, Kazdin (1977) reported that tokens have been used with severely mentally retarded persons for making their beds, taking showers, and self-cleaning skills. In addition, Wehman (1974) used a token system to teach 15 severely mentally retarded persons to wash their face and hands and to brush their hair.

Eating Several procedures exist for teaching mentally retarded persons various aspects of independent eating skills, including cooking or food preparation (Martin, Rusch, James, Decker, & Trtol, 1982; Matson, 1979; Robinson-Wilson, 1977), self-feeding skills (Azrin & Armstrong, 1973; Groves & Carroccia, 1971; Nelson, Cone, & Hanson, 1975), and in controlling inappropriate mealtime behavior (Barton, Guess, Garcia, & Baer, 1970). Most of these procedures have used a combination of chaining, reinforcement, and timeout procedures (Wehman & Bates, 1978) and can be used to maintain as well as to develop appropriate eating behavior (O'Brien, Bugle, & Azrin, 1972).

Groves and Carroccia (1971) taught self-feeding skills to severely mentally retarded persons who had previously never fed themselves, who used either no utensils or the wrong utensils when eating, and who demonstrated frequent inappropriate mealtime behavior such as throwing, hoarding, and grabbing food. These investigators taught self-feeding skills to these persons with a combination of procedures including shaping, prompting, and timeout.

Barton et al. (1970) reduced the undesirable mealtime behaviors (e.g., stealing and spilling food) of severely mentally retarded adolescents with a timeout procedure. When inappropriate behavior was displayed, the client was either removed from the table or the client's food tray was temporarily removed. Timeout procedures have been particularly effective when the client already has prerequisite self-feeding skills but demonstrates inappropriate mealtime behavior (Whitman & Scibak, 1979).

Azrin and Armstrong (1973) used overcorrection and reinforcement to teach 11 severely mentally retarded persons to eat properly. Azrin and Armstrong called their program the "mini-meal" because they divided the three daily meals into a number of shorter meals throughout the day. In this way, each client received numerous opportunities for training and practice. All 11 clients learned to eat properly with this system in an average of 5 days.

Johnson and Cuvo (1981) and Martin et al. (1982) used picture cues to train mildly and moderately mentally retarded clients to become more independent in meal preparation skills. Johnson and Cuvo (1981) trained four clients to use pictures to independently cook single food items, while Martin et al. (1982) taught three clients to independently prepare entire meals (each meal required that the clients complete between 48 and 76 separate steps).

Community Living Skills There is little doubt that mildly and moderately retarded persons can learn many community living skills, e.g., coin summation and change-making skills (Trace, Cuvo, & Criswell, 1977; Wunderlich, 1972), pedestrian skills (Page, Iwata, & Neef, 1976), and telephone skills (Leff, 1975). However, few investigators have taught community living skills to severely mentally retarded persons (Sowers et al., 1979; Vogelsberg & Rusch, 1979).

Sowers et al. (1979) were successful in teaching a severely mentally retarded adult to ride a city bus, and Certo, Schwartz, and Brown (1976) taught severely handicapped persons to ride a public bus when highly structured prompting and programming procedures were used. In addition, Vogelsberg and Rusch (1979) taught three severely handicapped school-age children to cross a partially controlled street.

Nietupski, Welch, and Wacker (in press) taught four moderately and severely mentally retarded adults to use a pocket calculator and picture prompts to purchase taxable and nontaxable items. The clients were provided with up to $20 and taught to use the calculator to subtract the price of various supermarket items until all assigned items were purchased or a negative subtotal was reached (in which case the final item was returned). Follow-up data indicated that the clients maintained their skills over a 3-month interval.

Vogelsberg, Anderson, Berger, Haselden, Mitwell, Schmidt, Skowron, Ulett, and Wilcox (1980) provided an excellent review of variables related to successful independent living and developed an inventory for use in selecting, setting up, and helping severely handicapped people to survive in independent living situations. Marholin, O'Toole, Touchette, Berger, and Doyle (1979) also provided valuable information on teaching community skills to mentally retarded persons, including the use of public transportation, restaurants, and stores.

Summary Most of the literature concerned with the self-help skills of severely mentally retarded persons has focused on basic skills such as toileting or eating skills. This emphasis has occurred because without the reliable acquisition of these skills, attempts at community placement would be difficult, at best. For most of the self-help skills described, reliable methods do seem to be available, although replication and maintenance studies are still needed.

However, so few attempts at community living skills have been reported that it is not possible to evaluate these programs. The investigations reported by Nietupski et al. (in press), Sowers et al. (1979) and Vogelsberg and Rusch (1979) are a major step forward, and it is hoped that more research in this area will be forthcoming.

EDUCATIONAL PROGRAMS AND SERVICES

It has been estimated that over 400,000 severely handicapped persons are in need of educational services (Sailor, Guess, & Lavis, 1975). Much of the research regarding the educational performance of mentally retarded individuals, however, has not been prescriptive, which limits the amount of definitive information available (Gardner, 1978). In addition, severely mentally retarded persons comprise a heterogeneous group (Sontag et al., 1977), which makes the development of educational prescriptions difficult. For example, Denny (1964) reported that groups based on a specified level of IQ frequently demonstrate greater variability in performance on any given task than do nonretarded persons of the same mental-age level. Similar findings were also reported by Milgram (1973).

An additional factor that has limited the appraisal of the educational performance of severely mentally retarded persons is that educational programming for these individuals has occurred only recently. Traditionally, special education programs and child guidance clinics showed minimal interest in the education of such persons because they were considered to be custodial and were therefore placed in state residential facilities at young ages (Morris, 1978; Wehman & Bates, 1978). As stated earlier, this attitude has changed in recent years, at least in part because of court and legislative decisions affirming the rights of all handicapped persons to public school services (Wehman & Bates, 1978).

A final factor that has acted to restrict our understanding is that many research investigations conducted on the educational skills of severely mentally retarded persons have focused only on comparisons between retarded and nonretarded groups and have not attempted to describe habilitation plans for severely mentally retarded persons (Baumeister & Kellas, 1971).

In recent years, the educational performance of severely mentally retarded persons has generated more attention, permitting the development of curricula and prescriptions for their education (see Brown et al., 1979; Morris, 1978; Wehman, 1979b; and Wehman & Bates, 1978, for suggestions). Existing curricula for severely mentally retarded persons reflect two identifiable approaches (Guess, Horner, Utley, Holvoet, Maxon, Tucker, & Warren, 1978). The first approach, referred to by Guess et al. (1978) as a "developmental logic," assumes the best method for teaching severely handicapped persons is to follow the same sequence in which nonretarded children learn (i.e., that all persons move through various developmental levels and that each level is prerequisite to the next). Therefore, advocates of this position (e.g., Haring & Bricker, 1976) have argued that specific behaviors cannot be taught independently from the child's current developmental level.

The second approach, representing a "remedial logic" (Guess et al., 1978), emphasizes the development of skills that will improve a child's ability to interact with the environment. Advocates of this position do not make assumptions regarding the order with which these skills should be taught.

Guess et al. (1978) reported that both of these approaches emphasize that the behaviors taught should be functional, i.e., that the behaviors should have immediate consequences for the child and are a natural part of the child's interaction with the environment. No attempt is made here to further elaborate on these approaches. Interested readers are referred to Guess et al. (1978), Guess, Sailor, and Baer (1974, 1977), and Haring and Bricker (1976) for more complete descriptions and analyses.

Suggestions for Curriculum Development

The traditional view of the educational curriculum as emphasizing reading, writing, and arithmetic must be altered for severely mentally retarded persons because of the priority to teach other behaviors such as self-help skills (Wehman & Bates, 1978). This is not to imply, however, that reading and arithmetic should not be taught to severely mentally retarded persons. Rather, the importance of teaching these skills must be weighed against the other skills severely mentally retarded students frequently need to acquire.

Irrespective of the content taught, several suggestions have been made regarding appropriate educational programming for severely mentally retarded persons. First, Brown et al. (1979) and Guess et al. (1978) suggested that the skills taught should promote as much independence as possible. Brown et al. suggested that even if the severely mentally retarded student is unable to participate fully in a task, he or she should be allowed to participate as much as possible. In addition, materials and devices used in the classroom should be adapted to promote independence.

A second suggestion by Brown et al. (1979) is that educational activities for severely mentally retarded persons should be age-appropriate. These authors noted that a 19-year-old severely mentally retarded individual is not identical to a 4-year-old nonretarded child, even if both have the same mental ages. The authors also stated that severely mentally retarded persons must be taught age-appropriate activities if eventual community placement is to be possible.

Third, the skills taught to severely mentally retarded persons should be functional (Brown et al., 1979; Guess et al., 1978; Orlansky, 1979). Brown et al. (1979) suggested that in determining what skills are to be taught to severely mentally retarded persons, teachers should consider the degree to which that skill enhances the child's ability to function in the natural environment. For example, if the child needs to learn fine-motor skills or develop better eye-hand coordination, it is more functional to have the child place keys into locks than pegs into boards. In addition to having immediate practical effects, instruction of functional skills should result in skills being retained for a longer duration (i.e., result in better maintenance) than nonfunctional skills (Guess et al., 1978).

Fourth, activities taught to severely mentally retarded persons should be conducted in natural contexts (Orlansky, 1979). For example, dressing and eating skills should be trained during times when these behaviors normally occur, not during arbitrary times of the day.

Fifth, severely mentally retarded persons should be provided the opportunity to freely and spontaneously explore their environments and to interact with their peers (Orlansky, 1979). Orlansky stated that while it is generally accepted that severely mentally retarded persons benefit from highly structured situations, some allowance should still be made for the possibility of independent and spontaneous activities. In addition, the necessity of one-to-one instruction has not been shown to always apply to severely mentally retarded learners. Storm and Willis (1978) compared small-group training with individualized instruction in teaching 18 imitative tasks to 12 severely mentally retarded adults. They reported group training to be as effective as individualized training when staff time was held constant (i.e., every student in the group instruction condition received 20 hours of training; students in the individualized condition received a total of 20 hours of training, but this amount of training was divided across the students). Favell, Favell, and McGimsey (1978) reported similar findings with severely mentally retarded adolescents.

A sixth and final suggestion regarding curriculum development for severely mentally retarded students is to include teaching strategies that increase the attention of these students to the relevant dimensions of the classroom tasks presented (Gardner, 1978). This suggestion is derived from the research of Zeaman and House (1963), who reported that the discrimination-learning deficits of many mentally retarded students occurred because of attentional deficits rather than basic learning deficits. Zeaman and House (1963) reported that when mentally retarded persons are confronted with a simple visual discrimination task, they frequently do not attend initially to the relevant visual cues necessary for task completion. Instead, these learners engage in trial and error behavior. However, once their attention is directed toward these cues, their learning rates do not differ from nonretarded children of comparable mental ages. According to this approach, the first step in training mentally retarded persons must therefore be to direct their attention to the relevant cues or dimensions of learning tasks. Gardner (1978) suggested that to increase the attention of mentally retarded persons, redundancy of cues (e.g., color coding of parts and exaggerating shape differences) should be used. His suggestions are supported by Gold (1972) and others concerned with vocational task performance.

Traditional Academic Skills Historically, programming for severely mentally retarded persons has not included reading or arithmetic skills because such persons were not considered capable of acquiring these skills (Wehman & Bates, 1978). As a result, few studies have been conducted on these skills.

In general, reading and mathematics instructional objectives should be based on the student's mental age, not chronological age (see Wehman & McLaughlin, 1981, for helpful suggestions in teaching these skills). Dorry and Zeaman (1973, 1975) taught moderately to severely mentally retarded persons a simple sight-word vocabulary with a fading procedure. The clients first received pretraining on a picture recognition task. Following pretraining, the pictures were paired with words. Finally, the pictures were faded until the subjects were reading the words independently. Using a procedure that included verbal and physical prompts and modeling, Rosenbaum and Breiling (1976) taught a severely handicapped child to comprehend sentences she was already able to sight read.

When instructing a severely mentally retarded student in traditional skills, the goal for instruction should always be functional. For example, if the goal for mathematics instruction is to increase the student's skills in purchasing, training with calculators may be more functional than traditional paper-and-pencil mathematics instruction. If possible, the training should also occur in a natural environment (e.g., a supermarket) to determine if the student uses the skill to facilitate ongoing performance. If training is conducted in the classroom, frequent generalization probes to the natural environment should be conducted. Nietupski et al. (in press) demonstrated that classroom training can generalize to natural environments, and provided a thorough description of how to conduct generalization probes.

Curriculum Programs In recent years, the educational performance of severely handicapped persons has generated more attention, resulting in the development of curricula for their education. Fredericks, Baldwin, Moore, Templeman, and Anderson (1980) reported on an educational model called the "Data-Based Classroom." This program, developed by Fredericks and his colleagues at the Oregon State System of Higher Education, has been replicated in more than 400 classroom sites in the United States. The program utilizes individualized programming procedures and emphasizes the development of self-help skills, motor development, language skills, and cognitive skills. All aspects of the program are developmentally sequenced and all contain task analyses of the skills to be learned. Of particular importance is the use of parents to continue instruction outside of the school environment.

Fredericks et al. (1980) tested the benefits of this program in two studies. The first study demonstrated that once this program was initiated with severely mentally retarded persons, the number of new skills acquired by the student increased considerably, while little improvement occurred without instruction. In the second study, the authors compared the progress of students in this program with similar students in other programs. Students enrolled in the "Data-Based Classroom" demonstrated significantly more gains in their skills.

Brown et al. (1979, p. 404) proposed what they called "current and subsequent environment-oriented curriculum development strategies." The authors discussed five major aspects of this approach. First, the approach deemphasizes the traditional focus upon the developmental discrepancies of severely mentally retarded persons, and focuses instead on age-appropriate functional skills. Second, the approach precisely describes the functional skill clusters required in a variety of natural environments. Third, it creates new curricular options that expand the boundaries of educational service delivery models. Fourth, the approach ensures that critical domestic, vocational, leisure, and community functioning skills are included in the educational curriculum. Fifth, instruction is provided in a variety of natural environments.

Guess et al. (1978) proposed the Functional Sequencing Model (FSM) for educational instruction. The FSM is a combination of developmental and behavioral/remedial approaches to instruction that concentrates on six domains of behavior: self-help, sensorimotor, language, social skills, academic skills, and vocational preparation. These six domains reflect content areas typically identified in assessment instruments (e.g., Balthazar, 1973; Nihara et al., 1974) and in existing curricula. In addition, the FSM is based on the notion of response generalization—i.e., responses that are similar topographically (physically similar responses, such as pulling down pants and pulling down on a towel dispenser) and functionally (two or more responses have different topographies but similar outcomes or meanings, such as saying "ball" and pointing to a ball) should coexist. In other words, topographically and/or functionally similar responses should not be taught separately; rather, once a pulling response is taught, for example, the subject should generalize this response across tasks and activities. Guess et al. (1978) stated that the major emphasis of the FSM is on teaching environmentally functional skills and on identifying and simultaneously teaching responses common to several tasks (e.g., grasping, pulling, etc.).

Problems in Instructional Programming Several interrelated and confounding deficiencies in the learning characteristics of severely mentally retarded learners add to the difficulty in providing instructional programming for them. For example, most nonretarded learners use imitation (observational learning) and various mediational strategies (e.g., clustering and rehearsal) spontaneously to facilitate the acquisition and retention of information. However, severely mentally retarded persons frequently do not spontaneously use either of these procedures to aid their learning (Gardner, 1978). As reported in the Communication Training section, imitation skills can be taught to severely mentally retarded persons (e.g., Garcia et al., 1971). However, most research on mediational strategies with mentally retarded persons has focused on mildly, mentally retarded subjects (see Gardner, 1978, and Kramer, Nagle, & Engle, 1980, for reviews). For example, Kramer et al. (1980) reported that mildly mentally retarded persons are able to use mnemonic strategies such as language mediators (Turnure & Thurlow, 1975), rehearsal (Turnbull, 1974), and various organizational strategies (Luszcs & Bacharach, 1975) to improve their memory skills. Winschel and Lawrence (1975) reported that the results of these studies hold potential for improving the educational performance of mentally retarded persons. Unfortunately, few studies have tested the use of mediational strategies with severely mentally retarded persons.

An exception to this is the research conducted by Meador and Rumbaugh (1981). They investigated whether severely handicapped persons could use hypothesis testing to mediate their performance on a discrimination task. The results indicated that the subjects were successful in using this strategy.

Two additional approaches to instruction that use mediational strategies may prove useful for severely handicapped learners. The first approach is to use picture cues. Spellman, DeBriere, Jarboe, Campbell, and Harris (1978) reported that picture prompts may promote maintenance of performance if the clients use pictures as a reference source. In other words, if a client "forgets" how to perform a task, and then uses previously trained pictures to prompt correct performance, the pictures serve as a reference source for the student.

A second approach is to teach clients to self-instruct (Karlan & Rusch, 1982) or self-label (Wacker & Greenebaum, in press). Karlan and Rusch (1982) reported that self-generated verbal instructions may be a viable maintenance procedure if the clients continue to instruct correct behavior following the termination of training. Wacker and Greenebaum (in press) reported that when moderately and severely mentally retarded students were taught to verbally label the critical feature of a prevocational sorting task, they independently (without further training) generalized their performance to a second task.

Another major problem in the literature on curriculum development for severely mentally retarded persons is that the contribution of the client to the success or failure of a program has seldom been considered (Morris, 1978; Orlansky, 1979). For example, Zigler (1966, 1969) provided illustrations of the possible contaminating effects of various cognitive and motivational variables on the performance of mentally retarded persons. Zigler reported that many of the studies used to infer learning or memory deficits in mentally retarded persons frequently did not control for motivational variables, and, therefore, that the validity of these findings may be questionable.

Guess et al. (1978) noted that the technology for teaching severely mentally retarded persons is more advanced than the knowledge of what to teach. It is still unclear what skills should be taught or when various skills should be programmed. In addition, Morris (1978) reported that few investigations have reported generalization and maintenance data. Therefore, it is still uncertain if those skills successfully learned by severely mentally retarded persons continue to be used following training.

Social Skills

Inadequate social behavior is often cited as a major behavioral deficit of severely mentally retarded persons, particularly if they are institutionalized (Mayhew, Enyart, & Anderson, 1978; Spradlin, Girardeau, & Corte, 1967). In fact, the lack of competent social behavior frequently distinguishes severely mentally retarded persons from nonretarded and other mentally retarded persons (Wehman, 1977; Wehman & Bates, 1978). Several reasons may account for the lack of appropriate social behavior in severely mentally retarded persons. First, severely mentally retarded persons lack many other behaviors that may be prerequisite for the development of social behaviors. For example, they frequently display poor eye contact (Morris, 1978; Morris & O'Neill, 1975). Second, many severely mentally retarded persons live in isolated institutional and community settings that may preclude opportunities for developing appropriate social behavior (Berkson & Romer, 1980; Birenbaum & Re, 1979). Third, opportunities for developing social relationships with staff members in institutional settings are frequently limited by chronically high staff turnover rates (Zaharia & Baumeister, 1978).

Severely mentally retarded persons, however, vary widely with respect to their social skills (Sparrow & Cicchetti, 1978). For example, enduring, intense, and complex friendships can occur among severely mentally retarded persons in both institutional and community settings (Landesman-Dwyer, Berkson, & Romer, 1979), and several approaches have been successful in increasing the social behavior of severely mentally retarded persons (Mayhew et al., 1978).

The following subsections briefly review investigations and suggestions regarding the social behavior of severely mentally retarded persons. Emphasis is placed on the development of social affiliations, play behavior, and leisure skills.

Social Affiliations Several investigations have reported on the influence of various characteristics of severely mentally retarded persons or their environments on the development of affiliation and friendship patterns. Landesman-Dwyer et al. (1979) reported that affiliations among mentally retarded adults are more strongly predicted by the size of the individual's living environment (i.e., group home) and the characteristics of the other residents living in that environment, than by the personal traits (e.g., sex, age, and IQ) of the resident. The results of the Landesman-Dwyer et al. (1979) study were that: 1) the amount of social interaction is not determined by sex or IQ level, 2) larger group homes resulted in more social interactions than did smaller homes, and 3) if the overall average of the IQ level within a group home is relatively high, all residents (including those with lower IQs) are more likely to spend time engaged in social interactions. The study was based on and supported previous findings that indicated that social interactions occurred more frequently in larger group homes than in smaller ones (Landesman-Dwyer, Stein, & Sackett, 1978; Sackett & Landesman-Dwyer, 1977). Sackett and Landesman-Dwyer (1977) reported that residents in smaller group homes (between six and nine residents) spent less time in didactic peer interactions and had a lower probability of having a "best friend" than those residing in larger group homes (between 18 and 20 residents).

Berkson and Romer (1980) investigated the effect of variables such as amount of exposure to other residents and similarity between residents (e.g., IQ levels) on choice of affiliation among mentally retarded persons. The findings supported those reported previously, i.e., the effects for IQ and sex were not significant or were accounted for primarily by residential segregation (e.g., all residents in a home were of the same IQ level).

Romer and Berkson (1980a,b) reported similar findings but also found that mentally retarded persons tended to affiliate most often with residents they had the most exposure to, irrespective of sex. Of the personal characteristics of the subjects investigated, age was the best predictor of affiliation (older subjects were less likely to affiliate). In addition, these investigators found that mentally retarded persons tended to affiliate with other residents who were moderately different from themselves in IQ but similar in physical attractiveness. These results and those of Landesman-Dwyer et al. (1979) indicate that if severely mentally retarded persons are segregated in group homes, their overall level of social interaction will be lower than if higher functioning mentally retarded persons are also present in these facilities.

Another factor that may affect the affiliations of severely mentally retarded persons is the occurrence of transfers (i.e., moving clients from one residence to another). Residential and work placements tend to change frequently for severely mentally retarded persons, and, if exposure is important for affiliation, affiliation patterns may be disrupted because of these transfers (Romer & Berkson, 1980a,b).

Carsrud et al. (1979) investigated the effects of environmental changes on 16 severely mentally retarded adolescents and adults. These residents were relocated involuntarily from an older, crowded living unit into a newer, uncrowded unit. The results suggested that the relocation did effect the social behaviors of the residents involved, causing an increase in both adaptive and maladaptive behavior. These results are consistent with those reported by Cohen et al. (1977), who noted that relocation promoted withdrawal and depression in higher-functioning mentally retarded persons and increases in both adaptive and maladaptive behavior in lower-functioning residents.

Cooperative Play and Social Interactions Few efforts have been reported on developing substantial cooperative play and social interactions in severely mentally retarded persons (Morris, 1978; Wehman & Bates, 1978). The development of these skills is important, not only because of their obvious influence on the child's everyday life, but also because they frequently result in many other positive effects. For example, Wehman (1979a) reported that teaching severely mentally retarded children to play appropriately with toys may facilitate: 1) the child's fine-motor skill development (Friedlander, Kamin, & Hesse, 1974), 2) the teacher's assessment of the child's cognitive functioning level (i.e., by inspecting the child's use of toy and play strategies), 3) the child's use of free time, and 4) the inhibition of inappropriate behavior if the behaviors connected with playing are incompatible with inappropriate behavior (Favell, 1973; Kissel & Whitman, 1977).

Several procedures exist for increasing severely mentally retarded children's independent play with toys (e.g., Favell, 1973; Kissel & Whitman, 1977; Wambold & Bailey, 1979; see also Wehman, 1979a, for suggestions and strategies for overcoming problems associated with teaching play behaviors). For example, Wambold and Bailey (1979) used prompting and encouragement of self-direction to teach six severely handicapped children to engage in independent play. These procedures were successful with five of the six children and on the average, increased the time spent in independent play activities by 24%. Morris and Dolker (1974) used physical guidance and modeling to teach a ball-rolling activity to two severely mentally retarded children, by using an imitation procedure (Burney, Russell, & Shores, 1977).

Several procedures have also attempted to increase the social interaction of severely mentally retarded persons. Whitman, Mercurio, and Caponigri (1970) used positive reinforcement (candy) to increase the amount of social interactions in severely mentally retarded children while they were playing a ball-rolling game. Stokes, Baer, and Jackson (1974) taught four severely mentally retarded persons a greeting response (waving their hands to greet others) by delivering food and giving praise contingent upon this response. Strain (1975), in an innovative investigation, increased the social behavior of eight severely handicapped preschoolers by using modeling and rehearsal strategies. The children were read stories regarding the social behavior of storybook characters, who the children could then imitate. After story time, the children were allowed to engage in free play. The amount of social play (e.g., sharing) increased for all children.

The use of nonhandicapped peers to mediate the behavior of severely handicapped students may also have merit. Strain (1977) increased the frequency of positive social behavior of three moderately retarded preschool boys by instructing a nonhandicapped peer (confederate) to initiate play. The confederate was taught to verbally prompt the boys to play, and generally set the occasion for appropriate social behavior. Similar findings were reported by Lancioni (1982) with elementary-age students.

Leisure Skills The development of leisure skills, including cooperative play and social interaction skills, is important for severely mentally retarded persons because these skills may facilitate increased proficiency in other aspects of their behavior, such as language or cognition. In addition, these skills may facilitate the acceptance of severely mentally retarded persons by their nonhandicapped peers (Wehman & McLaughlin, 1981). Severely mentally retarded persons, particularly those from institutions, have had minimal opportunities to develop leisure-time behaviors (Wambold & Bailey, 1979). In addition, although most severely mentally retarded persons have an abundance of free time (Wehman & McLaughlin, 1981), they tend to spend most of this time being idle or engaging in inappropriate behavior (Wambold & Bailey, 1979).

A few attempts at teaching active leisure skills to severely mentally retarded persons have been reported (e.g, Adkins & Matson, 1980; Johnson & Bailey, 1977). Adkins and Matson (1980) taught six moderately to severely mentally retarded institutionalized adults to make pot holders. This procedure was successful in increasing the active leisure time of these subjects. In addition, the procedures resulted in a positive side effect for one of the subjects by decreasing the amount of disruptive behavior previously exhibited, i.e., as active leisure-time participation increased, the amount of disruptive behavior decreased.

The current approach to teaching active leisure skills is to teach age-appropriate activities that generalize to natural environments. For example, Schleien, Wehman, and Kiernan (1981) and Hill, Wehman, and Horst (1982) taught severely handicapped persons to play a dart game and a pinball game, respectively. In both studies, the clients generalized their leisure skills to community settings. The importance of these studies is that the clients acquired leisure skills that increased their probability of interacting with nonhandicapped peers in social situations.

In determining the leisure skills to be taught to severely mentally retarded persons, Wehman and McLaughlin (1981) provide the following suggestions (Wehman & McLaughlin also provide an extensive leisure skill inventory for use with severely mentally retarded persons): 1) attempt to determine the leisure skill preferences of the clients, 2) determine the client's general level of functioning, 3) make sure the tasks are age-appropriate, and 4) ensure that there is support in the home environment for the leisure skills acquired.

Considerations Several basic training strategies have been used to increase the social behavior of severely handicapped persons. These strategies include the use of peers to mediate social behavior, directly training cooperative behavior (e.g., ball rolling), and directly training skills that may lead to increased social behavior (e.g., use of pinball machines). Regardless of the particular strategy used, two factors should always be considered when training social skills. First, the client needs to be specifically reinforced for engaging in appropriate social behavior. Each of the training procedures previously described reinforced the client when appropriate social behavior occurred. Although gains in social behavior can sometimes be achieved by modifying living environments, the gains achieved tend to be minimal if the clients are not consistently reinforced (Harris, Veit, Allen, & Chinsky, 1974; Murphy & Zahn, 1975).

Second, attention should be given to the natural consequences of appropriate social behavior. One reason for the lack of appropriate social behavior in many severely mentally retarded persons is the lack of naturally occurring reinforcement for engaging in this behavior (Dailey, Allen, Chinsky, & Veit, 1974; Mayhew et al., 1978; Warren & Mondy, 1971). Warren and Mondy (1971) reported that the staff in a state residential institution did not attend to the appropriate behavior of their clients 75%–80% of the time. Mayhew et al. (1978) reported they could increase or decrease appropriate social behavior in severely mentally retarded persons by simply attending to or ignoring such behavior. If we expect that clients will maintain social behavior in natural environments, then it is imperative that this behavior be encouraged and reinforced in the natural environment.

Inappropriate Behavior

Mentally retarded persons, particularly those who are or have been institutionalized, frequently engage in inappropriate behavior such as self-stimulatory and self-injurious behavior (Kazdin, 1978). It has been estimated that over 60% of institutionalized severely mentally retarded persons engage in some form of self-stimulatory behavior (Berkson & Davenport, 1962), with perhaps 7% demonstrating self-injurious behavior (Whitman & Scibak, 1979). Wehman and McLaughlin (1979) surveyed public and residential facilities regarding the behavior problems experienced by severely mentally retarded persons. The most frequent behavior problem encountered was noncompliance, but the most difficult behavior was self-stimulatory, or stereotypic, behavior.

Self-Stimulatory Behavior Self-stimulatory, or stereotypic, behavior involves repetitive body movements that serve no apparent purpose in the external environment (Harris & Wolchick, 1979). The etiology and function of this behavior remains debatable (Berkson, 1973). Examples of self-stimulatory behavior include rocking, arm waving, head weaving, and finger twirling (Cohen, Mayhew, & Clemens, 1980).

A number of techniques have been used to eliminate or decelerate self-stimulatory behavior, including physical punishment, timeout, differential reinforcement procedures, and overcorrection. The effects of these procedures are briefly described below (see Hobbs & Goswick, 1977, for a review of research on self-stimulation). Nonbehavioral procedures, such as the use of tranquilizers (Davis, Sprague, & Werry, 1969) or other medications are not reviewed.

Physical punishment procedures have been the most frequently used procedures to decrease self-stimulation, e.g., shock (Baumeister & Forehand, 1972; Lovaas, Schaeffer, & Simmons, 1965), slapping (Koegel, Firestone, Kramme, & Dunlap, 1974), and loud noise or reprimands (Baumeister & Forehand, 1972). However, the use of aversive punishment, despite its reported effectiveness, has been criticized for ethical and legal reasons and because its use may generate undesirable side effects such as withdrawal or aggression (Cohen et al., 1980).

Timeout procedures have also been used to reduce stereotypic behaviors (e.g., Pendergrass, 1972; Tharp & Wetzel, 1969). These procedures involve the contingent removal of the person from all sources of reinforcement when the inappropriate behavior is performed. Frequently, the length of the timeout interval can be very short and yet still be effective. For example, Pendergrass (1972) used a 2-minute timeout procedure to suppress stereotypic behavior in two mentally retarded children.

Two difficulties are associated with timeout procedures and may limit their usefulness. First, use of the procedure assumes that all sources of reinforcement can be removed, which is difficult with self-stimulatory behaviors because of their unknown etiology. Second, Solnick, Rincover, and Peterson (1977) demonstrated that the opportunity to engage in stereotypic behavior exists in timeout situations. As a result, the behavior may actually increase rather than decrease.

Reinforcement procedures have also been used to reduce stereotypic responding (e.g., Azrin, Kaplan, & Foxx, 1973; Repp, Deitz, & Deitz, 1976; Repp, Deitz, & Speir, 1974). Two types of reinforcement procedures have been most frequently used: differential reinforcement of other behaviors (DRO) and reinforcing incompatible behaviors (DRI). Repp et al. (1974) used a DRO procedure to reduce the stereotypic behavior of severely mentally retarded persons. Reinforcement was provided at the end of initially short time intervals during which no stereotypic behavior (e.g., rocking) occurred. The time intervals were gradually increased to longer time periods, leading to a marked reduction in the overall rate of stereotypic behavior. Azrin et al. (1973) reduced self-stimulatory behaviors in nine mentally retarded adults by employing a reinforcement of incompatible behaviors procedure. In this case, the incompatible behavior was appropriate use of work and play materials that the subjects had previously been using in nonfunctional stereotypic ways.

A final behavioral approach to reducing self-stimulation to be reviewed here is overcorrection (Foxx & Azrin, 1972). Overcorrection procedures are generally comprised of two components: 1) positive practice, in which a given set of desired behaviors is practiced repeatedly and 2) restitution, which requires the subject to restore the environment to a condition equal to or superior to that prior to the inappropriate behavior. (The reader should note that restitution is a particularly important ingredient when overcorrection is applied to disruptive behavior.)

Several studies have indicated that variants of the overcorrection procedure are effective in reducing stereotypic behavior (Azrin et al., 1973; Coleman, Whitman, & Johnson, 1979; Foxx & Azrin, 1973a; Higgs, Burns, & Meunier, 1980; Newton, Whorton, & Simpson, 1977). Azrin et al. (1973) reduced rocking and head-weaving behavior in severely mentally retarded adults to near-zero levels, using positive practice and reinforcement of incompatible behaviors. Coleman et al. (1979) reduced self-stimulatory behavior of a severely mentally retarded child while simultaneously increasing appropriate play behavior. Higgs et al. (1980) reduced self-stimulatory vocalizations with an overcorrection procedure that entailed the use of functional head-movement training, i.e., the child was required to move her head through a sequence of steps for 5 minutes every time she made an inappropriate verbalization.

Few studies have been conducted evaluating the relative effectiveness of these procedures. Two exceptions to this are the studies reported by Harris and Wolchick (1979) and Cohen et al. (1980). Cohen et al. compared a DRO procedure with an overcorrection procedure to reduce the finger twirling of an institutionalized severely mentally retarded child. The DRO procedure was found to be the more effective procedure. Harris and Wolchick (1979) reported different findings when they compared the effectiveness of timeout, DRO, and overcorrection procedures on the whirling, tapping, and repetitive movements of four autistic and severely mentally retarded boys. During the timeout procedure, the experimenters said, "No hand play," and turned their heads from the subject for 10 seconds. During the DRO procedure, the subjects were reinforced after every second response on an academic task if they were not engaged in self-stimulatory behavior. The overcorrection procedure required that the subject's hands be moved through an exaggerated hand clap pattern for 10 seconds. The results indicated that the overcorrection procedure was superior to the other procedures in that it led to an immediate and dramatic decrease in the self-stimulatory behavior of all four subjects. The timeout procedure had variable effects across subjects, and the DRO procedure had either no effect or actually resulted in an increase in the self-stimulatory behavior.

Clients who engage in self-stimulatory behavior may do so for different reasons, which may partially explain why different findings occur with the treatment procedures. For example, some clients may engage in stereotypic behavior because they receive attention. In this case, DRO or DRI procedures may have an immediate impact on the behavior. Other clients may engage in stereotypic behavior for just the opposite reason, i.e., to escape or avoid contact with staff. In this case, DRO or DRI procedures may not be effective, at least initially.

In most cases, the use of positive reinforcement is recommended as the treatment of choice. Positive reinforcement procedures are recommended because positive skills are trained, and if these skills are incompatible with the stereotypic behavior, they will continue to suppress the occurrence of the stereotypic behavior. If other treatment programs are selected to suppress stereotypic behavior, the practitioner will still need to consistently reinforce appropriate behavior to maintain the effects of treatment.

Self-Injurious Behavior Self-injurious behavior (SIB) is defined as a response that a person directs toward himself or herself that may result in tissue damage or permanent physical harm (Murphy, Ruprecht, & Nunes, 1979). As with self-stimulatory behavior, a number of possible antecedent conditions and etiologies have been offered as explanations (Tarpley & Schroeder, 1979). Besides being physically harmful, self-injurious behavior is very disruptive to programming attempts and is a relatively common phenomenon in institutionalized severely mentally retarded persons (Borreson, 1980; Rose, 1979). The most common forms of self-injurious behavior include scratching, head banging, biting, and gouging, but may include any conceivable response that the subject makes that is potentially harmful. Self-injurious behaviors are of concern to professionals working with severely mentally retarded persons because: 1) they may lead to permanent physical damage, 2) they may prohibit community placement, and 3) they may interfere with the acquisition of other, more appropriate behaviors (Kissel & Whitman, 1977; Koegel & Covert, 1972; Koegel et al., 1974).

Numerous behavior management techniques have been used to control self-injurious behavior (e.g., extinction, physical punishment, DRO, timeout, and reinforcing incompatible behavior). Some of these procedures are reviewed below; however, readers are also referred to Frankel and Simmons (1976) and Forehand and Baumeister (1976) for a more complete review, and to Smolev (1971) for a comprehensive review of early behavior management techniques.

Physical punishment procedures have been effective in controlling self-injurious behavior (e.g., Corte, Wolf, & Locke, 1971; Griffin, Locke, & Landers, 1975; Tanner & Zeiler, 1975). For example, Lovaas and Simmons (1969) and Corte et al. (1971) used contingent electric shock to reduce self-injurious behavior in mentally retarded persons, while others have used aromatic ammonia (Tanner & Zeiler, 1975) and hair tugging (Griffin et al., 1975). However, while the contingent use of intense physical punishment has frequently been an effective procedure in controlling self-injurious behavior, the use of most physical punishment procedures have been restricted (Martin, 1975; Tarpley & Schroeder, 1979). Physical punishment should only be used in extreme cases, and then only when proper human rights committees are available to monitor the program.

Timeout procedures have been reported to be more successful in controlling self-injurious behavior than extinction (ignoring the behavior) or reinforcement procedures, but not as successful as physical punishment (Murphy et al., 1979). Lucero, Frieman, Spoering, and Fehrenbacher (1976) decreased self-hitting in three severely mentally retarded persons by stopping them from eating (with physical restraints) for 15 seconds whenever self-injurious behavior was performed. Hamilton, Stephens, and Allen (1967) also used a combination of timeout and physical punishment procedures to reduce the destructive behavior of institutionalized severely mentally retarded residents. Murphy et al. (1979) used intermittent timeout with restraint and reinforcement of alternative behaviors to suppress self-injurious behavior in a severely mentally retarded adolescent. In addition, these results generalized to nontreatment settings.

The major problem connected with timeout procedures is that, in removing the subject from all sources of reinforcement, the subject is also frequently removed from educational and training environments. Although the length of time the subject is removed tends to be brief, this can be disruptive to training. The research reported by Murphy et al. (1979) is therefore of particular interest because the use of intermittent timeout procedures would be less disruptive (see also Clark, Rowbury, Baer, & Baer, 1973).

The effects of extinction and reinforcement procedures to control self-injurious behavior have been at least moderately successful, but equivocal findings have been reported (Nunes, Murphey, & Ruprecht, 1977; Rose, 1979). For example, Corte et al. (1971) reported that DRO was more effective than extinction but less effective than either physical punishment or overcorrection. However, Repp and Deitz (1974) found that DRO was an effective procedure, especially when it is combined with other procedures such as timeout or loss of reinforcers. In addition, Rose (1979) reduced the self-biting behavior of a severely handicapped child with a DRO procedure. The major advantage of reinforcement procedures is that they are not aversive and therefore have more practical implications for use in applied settings. However, it is not certain that these procedures are effective for controlling all self-injurious behavior, especially when compared with other procedures.

Overcorrection procedures have also been found to be effective in controlling self-injurious behavior (e.g., Agosta, Close, Hops, & Rusch, 1980; Azrin, Gottlieb, Hughart, Wesolowski, & Rahn, 1975; Harris & Romanczyk, 1976). For example, Harris and Romanczyk (1976) used overcorrection (guided head up and down) to decrease the head-banging behavior of a mentally retarded child. Agosta et al. (1980) used restitution and positive practice overcorrection to reduce the self-injurious behavior of a preschool child.

As previously discussed in the subsection on stereotypic behavior, the reasons for clients engaging in SIB may be variable. However, the use of positive reinforcement should be attempted initially because of the potential benefits to the client of this approach.

Prevention and early intervention are the keys to an effective program for SIB. Clients should be consistently reinforced for appropriate behavior and provided with structured schedules. If SIB still occurs, it should be treated immediately with DRO and DRI procedures. More restrictive forms of treatment are usually needed only when the SIB has been permitted to continue for long periods of time, or when the client has minimal opportunities or receives minimal reinforcement for engaging in other behavior.

Other Inappropriate Behavior Although self-stimulatory and self-injurious behaviors have been the most frequently investigated behaviors, the same procedures used to decrease these behaviors have also been used to decrease many other behaviors, e.g., aggressive behavior, disrobing, and noncompliance. Some of the findings with respect to these other behaviors are reviewed here.

A relatively common behavior that has a negative impact on the programming and placement of severely mentally retarded persons is aggressive behavior. Several procedures have been effective in controlling this behavior, including overcorrection (Foxx & Azrin, 1972; Polvinale & Lutzker, 1980), reinforcement (Polvinale & Lutzker, 1980; Repp & Deitz, 1974; Vukelich & Hake, 1971), and timeout (Bostow & Bailey, 1969; Calhoun & Matherne, 1975; Firestone, 1976; Noll & Simpson, 1979; Pendergrass, 1972). Foxx and Azrin (1972) used overcorrection to decrease the disruptive behavior (e.g., overturning a bed) of a severely mentally retarded client. The overcorrection procedure required the client to return the bed to its correct position (restitution) and then to straighten all other beds on the ward (positive practice). Polvinale and Lutzker (1980) reported that the combined use of DRO and overcorrection was effective in eliminating the aggressive and self-stimulatory behaviors of a severely mentally retarded boy. Pendergrass (1972) used the timeout procedure for intervals of 2 minutes to control the aggressive behavior (e.g., biting, hitting, and kicking) of two severely mentally retarded persons.

Other behaviors that have been reduced or eliminated using behavioral procedures include: 1) noncompliance (Mithaug, 1979a; Mithaug & Hanawalt, 1977), 2) hyperactive behavior (Evans, 1979; Forehand & Baumeister, 1970), 3) chronic rumination (Jackson, Johnson, & Ackron, 1975; Libby & Phillips, 1979), 4) public disrobing (Durana & Cuvo, 1980; Foxx, 1976; Paul & Miller, 1971), 5) theft (Azrin & Wesolowski, 1974), and 6) irrational statements (Kazdin, 1971).

Considerations Clearly, many different procedures are available and have been tested for controlling any number of inappropriate behaviors of severely mentally retarded persons. Deciding which procedure to use is dependent on many factors, including: the controlling stimuli of the behavior, the resources and time available, the urgency of treatment, and ethical and legal considerations. There is a need for more comparative research investigating the relative effectiveness of the procedures described. Almost all of the procedures have been reported to be effective when investigated in isolation. However, it is still unclear which procedures are most effective in controlling a given behavior in terms of both the immediate reduction of the behavior and to the maintenance or generalization of treatment effects.

Hobbs and Goswick (1977), in reviewing the research with respect to self-stimulation, noted that few studies have examined generalization or maintenance effects. Of the few studies in this section that reported data on generalization or maintenance, the findings were equivocal. Lack of generalization or maintenance effects is not particular to procedures dealing with inappropriate behavior or to severely mentally retarded persons (see Stokes & Baer, 1977). Concern over the issue of generalization was expressed with respect to almost every topic covered in this chapter. Research is needed to examine the necessary conditions for promoting generalization with severely mentally retarded persons.

CONCLUSION

The concept of severe/profound mental retardation is multifaceted and the members who comprise this group are heterogeneous. Any attempt to precisely characterize a severely mentally retarded person is futile, except to the extent that certain aspects of the person's intellectual functioning and adaptive behavior are known.

This chapter addressed the issues surrounding severe/profound mental retardation, first by distinguishing components of the definition (e.g., IQ and adaptive behavior) and then by presenting specific behavioral characteristics commonly investigated with this population (e.g., vocational behavior and communication skill). Information from both approaches allows for a more complete understanding of what constitutes severe/profound mental retardation and of how to train various skills to persons with such handicaps. Such information is further necessary to assist in developing more normalized life situations for these individuals.

However, our current knowledge on how best to achieve normalization is far from complete. We still need much more insight on what to teach, on how to optimally sequence instruction, and on where instruction should take place. Moreover, we have yet to define our instructional goals, except in broad terms, such as in relation to normalization or community placement.

REFERENCES

Adkins, J., & Matson, J. Teaching institutionalized mentally retarded adults socially appropriate leisure skills. *Mental Retardation*, 1980, *18*, 249–252.

Agosta, J., Close, D., Hops, H., & Rusch, F. Treatment of self-injurious behavior through overcorrection procedures. *Journal of The Association for the Severely Handicapped*, 1980, *5*, 5–12.

Allen, R., Cortazzo, A., & Adams, C. Factors in adaptive behavior checklist for use with retardates. *Training School Bulletin*, 1970, *67*, 144–157.

Azrin, N., & Armstrong, P. The "mini-meal"—A method for teaching eating skills to the profoundly retarded. *Mental Retardation*, 1973, *11*, 9–13.

Azrin, N., & Foxx, R. A rapid method of toilet training the institutionalized retarded. *Journal of Applied Behavior Analysis*, 1971, *4*, 89–99.

Azrin, N., Gottlieb, L., Hughart, L., Wesolowski, M., & Rahn, T. Eliminating self-injurious behavior by educative procedures. *Behavior Research and Therapy*, 1975, *13*, 101–111.

Azrin, N., Kaplan, S., & Foxx, R. Autism reversal: Eliminating stereotyped self stimulation of retarded individuals. *American Journal of Mental Deficiency*, 1973, *78*, 241–248.

Azrin, N., Schaeffer, R., & Wesolowski, M. A rapid method of teaching profoundly retarded persons to dress by a reinforcement-guidance method. *Mental Retardation*, 1976, *14*, 29–33.

Azrin, N., & Wesolowski, M. Theft reversal: An overcorrection procedure for eliminating stealing by retarded persons. *Journal of Applied Behavior Analysis*, 1974, *7*, 577–581.

Baer, D., & Guess, D. Receptive training of adjectival inflections in mental retardates. *Journal of Applied Behavior Analysis*, 1971, *4*, 129–139.

Baer, D., & Guess, D. Teaching productive noun suffixes to severely retarded children. *American Journal of Mental Deficiency*, 1973, *77*, 498–505.

Baker, D. Severely handicapped: Toward an inclusive definition. *AAESPH Review*, 1979, *4*, 52–65.

Balthazar, E. *Balthazar Scales of Adaptive Behavior*. Champaign, IL: Research Press, 1971.

Balthazar, E. *The Balthazar Scales of Adaptive Behavior. Section II. The scales of social adaptation*. Palo Alto, CA: Consulting Psychologists Press, 1973.

Baroff, G. On "size" and the quality of residential care: A second look. *Mental Retardation*, 1980, *18*, 113–117.

Barton, E., Guess, D., Garcia, E., & Baer, D. Improvement of retardates' mealtime behaviors by time-out procedures using multiple baseline techniques. *Journal of Applied Behavior Analysis*, 1970, *3*, 77–84.

Bateman, S. Application of Premack's generalization on reinforcement to modify occupational behavior in two severely retarded individuals. *American Journal of Mental Deficiency*, 1975, *79*, 604–610.

Bates, E., Benigni, L., Bretherton, I., Camaioni, L., & Volterra, V. From gesture to the first word: On cognitive and social prerequisites. In: M. Lewis & L. Rosenblum (eds.), *Interaction, conversation, and the development of language*. New York: John Wiley & Sons, 1977.

Baumeister, A., & Forehand, R. Effects of contingent shock and verbal command on body rocking of retardates. *Journal of Clinical Psychology*, 1972, *28*, 586–590.

Baumeister, A., & Kellas, G. Process variables in the paired-associate learning of retardates. In: N. Ellis (ed.), *International review of research in mental retardation*, Vol. 5. New York: Academic Press, 1971.

Becker, R. Job training placement for retarded youth: A survey. *Mental Retardation*, 1976, *14*, 7–9.

Bell, N. IQ as a factor in community lifestyle of previously institutionalized retardates. *Mental Retardation*, 1976, *14*, 29–33.

Bellamy, G. Habilitation of the severely and profoundly retarded: A review of research on work productivity. In: G. Bellamy (ed.), *Habilitation of severely and profoundly retarded adults*. Eugene, OR: University of Oregon Center on Human Development, 1976.

Bellamy, G., Inman, D., & Horner, R. Design of vocational habilitation services for the severely retarded: The specialized training program model. In: G. Hamerlynck (ed.), *Applied behavior analysis techniques for the developmentally disabled*. New York: Brunner-Mazel, 1978.

Bellamy, G., Inman, D., & Yeates, J. Workshop supervision: Evaluation of a procedure for production management with the severely retarded. *Mental Retardation*, 1978, *16*, 317–319.

Bellamy, G., Peterson, L., & Close, D. Habilitation of the severely and profoundly retarded: Illustrations of competence. *Education and Training of the Mentally Retarded*, 1975, *10*, 174–186.

Berger, S. A clinical program for developing multi-modal language responses with atypical deaf children. In: J. McLean, D. Yoder, & R. Schiefelbusch (eds.), *Language intervention with the retarded*. Baltimore: University Park Press, 1972.

Berkson, G. Visual defect does not reduce stereotyped movements. *American Journal of Mental Deficiency*, 1973, *78*, 89–94.

Berkson, G., & Davenport, R., Jr. Stereotyped movements of mental defectives. I: Initial survey. *American Journal of Mental Deficiency*, 1962, *66*, 849–852.

Berkson, G., & Landesman-Dwyer, S. Behavioral research on severe and profound mental retardation (1955–1974). *American Journal of Mental Deficiency*, 1977, *81*, 428–454.

Berkson, G., & Romer, D. Social ecology of supervised communal facilities for mentally disabled adults. I. Introduction. *American Journal of Mental Deficiency*, 1980, *85*, 219–228.

Berlin, C. Biology and retardation. In: J. Neisworth & R. Smith (eds.), *Retardation: Issues, assessment, and intervention*. New York: McGraw-Hill Book Co., 1978.

Birenbaum, A., & Re, M. Resettling mentally retarded adults in the community—almost four years later. *American Journal of Mental Deficiency*, 1979, *83*, 323–329.

Blatt, B. *Exodus from pandemonium: Human abuse and a reformation of public policy*. Boston: Allyn and Bacon, 1970.

Blatt, B., & Kaplan, F. *Christmas in purgatory: A photographic essay on mental retardation*. Boston: Allyn and Bacon, 1966.

Bloom, L., & Lakey, M. *Language development and language disorders*. New York: John Wiley & Sons, 1978.

Bonvillian, J., & Nelson, K. Development of sign language in autistic children and other language handicapped individuals. In: P. Siple (ed.), *Understanding language through sign language research*. New York: Academic Press, 1978.

Borreson, P. The elimination of a self-injurious avoidance response through a forced running consequence. *Mental Retardation*, 1980, *18*, 73–77.

Bostow, D., & Bailey, J. Modifications of severe disruptive and aggressive behavior using brief time-out and reinforcement procedures. *Journal of Applied Behavior Analysis*, 1969, *2*, 31–37.

Bradley, B. Deinstitutionalization: Social justice or political expedient? *Amicus*, 1980, *5*, 82–87.

Bricker, D. Imitative sign training as a facilitator of word-object association with low functioning children. *American Journal of Mental Deficiency*, 1972, *76*, 509–516.

Bricker, D., Dennison, L., & Bricker, W. *A language intervention program for developmentally disabled young children*. Miami: Mailman Center for Child Development, 1976.

Bricker, W., & Bricker, D. A program of language training for the severely handicapped child. *Exceptional Children*, 1970, *37*, 101–112.

Bricker, W., & Bricker, D. An early language training strategy. In: R. Schiefelbusch & L. Lloyd (eds.), *Language perspectives—Acquisition, retention, and intervention*. Baltimore: University Park Press, 1974.

Brolin, D. *Vocational preparation of retarded citizens*. Columbus, OH: Charles E. Merrill Publishing Co., 1976.

Brown, L., Bellamy, G., Perlmutter, L., Sackowitz, P., & Sontag, E. The development of quality, quantity, and durability in the work performance of retarded students in a public school prevocational workshop. *Training School Bulletin*, 1972, *68*, 58–69.

Brown, L., Branston, M., Hamre-Nietupski, S., Pumpian, I., Certo, N., & Gruenewald,

L. A strategy for developing chronological age appropriate and functional curricular content for severely handicapped adolescents and young adults. *Journal of Special Education*, 1979, *13*, 81–90.

Brown, L., Branston-McClean, M., Baumgart, D., Vincent, L., Falvey, M., & Schroeder, J. Using the characteristics of current and subsequent least restrictive environments in the development of curricular content for severely handicapped students. *AAESPH Review*, 1979, *4*, 407–424.

Brown, L., Jones, S., Troccolo, E., Heiser, C., Bellamy, G., & Sontag, E. Teaching functional reading to young trainable students: Toward longitudinal objectives. *Journal of Special Education*, 1972, *6*, 237–246.

Brown, L., & Pearce, E. Increasing the production of trainable retarded students in public school simulated workshop. *Education and Training of the Mentally Retarded*, 1970, *5*, 15–22.

Burney, J., Russell, B., & Shores, R. Developing social responses in two profoundly retarded children. *AAESPH Review*, 1977, *2*, 53–60.

Butterfield, E. Basic facts about public residential facilities for the mentally retarded. In: R. Kugel & W. Wolfensberger (eds.), *Changing patterns in residential services for the mentally retarded*. Washington, D.C.: U.S. Government Printing Office, 1969.

Cain, L., Levine, S., & Freeman, F. *The Cain-Levine Social Competency Scale*. Palo Alto, CA: Consulting Psychologists Press, 1963.

Calhoun, K., & Matherne, P. The effects of varying schedules of time-out on aggressive behavior of a retarded girl. *Journal of Behavior Therapy and Experimental Psychiatry*, 1975, *6*, 139–143.

Carrier, J., Jr. Nonspeech noun usage training with severely and profoundly retarded children. *Journal of Speech and Hearing Research*, 1974, *17*, 510–517.

Carsrud, A., Carsrud, K., Henderson, D., Alisch, L., & Fowler, A. Effects of social and environmental change on institutionalized mentally retarded persons: The relocation syndrome reconsidered. *American Journal of Mental Deficiency*, 1979, *84*, 266–272.

Cartwright, G., & Cartwright, C. Definition and classification approaches. In: J. Neisworth & R. Smith (eds.), *Retardation: Issues, assessment, and intervention*. New York: McGraw-Hill Book Co., 1978.

Certo, N., Schwartz, R., & Brown, L. Teaching severely handicapped students to ride a public bus. In: N. Haring & L. Brown (eds.), *Teaching the severely handicapped*, Vol. 2. New York: Grune & Stratton, 1976.

Clark, H., Rowbury, T., Baer, A., & Baer D. Timeout as a punishing stimulus in continuous and intermittent schedules. *Journal of Applied Behavior Analysis*, 1973, *6*, 443–455.

Clark, J., Greenwood, L., Abramowitz, D., & Bellamy, G. Summer jobs for vocational preparation of moderately and severely retarded adolescents. *Journal of the Association for the Severely Handicapped*, 1980, *5*, 24–37.

Close, D., Irvin, L., Prehm, H., & Taylor, V. Systematic correction procedures in vocational-skill training of severely retarded individuals. *American Journal of Mental Deficiency*, 1978, *83*, 270–275.

Coffman, T., & Harris, M. Transition shock and adjustments of mentally retarded persons. *Mental Retardation*, 1980, *18*, 3–7.

Cohen, H., Conroy, J., Frazer, D., Snelbecker, G., & Spreat, S. Behavioral effects of interinstitutional relocation of mentally retarded residents. *American Journal of Mental Deficiency*, 1977, *82*, 12–18.

Cohen, R., Mayhew, G., & Clemens, D. Comparison of topographically similar and dissimilar positive practice and a DRO procedure in the management of stereotypic behavior. *Journal of The Association for the Severely Handicapped*, 1980, *5*, 294–302.

Coleman, R., Whitman, T., & Johnson, M. Suppression of self-stimulatory behavior of a profoundly retarded boy across staff and settings: An assessment of situational generalization. *Behavior Therapy*, 1979, *10*, 266–280.

Colwell, L., Richards, E., McCarver, R., & Ellis, N. Evaluation of self-help habit training of the profoundly retarded. *Mental Retardation*, 1973, *11*, 14–18.

Connis, R. The effects of sequenced pictures, self-recording, and praise on the job task sequencing of retarded adults. *Journal of Applied Behavior Analysis*, 1979, *12*, 355–361.

Conroy, J. Trends in deinstitutionalization of the mentally retarded. *Mental Retardation*, 1977, *15*, 44–46.

Corte, H., Wolf, M., & Locke, B. A comparison of procedures for eliminating self-injurious behavior of retarded adolescents. *Journal of Applied Behavior Analysis*, 1971, *4*, 201–213.

Crawford, J., Aiello, J., & Thompson, D. Deinstitutionalization and community placement: Clinical and environmental factors. *Mental Retardation*, 1979, *17*, 59–63.

Crosson, J. A technique for programming sheltered workshop environments for training severely retarded workers. *American Journal of Mental Deficiency*, 1969, *73*, 814–818.

Cuvo, A., Leaf, R., & Borakove, L. Teaching janitorial skills to the mentally retarded: Acquisition, generalization, and maintenance. *Journal of Applied Behavior Analysis*, 1978, *11*, 345–355.

Dailey, W., Allen, G., Chinsky, J., & Veit, S. Attendant behavior and attitudes toward institutionalized retarded children. *American Journal of Mental Deficiency*, 1974, *78*, 586–591.

Davis, K., Sprague, R., & Werry, J. Stereotyped behavior and activity level in severe retardates: The effect of drugs. *American Journal of Mental Deficiency*, 1969, *73*, 721–727.

Dennis, W., & Sayegh, B. The effects of supplementary experiences upon the behavioral development of infants in institutions. *Child Development*, 1965, *36*, 81–90.

Denny, M. Research in learning and performance. In: H. Stevens & R. Heber (eds.), *Mental retardation: A review of research*. Chicago: University of Chicago Press, 1964.

DeVellis, R. Learned helplessness in institutions. *Mental Retardation*, 1977, *15*, 10–13.

Dingman, H., & Tarjan, G. Mental retardation and the normal distribution curve. *American Journal of Mental Deficiency*, 1960, *64*, 991–994.

Doll, E. *Measurement of social competence: A manual for the Vineland Social Maturity Scale*. Washington, D.C.: American Association on Mental Deficiency, 1969.

Dorry, G., & Zeaman, D. The use of a fading technique in paired-associate teaching of reading vocabulary with retardates. *Mental Retardation*, 1973, *11*, 3–6.

Dorry, G., & Zeaman, D. Teaching a simple reading vocabulary to retarded children: Effectiveness of fading and nonfading procedures. *American Journal of Mental Deficiency*, 1975, *79*, 711–716.

Durana, I., & Cuvo, A. A comparison of procedures for decreasing public disrobing of an institutionalized, profoundly retarded woman. *Mental Retardation*, 1980, *18*, 185–188.

Evans, R. The reduction of hyperactive behavior in three profoundly retarded adolescents through increased stimulation. *AAESPH Review*, 1979, *4*, 259–263.

Eyman, R., & Borthwick, S. Patterns of care for mentally retarded persons. *Mental Retardation*, 1980, *18*, 63–66.

Eyman, R., Tarjan, G., & Cassady, M. Natural history of acquisition of basic skills by hospitalized retarded patients. *American Journal of Mental Deficiency*, 1970, *75*, 120–129.

Falvey, M., Brown, L., Lyon, S., Baumgart, D., & Schroeder, J. Strategies for using cues and correction devices. In: W. Sailor, B. Wilcox, & L. Brown (eds.), *Methods of instruction for severely handicapped students*. Baltimore: Paul H. Brookes Publishing Co., 1980.

Favell, J. Reduction of stereotypes by reinforcement of toy play. *Mental Retardation*, 1973, *2*, 21–23.
Favell, J., Favell, J., & McGimsey, J. Relative effectiveness and efficiency of group vs. individual training of severely retarded persons. *American Journal of Mental Deficiency*, 1978, *83*, 104–109.
Firestone, P. The effects and side-effects of timeout on an aggressive nursery school child. *Journal of Behavior Therapy and Experimental Psychiatry*, 1976, *7*, 79–81.
Fisher, J., & Zeaman, D. An attention-retention theory of retardate discrimination learning. In: N. Ellis (ed.), *International review of research in mental retardation*, Vol. 6. New York: Academic Press, 1973.
Forehand, R., & Baumeister, A. Effects of variations in auditory-visual stimulation on the activity levels of severe mental retardates. *American Journal of Mental Deficiency*, 1970, *74*, 470–474.
Forehand, R., & Baumeister, A. Deceleration of aberrant behavior among retarded individuals. In: M. Hersen, R. Eisler, & P. Miller (eds.), *Progress in behavior modification*. New York: Academic Press, 1976.
Foxx, R. The use of overcorrection to eliminate the public disrobing (stripping) of retarded women. *Behavior Research and Therapy*, 1976, *14*, 53–61.
Foxx, R., & Azrin, N. Restitution: A method of eliminating aggressive-disruptive behavior of retarded and brain damaged patients. *Behavior Research and Therapy*, 1972, *10*, 15–27.
Foxx, R., & Azrin, N. The elimination of autistic self-stimulatory behavior by overcorrection. *Journal of Applied Behavior Analysis*, 1973, *6*, 1–14. (a)
Foxx, R., & Azrin, N. *Toilet training the retarded*. Champaign, IL: Research Press, 1973. (b)
Frankel, F., & Simmons, J. Self-injurious behavior in schizophrenic and retarded children. *American Journal of Mental Deficiency*, 1976, *80*, 512–522.
Fredericks, B., Baldwin, V., Moore, W., Templeman, T., & Anderson, R. The teaching research data-based classroom model. *Journal of The Association for the Severely Handicapped*, 1980, *5*, 211–223.
Friedlander, B., Kamin P., & Hesse, G. Operant therapy for prehension disabilities in moderately and severely retarded young children. *Training School Bulletin*, 1974, *71*, 101–108.
Frisch, S., & Schumaker, J. Training generalized receptive prepositions in retarded children. *Journal of Applied Behavior Analysis*, 1974, *7*, 611–621.
Fristoe, M., & Lloyd, L. Manual communication for the retarded and others with severe communication impairment: A resource list. *Mental Retardation*, 1977, *15*, 18–21.
Fristoe, M., & Lloyd, L. A survey of the use of non-speech systems with the severely communication impaired. *Mental Retardation*, 1978, *16*, 99–103.
Fristoe, M., & Lloyd, L. Non-speech communication. In: N. Ellis (ed.), *Handbook of mental deficiency: Psychological theory and research* (2nd ed.). New York: Lawrence Earlbaum Associates, 1979. (a)
Fristoe, M., & Lloyd, L. Signs used in manual communication training with persons having severe communication impairment. *AAESPH Review*, 1979, *4*, 364–373. (b)
Gage, M., Fredericks, H., Baldwin, B., Moore, W., & Grove, D. Group homes for handicapped children. In: N. Haring & D. Bricker (eds.), *Teaching the severely handicapped*, Vol. 3. Seattle, WA: American Association for the Education of the Severely and Profoundly Handicapped, 1978.
Garcia, E. The training and generalization of a conversational speech form in nonverbal retardates. *Journal of Applied Behavior Analysis*, 1974, *7*, 137–149.
Garcia, E., Baer, D., & Firestone, I. The development of generalized imitation within topographically determined boundaries. *Journal of Applied Behavior Analysis*, 1971, *4*, 101–112.

Garcia, E., & DeHaven, E. Use of operant techniques in the establishment and generalization of language: A review and analysis. *American Journal of Mental Deficiency*, 1974, *79*, 169–178.

Garcia, E., Guess, D., & Byrnes, J. Development of syntax in a retarded girl using procedures of imitation, reinforcement, and modeling. *Journal of Applied Behavior Analysis*, 1973, *6*, 299–311.

Gardner, J. *The Comprehensive Behavior Checklist: Manual.* Columbus, OH: Columbus State Institute, 1970.

Gardner, W. Research in learning and performance characteristics of the mentally retarded. In: J. Neisworth & R. Smith (eds.), *Retardation: Issues, assessment, and intervention.* New York: McGraw-Hill Book Co., 1978.

Gearheart, B., & Litton, F. *The trainable retarded, a foundations approach* (2nd ed.). St. Louis: C.V. Mosby Co., 1979.

Gold, M. Stimulus factors in skill training of retarded adolescents on a complex assembly task: Acquisition, transfer, and retention. *American Journal of Mental Deficiency*, 1972, *76*, 517–526.

Gold, M. Factors affecting production by the retarded: Base rate. *Mental Retardation*, 1973, *11*, 41–45. (a)

Gold, M. Research on the vocational habilitation of the retarded: The present, the future. In: N. Ellis (ed.), *International review of research in mental retardation*, Vol. 6. New York: Academic Press, 1973. (b)

Gold, M. Task analysis of a complex assembly task by the retarded blind. *Exceptional Children*, 1976, *43*, 78–84.

Gold, M., & Barclay, C. The effects of verbal levels on the acquisition and retention of a complex assembly task. *Training School Bulletin*, 1973, *70*, 38–43. (a)

Gold, M., & Barclay, C. The learning of difficult visual discriminations by the moderately and severely retarded. *Mental Retardation*, 1973, *11*, 9–11. (b)

Goodman, L., Wilson, P., & Bornstein, J. Results of a national survey of sign language programs in special education. *Mental Retardation*, 1978, *16*, 104–106.

Griffin, J., Locke, B., & Landers, W. Manipulation of potential punishment parameters in the treatment of self-injury. *Journal of Applied Behavior Analysis*, 1975, *8*, 458–459.

Griffith, P., & Robinson, J. Influence of iconicity and phonological similarity of sign learning by mentally retarded children. *American Journal of Mental Deficiency*, 1980, *85*, 291–298.

Grinnel, M., Detamore, K., & Lippke, B. Sign it successful—Manual English encourages expressive communication. *Teaching Exceptional Children*, 1976, *8*, 123–124.

Grossman, J. (ed.). *Manual on terminology and classification in mental retardation.* Washington, D.C.: American Association on Mental Deficiency, 1977.

Groves, I., & Carroccia, D. A self-feeding program for the severely and profoundly retarded. *Mental Retardation*, 1971, *9*, 10–12.

Gruber, B., Reeser, R., & Reid, D. Providing a less restrictive environment for profoundly retarded persons by teaching independent walking skills. *Journal of Applied Behavior Analysis*, 1979, *12*, 285–297.

Guess, D., Horner, R., Utley, B., Holvoet, J., Maxon, D., Tucker, D., & Warren, S. A functional curriculum sequencing model for teaching the severely handicapped. *AAESPH Review*, 1978, *3*, 202–215.

Guess, D., Sailor, W., & Baer, D. To teach language to retarded children. In: R. Schiefelbusch & L. Lloyd (eds.), *Language perspectives—Acquisition, retention, and intervention.* Baltimore: University Park Press, 1974.

Guess, D., Sailor, W., & Baer, D. A behavioral-remedial approach to language training for the severely handicapped. In: E. Sontag, J. Smith, & N. Certo (eds.), *Educational programming for the severely and profoundly handicapped.* Reston, VA: Division on Mental Retardation, The Council for Exceptional Children, 1977.

Guess, D., Sailor, W., Rutherford, G., & Baer, D. An experimental analysis of linguistic development: The productive use of the plural morpheme. *Journal of Applied Behavior Analysis*, 1968, *1*, 297–306.

Hagen, C., Porter, W., & Brink, J. Nonverbal communication: An alternative mode of communication for the child with severe cerebral palsy. *Journal of Speech and Hearing Disorders*, 1973, *38*, 448–455.

Hamilton, J., Stephens, L., & Allen, P. Controlling aggressive and destructive behavior in severely retarded institutionalized residents. *American Journal of Mental Deficiency*, 1967, *71*, 852–856.

Haring, N., & Bricker, D. Overview of comprehensive services for the severely/profoundly handicapped. In: N. Haring & L. Brown (eds.), *Teaching the severely handicapped*, Vol. 1. New York: Grune & Stratton, 1976.

Harlow, H. Forward. In: N. Robinson & H. Robinson (eds.), *The mentally retarded child* (2nd ed.). New York: McGraw-Hill Book Co., 1976.

Harris, J., Veit, S., Allen, G., & Chinsky, J. Aide-resident ratio and ward population density as mediators of social interaction. *American Journal of Mental Deficiency*, 1974, *79*, 320–326.

Harris, S. Teaching language to nonverbal children with emphasis on problems of generalization. *Psychological Bulletin*, 1975, *82*, 565–580.

Harris, S., & Romanczyk, R. Treating self-injurious behavior of retarded child by overcorrection. *Behavior Therapy*, 1976, *7*, 235–239.

Harris, S., & Wolchick, S. Suppression of self-stimulation: Three alternative strategies. *Journal of Applied Behavior Analysis*, 1979, *12*, 185–198.

Harris-Vanderheiden, D., Brown, W., MacKenzie, P., Reinin, S., & Schiebel, C. Symbol communication for the mentally handicapped. *Mental Retardation*, 1975, *13*, 34–37.

Hayward, J., & Tapp, J. Experience and the development of adaptive behavior. In: N. Ellis (ed.), *International review of research in mental retardation*, Vol. 1. New York: Academic Press, 1966.

Heal, L., Sigelman, C., & Switsky, H. Research on community residential alternatives for the mentally retarded. In: N. Ellis (ed.), *International review of research in mental retardation*, Vol. 9. New York: Academic Press, 1974.

Helland, C., Patuck, R., & Klein, M. A comparison of self-and external reinforcement with the trainable mentally retarded. *Mental Retardation*, 1976, *14*, 22–23.

Higgs, R., Burns, G., & Meunier, G. Eliminating self-stimulatory vocalizations of a profoundly retarded girl through overcorrection. *Journal of The Association for the Severely Handicapped*, 1980, *5*, 264–269.

Hill, J., Wehman, P., & Horst, G. Toward generalization of appropriate leisure and social behavior in severely handicapped youth: Pinball machine use. *Journal of The Association for the Severely Handicapped*, 1982, *6*, 38–44.

Hobbs, S., & Goswick, R. Behavioral treatment of self-stimulation: An examination of alternatives to physical punishment. *Journal of Clinical Child Psychology*, 1977, *6*, 20–23.

Hodges, P., & Deich, R. Teaching an artificial language to nonverbal retardates. *Behavior Modification*, 1978, *2*, 489–509.

Hollis, J., & Carrier, J., Jr. Research implications for communication deficiencies. *Exceptional Children*, 1975, *42*, 405–412.

Hopper, C., & Helmick, R. Nonverbal communication for the severely handicapped: Some considerations. *AAESPH Review*, 1977, *2*, 47–52.

Horner, R., & Keilitz, I. Training mentally retarded adolescents to brush their teeth. *Journal of Applied Behavior Analysis*, 1975, *8*, 301–309.

Horner, R., Lahren, B., Schwartz, T., O'Neill, C., & Hunter, J. Dealing with low production rates of severely retarded workers. *AAESPH Review*, 1979, *4*, 202–212.

Hunter, J., & Bellamy, G. Cable harness construction for severely retarded adults: A demonstration of training techniques. *AAESPH Review*, 1976, *1*, 2–13.

Inhelder, B. Some pathologic phenomena analyzed in the perspective of developmental psychology. In: B. Inhelder & H. Chapman (eds.), *Piaget and his school*. New York: Springer-Verlag, 1976.

Intagliata, J., Kraus, S., & Willer, B. The impact of deinstitutionalization on a community based service system. *Mental Retardation*, 1980, *18*, 305–307.

Intagliata, J., Wilder, B., & Cooley, F. Cost comparison of institution and community based alternatives for mentally retarded persons. *Mental Retardation*, 1979, *17*, 154–156.

Irvin, L., & Bellamy, G. Manipulation of stimulus features in vocational-skill training of severely retarded individuals. *American Journal of Mental Deficiency*, 1977, *81*, 486–491.

Jackson, G., Johnson, C., & Ackron, G. Food satiation as a procedure to decelerate vomiting. *American Journal of Mental Deficiency*, 1975, *80*, 223–227.

Jancar, J., & Simon, G. Causes and prevention. In: G. B. Simon (ed.), *The modern management of mental handicap: A practice manual*. Lancaster, England: MTP Press Limited, 1980.

Janssen, C., & Guess, D. Use of function as a consequence in training receptive labeling to severely and profoundly retarded individuals. *AAESPH Review*, 1978, *3*, 246–258.

Johnson, B., & Cuvo, A. Teaching mentally retarded adults to cook. *Behavior Modification*, 1981, *5*, 187–202.

Johnson, J., & Mithaug, D. A replication survey of sheltered workshop entry requirements. *AAESPH Review*, 1978, *3*, 116–122.

Johnson, M., & Bailey, J. The modification of leisure behavior in a half-way house for retarded women. *Journal of Applied Behavior Analysis*, 1977, *10*, 273–282.

Jones, A., & Robson, L. Language training the severely mentally handicapped. In: N. Ellis (ed.), *Handbook of mental deficiency, psychological theory, and research* (2nd ed.). New York: Lawrence Erlbaum Associates, 1979.

Karan, O. Graduated habilitation programming for the severely developmentally disabled. *Rehabilitation Literature*, 1977, *38*, 322–327.

Karen, R., Eisner, M., & Endres, R. Behavior modification in a sheltered workshop for severely retarded students. *American Journal of Mental Deficiency*, 1974, *79*, 338–347.

Karen, R., & Maxwell, S. Strengthening self-help behavior in the retardate. *American Journal of Mental Deficiency*, 1967, *71*, 546–550.

Karlan, G., & Rusch, F. Correspondence between saying and doing: Some thoughts on defining correspondence and future directions for application. *Journal of Applied Behavior Analysis*, 1982, *15*, 151–162.

Kaufman, M. The effects of institutionalization on development of stereotyped and social behaviors in mental defectives. *American Journal of Mental Deficiency*, 1967, *71*, 581–585.

Kazdin, A. The effect of response cost in suppressing behavior in a pre-psychotic retardate. *Journal of Behavior Therapy and Experimental Psychiatry*, 1971, *2*, 137–140.

Kazdin, A. *The token economy: A review and evaluation*. New York: Plenum Publishing Corp., 1977.

Kazdin, A. Behavior modification in retardation. In: J. Neisworth & R. Smith (eds.), *Retardation: Issues, assessment, and intervention*. New York: McGraw-Hill Book Co., 1978.

Kazdin, A., & Erickson, L. Developing responsiveness to instructions in severely and profoundly retarded residents. *Journal of Behavior Therapy and Experimental Psychiatry*, 1975, *6*, 17–21.

Kissel, R., & Whitman, T. An examination of the direct and generalized effects of a play-training and overcorrection procedure upon the self-stimulatory behavior of a profoundly retarded boy. *AAESPH Review*, 1977, *2*, 131–146.

Koegel, R., & Covert, A. The relationship of self-stimulation to learning in autistic children. *Journal of Applied Behavior Analysis*, 1972, *5*, 381–387.

Koegel, R., Firestone, P., Kramme, D., & Dunlap, G. Increasing spontaneous play by suppressing self-stimulation in autistic children. *Journal of Applied Behavior Analysis*, 1974, *7*, 521–528.

Kohl, F., Karlan, G., & Heal, L. Effects of pairing manual signs with verbal cues upon the acquisition of instruction-following behaviors and the generalization to expressive language with severely handicapped students. *AAESPH Review*, 1979, *4*, 291–300.

Koop, S., Martin, G., Yu, D., & Suthons, E. Comparison of two reinforcement strategies in vocational-skill training of mentally retarded persons. *American Journal of Mental Deficiency*, 1980, *84*, 616–626.

Kopchick, G., & Lloyd, L. Total communication programming for the severely language impaired: A 24-hour approach. In: L. Lloyd (ed.), *Communication assessment and intervention strategies*. Baltimore. University Park Press, 1976.

Kramer, J., Nagle, R., & Engle, R. Recent advances in mnemonic strategy training with mentally retarded persons: Implications for educational practice. *American Journal of Mental Deficiency*, 1980, *85*, 306–314.

Kugel, R., & Shearer, A. Towards further change. In: R. Kugel & W. Wolfensberger (eds.), *Changing patterns in residential services for the mentally retarded*. Washington, D.C.: Superintendent of Documents, 1976.

Kugel, R., & Wolfensberger, W. (eds.) *Changing patterns in residential services for the mentally retarded*. Washington, D.C.: U.S. Government Printing Office, 1969.

Lancioni, G. Normal children as tutors to teach social responses to withdrawn mentally retarded schoolmates: Training, maintenance, and generalization. *Journal of Applied Behavior Analysis*, 1982, *15*, 17–40.

Landesman-Dwyer, S., Berkson, G., & Romer, D. Affiliation and friendship of mentally retarded residents in group homes. *American Journal of Mental Deficiency*, 1979, *83*, 571–580.

Landesman-Dwyer, S., Sackett, G., & Kleinman, J. Relationship of size to resident and staff behavior in small community residences. *American Journal of Mental Deficiency*, 1980, *85*, 6–17.

Landesman-Dwyer, S., Stein, J., & Sackett, G. A behavioral and ecological study of group homes. In: G. Sackett (ed.), *Observing behavior, Vol. 1: Theory and applications in mental retardation*. Baltimore: University Park Press, 1978.

Leff, R. Teaching TMR children and adults to dial the telephone. *Mental Retardation*, 1975, *13*, 9–11.

Levett, L. A method of communication for nonspeaking severely subnormal children. *British Journal of Disorders of Communication*, 1969, *4*, 64–66.

Libby, D., & Phillips, E. Eliminating rumination behavior in a profoundly retarded adolescent: An exploratory study. *Mental Retardation*, 1979, *17*, 94.

Lloyd, L. (ed.). *Communication assessment and intervention strategies*. Baltimore: University Park Press, 1976.

Lovaas, O., Schaeffer, B., & Simmons, J. Building social behavior in autistic children by use of electric shock. *Journal of Experimental Research in Personality*, 1965, *1*, 99–109.

Lovaas, O., & Simmons, J. Manipulation of self-destruction in three retarded children. *Journal of Applied Behavior Analysis*, 1969, *2*, 143–157.

Lucero, W., Frieman, J., Spoering, K., & Fehrenbacher, J. Comparison of three procedures in reducing self-injurious behavior. *American Journal of Mental Deficiency*, 1976, *80*, 548–554.

Luszcs, M., & Bacharach, B. List organization and rehearsal instructions in recognition memory of retarded adults. *American Journal of Mental Deficiency*, 1975, *80*, 57–62.

Lynch, K. Toward a skill-oriented prevocational program for trainable and severely mentally impaired students. In: T. Bellamy, G. O'Connor, & O. Karan (eds.), *Vocational habilitation of the developmentally disabled: Contemporary service strategies*. Baltimore: University Park Press, 1979.

MacAndrew, C., & Edgerton, R. The everyday life of institutionalized idiots. *Human Organization*, 1964, *23*, 312–318.

McCarver, R., & Craig, E. Placement of the retarded in the community: Prognosis and outcome. In: N. Ellis (ed.), *International review of research in mental retardation*, Vol. 7. New York: Academic Press, 1974.

MacMillan, D. *Mental retardation in school and society*. Boston: Little, Brown, & Co., 1977.

Mahoney, K., VanWagenen, R., & Meyerson, L. Toilet training of normal and retarded children. *Journal of Applied Behavior Analysis*, 1971, *4*, 173–181.

Malgady, R., Barcher, P., Davis, J., & Towner, G. Validity of the vocational adaptation rating scale: Prediction of mentally retarded workers' placement in sheltered workshops. *American Journal of Mental Deficiency*, 1980, *84*, 633–640.

Marholin, D., O'Toole, K., Touchette, P., Berger, P., & Doyle, D. "I'll have a Big Mac, large fries, large Coke, and apple pie" . . . or teaching adaptive community skills. *Behavior Therapy*, 1979, *10*, 236–248.

Marozas, D., May, D., & Lehman, L. Incidence and prevalence: Confusion in need of clarification. *Mental Retardation*, 1980, *18*, 229–230.

Martin, A., & Morris, J. Training a work ethic in severely mentally retarded workers—Providing a context for the maintenance of skill performance. *Mental Retardation*, 1980, *18*, 67–71.

Martin, G., Kehoe, B., Bird, E., Jensen, V., & Darbyshire, M. Operant conditioning in dressing behavior. *Mental Retardation*, 1971, *9*, 27–31.

Martin, G., Pallotta-Cornick, A., Johnstone, G., & Goyos, A. A supervisory strategy to improve work performance for lower functioning retarded clients in a sheltered workshop. *Journal of Applied Behavior Analysis*, 1980, *13*, 183–190.

Martin, J., Rusch, F., James, V., Decker, P., & Trtol, K. The use of picture cues to establish self-control in the preparation of complex meals by mentally retarded adults. *Applied Research in Mental Retardation*, 1982, *3*, 105–119.

Martin, R. *Legal challenges to behavior modification: Trends in schools, corrections, and mental health*. Champaign, IL: Research Press, 1975.

Matson, J. A field tested system of training meal preparation skills to the retarded. *British Journal of Mental Subnormality*, 1979, *25*, 14–18.

Mayhew, G., Enyart, P., & Anderson, J. Social reinforcement and the naturally occurring social responses of severely and profoundly retarded adolescents. *American Journal of Mental Deficiency*, 1978, *83*, 164–170.

Meador, D., & Rumbaugh, D. Quality of learning of severely retarded adolescents. *American Journal of Mental Deficiency*, 1981, *85*, 404–409.

Meyers, E., Nihira, K., & Zetlin, A. Adaptive behavior. In: N. Ellis (ed.), *Handbook of mental deficiency, psychological theory and research*. New York: Lawrence Erlbaum Associates, Inc., 1979.

Michaelis, C. Communication with the severely and profoundly handicapped: A psycholinguistic approach. *Mental Retardation*, 1978, *16*, 346–349.

Milgram, N. Cognition and language in mental retardation: Distinctions and implications. In: D. Routh (ed.), *The experimental psychology of mental retardation*. Chicago: Aldine Publishing Co., 1973.

Miller, J. On specifying what to teach: The movement from structure, to structure and meaning, to structure and meaning and knowing. In: E. Sontag, J. Smith, & N. Certo (eds.), *Educational programming for the severely and profoundly handicapped*. Reston, VA: Division of Mental Retardation, The Council for Exceptional Children, 1977.

Miller, J. Assessing children's language behavior: A developmental process approach. In: R. Schiefelbusch (ed.), *The basis of language intervention*. Baltimore: University Park Press, 1978.

Minge, M., & Ball, T. Teaching self-help skills to profoundly retarded patients. *American Journal of Mental Deficiency*, 1967, *71*, 864–868.

Mithaug, D. Case studies in the prevocational training and behavior management of severely handicapped adults. *AAESPH Review*, 1978, *3*, 132–143.

Mithaug, D. A comparison of procedures to increase responding in three severely retarded, noncompliant young adults. *AAESPH Review*, 1979, *4*, 66–80. (a)

Mithaug, D. The relation between programmed instruction and task analysis in the prevocational training of severely and profoundly handicapped persons. *AAESPH Review*, 1979, *4*, 162–178. (b)

Mithaug, D., & Hagmeier, L. The development of procedures to assess prevocational competencies in severely handicapped young adults. *AAESPH Review*, 1978, *3*, 94–115.

Mithaug, D., Hagmeier, L., & Haring, N. The relationship between training activities and job placement in vocational education of the severely and profoundly handicapped. *AAESPH Review*, 1977, *2*, 89–109.

Mithaug, D., & Hanawalt, D. Employing negative reinforcement to establish and transfer control of a severely retarded and aggressive nineteen-year-old girl. *AAESPH Review*, 1977, *2*, 37–49.

Mithaug, D., & Hanawalt, D. The validation of procedures to assess prevocational task preferences in retarded adults. *Journal of Applied Behavior Analysis*, 1978, *11*, 153–162.

Mithaug, D., & Haring, N. Community vocational and workshop placement. In: N. Haring & L. Brown (eds.), *Teaching the severely handicapped*, Vol. 2. New York: Grune & Stratton, 1976.

Mithaug, D., & Mar, D. The relation between choosing and working prevocational tasks in two severely retarded young adults. *Journal of Applied Behavior Analysis*, 1980, *13*, 177–182.

Mithaug, D., Mar, D., Stewart, J., & McCalmon, D. Assessing prevocational competencies of profoundly, severely, and moderately retarded persons. *Journal of The Association for the Severely Handicapped*, 1980, *5*, 270–283.

Mithaug, D., & Stewart, J. *Match-sort-assemble: A prevocational program for handicapped children and adults*. Seattle: Exceptional Education, 1978.

Morris, R. *Behavior modification with children: A systematic guide*. Cambridge, MA: Winthrop, 1976.

Morris, R. Treating mentally retarded children: A prescriptive approach. In: A. Goldstein (ed.), *Prescriptions for child—mental health and education*. New York: Pergamon Press, 1978.

Morris, R., & Dolker, M. Developing cooperative play in socially withdrawn retarded children. *Mental Retardation*, 1974, *12*, 24–27.

Morris, R., & O'Neill, J. Developing eye contact in severely and profoundly retarded youth. *Mental Retardation*, 1975, *13*, 42–43.

Morton, R., & Hebel, J. *A study guide to epidemiology and biostatistics*. Baltimore: University Park Press, 1978.

Murphy, G., Steele, K., Gilligan, T., Yeon, J., & Spare, D. Teaching a picture language to a nonspeaking retarded boy. *Behavior Research and Therapy*, 1977, *15*, 198–201.

Murphy, M., & Zahn, D. Effects of improved ward conditions and behavioral treatment on self-help skills. *Mental Retardation*, 1975, *13*, 24–27.

Murphy, R., Ruprecht, M., & Nunes, D. Elimination of self-injurious behavior in a profoundly retarded adolescent using intermittent time-out, restraint, and blindfold procedures. *AAESPH Review*, 1979, *4*, 334–345.

National Center for Law and the Handicapped, Inc., Legal Staff. The right to habilitation in the community. *Amicus*, 1980, *5*, 73–81.

Nelson, G., Cone, J., & Hanson, C. Training correct utensil use in retarded children: Modeling vs. physical guidance. *American Journal of Mental Deficiency*, 1975, *80*, 114–122.

Newton, R., Whorton, D., & Simpson, R. The modification of self-stimulatory verbalizations in an autistic child through the use of an overcorrection procedure. *AAESPH Review*, 1977, *2*, 157–163.

Nietupski, J., & Hamre-Nietupski, S. Teaching auxiliary skills to severely handicapped students. *AAESPH Review*, 1979, *4*, 107–124.

Nietupski, J., Scheutz, G., & Ockwood, L. The delivery of communication therapy services to severely handicapped students: A plan for change. *Journal of The Association for the Severely Handicapped*, 1980, *5*, 13–23.

Nietupski, J., Welch, J., & Wacker, D. Acquisition, maintenance, and transfer of grocery item purchasing skills by moderately and severely handicapped students. *Education and Training of the Mentally Retarded*, in press.

Nihira, K., Foster, R., Shellhaas, M., & Leland, H. *AAMD Adaptive Behavior Scale*. Washington, D.C.: American Association on Mental Deficiency, 1969.

Nihira, K., Foster, R., Shellhaas, M., & Leland, H. *AAMD Adaptive Behavior Scale, 1974 revision*. Washington, D.C.: American Association on Mental Deficiency, 1974.

Nihira, L., & Nihira, K., Jeopardy in community placement. *American Journal of Mental Deficiency*, 1975, *79*, 538–544.

Noll, M., & Simpson, R. The effects of physical time-out on the aggressive behaviors of a severely emotionally disturbed child in a public school setting. *AAESPH Review*, 1979, *4*, 399–406.

Nunes, D., Murphey, R., Ruprecht, M. Reducing self-injurious behavior of severely retarded individuals through withdrawal of reinforcement procedures. *Behavior Modification*, 1977, *1*, 499–516.

Nutter, D., & Reid, D. Teaching retarded women a clothing selection skill using community norms. *Journal of Applied Behavior Analysis*, 1978, *11*, 475–487.

O'Brien, F., Bugle, L., & Azrin, N. Training and maintaining a retarded child's proper eating. *Journal of Applied Behavior Analysis*, 1972, *5*, 67–72.

O'Neill, C., & Bellamy, G. Evaluation of a procedure for teaching saw chain assembly to a severely retarded woman. *Mental Retardation*, 1978, *16*, 36–40.

Orlansky, M. Sam's day: A simulated observation of a severely handicapped child's educational program. *AAESPH Review*, 1979, *4*, 251–258.

Page, T., Iwata, B., & Neef, N. Teaching pedestrian skills to retarded persons: Generalization from the classroom to the natural environment. *Journal of Applied Behavior Analysis*, 1976, *9*, 433–444.

Paul, H., & Miller, J. Reduction of extreme deviant behaviors in a severely retarded girl. *Training School Bulletin*, 1971, *67*, 193–197.

Pendergrass, B. Time out from positive reinforcement following persistent, high rate behavior in retardates. *Journal of Applied Behavior Analysis*, 1972, *5*, 85–91.

Plotkin, R., & Gill, K. Invisible manacles: Drugging mentally retarded people. *Stanford Law Review*, 1979, *31*, 637–678.

Polvinale, R., & Lutzker, J. Elimination of assaultive and inappropriate sexual behavior by reinforcement and social-restitution. *Mental Retardation*, 1980, *18*, 27–30.

Potter, J., Biacchi, A., & Richardson, E. Simulating real-life situations in a classroom setting: The Montgomery County training module. In: E. Sontag, J. Smith, & N. Certo (eds.), *Educational programming for the severely and profoundly handicapped*. Reston, VA: The Division on Mental Retardation, The Council for Exceptional Children, 1977.

President's Commission on Mental Retardation. *Changing patterns in residential services for the mentally retarded*. Washington, D.C.: Superintendent of Documents, 1975.

Quinones, W. A test battery for assessing the vocational competency of moderately mentally retarded persons. *Mental Retardation*, 1978, *16*, 412–416.

Raynes, N. The less you've got the less you get: Functional grouping, a cause for concern. *Mental Retardation*, 1980, *18*, 217–220.

Reich, R. Gestural facilitation of expressive language in moderately/severely retarded preschoolers. *Mental Retardation*, 1978, *16*, 113–117.

Reid, D., & Hurlbut, B. Teaching nonvocal communication skills to multiply handicapped retarded adults. *Journal of Applied Behavior Analysis*, 1977, *10*, 591–603.

Repp, A., & Deitz, S. Reducing aggressive and self-injurious behavior of institutionalized retarded children through reinforcement of other behaviors. *Journal of Applied Behavior Analysis*, 1974, *7*, 313–325.

Repp, A., Deitz, S., & Deitz, D. Reducing inappropriate behaviors in classrooms and in individual sessions through DRO schedules of reinforcement. *Mental Retardation*, 1976, *14*, 11–15.

Repp, A., Deitz, S., & Speir, N. Reducing stereotypic responding of retarded persons by the differential reinforcement of other behaviors. *American Journal of Mental Deficiency*, 1974, *79*, 279–284.

Retish, P., Hoy, M., & Boaz, B. Systems Unlimited—Normalization exemplified. *Mental Retardation*, 1978, *16*, 313–316.

Reuter, J., Archer, F., Dunn, B., & White, C. Social milieu of a residential treatment center for severely or profoundly handicapped young children. *American Journal of Mental Deficiency*, 1980, *84*, 367–372.

Revell, W., Jr., & Wehman, P. Vocational evaluation of severely and profoundly retarded clients. *Rehabilitation Literature*, 1978, *39*, 226–231.

Richardson, S. Language training for mentally retarded children. In: R. Schiefelbusch, R. Copeland, & J. Smith (eds.), *Language and mental retardation: Empirical and conceptual considerations*. New York: Holt, Rinehart & Winston, 1977.

Risley, T., & Wolf, M. Establishing functional speech in echolalic children. *Behavior Research and Therapy*, 1967, *5*, 73–88.

Robinson, N., & Robinson, H. *The mentally retarded child* (2nd ed.). New York: McGraw-Hill Book Co., 1976.

Robinson-Wilson, M. Picture recipe cards: An approach to teaching severely and profoundly retarded adults to cook. *Education and Training of the Mentally Retarded*, 1977, *12*, 69–73.

Rogers, S. Characteristics of the cognitive development of profoundly retarded children. *Child Development*, 1977, *48*, 837–843.

Romer, D., & Berkson, G. Social ecology of supervised communal facilities for mentally disabled adults. II. Predictors of affiliation. *American Journal of Mental Deficiency*, 1980, *85*, 229–242. (a)

Romer, D., & Berkson, G. Social ecology of supervised communal facilities for mentally disabled adults. III. Predictors of social choice. *American Journal of Mental Deficiency*, 1980, *85*, 243–252. (b)

Rose, T. Reducing self-injurious behavior by differentially reinforcing other behaviors. *AAESPH Review*, 1979, *4*, 179–186.

Rosen, M., Clark, G., & Kivitz, M. *The history of mental retardation*, Vol. 1. Baltimore: University Park Press, 1976.

Rosen, M., Kivitz, M., Clark, G., & Floor, L. Prediction of postinstitutional adjustment of mentally retarded adults. *American Journal of Mental Deficiency*, 1980, *74*, 726–734.

Rosenbaum, M., & Breiling, J. The development and functional control of reading-comprehension behavior. *Journal of Applied Behavior Analysis*, 1976, *9*, 323–333.

Rusch, F., & Close, D. Overcorrection: A procedural evaluation. *AAESPH Review*, 1976, *1*, 32–45.

Rusch, F., Schutz, R., & Agran, M. Validating entry-level survival skills for service occupations: Implications for curriculum development. *Journal of The Association for the Severely Handicapped*, 1982, *7*, 32–41.

Sackett, G., & Landesman-Dwyer, S. Toward an ethology of mental retardation. In: P. Mittler (ed.), *Research to practice in mental retardation, Vol. II: Education and training*. Baltimore: University Park Press, 1977.

Sailor, W., Guess, D., & Lavis, L. Training teachers for education of the severely handicapped. *Education and Training of the Mentally Retarded*, 1975, *10*, 201–203.

Salvia, J. Perspectives on the nature of retardation. In: J. Neisworth & R. Smith (eds.), *Retardation: Issues, assessment, and intervention*. New York: McGraw-Hill Book Co., 1978.

Sattler, J. *Assessment of children's intelligence*. Philadelphia: W.B. Saunders Co., 1974.

Schalock, R., Harper, R., & Genung, T. Community integration of mentally retarded adults: Community placement and program success. *American Journal of Mental Deficiency*, 1981, *85*, 478–488.

Scheerenberger, R. *Deinstitutionalization and institutional reform*. Springfield, IL: Charles C Thomas, 1976.

Schiefelbusch, R. Language development and language modification. In: N. Haring & R. Schiefelbusch (eds.), *Methods in special education*. New York: McGraw-Hill Book Co., 1967.

Schleien, S., Wehman, P., & Kiernan, J. Teaching leisure skills to severely handicapped adults: An age-appropriate darts game. *Journal of Applied Behavior Analysis*, 1981, *14*, 513–519.

Schreiner, J. Prediction of retarded adults' work performance through components of general ability. *American Journal of Mental Deficiency*, 1978, *83*, 77–79.

Schroeder, S. Parametric effects of reinforcement frequency, amount of reinforcement, and required response force on sheltered workshop behavior. *Journal of Applied Behavior Analysis*, 1972, *5*, 431–441.

Seligman, M. *Helplessness: On depression, development, and death*. San Francisco: Freeman, 1975.

Simeonsson, R., & Wiegerink, R. Early language intervention: A contingent model. *Mental Retardation*, 1974, *12*, 7–11.

Smith, R. *An introduction to mental retardation*. New York: McGraw-Hill Book Co., 1971.

Smith, R., Neisworth, J., & Greer, J. Classification and individuality. In: J. Neisworth & R. Smith (eds.), *Retardation: Issues, assessment, and intervention*. New York: McGraw-Hill, Inc., 1978.

Smolev, S. Use of operant techniques for the modification of self-injurious behavior. *American Journal of Mental Deficiency*, 1971, *76*, 295–305.

Snyder, L., Lovitt, T., & Smith, J. Language training for the severely retarded: Five years of behavior analysis research. *Exceptional Children*, 1975, *42*, 7–15.

Solnick, J., Rincover, A., & Peterson, C. Some determinants of the reinforcing and punishing effects of timeout. *Journal of Applied Behavior Analysis*, 1977, *10*, 415–424.

Sontag, E., Smith, J., & Sailor, W. The severely/profoundly handicapped: Who are they? Where are we? *Journal of Special Education*, 1977, *11*, 5–11.

Sowers, J., Rusch, F., Connis, R., & Cummings, L. Teaching mentally retarded adults to time manage in a vocational setting. *Journal of Applied Behavior Analysis*, 1980, *13*, 119–128.

Sowers, J., Rusch, F., & Hudson, C. Training a severely retarded young adult to ride the city bus to and from work. *AAESPH Review*, 1979, *4*, 15–23.

Sparrow, S., & Cicchetti, D. Behavior rating inventory for moderately, severely, and profoundly retarded persons. *American Journal of Mental Deficiency*, 1978, *82*, 365–374.

Spellman, C., DeBriere, T., Jarboe, D., Campbell, S., & Harris, S. Pictorial instruction: Training daily living skills. In: M. Snell (ed.), *Systematic instruction of the moderately and severely handicapped*. Columbus, OH: Charles E. Merrill Publishing Co., 1978.

Spooner, F., & Hendrickson, L. Acquisition of complex assembly skills through the use of systematic training procedures. *AAESPH Review*, 1976, *1*, 14–25.

Spradlin, J. Language and communication of mental defectives. In: N. Ellis (ed.), *Handbook of mental deficiency*. New York: McGraw-Hill Book Co., 1963.

Spradlin, J., Girardeau, F., & Corte, H. Social and communication behaviors of retarded adolescents in a two-person situation. *American Journal of Mental Deficiency*, 1967, *72*, 473–481.

Sternberg, L., Battle, C., & Hill, J. Prelanguage communication programming for the severely and profoundly retarded. *Journal of The Association for the Severely Handicapped*, 1980, *5*, 224–233.

Stevens-Long, J., & Rasmussen, M. The acquisition of simple and compound sentence structure in an autistic child. *Journal of Applied Behavior Analysis*, 1974, *7*, 473–474.

Stodden, R., Casale, J., & Schwartz, S. Work evaluation and the mentally retarded: Review and recommendations. *Mental Retardation*, 1977, *15*, 25–27.

Stokes, T., & Baer, D. An implicit technology of generalization. *Journal of Applied Behavior Analysis*, 1977, *10*, 349–367.

Stokes, T., Baer, D., & Jackson, R. Programming the generalization of a greeting response in four retarded children. *Journal of Applied Behavior Analysis*, 1974, *7*, 599–610.

Storm, R., & Willis, J. Small group training as an alternative to individual programs for profoundly retarded persons. *American Journal of Mental Deficiency*, 1978, *83*, 283–288.

Strain, P. Increasing social play of severely retarded preschoolers through socio-dramatic activities. *Mental Retardation*, 1975, *13*, 7–9.

Strain, P. An experimental analysis of peer social initiations on the behavior of withdrawn preschool children: Some training and generalization effects. *Journal of Abnormal Child Psychology*, 1977, *5*, 445–455.

Stremel-Campbell, K., Cantrell, D., & Halle, J. Manual signing as a language system and as a speech initiator for the nonverbal severely handicapped student. In: E. Sontag, J. Smith, & N. Certo (eds.), *Educational programming for the severely and profoundly handicapped*. Reston, VA: Division on Mental Retardation, The Council for Exceptional Children, 1977.

Striefel, S., Bryan, K., & Aikins, D. Transfer of stimulus control from motor to verbal stimuli. *Journal of Applied Behavior Analysis*, 1974, *7*, 123–135.

Striefel, S., & Wetherby, B. Instruction following behavior of a retarded child and its controlling stimuli. *Journal of Applied Behavior Analysis*, 1973, *6*, 663–670.

Striefel, S., Wetherby, B., & Karlan, G. Establishing generalized verb-noun instruction-following skills in retarded children. *Journal of Experimental Child Psychology*, 1976, *22*, 247–260.

Sutter, P., Mayeda, T., & Call, T. Comparison of successful and unsuccessful community placed mentally retarded persons. *American Journal of Mental Deficiency*, 1980, *85*, 262–267.

Tanner, B., & Zeiler, M. Punishment of self-injurious behavior using aromatic ammonia as the aversive stimulus. *Journal of Applied Behavior Analysis*, 1975, *8*, 53–57.

Tarpley, N., & Schroeder, S. Comparison of DRO and DRI on rate of suppression of self-injurious behavior. *American Journal of Mental Deficiency*, 1979, *84*, 188–194.

Tharp, R., & Wetzel, R. *Behavior modification in the natural environment.* New York: Academic Press, 1969.

Thompson, T., & Carey, A. Structured normalization: Intellectual and adaptive behavior changes in a residential setting. *Mental Retardation*, 1980, *18*, 193–197.

Throne, J. Deinstitutionalization: Too wide a swath. *Mental Retardation*, 1979, *17*, 171–175.

Tizard, J. *Community services for the mentally handicapped.* London: Oxford University Press, 1964.

Topper, S. Gesture language for a non-verbal severely retarded male. *Mental Retardation*, 1975, *13*, 30–31.

Trace, M., Cuvo, A., & Criswell, J. Teaching coin equivalence to the mentally retarded. *Journal of Applied Behavior Analysis*, 1977, *10*, 85–92.

Treffry, D., Martin G., Samels, J., & Watson, C. Operant conditioning of grooming behavior of severely retarded girls. *Mental Retardation*, 1970, *8*, 29–33.

Turnbull, A. Teaching retarded persons to rehearse through cumulative overt labeling. *American Journal of Mental Deficiency*, 1974, *79*, 331–337.

Turnure, J., & Thurlow, M. The effects of structural variations in elaborations on learning by EMR and nonretarded children. *American Journal of Mental Deficiency*, 1975, *79*, 632–639.

Twardosz, S., & Baer, D. Training two severely retarded adolescents to ask questions. *Journal of Applied Behavior Analysis*, 1973, *6*, 655–661.

Umbreit, J. Effects of developmentally sequenced instructions on the rate of skill acquisition of severely handicapped students. *Journal of The Association for the Severely Handicapped*, 1980, *5*, 121–129.

Usdane, W. The placement process in the rehabilitation of the severely handicapped. *Rehabilitation Literature*, 1976, *37*, 162–165.

Vail, D. *Dehumanization and institutional care.* Springfield, IL: Charles C Thomas, 1967.

Vanderheiden, B., & Grilley, K. (eds.). *Nonvocal communication techniques and aids for the severely physically handicapped.* Baltimore: University Park Press, 1976.

Vogelsberg, R., Anderson, J., Berger, P., Haselden, T., Mitwell, S., Schmidt, C., Skowron, A., Ulett, D., & Wilcox, B. Programming for apartment living: A description and rationale of an independent living skills inventory. *Journal of The Association for the Severely Handicapped*, 1980, *5*, 38–54.

Vogelsberg, R., & Rusch, F. Training severely handicapped students to cross partially controlled intersections. *AAESPH Review*, 1979, *4*, 264–273.

Vogelsberg, R., Williams, W., & Friedl, M. Facilitating systems change for the severely handicapped: Secondary and adult services. *Journal of The Association for the Severely Handicapped*, 1980, *5*, 73–85.

Vukelich, R., & Hake, D. Reduction of dangerously aggressive behavior in a severely retarded resident through a combination of positive reinforcement procedures. *Journal of Applied Behavior Analysis*, 1971, *4*, 215–225.

Wacker, D., & Berg, W. Effects of picture prompts on the acquisition of complex vocational tasks by mentally retarded adolescents. *Journal of Applied Behavior Analysis*, in press.

Wacker, D., & Greenebaum, F. Efficacy of a verbal training sequence on the sorting performance of moderately and severely retarded adolescents. *American Journal of Mental Deficiency*, in press.

Walls, R., & Werner, T. Vocational behavior checklists. *Mental Retardation*, 1977, *15*, 30–35.

Walls, R., Werner, T., Bacon, A., & Zane, T. Behavior checklists. In: R. Hawkins & J. Cone (eds.), *Behavioral assessment: New directions in clinical psychology*. New York: Brunner-Mazel, 1977.

Wambold, C., & Bailey, R. Improving the leisure-time behaviors of severely/profoundly mentally retarded children through toy play. *AAESPH Review*, 1979, *4*, 237–250.

Warren, S., & Mondy, L. To what behaviors do attending adults respond? *American Journal of Mental Deficiency*, 1971, *75*, 449–455.

Wehman, P. Maintaining oral hygiene skills in geriatric retarded women. *Mental Retardation*, 1974, *12*, 20.

Wehman, P. Vocational training of the severely retarded: Expectations and potential. *Rehabilitation Literature*, 1976, *37*, 233–236.

Wehman, P. *Helping the mentally retarded acquire play skills: A behavioral approach*. Springfield, IL: Charles C Thomas, 1977.

Wehman, P. Instructional strategies for improving toy play skills of severely handicapped children. *AAESPH Review*, 1979, *4*, 225–235. (a)

Wehman, P. *Curriculum design for severely and profoundly handicapped students*. New York: Human Sciences Press, 1979. (b)

Wehman, P., & Bates, P. Education curriculum for severely and profoundly handicapped persons: A review. *Rehabilitation Literature*, 1978, *39*, 2–14.

Wehman, P., Hill, J., & Koehler, F. Helping severely handicapped persons enter competitive employment. *AAESPH Review*, 1979, *4*, 274–290.

Wehman, P., & McLaughlin, P. Teachers' perceptions of behavior problems with severely and profoundly handicapped students. *Mental Retardation*, 1979, *17*, 20–21.

Wehman, P., & McLaughlin, P. *Vocational curriculum for developmentally disabled persons*. Baltimore: University Park Press, 1980.

Wehman, P., & McLaughlin, P. *Program development in special education*. New York: McGraw-Hill Book Co., 1981.

Wehman, P., Renzaglia, A., & Schutz, R. Behavioral training strategies in sheltered workshops for the severely developmentally disabled. *AAESPH Review*, 1977, *2*, 24–36.

White, W., & Wolfensberger, W. The evolution of dehumanization in our institutions. *Mental Retardation*, 1969, *7*, 5–9.

Whitman, T., Mercurio, J., & Caponigri, B. Development of social responses in two severely retarded children. *Journal of Applied Behavior Analysis*, 1970, *3*, 133–138.

Whitman, T., & Scibak, J. Behavior modification research with the severely and profoundly retarded. In: N. Ellis (ed.), *Handbook of mental deficiency, psychological theory, and research* (2nd ed.). New York: Lawrence Erlbaum Associates, 1979.

Whitman, T., Zakaras, M., & Chardos, S. Effects of reinforcement and guidance procedures on instruction-following behavior of severely retarded children. *Journal of Applied Behavior Analysis*, 1971, *4*, 283–290.

Wilbur, R. *The linguistics of manual languages and manual systems*. Baltimore: University Park Press, 1976.

Williams, W., & Gotts, E. Selected considerations on developing curriculum for severely handicapped students. In: E. Sontag, J. Smith, & N. Certo (eds.), *Educational programming of the severely and profoundly handicapped*. Reston, VA: Division on Mental Retardation, The Council for Exceptional Children, 1977.

Winschel, J., & Lawrence, E. Short-term memory: Curricular implications for the mentally retarded. *Journal of Special Education*, 1975, *9*, 395–408.

Wolfensberger, W. *Normalization. The principle of normalization in human services*. Toronto: National Institute on Mental Retardation, 1972.

Wunderlich, R. Programmed instruction: Teaching coinage to retarded children. *Mental Retardation*, 1972, *10*, 21–23.

Zaharia, E., & Baumeister, A. Technician turnover and absenteeism in public residential facilities. *American Journal of Mental Deficiency*, 1978, *82*, 580–593.

Zeaman, D., & House, B. The role of attention in retardate discrimination learning. In: N. Ellis (ed.), *Handbook of mental deficiency, psychological theory and research*. New York: McGraw-Hill Book Co., 1963.

Zigler, E. Research on personality structure in the retardate. In: N. Ellis (ed.), *International review of research in mental retardation*, Vol. 1. New York: Academic Press, 1966.

Zigler, E. Developmental versus difference theories in mental retardation and the problem of motivation. *American Journal of Mental Deficiency*, 1969, *73*, 536–556.

Zweiban, S. Indicators of success in learning a manual communication mode. *Mental Retardation*, 1977, *15*, 47–49.

DISCUSSION QUESTIONS

1. What are the dimensions of the AAMD definition of mental retardation? How are these components defined and explicated?
2. What are the differences between a classification approach and a descriptive approach to describing severely and profoundly mentally retarded individuals? What are the advantages of each approach, separately and in combination?
3. What are the dimensions of developmental disabilities as defined by the Developmental Disabilities Amendments of 1978 (PL 95-602)?
4. How might the terms incidence and prevalence be differentiated?
5. What major time frames are considered in discussing biologically caused mental retardation? What are some of the etiologically significant conditions that occur at each of these stages?
6. What are the most common medical causes of mental retardation? For each general cause, cite specific examples of conditions that may lead to mental retardation.
7. What is meant by classification by syndrome? What are examples of syndromes associated with mental retardation?
8. What arguments can be articulated that support or reject the deinstitutionalization of severely and profoundly mentally retarded individuals?
9. What is meant by the normalization of the lives of mentally retarded persons? How might the lives of mentally retarded persons be normalized in the community and in institutional settings?
10. What procedures, policies, and programs are required to make placement in the community as successful as possible?
11. What is the major reason for the failure of traditional assessments of vocational potential? What are some of the new approaches and what are their problems?
12. What are some of the common training strategies that help severely and profoundly mentally retarded individuals acquire vocational skills? What are examples of the specific skills taught to this population?
13. What are some of the typical approaches to the development of oral communication skills in severely and profoundly mentally retarded persons?
14. What are some of the typical approaches to the use of nonspeech communication systems?
15. What skills are usually included under the rubric of self-help skills? What are some of the approaches that have been used and recommended for their acquisition?
16. What are several approaches to curriculum development for the severely and profoundly mentally retarded population? What are some of the problems facing curriculum developers?
17. What social, interpersonal, and community living skills are needed by severely and profoundly mentally retarded individuals? How might these skills be acquired?
18. What are some of the inappropriate behaviors manifested by some severely and profoundly mentally retarded persons? How might these behaviors be stopped?

Chapter 3

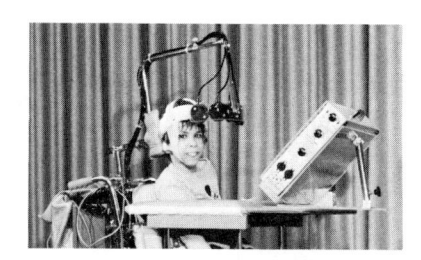

Severely and Profoundly Physically Handicapped Students

Olive Scola Smith

CHAPTER OBJECTIVES

After reading this chapter, you should be able to:

1. Define what is meant by the term *severely handicapped* and discuss its various parameters.
2. Discuss interdisciplinary and transdisciplinary approaches and their presumed advantages.
3. Describe curricula elements that are appropriate to the total education of severely and profoundly physically handicapped students.
4. Give examples of model programs for severely and profoundly physically handicapped students.
5. Present the most common symptoms, cite the incidence, discuss significant etiologic factors, and describe the most recent treatment strategies for the following conditions:
   a. Congenital deformities
   b. Neurological disorders

c. Life-threatening and fatal illnesses
d. Cardiac disorders
e. Blood disorders
f. Orthopaedic handicaps
g. Residua of accidents

Parents and educators agree that a serious need exists to provide adequate services to severely handicapped children. National figures indicate that this group represents approximately 2% of the total population (Brown, Wilcox, Sontag, Vincent, Dodd, & Gruenewald, 1977). PL 94-142, the Education for All Handicapped Children Act of 1975, mandates that the public schools provide programs for these youngsters. Zero exclusion is the common goal as school districts strive to meet the Act's requirements.

School administrators must facilitate the transition of severely physically handicapped children into the public schools by making specialized equipment available to them and by modifying existing school buildings so that they are barrier-free (Orelove & Hanley, 1979). Through preservice and inservice preparation programs, staff members must also be appropriately trained to work with severely handicapped students. In addition, the general community must not only be informed about services for severely handicapped persons, but it must also be involved in the planning and design of such services, and sensitized, as well, to the increasingly popular concepts of deinstitutionalization and normalization. Educators engaged in planning programs will find it necessary to discard isolated program models in favor of coordinated service models that encourage a facilitative and reinforcing environment/ecosystem to meet the multidimensional needs of severely handicapped children (Apter, 1977).

Historically, services to severely physically handicapped persons were based upon the medical model, with the physician providing a label, a presumed etiology, a treatment plan, and hypothesized prognosis. With heightened awareness in the 1970s of the life-skills needs of severely handicapped individuals, an educational model has evolved that shuns labels unless they have a direct influence on educational programming or management. Practitioners working with physically handicapped individuals, however, frequently find that labels have significance because they communicate specific behavioral correlates, e.g., a child possessing a severe (Class 4) bilateral hearing loss cannot be expected to follow conversations without a hearing aid. The current educational model emphasizes the description of relevant or target behaviors, their observation in a given student, and individualized program planning to develop those behaviors that are not consistently or independently demonstrated by the student in question. Since students with various types and degrees of physically handicapping conditions are entering public school programs in greater numbers, the demands on educators are intensified. The challenge is to structure and program an environment that will facilitate the acquisition of basic functional skills (Bender & Valletutti, 1982; Valletutti & Bender, 1982) and to reduce stress or frustration while providing as normal a setting as possible (Baker, 1980).

DEFINING THE SEVERELY AND PROFOUNDLY PHYSICALLY HANDICAPPED POPULATION

The American Association for the Education of the Severely/Profoundly Handicapped (now The Association for the Severely Handicapped) published a review by Baker (1979) of 23 journal articles written in 1976 and 1977 defining the severely handicapped population. In her review, Baker noted that although public schools are beginning to develop programs for severely handicapped individuals, there was no single unifying criterion that delimited the term *severely handicapped*. She proposed the following definition:

> [A severely handicapped person] is one whose ability to provide for his or her own basic life-sustaining and safety needs is so limited relative to the proficiency expected on the basis of chronological age, that it could pose a serious threat to his or her survival (p.60).

Baker further identified four major categories of severely handicapped individuals: severe/profound mental retardation; severe emotional disturbance; severe orthopaedic/physical impairment; and multiple handicapping conditions.

Kirk and Gallagher (1983) describe the category of physical handicaps and other health impairments by characterizing it as "a variety of nonsensory conditions that affect the child's well-being and that can create special educational problems centering around mobility, physical vitality, and self-image. Included in this broad category are conditions such as congenital malformations, epilepsy, muscular dystrophy, asthma, rheumatic fever, cerebral palsy (uncomplicated by mental retardation), and diabetes" (p. 447). The legal definitions that refer to the physically handicapped incorporate two subgroups of this population: the orthopaedically impaired and other health impaired.

1. "Orthopaedically impaired" means a severe orthopaedic impairment which adversely affects a child's educational performance. The term includes impairments caused by congenital anomaly (e.g., clubfoot, absence of some member, etc.), impairments caused by disease (e.g., poliomyelitis, bone tuberculosis, etc.), and impairments from other causes (e.g., cerebral palsy, amputations, and fractures or burns which cause contractures) (*Federal Register,* 1977a).
2. "Other health impaired" means (i) having an autistic condition which is manifested by severe communication and other developmental and educational problems; or (ii) having limited strength, vitality or alertness, due to chronic or acute health problems such as a heart condition, tuberculosis,

rheumatic fever, nephritis, asthma, sickle cell anemia, hemophilia, epilepsy, lead poisoning, leukemia, or diabetes, which adversely affects a child's educational performance (*Federal Register,* 1981).

Physical handicaps can be manifested on a continuum of occurrence from mild to profound. In order for a physical impairment to be subsumed under the rubric of severely handicapped, the individual so handicapped requires an educational program that establishes and develops basic social, self-help, and communication skills which make it possible for the individual to survive in a supervised and protected environment (Sontag, Smith, & Sailor, 1977).

A serious physical or medical impairment does not necessarily lead to the description of a child as being severely handicapped unless the individual cannot provide for life-sustaining and safety needs. The severely physically handicapped persons described later in this chapter are those who require specialized programming because of defects of the nervous system, muscles, bones, or joints, or because they have other health impairments (e.g., cardiac, kidney, or blood disorders). Frequently, physically handicapped individuals are stigmatized because their visible defects suggest to uninformed and biased observers that they are intellectually restricted or incompetent. Intellectual functioning may or may not be impaired. Educators working with severely physically handicapped students must be able to devise a program that accommodates a variety of handicaps, must assume partial responsibility for supervision of medical problems, and must function as a fully participating member of a transdisciplinary team.

INTERDISCIPLINARY AND TRANSDISCIPLINARY APPROACHES

Severely physically handicapped persons require the services of a variety of professional disciplines to provide them with the multidimensional education and treatment services they need. The demands of lifelong, comprehensive care have made it clear that fragmented and isolated services cannot be tolerated and interdisciplinary cooperation must be fostered. "Interdisciplinary communication is prerequisite to the interdisciplinary cooperation needed to identify goals for clients and to prescribe treatment priorities, sequences, strategies, implementation processes, materials, and evaluative procedures" (Valletutti & Christoplos, 1977, p. 1).

The need for an interdisciplinary approach to therapeutic services was first recognized by health care professionals working in a variety of health care facilities, including community mental health centers, diagnostic and evaluative clinics, intermediate care facilities (ICFs), group homes, and university affiliated facilities (UAFs) (Elder & Magrab, 1979). The recognition of the importance of an interdisciplinary approach to human services is exemplified in the federal standards for staffing intermediate care facilities for mentally retarded persons and or receiving Title XIX reimbursement for services. Evaluation for residency and the design and evaluation of an individualized habilitation program must be accomplished by an interdisciplinary team (*Federal Register*, 1977b). Moreover, Public Law 94-142, the Education for All Handicapped Children Act, requires the development of an individualized education program (IEP) that must include both special education and related services. The provision of necessary related services emphasizes the need for interdisciplinary evaluation and program planning (*Federal Register*, 1977a).

With increasing attention directed toward the educational and habilitative needs of severely handicapped students, and advances in knowledge, educational specialists in this area of human services have emerged. These generalists, who are cross- or transdisciplinary, have reaped the benefits of interdisciplinary training, and are increasingly able to manage the multidisciplinary problems of severely handicapped individuals in a transdisciplinary style. The increasing attention to transdisciplinary approaches is a direct reaction to the high cost and purported disadvantages of the interdisciplinary approach, including: duplication of effort, lack of appropriate follow through, absence of effective and efficient interaction skills, the effect of specialized treatments on total developmental progress, the tendency to inhibit creative approaches, and the predilection of experts to engage in disputes of territorial rights (Ruben, Plovnick, & Fry, 1975; Valletutti & Christoplos, 1977). In calling for a transdisciplinary approach, Valletutti & Christoplos, (1977) suggest, "In the interest of serving clients, members of each discipline should be willing, whenever possible, to relinquish certain roles and their own specialized skills to others" (p. 5).

Thus, the transdisciplinary treatment and education model may also be considered appropriate for this population. It attempts to break down traditional disciplinary boundaries, encourages communication among team members, and permits sharing of information and knowledge for the benefit of the client (McCormick & Goldman, 1979). This approach lessens the tendency to provide fragmented services and helps to eliminate duplication. Within this model, representatives of the disciplines may be provided a rich opportunity to grow professionally and to develop many skills, while at the same time providing more effective and efficient service delivery to students. Team members' time can also be used more economically, reaching greater numbers of children with a variety of handicaps. The constant exchange of information and feedback assists in the ongoing modification and evaluation of individualized education programs (IEPs). Thus, by addressing multiple handicaps at the same time, the transdisciplinary approach is seen as a promising alternative to the traditional method in which a child undergoes a series of separate evaluations and treatment by different disciplines.

Meeting Equipment Needs

In terms of providing for a severely physically handicapped student's need for specialized classroom devices or equipment, transdisciplinary cooperation is particularly helpful. Children with severe physical disabilities often require specially designed devices to assist them in functioning as independently as possible (Scheuerman, 1976) in areas of mobility, communication, and feeding. Although there are many commercial suppliers of this equipment, it frequently becomes the task of the teacher, physical therapist, occupational therapist, or physical education trainer to modify available materials for use with individual children. The assistance of maintenance personnel or someone skilled in carpentry or design is also helpful.

The growth of scientific technology, electronics, and computerized equipment has done much to assist the severely physically handicapped population. In the past few years, space-age prosthetics, electronic sensory devices, specially equipped vans, and audiovisual equipment have been designed to augment the program needs of such students. In addition, the increasing presence of physical and occupational therapists and speech/language pathologists on the school team has helped severely physically handicapped individuals develop self-care skills. Systems for nonverbal communication and assessment have provided educators with new methods of determining functioning levels and of creating appropriate programs for severely handicapped students.

Physician's Role

Until the mandates of PL 94-142 required the education of the severely physically handicapped population in the least restrictive environment, most of these students were treated in health care settings or in private facilities with a strong medical orientation. Educators working in these programs, of necessity, became familiar with the medical model and with medical practice as primarily demonstrated by pediatricians, orthopaedists, neurologists, physiatrists, and psychiatrists. With the advent of public school-based programs, the role of physicians became more vague and was less familiar to educators unacquainted with the comprehensive health service needs of their students and with the professional disciplines required to implement them. While most special educators have long appreciated the essential role of the traditional therapies (occupational, physical, and speech-language) and have recently become increasingly cognizant of the more esoteric therapies of art, dance, music, drama, and therapeutic recreation, they are not nearly as aware and informed of the role of physicians in the nonmedical setting of the school. Certainly, the "hands-on" delivery of related services is more frequently accomplished by various nonmedical human service professionals. Nevertheless, the role of the physician in providing quality service to severely physically handicapped students and consultative services to their teachers must be kept in perspective and must not be minimized.

The pediatrician is a critical team member, as he or she has the primary responsibility for guiding parents through the early diagnostic phase and for helping to prepare them for the numerous medical problems that tend to arise with severely handicapped children (Howard, 1982). The present emphasis on deinstitutionalization and the federal mandate for an appropriate educational experience tend to broaden the role of the physician. Where the physician once interacted primarily with the child and parent, collaboration with other disciplines and community agencies is now standard procedure in programming for severely handicapped children. The quality and complexity of physician-patient and physician-parent relationships have thus assumed new dimensions and directions in the determination of appropriate services for handicapped children. The physician's willingness to be involved determines the extent to which he or she can be a child advocate in the course of developing a support system for the child (Wolraich, 1982).

As a team member, the physician adds a much-needed perspective in the determination of a physically handicapped child's individualized education program. The pediatrician's input can be valuable in reviewing children's medical problems, medication, etiology and prognosis, and the effects of medication on behavior and learning (Levine, 1982). A close relationship between the school and pediatrician is necessary with respect to medical problems that may aggravate or accompany learning problems—for example, allergies that require ongoing medication; seizure disorder medication that causes side effects; and ear infections and transient hearing loss resulting in language delays.

As the role of health care workers and physicians has grown, many hospitals have developed clinics or child evaluation centers for handicapped and at-risk infants. These centers provide diagnostic, assessment, and management services, utilizing a team approach that varies with the nature and severity of cases. The team may include a psychologist, psychiatrist, speech and hearing therapist, physical therapist, occupational therapist, pediatric neurologist, developmental pediatrician, social worker, nutritionist, learning consultant, and pediatric nurse. One of these professionals may be designated the case manager in providing referral and consultation services and developing interagency coordination. The parents, also, are active team members throughout evaluation, program development, and placement of the handicapped child. Generally, physicians associated with large hospital-based clinic programs have adapted to the diverse and expanded role of the pediatric interventionist. The tasks of diagnosis, medical care, counseling of parents, collaborating with other agencies and programs, and functioning as a member of an early intervention team may all be assumed by a pediatrician (Bennett, 1982).

In the past several years the U.S. Department of Education has supported a series of programs designed to prepare physicians in caring for handicapped children. The Children's Hospital Medical Center in Boston, for example, provides a month of intensive training that includes visits to various community programs, supervised clinical experience, and review of case studies (Levine, 1982). The American Academy of Pediatrics has also sponsored nationwide workshops on handicapped children for practicing pediatricians. In addition, the Office of Special Education (now Special Education Programs) has supported a curriculum development project at Ohio State University's Nisonger Center. The Nisonger Center's training program for future pediatricians is now being implemented in many training centers throughout the nation. And at the University of Arkansas, a program model of personnel preparation is underway in which university special education and pediatric faculty members work together to train teachers in the medical aspects of educational disabilities. One of the program's required courses, "Medical Problems in Child Development," is taught jointly by a special educator and a pediatrician. The course introduces teachers to the medical and emotional aspects of handicaps and of treatments for handicapped children, thus helping to sensitize teachers to dimensions other than the purely educational in dealing with students' handicaps.

The increase in communication between physicians, teachers, and child study team members that is occurring with the admission of severely physically handicapped children to school programs will intensify as programs strive for zero exclusion. As roles of professionals continue to expand and intermesh, a common framework of understanding becomes essential (Freund, Casey, & Bradley, 1982). Educators and physicians alike have become increasingly aware of their training needs under the mandates of PL 94-142. As service providers move toward the transdisciplinary team concept and territories become less rigidly demarcated, the chance for professionals and parents to develop and implement more effective individualized education programs for children is greatly enhanced.

Screening

A transdisciplinary approach is also valid for the screening process, as such an approach affords the most efficient use of consultants, social workers, program administrators, and leaders, all of whom provide services in a number of areas depending upon time and availability. A specialist in severely physically handicapping conditions, such as a nurse, can be invaluable in the process of triage, i.e., the process of determining priorities of need and meeting those needs with appropriate services (Gordon-Davis & Strasser, 1977). Although an effort is made under the transdisciplinary approach to assign screening to the most appropriate professional in terms of the presenting problem, these arrangements are not always possible—in which case, appropriate arrangements with another professional can be made. Or, if the services of a particular discipline are required, a scheduling change may be advisable.

Fundamental to the transdisciplinary approach is that team members are encouraged to share information and skills at every level of service delivery, from referral through program provision to parent contact (Lyon & Lyon, 1980), in order to ensure program continuity in the possible absence of representatives of specific disciplines. The dividends of such improved communication are inevitably felt throughout the entire program. The transdisciplinary approach also permits the use of various professionals in many classroom situations, thus reducing costs and avoiding compartmentalization, which leads to segmentation of program provision. In striving for a "least restrictive environment," the role-release approach, in which traditional roles are eschewed, facilitates the student's movement through programs and once rigidly assigned domains (Lyon & Lyon, 1980).

EDUCATIONAL PROGRAMS AND SERVICES

Implementing a meaningful educational program for severely physically handicapped students is a complex task requiring the collective wisdom of educators and other members of the transdisciplinary team, including parents and, whenever feasible, the students themselves. Research indicates that the superiority of one curriculum over another does not determine program effectiveness (Karnes, 1973; Weikert, Epstein, Schweinhart, & Bond, 1978). Rather, the ongoing process of monitoring for changed behaviors and continuously adjusting the program plan contribute to effective individualized education programs for specific children. Certainly a well-structured curriculum with a built-in evaluation procedure provides a base for program implementation, from which the teacher may individualize for severely handicapped children.

Providing for Medical Needs

It is important to mention at the outset, however, that no instructional planning can be carried out for severely physically handicapped children without a thorough interpretation of medical information. For example, the following factors may influence program planning:

1. Seizure activity, medications, allergies, susceptibility to illness, strength, and special feeding instructions may necessitate programming and scheduling modifications.
2. Heart defects may require monitoring or curtailment of particular activities.
3. Cleft palate, faulty heart valve, and club foot may be recommended for further study and possible surgery, requiring changes in the program.
4. Congenital or degenerative problems may require planning to maintain functioning levels.
5. Medications and their side effects must be identified in terms of motor activities, feedings, and the like.
6. Physical deformities or limb paralysis may require instruction to be planned around working extremities.
7. Allergies must be considered in any feeding program.
8. Alterations in work, play, and rest schedules will be needed according to health problems of the individual child.
9. Spastic and athetoid children require different therapy programs.
10. The use of prosthetic devices must be considered.

11. Positioning and handling techniques will vary, depending upon specific physical problems.
12. Specially prescribed feeding techniques are needed for particular types of anomalies (e.g., cleft palate, Down's syndrome, and cerebral palsy).

Programs for severely physically handicapped children must also include preventive intervention to counteract the effects of severe handicapping conditions (see individual descriptions of handicapping conditions later in this chapter). Proper physical handling of handicapped individuals by staff and parents must be a program priority and may require special training for caregivers.

Philosophical Framework

While recognizing, then, that a child's medical needs may require certain alterations in the curriculum, a major factor in selecting a curriculum involves ensuring that the curriculum's philosophical framework complements that of the agency. Hankerson (1980) cautioned that all persons involved with a program should be provided a thorough orientation in its philosophical base, since this philosophy determines, in part, the goals selected for a student. Hankerson presented a five-step method for analyzing a curriculum's philosophy in terms of program efficacy. It is extremely important that the philosophy, goals, and objectives of the educational model be in accord with the needs and expectations of the immediate community (Hankerson, 1980); this is especially true when minority or culturally diverse populations are being served. In addition to the discussion in this chapter, the reader is referred to Hankerson (1980) for a review of basic strategies for developing an educational model and a list of activities involved in planning and administering an early childhood program.

Interaction of Caregivers

Another equally important element of a good program involves providing for the interaction of caregivers. Parents and staff may either facilitate or retard development of severely physically handicapped children. They must not only provide appropriate stimulation activities to allow for a child's growth, but they must be sensitive to the level and quality of the child's response to these activities. By ensuring ongoing staff responsiveness to the minute changes in the developmental level of severely handicapped students, programs provide a reinforcing atmosphere for the child when a new skill emerges.

Maximizing Opportunities for Learning

The environment in each learning site is the key to maximizing curriculum effectiveness. In structuring the environment, planners must assure that it remains functional. The environment should be viewed as an educational tool where specified tasks may be performed in a supportive, therapeutic milieu that fosters social interaction (Bayes & Francklin, 1971). Baker (1980) concluded that the physical environment has a powerful influence on human behavior. A supportive yet challenging environment where normal interaction with nonhandicapped as well as handicapped persons can take place seems optimally beneficial. Within that environment, adequate staff is needed to provide required stimulation activities and to act as natural reinforcers for teaching skills. Individual progress is best achieved in surroundings where the staff is able to control an excess of nonfunctional behavior and where positive social interaction is a goal (Lathey, 1978) (see also Chapter 2 for specific methods for reducing and eliminating inappropriate behavior). To measure students' progress, a criterion-referenced assessment device with developmental milestones specified in program skill areas provides a guide for writing objectives and monitoring progress. It is recommended that skill areas be broken down into subskills and task analyzed to aid classroom staff in providing individualized programs to low-functioning children. For severely physically handicapped children, program planning must remain as individualized as possible.

A program for severely physically handicapped children must include observations of the ecology of each family unit, in order that program development and implementation may reflect children's total needs and deficits. As stated, cooperation among agencies and service providers is essential. A program's primary purpose is to improve the life situation for each handicapped child, while helping him or her to attain varying levels of independence. While one child's level may peak with the achievement of chewing or grasping, another child may progress to a standing position or to speaking in short sentences. The omission of one vital component of a child's program frequently has negative effects on the attainment of other skills. Thus, in order to realize each child's potential, program planners must seek out and coordinate services, thus enabling progress through interrelated experiences. Evaluation of services and of children's progress must also be ongoing in order to maximize client growth. The overall planning is, by nature, complex and open-ended, and requires a case manager to provide structure and supervision.

Cognitive Development

A program of cognitive development should be designed to include functional, reality-based situations for severely, physically handicapped children, thus helping them to organize and interact appropriately with their environment. In the developmental classroom, however, this engineered learning module should avoid being superficial and, instead, should be provided as a natural part of the daily living experience. In relating to others and in the sensory experience of people and objects, nonhandicapped children naturally gain a sense of body awareness, perceive certain causal relationships, and come to recognize the impact of their actions in various situations. Severely physically impaired children, on the other hand, often require increased and prolonged stimulation through many senses to experience cognitive growth. Careful planning and appropriate physical environments are critical to effective cognitive development for severely physically handicapped children.

Community Education Model

Community education, based on ecological theory as described by Apter (1977) (which studies the interaction between organisms and the environment in a variety of life settings), is another important element in effective program development. To support mainstreaming efforts, many educators are moving away from segregated programs and are adapting the existing environment for children with special needs. A system of community education complements ecological theory by allowing for continuous learning experiences using a variety of community facilities. Implicit in the model is that education is not the sole responsibility of the public schools; instead, input from many agencies may be integrated into the program. Swap (1974) describes the establishment of harmonious ecosystems whereby human needs are met through multiple programs, individualized goal setting, and the valuing of human differences. The community special education model places the school in the position of a mental health center (Stickney, 1968), with the school assuming the major role of coordinating delivery of comprehensive services for handicapped individuals. Thomas and Marshall (1977) present an ecological model for clinically evaluating and coordinating services to handicapped children. In this model, a multidisciplinary, medically-based program provides the focal point for interaction and communication, and provides the coordinating point for the child's program. Such a model can reach out to utilize the available resources in the community, rather than having to wait for traditional services (e.g., special education, vocational services, and sheltered workshops) to begin. The model identifies commonalities in services for children with handicaps and reviews them according to the following areas: information gathering; data pooling; initial programming; and periodic assessment and program modification.

Integration

Integration between handicapped and nonhandicapped children is also important to a sound curriculum. A side-by-side approach to integration, systematically incorporated into a program for severely handicapped youngsters, is described by Thomason and Arkell (1980) and has been merged into the Albuquerque (New Mexico) Public Schools. The side-by-side sites (a regular school adjacent to a special school) are dispersed throughout the school system, permitting frequent interaction between severely handicapped and nonhandicapped students, and facilitating development of comprehensive medical services. Community awareness of and acceptance of severely handicapped children has also increased; transportation and architectural changes, however, remain to be resolved. The opportunity for peer imitation (Snyder, Apolloni, & Cooke, 1977) is one of the most commonly stated justifications for integrating handicapped and nonhandicapped children. The development of an attitude of acceptance toward handicapped students by nonhandicapped students and the overcoming of anxieties felt toward handicapped children, however, may represent the most positive results of integration of any cited in the literature. Anastasiow (1981) recommended a human development or life-skills program for youngsters in the early grades that provides students with experiences involving handicapped as well as nonhandicapped peers. Anastasiow cautioned teachers to understand that the child, caregiver(s), and physical environment comprise a transactional network and that none of the elements in the network can be omitted. Anastasiow also recommended that in order for the child to achieve his or her maximum potential, a task-analysis approach be used in program implementation, while a cognitive approach be used as a theoretical basis for the program.

Other Approaches

Regarding other types of programs, Orlansky (1979) described a program for severely handicapped children that uses strictly behavioral techniques. Work stations, prescriptive teaching programs, and lists of reinforcers for each child are established by the teacher. An intense, systematic, individualized, instructional experience is provided, and precise behavioral terms are used to record performance. This approach differs considerably from the natural environment approach, and the teacher structures intervention at preestablished time intervals. When working on an objective such as eliminating self-injurious behavior, for example, the staff person monitors behavior only at set times.

Haring (1977) described a systematic instructional model that is purported to produce significant gains across basic skill and academic areas.

Finally, McCormick and Goldman (1979) described a transdisciplinary service delivery model based on training evaluation procedures and applied behavior analysis. The model incorporates one primary service implementor, with team members serving as consultants. Intervention strategies are designed and measured to accommodate learning-related differences. Caregiving activities may also be used as a vehicle for instruction, with consultants combining instructional goals (e.g., movement exercises with self-care activities).

Although many program models have emerged, Williams, Brown, and Certo (1976) point out that all programs seek to answer a basic set of questions about their clients. Answers to these questions listed below form the basis of program planning and should produce developmental changes in functioning levels and life-styles of severely physically handicapped children.

1. What skill does a teacher intend for a student to perform?
2. Why does the teacher want the student to perform the skill?
3. How does the teacher empirically verify that the skill is being taught?
4. How does the teacher intend to teach the skill?
5. Can the student perform the skill at a situationally accepted rate?
6. What does the teacher intend to use as instructional materials in order for the skill to be acquired?

7. Can the student perform the skill across person, place, instructional materials, and language cues?
8. Can the student perform the skill without directions from a person in authority?

To assist in program provision, a brief review of the most common severely physically handicapping conditions follows. Note that while not all forms of the handicapping conditions described can in themselves be considered severe handicaps, it is often the case that several different conditions occur together, thus creating severe and profound problems for the affected individual.

For definitions of unfamiliar terms in the descriptions of conditions, readers are referred to the glossary at the end of this chapter.

CONGENITAL DEFORMITIES

Arthrogryposis (Amyoplasia Congenita)

Description Arthrogryposis is an abnormality associated with autosomal recessive genes. Mental retardation is a symptom, with fixation of the joints the most distinctive and constant clinical feature. Underlying pathology is varied and may involve the spinal cord, muscles, or joints. When the disorder is associated with congenital muscular dystrophy, a characteristic posture of flexion at the hips and knees and adduction of the legs has been observed. AMC is the term used for a special form of this disease, in which there is congenital stiffness of one or more joints associated with hypoplasia of the attached muscles. The term *multiple congenital articular rigidities* is also used to identify this disorder, involving thick, inelastic articular capsules and atrophic muscle fibers with some fibrosis and fatty infiltration. Dislocation of the hip and other joints is common, the result of incomplete fibrous ankylosis. Certain muscle groups may be underdeveloped or absent; the wrists and fingers are flexed and club feet are present. Elbows and knees described as cylindrical are usually ankylosed in extension, although fixation of the knees in flexion also occurs. The skin appears thickened, wrinkled, and flabby. The arms are rotated inward, the thighs outward. The anomaly consists of incomplete fusion of many or all of the joints, except those of the spine and jaw.

Incidence The disorder appears sporadically, but familial cases have been observed; frequency is designated as rare.

Etiology Frequent association with such malformations as defects of the hard and/or soft palate or vertebrae and absence of the sacrum and fibula(ae) indicate origin early in embryonic life before intrauterine pressure (once considered a causative agent) becomes a factor. It may be related to fetal paralysis or to an inadequate amount of amniotic fluid, causing the fetus to be in a fixed position for a long period of time.

Treatment Treatment may consist of massage and passive movements, with gradual correction of deformities through splints, casts, and orthopaedic surgery. Since muscle strength is poor, mobilization of the joints by physical therapy alone is not effective. If joints of the upper extremities can be mobilized, dynamic bracing may be needed for functional positioning before ambulation is possible. Orthopaedic treatment may improve posture to a degree, but little or no change in muscle power is expected.

Club feet are often difficult to correct, and surgery is frequently recommended. Heel cord lengthening, posterior capsulectomies of the ankle joints, and medial release operations may be needed to put the stiff foot into a functional position. If legs are not in full extension, multiple plaster wedging may be indicated to enable the patient to wear long leg braces. When hips are dislocated, correction may not be needed. Bilateral dislocation of the hips is not a major obstacle to ambulation in severely disabled patients.

The prognosis for independent living is poor. School programming may involve placement in a class for multiply handicapped, severely handicapped, or orthopaedically handicapped individuals.

Spina Bifida

Description Spina bifida occurs when one or more of the vertebral arches fails to unite during the embryonic stages of the spinal cord's development. The defect may be present anywhere between the head and lowest part of the back. The mildest form is spina bifida occulta (hidden), characterized by a dimple or hair tuft on the lower spine, indicating the presence of radiographic defects in the sacral area. Defects have been commonly found in otherwise normal individuals and are said to diminish with age. When a sac containing spinal column material protrudes or herniates, a meningocele is present. A meningomyelocele indicates the presence of portions of the spinal cord or nerve roots. If the herniated sac contains spinal cord materials only, it is known as a myelocele.

Meningocele Meningoceles comprise about 10% of all spina bifida cystica (meningocele or meningomyelocele) cases. The meningocele is a cystic lesion in the midline of the back that contains meninges and nerve roots but is free of central nervous system tissue. The meningocele is covered with skin, and studies imply that there is no progressive neurological symptomatology. Meningoceles have similar frequency of occurrence in the cervical, thoracic, and lumbar spines. The chance of lesions occurring in the cervical or thoracic regions is greater.

Meningomyelocele The neural ectoderm that develops into a spinal cord and nerve roots appears to be connected to the epithelium, resulting in a malformed spinal cord, incompletely formed meninges, and a sac containing cerebrospinal fluid. The fluid leaks initially from the membrane, which begins to dry after birth. The accumulation of fluid may create a large sac unless surgical closure of the defect is initiated. Meningomyelocele is associated with defects of the brain stem and cerebellum in almost all cases. A number of other developmental anomalies of the neural tissues may coexist (e.g., aqueducted stenosis and arrested migration of cerebral neurons). Hydrocephalus develops in about 90% of affected children.

Some neurological deficit may be present in the limbs and general area below the mass. There is a general loss of sphincter control, and urinary flow may be spontaneous when the infant cries. Legs may be flaccid and hips congenitally dislocated. Immobility of the ankles and inverted feet may also be present. Paralysis is associated with meningomyelocele in various degrees, occurring below the site of the lesion.

The most frequent site of spinal cord malformation is the lumbar area. Because the cord at this level encompasses the nerve supply to the lower extremities controlling muscle strength, sensation, and bowel and bladder function, there are serious defects in these areas. A wide variety of problems may be present and must be determined by neurosurgical exploration. As the spinal cord migrates with growth, the brain stem becomes compressed and creates more serious problems, including hydrocephaly and pressure on the brain stem, affecting respiration and heart rate. Congenital heart disorders and club feet are frequently found among those suffering from spina bifida.

Incidence The incidence of spina bifida occulta is said to occur in 5% to 25% of the normal population. Spina bifida cystica (meningocele and meningomyelocele) varies in frequency to some degree in countries populated by Caucasians. The highest incidence is reported among the Welsh and Irish. There is a reported incidence of 4.2 individuals per 1,000 live births in Ireland, 2.8 per 1,000 in Buckinghamshire, and 1.5 per 1,000 in southeastern England (Rudolph, 1977). The incidence in the United States is 3 in 1,000 live births (Myers, 1975). Lower socioeconomic groups seem to be affected more frequently, and a genetic element may be present. There is a considerably higher risk of abnormal children of subsequent pregnancies in families in which spina bifida has occurred. The more extensive types of spina bifida have been reported in 1 to 4 infants per 1,000 live births.

As stated, in almost all cases of meningomyelocele, there is an associated defect of the brain stem and cerebellum (Arnold-Chiari malformation), which consists of downward displacement into the cervical spinal canal of parts of the cerebellum, fourth ventricle, and medulla oblongata. Hydrocephalus develops in about 90% of affected children as a result of the Arnold-Chiari malformation. This may also lead to medullary and lower cranial nerve dysfunction, resulting in difficulty in swallowing and atrophy of the tongue.

Etiology In 1967, Laurence (Rudolph, 1977) studied 179 families of spina bifida children, and no evidence of any abnormal influence on pregnancy (e.g., drugs, X rays, or diet) could be extracted. The possibility of prenatal insults sustained during the first month of pregnancy may be a factor in the incidence of spina bifida. While no single genetic pattern is viewed as conclusive, spina bifida occurs with increased frequency in some families. Many factors have been implicated as causative agents, including maternal age, radiation, diet, and excessive vitamin intake, but there is no clear-cut evidence to support these implications. By the 4th week of fetal life the canal in the spinal cord closes, and the spinal column closes at 12 weeks. As indicated by most researchers, the causative agents for spina bifida must be operative very early in fetal life.

Treatment A complete neurological assessment of the infant should be carried out shortly after birth. Prompt surgical closure of the skin defect, preferably within 48 hours after birth, may prevent meningeal infection. After closure, the infant must be carefully observed for hydrocephalus, which can also be treated surgically. There are a number of surgical procedures for treatment of urinary problems, including construction of an ileal loop bladder and a ureterostomy. Orthopaedic surgery is sometimes helpful to correct hip and foot deformities but should not be done unless the child has a chance of normal function. Children with spina bifida require ongoing monitoring and care from an interdisciplinary team in a clinical setting.

Since many children with spina bifida have normal intelligence, it is possible for some to attend regular class; however, they require a variety of supportive services. Children with good verbal ability sometimes manifest perceptual problems in the classroom. Lack of adequate transportation and accessible school buildings may also limit educational experiences. Children with spina bifida often have problems adjusting socially. Incontinence and hydrocephalus, repeated hospitalization, limited mobility, social immaturity, and dependence may have adverse effects on the child's acceptance by peers and teachers. The various functioning levels, strengths, and weaknesses of these children necessitate an individualized approach even when the child remains in a regular class (Lauder, Kanthor, Myers, & Resnick, 1979).

Congenital Dislocation of the Hip

Description Congenital dysplasia of the hip is marked by the abnormal development of the hip joint. The head of the femur may be partially or completely dislocated from the acetabulum. If congenital dysplasia is present with dislocation, the dislocation may be noted at birth. When the flexed hip is abducted the femur may slip in and out of the acetabulum, causing an obvious click on entry and exit. In the normal infant adduction can be continued to 90% without incident, but a resistance may be felt at 60% with dislocation, when congenital dislocation exists. Straight-leg raising is greatly increased when dislocation is present. In a standing child, the pelvis drops on the normal side as the trunk dips when weight is put on the involved leg. A "duck waddle" gait is caused by bilateral dislocation of the hip.

True dislocation is not evident at birth, but usually develops within 4 months. Deficiencies may include shallowness of the weight-bearing quadrant and excessive anteversion of the femoral neck. Prior to dislocation there may be abnormal splinting of the affected hip, diminished movement, flexion of the thigh, and limited abduction of the hip. Following dislocation all of the above findings are present, in addition to marked asymmetry of knee folds, external rotation of the leg, shortening of the involved leg, a clicking sound on abduction, and delay in learning to walk. X rays will show dislocation of the femur upward and laterally.

Ortolani's sign or maneuver helps to diagnose the presence of congenital dysplasia. The legs are adducted, with hips and knees extended. As stated, adduction can be continued to 90% without incident in normal infants. With dislocation, resistance may be sensed at 60% of flexion, while the other leg is held fixed to stabilize the pelvis. As the dislocated femoral head slips back into the acetabular fossa, dislocation can be identified. Telescoping is present when moving the head of the femur back and forth on the side of the ileum.

Incidence In most ethnic groups the incidence of congenital dysplasia of the hip is 1.5 infants in 1,000 live births (Barnett & Einhorn, 1972). Black infants, however, are rarely affected. The problem is six to seven times more frequent in girls, and the left hip is more often involved. The term *congenital dislocation of the hip* refers to those cases occurring after 4 months of age when hips are subjected to weight bearing and locomotion. There is evidence of high familial incidence in some geographic areas of the world, which may reflect practices such as binding and swaddling (Nelson, 1979).

Etiology The cause of congenital dysplasia of the hip is unknown. Researchers conjecture that abnormal development of the joint may be caused by the fetal position or by genetic factors. It is further suggested that hormonal influences may affect abnormal relaxation of the capsule and ligaments of the joint.

A popular hypothesis suggests that congenital dysplasia of the acetabulum predisposes to dislocation. Investigators in Sweden have postulated a delay in the development of enzyme systems that help in the degradation of transplacentally transmitted maternal hormones that induce relaxation of the ligaments (Barnett & Einhorn, 1972). A comparison of urine hormone assays from newborns with and without dislocation appears to support the hormonal hypothesis. Management based partly on this concept has reportedly been effective in decreasing the disease in Sweden.

Treatment Treatment may consist of closed reduction of the hip and maintenance of the reduction through immobilization (hip spica cast). Beyond 12 to 18 months, operative reduction is necessary. Diagnosis and treatment must begin early to be effective. Diagnosis is aided by clinical findings (Barlow's signs) in the first week of life and by limitation of abduction of the flexed hip. It is essential that the physician abduct the flexed hips of the infant regularly during the first year. Closed manipulative reduction should be accomplished without anesthesia, as too much force may be exerted, causing damage to the hip. If reduction is obtained, it is maintained by a plaster cast. If X rays indicate that manipulative reduction is imperfect, open reduction (surgical) should be performed. These operations have been performed at 2 to 6 years of age. Skeletal maturity may necessitate reconstructive procedures.

In newborns, the position of reduction is maintained by placing the child in a simple padded splint that holds the femurs in abduction and allows external rotation for weekly or monthly periods. Within 2 to 3 weeks the exit and entrance clicks may no longer be heard. After 6 weeks, the splints are no longer needed, and the joint is stable if reduction is successful. Abduction splint management appears to be the most effective and least complicated treatment prior to ambulation. Treatment of older children may necessitate stretching of the soft tissues by traction and manipulation under anesthesia. In this way the femoral head can be replaced in the acetabular fossa. Plaster casts are required to maintain the position because of the shallowness of the acetabulum.

With extensive reduction and rotation, the capsule of the hip is pulled tight, and the vascular supply to the head may be diminished. Up to 30% of older patients treated with rigid casts may have complications resulting from this problem. For example, arthritic changes in middle life have developed in patients treated by manipulative methods late in childhood. Follow up of individuals treated in the newborn period by simpler methods suggests that fewer complications arise. Children who do not respond to relatively gentle manipulative procedures and who demonstrate complications require more complex surgical procedures. The examination of the hips for dislocatability in newborns should be a part of the regular pediatric developmental examination.

Placement in a class for orthopaedically handicapped persons may be suggested, depending on the severity of the handicapping condition.

Osteogenesis Imperfecta

Description The congenital form of osteogenesis imperfecta is severe, occurs sporadically, and is characterized by countless fractures and ribbon-like bone shadows. In osteogenesis imperfecta tarda, fractures appear later in life with marked bone atrophy. There may be one or more fractures present at birth. In both forms, inadequate mineralization of the calvarium is seen but is more severe in the congenital form. Associated abnormalities are more commonly found in the tarda form: dental deficiencies of enamel and dentin, osteosclerosis with deafness, and blue-colored sclerae. Bone fractures can result from very minor movements such as position changes and ambulation. Dwarfism may result from improper healing, frequent refracturing, and restricted mobility.

Osteogenesis imperfecta is a generalized disorder of connective tissue, with clinical manifestations in the skeleton, joints and ligaments, teeth, sclerae, and skin. The fractures that characterize this illness frequently involve the long bones of the legs. Although susceptibility to fractures is said to diminish after puberty, it may return with pregnancy, menopause, or during periods of inactivity. Characteristics include shortened extremities, triangular face, domed forehead with overhanging occiput, and "hourglass" vertebrae. Abnormalities in the ligaments and tendons lead to loose-jointedness, while tendons may rupture with mild stress. Teeth may be small, misshapen, and blue-yellow. The skin tends to be thin, translucent, and easily bruised. Hernias occur frequently and cardiovascular disorders are common.

Although diagnosis is fairly obvious when blue sclerae, pathological fractures, and deafness are present, only 60% of those affected have clinical bone disease. There are several distinct syndromes with genetic and clinical heterogeneity. Variability, however, may occur among family members. When the legs are short and the head quite large, osteogenesis imperfecta may resemble achondroplasia.

Incidence Incidence seems to be approximately 1 individual in every 20,000 live births. Deafness is present in about 35% of patients in the fourth decade and in about 50% of patients in the fifth decade (Menolascino & Egger, 1978). Infants with severe osteogenesis imperfecta congenita are frequently stillborn or die in infancy.

Etiology As with other inherited disorders of connective tissues, there is clinical and genetic heterogeneity. Osteogenesis imperfecta tarda and osteogenesis imperfecta congenita are genetically based, but patterns of inheritance are not well defined. Cases occur sporadically, with some patients autosomal recessive and others autosomal dominant. While some patients may have very mild symptoms (e.g., blue sclerae), others in the same family may have multiple fractures. There appear to be two forms of osteogenesis imperfecta congenita: one probably dominant, with thin bones, and the other, recessive, with thick bones.

Treatment No specific therapy is known. Careful orthopaedic management is necessary, and immobilization should be avoided. Because of low serum pyrophosphate levels and excessive urinary pyrophosphate excretion, therapy with magnesium salts is often employed. The initial enthusiasm for this treatment, however, is waning, as results have not been conclusive. Since fractures are less frequent after puberty, endocrine therapy to induce early puberty has been employed but has produced questionable results. It is necessary to examine both apparently healthy parents of a child with an autosomal dominant disorder before considering the possibility of a mutation. On careful examination, the "skipped generation" often shows mild manifestations of the disorder.

Whether or not a youngster with osteogenesis imperfecta is placed in a class for regular, multiply handicapped, orthopaedically handicapped, or hearing impaired students depends upon individual needs.

NEUROLOGICAL DISORDERS

Cerebral Palsy

Description Cerebral palsy appears to have a much higher incidence among premature infants. In a study done by Eastman (1962), 31.2% of 753 persons afflicted with cerebral palsy were born before full term. Research relating cerebral palsy and prematurity supports the concept that prematurity is often associated with neurological damage and mental retardation. By definition, cerebral palsy is the result of a static lesion of the brain that has no cure; the clinical picture, however, can change with time. Spasticity may not become apparent until late in the first year, and the possibility of contractures increases without proper management. Untreated individuals with spasticity may become wheelchair-bound, while seizure disorders may add to the degree of disablement. Intelligence is said to be lower when cerebral palsy is associated with a seizure disorder. In addition, a variety of speech disorders may occur in children with cerebral palsy. Articulatory disturbances, speech delays, degrees of aphasia, apraxias, and rhythm abnormalities may be part of the clinical picture. Visual handicaps are common and important to programming, due to the high incidence of strabismus, refractive errors, and visual-field defects. Deafness is fairly uncommon, except in children with athetosis (due to kernicterus).

Children with cerebral palsy may be classified according to the predominant clinical manifestations. These children represent a group of diverse syndromes affecting the brain with impaired motor function. Gross malformations may be found in almost one-third of children with cerebral palsy, while cortical or subcortical changes, sometimes microscopic, may be noted in others. Cortical changes, when present, are found more commonly in the group acquiring cerebral palsy postnatally. Subcortical abnormalities result from perinatal complications. The following syndromes have been noted:

Spastic Cerebral Palsy
    Spastic hemiplegia
    Spastic tetraplegia or quadriplegia
    Spastic diplegia
    Atonic diplegia
    Spastic paraplegia
    Monoplegias and triplegias
Dyskinetic Cerebral Palsy
    Athetosis
    Other forms
Ataxic Cerebral Palsy
Mixed Syndromes

Spastic Cerebral Palsy Spastic cerebral palsy involves the upper motor neurons and is characterized by increased tone of the involved musculature, exaggerated deep-tendon reflexes, clonus, abnormal reflexes, and a tendency to develop contractures. Six types are described below:

    Spastic hemiplegia Both extremities on one side are involved in spastic hemiplegia, the upper extremities more severely involved than the lower. There is usually weakness of peripheral muscles (especially wrist and ankle) and increased deep-tendon and periosteal reflexes in the involved arm and leg. Because of peripheral muscle weakness and the tendency to develop contractures, the upper extemity tends to be fixed at the elbow, wrist, and fingers. In mildly afflicted children, the handicap may not be apparent while the patient rests in a sitting position, but walking or running may accentuate the abnormal position. Supination of the outstretched arm may elicit spasticity in the mildest cases, with flexion of the elbow on the involved side. Children tend to walk on toes more than heels, which results in circumduction of the affected leg to compensate for apparent lengthening. Running may reveal functional asymmetry, the child's shoes may show wear on the involved side, with scuffing of the toes and a lack of wear on the heels. The upper extremities may be shorter in length, with reduced muscle volume. The involved hand may show sensory impairment and an inability to discriminate objects. There may also be evidence of a central facial weakness.

Spastic tetraplegia or quadriplegia Characteristics described for hemiplegia are present symmetrically in the spastic quadriplegic; in other words, all four extremities are affected to a similar degree. Tightness of hip adductors and hamstring muscles is generally more distinct than in hemiplegia. Spasticity may be more marked in the arms than in the legs. The terms *double hemiplegia* and *tetraplegia* may be used in describing children with equal involvement in all four extremities. Children may manifest pseudobulbar palsy with dysarthric speech, impaired swallowing, and restricted lingual protrusion with a gag reflex present.

Spastic diplegia Greater involvement of the lower limbs characterizes spastic diplegia. The distinction between tetraplegia and diplegia is not always clear and may be determined by individual judgment regarding the degree of involvement of the upper and lower extremities. Spastic diplegia is frequently the result of prematurity; the arms and hands may appear to be uninvolved, while slightly abnormal findings appear later.

Atonic diplegia A variant form of spastic diplegia, atonic diplegia is characterized by marked delay in all motor milestones. There is obvious decreased tone in the muscles of the lower extremities, with an increased range of passive movement. When a child is suspended upright under the arms, flexion of the hips is a characteristic sign. A diagnosis of atonic diplegia must be made on children between 6 months and 4 years of age, because in the older child hypertonicity supervenes and hyperextensibility wanes.

Spastic paraplegia This form of cerebral palsy involves both legs to a marked degree, but there is no disablement of the upper extremities. Spastic paraplegia most often stems from spinal cord pathology and is characterized by adduction spasms of thighs, resulting in a scissoring gait. A tightening of the heel cords and tendency to flexion contracture of the knees result in a toe gait. Diplegia and paraplegia may be difficult to separate, since the hand involvement in diplegia is difficult to discern.

Monoplegias and triplegias These are relatively rare conditions but can be detected by the involvement of one or three extremities. In triplegia, all extremities with the exception of one arm are generally involved.

Dyskinetic Cerebral Palsy Impairment of volitional activity, with uncontrollable and haphazard movements that dissipate when the child is asleep, characterize dyskinetic cerebral palsy. Lesions of the basal ganglia cause this problem, and the most common type is athetosis. Athetosis expresses itself in slow, writhing movements usually involving all extremities as well as the face, the neck, and possibly the trunk. This constant movement is less apparent when the patient is relaxed, and appears to increase with excitement or tension. Athetosis generally involves all extremities to some degree, with rare cases identified in which one extremity may be involved. Hypertrophy of some muscles (e.g., neck) is fairly common due to the continuous movement of extremities and trunk. Athetosis due to kernicterus may be associated with nerve deafness and paresis of upward gaze.

Ataxic Cerebral Palsy Related to a static lesion of the cerebellum or its pathways, ataxic cerebral palsy shows little progression from its onset early in childhood. This form of cerebral palsy has the best prognosis for functional improvement. Characteristics include a wide-based gait, difficulty in turning rapidly, poor performance of fast repetitive movements, and problems with neurological tests involving finger-to-finger and finger-to-nose pointing.

Mixed Forms of Cerebral Palsy In some children, mixed forms of cerebral palsy have been detected. Combinations of spasticity and athetosis are found frequently. Ataxia combined with athetosis has also been identified. Cases of mixed forms can be identified through careful study, and treatment must be planned according to individual need.

Incidence Cerebral palsy is a relatively common disorder, with estimates of occurrence ranging from 0.6 to 2.4 individuals per 1,000 births (Isselbacher, Adams, Braunwald, Petersdorf, & Wilson, 1980). Cerebral palsy is the most frequent cause of permanent physical disability in children. Incidence in the United States ranges from 1.6 to 5 individuals per 1,000 individuals. Prenatal factors such as rubella, toxemia, maternal drug ingestion, genetic factors, and threatened abortion account for about 10% of all cases of cerebral palsy. Cerebral palsy occurs in premature infants three times more often than in full-term infants (Davis & Hill, 1980). Slightly more males than females are affected. Gross malformations are present in about one-third of children with cerebral palsy, with 25% to 35% having seizure disorders. Seizures are more common in postnatally acquired forms of cerebral palsy. The incidence of mental retardation may be as low as 25% and as high as 75%; it is higher when associated with a seizure disorder (Isselbacher et al., 1980). Visual perception problems are common among cerebral palsied children, in addition to a high incidence of strabismus. Of all children with cerebral palsy, 70% are spastic, 15% athetoid, 5% ataxic, and the remaining 10% mixed types. The incidence of athetosis and ataxia has been decreasing, according to figures from the Columbia-Presbyterian Medical Center in New York (Rudolph, 1977).

Cerebral palsy has increased in highly developed countries because of medical advances that save the lives of premature and seriously handicapped infants. Today, children with chronic, nonprogressive lesions are being recognized with increasing frequency; cerebral palsy affects nearly 400,000 children. Approximately 5% of all children have seizures at some time during the early years. More studies are needed, but available figures illustrate that cerebral palsy is a widespread problem.

Etiology Chronic nonprogressive cerebral dysfunction results from numerous causes and manifests in a variety of clinical syndromes. Clinical prognosis is determined by the time of occurrence and the site and extent of the lesion. The nervous system is more susceptible to insults occurring during the first trimester of pregnancy. Diffuse cerebral involvement results in mental retardation; small lesions that interfere with normal cerebral maturation also result in intellectual deficit. Impairment of parts of the brain controlling sight and hearing causes weaknesses in those areas, while convulsions result most commonly from cortical lesions. A focal lesion or diffuse cerebral involvement results in speech disturbances. The combinations and varieties of brain lesions present different patterns in the determination of the various types of cerebral palsy. In many children with cerebral palsy, the cause of their impairment may not be evident. Although a particular syndrome (e.g., spastic diplegia) may occur as an isolated clinical phenomenon, a mental deficit, seizures, visual handicap, behavioral disturbance, and other problems may accompany the motor deficit. The cause of the accompanying deficits may not be apparent. The fetus may have been affected by faulty implantation of the ovum, chromosomal anomalies, infection, trauma, radiation, toxic substances, or maternal toxemia or diabetes. In the perinatal period anoxia and trauma are the most common causes, and in the postnatal period infections, toxins, and vascular disease may be factors. Vascular complications are often the result of asphyxia. Kernicterus is recognized as one of the causes of athetosis. The use of exchange transfusions and administration of gamma-globulin may decrease the possibility of kernicterus. Postnatally, infections such as meningitis and encephalitis may damage the brain, while dehydration, subsequent venous thrombosis and arterial occlusions before or after birth may cause infantile hemiplegia.

Treatment Treatment for cerebral palsied children is as heterogeneous as the children themselves. Although 50% to 60% of children with cerebral palsy may be retarded, 40% to 50% may be intellectually capable of functioning in a regular school program. Physical and occupational therapists play a major role in the treatment programs of cerebral palsied children. At times, early intervention by these therapists may be a major factor in preventing the need for surgery. Operations are performed to stabilize various joints, and tendon releases assist the patient in decreasing spasticity. Physical therapy programs frequently utilize the Bobath method to inhibit primitive reflexes and facilitate postural reflexes. The Bobath treatment system is based on neurophysiology and is concerned with the inhibition of abnormal reflexes and the facilitation of the normal patterns of motion and postural reactions. Many therapists, using neurodevelopmental therapy, have been successful in reducing spasticity and promoting more normal postural and movement reactions. Techniques of proprioceptive and tactile stimulation are promoted by Bobath and Bobath (1972) for use with ataxic and some athetoid children. These techniques are also used when there is a sensory deficit or when the child does not know how to move because of lack of previous sensorimotor experiences or apraxia. The techniques of stimulation must be combined with reflex-inhibiting patterns that are accompanied by careful stimulation when postural tone is low. Abnormal reactions must be anticipated and stopped before they gain momentum. The main techniques of this approach include weight-bearing resistance, placing and holding, and tapping. All of the techniques may elicit abnormal motor responses in patients, and therapists must use reflex-inhibiting postural patterns to prevent tonic reflex activity.

In preparing the cerebral palsied child for speech, four areas of motor development may require therapy. The development of head control and stabilization of the neck aid in efficient respiration. Motor precision and oral-perceptual skills occur as the child learns to eat foods, paving the way for articulation. The babbling stage is a precursor of meaningful speech. All of these motor activities, however, may be disrupted by early primitive reflex patterns. Neurodevelopmental treatment attempts to inhibit abnormal and primitive reflexes, while activating more normal postural reactions of righting and equilibrium. As the child experiences more normal postural adjustments, external controls are reduced and the child carries out the movement independently. When abnormal reflexes such as tongue and jaw thrusting are decreased, more normal reactions may be seen with feeding, babbling, and language. Prespeech therapy programs have gained increasing acceptance and respectability.

To implement a therapeutic feeding program for cerebral palsied children, care must be given to the selection of appropriate textures of foods in order to stimulate particular activities. For example, softer foods are sucked and swallowed; harder foods are bitten and chewed. Other sensory properties of foods must also be considered. Taste, smell, and temperature of a given food will stimulate the child to either reach eagerly for it or violently reject it. Children with swallowing difficulties may be able to handle thicker foods more efficiently than thin foods. Yoghurt, for example, may be substituted for milk (milk increases the amount of mucous or saliva, which further inhibits swallowing) and foods that form a solid mass when chewed may be easier to swallow than those that break up easily. When cheek and tongue action is inefficient, foods that separate easily should be avoided. The speech or occupational therapist skilled in prespeech and feeding techniques plays a major role in the cerebral palsied child's treatment program.

Many children with cerebral palsy (25% to 35%) also suffer from seizure disorders, which may be further incapacitating. The spastic group has a higher incidence of seizures; 20% of children with hemiplegia suffer from seizures. Seizures may be evident in early infancy but become more visible in early childhood. The type of seizure may be related to age of onset, beginning with infantile spasms; grand mal, focal, multifocal, and psychomotor seizures are seen later. Careful selection of drugs for seizure activity and control of movement disorders may be a major part of the treatment program. The medical representative must be a part of any intervention team for cerebral palsied children. Medications such as Dantrium, used for relaxation of the skeletal muscles, may be effective, and anticonvulsants may be administered on a daily basis for seizure disorders.

Common laboratory tests such as urinalyses, blood counts, and sedimentation rates do not contribute to the diagnosis of cerebral palsy. Roentgenograms of the skull should be done routinely, as asymmetries may be detected in hemiplegic children and relative microcephaly may be noted. Abnormal electroencephalograms (EEGs) are common with cerebral palsied children whether seizures are present or not. Spike-seizure discharge is frequently a pattern noted in EEG readings. Spasticity may not be apparent in the young child with cerebral palsy but, without treatment, may increase in time to the point of severe contractures. Surgical and nonsurgical (e.g., neurodevelopmental treatment) means are used to counteract the disabling effects of contractures. Short leg braces, an "A frame" that separates the legs during resting hours, various splints, and stretching exercises may be used in the individual therapy programs of children. Specific functional improvement should be expected to result from surgery, and careful examination and an extended period of observation and therapy should be provided prior to any surgical procedure. A variety of orthopaedic procedures have been devised for the correction of contractures that do not respond readily to corrective measures. While exercises and appliances are sufficient in some cases, they may not be effective in others (e.g., athetosis). Significant mental retardation is another factor that may interfere with treatment.

Cerebral palsy symptoms range from slight hand tremors to complete paralysis, with perceptual, speech, and intellectual involvement among the possible accompanying problems. Of great importance for program planning is recognition of the uniqueness and variability of the individual's involvement. Concomitant medical problems, seizure disorders, motor handicaps, and visual deficits dramatize the need for specific individualized treatment plans and place unusual demands on staff persons. The range and versatility of dysfunction make treatment and educational programming very difficult. Prognosis and program expectations must be deferred until each child has been studied for rate of development and until methods have been determined for the acquisition of program information. When skill development is hindered because of severe motor, visual, intellectual, or medical problems, alternate means of teaching must be devised through careful study and observation.

Many children with cerebral palsy have spent their early years as social isolates. Their daily lives may consist of hours of therapy, lengthy travel to treatment centers, and long sessions with complex equipment. Evaluations are endless, and early hopes for achievement of developmental milestones may cloud the picture for some parents and interfere with program possibilities. As a result of a cerebral palsied child's small stature, delays in various skill areas, or restricted intelligence, the child's parents may develop problems in acceptance and, consequently may infantilize the child. Thus, children with cerebral palsy may seem more infantile for a longer time period and may not have a true awareness of their handicapping condition until adolescence, at which time, social and vocational problems may surface because of the lack of independent living skills. The usual outlets, such as sports, dances, parties, telephone conversations, and social contacts, may not be available for these teenagers; educators and parents must be sensitive and understanding during these critical years. Cerebral palsied adolescents often make important decisions at this period about their future lives; withdrawal from competition or renewed efforts to achieve may be important choices made at this time.

The cerebral palsied child is a challenge to the educator. Whenever possible, a regular school program is most desirable, but diagnosis may indicate the need for alternate programming. Forty to fifty percent of cerebral palsied children may be capable of functioning in a regular school program. Many persons with mild forms of cerebral palsy need no specialized education program. Any educational plan must consider the particular constellation of physical, perceptual, behavioral, and cognitive patterns of each child. A critical feature must be the periodic evaluation or ongoing monitoring of the child's program. The abilities and needs of the child with cerebral palsy change with development, medical treatment, intervention strategies, and therapy. The various types of language impairment may respond to special language programs, while technological techniques may be more effective in programs for noncommunicative students. Motor impairments may require students to use head pointers, individualized wheelchairs, electronic devices, and an endless variety of adaptive equipment. In addition, the provision of physical therapy within the daily program may be a critical factor. It is important that every aspect of the type and severity of each child's involvement be considered in program planning and management. Programming for this group of youngsters is difficult and requires significant expenditure of time if optimum results are to be realized.

Epilepsy

Description A seizure is an episode of cerebral dysfunction produced by abnormal, excessive neuronal discharge occurring in the brain (Rudolph, 1977). It may manifest as a change in the state of consciousness, an abnormal sensory experience, disordered motor activity, or a disturbance of intellectual and behavioral functions. When seizures are recurrent, the condition is called epilepsy. The term *convulsion* implies widespread abnormal motor activity; while all convulsions are not epileptic, many types of epilepsy do not include convulsions. When symptoms, such as whininess and irritability, appear days or hours before a seizure, they are referred to as a *prodrome*. An *aura* is the sensation recognized by the patient as a warning signal of an epileptic attack and is habitual in nature and occurrence. The aura is the beginning of the abnormal neuronal discharge and can be a helpful sign in the care and treatment of epilepsy.

Grand Mal Seizures Seizures that involve both sides of the body with tonic and clonic phases of the muscular spasms are known as grand mal seizures. Paleness, dilated pupils, eyeballs rolling upward, head thrown backward, and stiffened limbs precede the attack, followed by a sudden loss of consciousness. A short cry may be heard, the tongue may be severely bitten, and the victim may lose bowel and bladder control. After a period of clonic jerking, the victim may lapse into a semicoma and the musculature becomes generally limp. Upon awakening, the patient may have a severe headache or feel dazed or confused. When grand mal seizures occur in series and the patient does not regain consciousness, the condition is called *status epilepticus*. Because of the serious nature of these persistent seizures, (irreversible brain damage or death can occur), hospital treatment is recommended.

Petit Mal Seizures Petit mal seizures may involve brief periods of staring and transient loss of consciousness. The person may appear vacuous and disinterested during episodes; eyelids flutter or droop, and the patient may drop articles held in the hands or mouth. This type of seizure varies widely in frequency from once or twice a month to numerous times a day.

Seizures are rarely evident prior to 3 years of age but may increase or decrease in frequency during childhood and adolescence. The victim may experience dizzy spells and may not be aware that he or she has had a convulsion at all. Petit mal seizures present problems in the classroom setting because the victim experiences a lapse of time, does not follow the instructional program, and often is accused of daydreaming or inattentiveness. The cause of this type of seizure is unknown, but it is felt that it originates deep in the brain. The patient has intact intelligence in most instances.

Myoclonic and Akinetic Seizures Myoclonic jerks affecting a particular group of muscles on one side or in one extremity characterize myoclonic and akinetic seizures. Myoclonic seizures may occur in conjunction with other forms of epilepsy, such as petit mal, in which the victim experiences slow rhythmic jerks of the eyelid, neck, or arms. Akinetic seizures are associated with a general loss of postural tone and differ from single or repeated myoclonic jerks. In young children, the seizures resemble infantile myoclonic seizures and may be called *motor petit mal* or *jackknife* seizures. The massive myoclonic spasms last from 5 to 10 seconds and tend to occur in series in early childhood; a long series of myoclonic jerks may develop into grand mal attacks. Cerebral dysrhythmia attests to the presence of epilepsy; it is believed to occur because of the sudden release from inhibitory control of motor centers in the midbrain.

Focal Seizures Depending upon the location of brain damage, focal seizures may be sensory or motor. Focal or localized seizures may involve the entire body or may only affect a particular area of the body. Clinical manifestations are on the side opposite the site of epileptic discharge in the brain. A focal motor seizure begins in one part of the body and spreads to others in a pattern known as a *Jacksonian march*. Many times an attack is brief and remains in one area; consciousness is lost in cases when a general convulsion follows an extensive, rapid spread of localized seizures. Masticatory seizures are evidenced by chewing movements of the swallowing mechanism as well as salivation. Sensory seizures consist of disturbances of the senses, in which numbness or tingling is experienced in the arms and legs. Other sensory areas such as vision, smell, and hearing may be affected, with victims experiencing bright lights or blindness, loud noises, or deafness.

Psychomotor Seizures Because they consist of purposeful motor acts that are inappropriate, psychomotor seizures are difficult to recognize and control. The seizures often come without warning but may be preceded by abdominal pain or headache. The victim may have hallucinations or perceptual illusions or experience a dreamy state. Purposeful but inappropriate behaviors may include grimacing, laughing, walking about, or speaking in a babbling manner. Tonic or clonic movements are generally not present, but a state of confusion and fright may be experienced by the victim. Seizure discharge usually originates in the temporal lobe. Atrophic lesions due to birth injury or postnatal trauma are far more common than expanding lesions. The seizure may last a few minutes, during which rapid pulse, perspiration, pallor, or blushing may be noted in the patient. Learning disorders or behavioral problems may be observed and require specialized therapy (medication and counseling).

Other types of seizure patterns exist and may be difficult to identify. They include seizures in which vital body signs change temporarily. Seizures may occur in response to a specific smell, strain of music, or sample of reading material. This phenomenon is known as *reflex epilepsy* and is rare. Some researchers indicate that seizures may be self-induced at times by hyperventilation or through the induction of a hypnotic state. This action is generally felt to be a behavioral problem and is not responsive to medication.

Incidence Epilepsy occurs in approximately .5% of the population, affecting at least one million Americans (Menolascino & Egger, 1978). One out of 20 persons experiences convulsions at some time in his or her life. The chances are 1 in 10 that an offspring of epileptics will be similarly involved. Among retarded individuals, the incidence of epilepsy is higher than .5%. It is a common symptom in many of the major syndromes associated with mental retardation (Menolascino & Egger, 1978). However, many individuals afflicted with epilepsy are not handicapped; drug therapy and ongoing treatment by a physician have provided excellent results in the control of seizure activity.

Etiology The general cause of epilepsy is unknown, but the condition may be divided into two major groups. Genetic epilepsies can be identified by the absence of a structural lesion of the brain and a tendency toward the presence of genetically inherited cerebral dysrhythmia. Symptomatic epilepsies are associated with metabolic disorders of the brain caused by developmental problems, injury, or illness. In 4% to 8% of epileptic persons, there may be a hereditary factor; in the absence of seizures, a low-seizure threshold may be evidenced. In all cases of epilepsy a structural or metabolic disturbance in the brain is noted. The blood supply to the intermediate zone (where there is a weakened number of surviving cells) is threatened, and the unstable cells become a site for epileptic activity. The basic mechanism of seizure discharge appears to be prolonged depolarization with hyperactive and hypersynchronous discharge from abnormal neurons. Biochemical bases for epilepsy have been studied but are not clearly understood. There appear to be cyclic factors (e.g., menstruation) that trigger epileptic attacks. Triggering mechanisms in the environment, in the senses, and at times, those that are self-induced, may be factors in attacks.

Treatment Epilepsy responds to drug therapy and the administration of anticonvulsant drugs in approximately 70% to 85% of patients (Rudolph, 1977). Phenobarbital, first used in 1912, remains effective in many cases. The introduction of Dilantin in 1936 and other broad-spectrum drugs, tranquilizers, amphetamines, and more specific adrenal steroids have all helped in the control of epilepsy. Rudolph (1977) lists drugs of choice for various seizure types:

1. Motor, focal, psychomotor, and convulsive epilepsy
    Dilantin
    phenobarbital or Mebaral
    Mysoline
    Mesantoin
    Celontin
    Phenurone
2. Petit mal
    Zarontin
    Tridione
    Valium
    Diamox
    Dilantin
    Aralen
3. Minor motor
    ACTH or adrenal corticosteroids
    Zarontin
    Tridione
    Dexedrine
    meprobamate
    Valium

Gemonil
Celontin
4. Status epilepticus
Valium
sodium pentobarbital
sodium phenobarbital
paraldehyde
volatile anesthetics

Drugs, however, are only part of the treatment plan. Identification of and removal of the precipitating factors must be attempted, while a counseling program is highly recommended. Often the individual with epilepsy feels a sense of social isolation and embarrassment because others may witness the attacks. Because of the fictions and "old wives' tales" associated with this illness, guidance for the victim and his or her family is often essential. Because of the fear experienced in anticipation of or following an attack, behaviors may emerge in patients with epilepsy that suggest the presence of a personality disorder. In many instances, these may be compensatory reactions to a known element in the person's life, especially when seizures are not entirely controlled.

Vocational and educational choices are also determined in part by the incidence of seizures. Emergency first aid for the grand mal sufferer must be learned by family and educators. An actively convulsing person must be removed from dangerous places in schools and work areas and placed in a horizontal position. Clearing of the airways, removal of objects from the mouth, and the insertion of a padded object to protect the tongue is recommended. Gently restraining the patient may also be necessary. Those persons afflicted with grand mal seizures may have to limit vocational choices whenever heavy machinery or vehicles are involved. Driving an automobile, swimming, riding a horse, and other active sports must be decided on an individual basis through doctor, patient, and family interaction. As the youngster reaches adolescence, there is an increased need for independence, socialization, and admiration. Acute sensitivity to the seizure disorder may be felt at this point, accompanied by a need to deny the illness or the need for medication. This time is generally a period of testing for both parents and the afflicted child, and can shape the course of his or her behavior into adulthood. Parents must remember to permit as much normalcy as possible and assist the maturing child to self-sufficiency.

Spinal Cord Injuries

Description In cases where birth is extremely difficult and force is needed to aid the delivery, spinal cord injuries are possible. The infant may have a weak cry, prominent abdomen, and intercostal paralysis. The lower extremities may appear flaccid, abducted, and lifeless. Although sensory evaluation is difficult, there may be decreased responsiveness; upper extremity movements may be limited to the shoulder and forearm area. Hyperflexia may occur upon stimulation; total flexion of the involved areas may be mistaken for return of function. Respiratory, urinary, and skin infections may occur in this initial stage and are sometimes fatal. The extent and characteristics of the paraplegia (i.e., flaccidity or spasticity) depend upon the spinal cord defect. There is normally no decrease in intelligence, but victims rarely walk or sit without support. Upper extremities may be free from damage, although surgery may be needed in older children for normal urinary and sphincter control. Orthopaedic problems may also necessitate surgical treatment. Spinal cord injuries in the upper spine affect most bodily organs to some degree, requiring treatment by a variety of specialists. The newborn requires immediate airway attention and bowel and bladder care. Antibiotics may be needed if long-term catheterization is required.

Damage to the vertebral column is found more frequently when trauma to the spinal cord takes place in older children. The patient must be handled in such a manner that additional injury is not caused by improper posture or movement of the vertebrae. Because spinal cord injury at this age is often the result of serious accidents, other bodily injuries may have occurred. Surgery may be indicated in open injuries, while closed-cord injuries may receive nonsurgical treatment. Care to avoid heavy sedatives is essential at this time, since they may mask neurological changes critical to diagnosis. There is no way of knowing whether early spinal cord injury is due to contusion or whether the lesion is one of frank anatomic discontinuity. In severe lesions of the vertebrae, physiological loss of cord function above the uppermost visible vertebral injury occurs.

Plexus injury is most commonly the result of birth trauma. The plexus has points of fascial fixation to the first rib medially and the caracoid process of the scapula laterally. Injuries in this area may occur with breech or cephalic deliveries. Treatment includes bracing and passive exercises to restore full range of motion. Eighty percent of these patients will have complete recovery within months. Lower plexus root injuries have a less favorable prognosis, and a longer recovery period is required.

Serratus anterior palsy is caused by injury to the long thoracic nerve (nerve of Bell) and is usually the result of pressure on the shoulder. This injury is often associated with pitching in baseball, weight lifting, or carrying heavy objects. Treatment with a simple arm sling accompanied by range of motion exercises often assists in full functional recovery.

Radial nerve injury is most commonly a result of fracture through the middle third of the humerus. There is marked weakness of the brachioradialis and the extensors of the wrist and fingers. Sensation is lost in an area between index finger and thumb, and it may be difficult to tell whether the nerve has been lacerated and/or severed. Tendon transplantation may be necessary when permanent damage exists. Ulnar and median nerve damage may be caused by laceration, and may result in sensory loss in the forearm, fingers, and thumb. Peripheral nerve injuries affecting the lower extremities almost always involve the sciatic nerve and its branches. The sciatic nerve is located between the ischial tuberosity and the greater trochanter under the gluteus maximus muscle. In infancy, intragluteal injections should be avoided because of the possibility of injury. Lesions produce paralysis of the foot and loss of flexion in the leg. There may be a sensory loss below the knee, a foot drag, and an absence of ankle jerk. When injuries occur in infancy, extremities may be short and small due to a lack of stimulation in the muscular tendon mount. Stimulation is essential to bone growth. High lesions rarely show recovery and may be associated with marked permanent disability.

Diseases of the spinal cord are not common but require prompt diagnosis and treatment for best results. Spinal epidural abscess is usually staphylococcal in origin, with severe pain, rigidity, paraparesis, and loss of bladder and bowel control. Systemic evidence of infection may not be obvious; however, myelography may be necessary to document spinal cord pressure. Treatment includes neurosurgery and prompt drainage of the abscess to prevent paraplegia.

Vascular anomalies of the spinal cord may cause sudden spinal cord dysfunction if there is rupture of the damaged blood vessel with hemorrhage into the spinal cord. When bleeding is massive, nuchal rigidity occurs; cerebrospinal fluid may be bloody or protein content elevated. A wine-purple stain may cover the skin corresponding to the level of vascular malformation. Surgery to remove the malformation may not be successful.

Incidence Injury to the vertebral column and spinal cord account for less than 5% of childhood injuries. The bony structure around the spinal cord assists in protecting it from injury. Because of its mobility, the cervical spine is a common site of spinal injury at any age. The thoracic vertebrae are supported by the trunk, and the spinal cord is smaller in this area, affording even greater protection. The lumbar spine is given additional support by the pelvis, but there is somewhat less protection in the lower thoracic and upper lumbar areas.

Cord transections may contribute to childhood respiratory paralysis; with extensive paralysis of the diaphragm, death may occur. Diseases of the spinal cord are uncommon in childhood, but when they exist they cause compression of the cord, which must be treated promptly. Injuries to the peripheral nerves are not common in childhood, but recovery is better in children than in adults through spontaneous resolution and surgery.

There are 7,000 to 10,000 cases of spinal cord injuries yearly, resulting in up to 3,000 deaths (Thomas, 1974). Forty-two percent of the injuries are incomplete lesions, in which some neurological recovery is possible. Patients with severe spinal cord lesions live longer today than they did in the early 1900s. The total number of cases in the United States was estimated at 125,000 in 1974 (Thomas, 1974). Most injuries to the spinal cord occur among the young, often as a result of birth trauma or accidents.

Etiology Spinal cord injuries in childhood are due to breech or difficult deliveries, automobile accidents, and diving injuries. They are associated with fracture or dislocation of vertebrae. Any force changing the normal relationship of arm, shoulder, and neck may result in plexus injury. Birth trauma is a frequent cause of spinal cord injury. Injury to the thoracic segments of the vertebral column is usually the result of direct severe trauma; the prognosis is poor because of the rich blood supply in the thoracic area. Peripheral nerve injuries are uncommon in childhood and are due to damage to the brachial plexus or sciatic nerve. There is greater distal involvement and more diffuse damage with injuries to older children. Severe trauma results in a degree of hemmorhage and scarring that sometimes precludes functional recovery in injuries to the brachial plexus.

Treatment Treatment of spinal cord injuries varies with the type, site, and extent of damage. When the lesion is extensive, a long period of treatment and habilitation may be necessary. School programming for the young quadriplegic or paraplegic may require specialized equipment, respirators, and a variety of intervention techniques. Among young adults, hospitalization is long and costly, and extensive therapy programs may span years of treatment. The loss of independence and a reduction in the quality of life following a serious spinal cord injury may result in a need for extensive counseling among young adults. Rehabilitation is costly, slow, and complicated by continuous medical problems (e.g., urinary and respiratory). Research continues in this habilitation area, particularly concerning the use of electrophrenic respirators and specially equipped transportation systems. Behavior modification techniques have been used to counteract severe depression and emotional problems. Large companies (e.g., International Business Machines [IBM]) are cooperating in training severely disabled persons for home-bound employment as computer programmers (Thomas, 1974). Community outreach and education services for severely disabled persons are being planned by model programs. Such programs are being aided by projects around the United States that are accumulating a data bank of research to assist in future planning for this population.

LIFE-THREATENING AND FATAL ILLNESSES

Cystic Fibrosis

Description Cystic fibrosis is the most common cause of chronic lung disease in children. Diagnosis generally relies on the measurement of "sweat" electrolytes because of the large amount of sodium and chloride found in the sweat of afflicted individuals. Pulmonary involvement is noted first by the coughing caused by mucous secretions. Chest rales and widespread bronchiolar involvement accompanied by wheezing are noted as the disease progresses. Meconium ileus is present at birth in close to 15% of cases; meconium in the intestinal tract is not digested because of inadequate pancreatic enzymes in the bowel. The infant may have a ravenous appetite but have symptoms pointing to a deficiency of fat-soluble vitamins, with indications of rectal prolapse. Cystic fibrosis should be considered a possibility in chronically ill infants with gastrointestinal symptoms suggestive of malabsorption, when such symptoms are accompanied by recurrent pulmonary infection. Nasal polyps, severe abdominal cramping, rectal prolapse, and a high level of sodium and chloride in the sweat assist in diagnosing cystic fibrosis.

In cystic fibrosis, the involvement of various organs occurs at different ages. The lungs, pancreas, liver, intestines, sweat glands, nasal sinuses, salivary glands, and male and female genital tracts may be involved. Morphologic changes are secondary to the obstruction of the ducts of the mucus-secreting organs of the body. The most consistent abnormality is the altered function of the exocrine sweat glands. Blocked and dilated ducts, with fatty tissue eventually replacing normal pancreatic tissue, are structural changes seen in the pancreas. The salivary glands may be similarly affected and the liver may develop focal lesions from bile that contains mucous plugs. The lungs may develop hyperinflation and bronchiolitis as cystic fibrosis progresses, increasing obstruction of airflow and recurrence of bacterial pneumonia. Congestive heart failure may be an ultimate result due to pulmonary hypertension. The reproductive organs may be involved in various ways; there may be distention of the epithelial cells of the cervical glands in females and abnormalities of the vas deferens or seminal vesicles in males. Some children show normal growth and development in the first decade but develop pulmonary disease in the second decade. Decrease of appetite and energy, weight loss or lack of gain, increased cough and sputum production, and low-grade fever are symptoms of pulmonary infection. There is, however, a marked variation in the age of onset of cystic fibrosis, which complicates diagnosis.

Incidence   Cystic fibrosis occurs in approximately 1 infant in 3,000 live births and is the most common cause of chronic lung disease in children (Myers, 1975). The disease has been reported in all racial groups, but is highest in Caucasian families of central European background. Among American blacks the estimated occurrence is 1 in 12,000 births; it is rare among American Indians and much less common in persons of Asian ancestry.

Etiology   Cystic fibrosis is transmitted as a Mendelian recessive disorder when both parents are carriers. Researchers believe that a single mutant allele may cause the disease, but this is not conclusive. When a child with cystic fibrosis is born into a family, there is a 25% higher likelihood of subsequent offspring also being affected. Cystic fibrosis is an inherited disorder, and genetic counseling may be indicated for families in which the disease is present.

Treatment   Treatment programs for cystic fibrosis have been effective in prolonging life, but there is no known cure. Approximately 50% of patients live into the second decade, and close to 20% survive beyond 15 years of age (Rudolph, 1977). Symptoms may be alleviated through treatment, but treatment plans remain controversial because of the lack of scientific evidence regarding their efficacy. Cystic fibrosis is a demanding disease and alters the life-styles of entire families because of costs, attention, and time involved in treatment. Parents must be made aware of the treatment outlook of cystic fibrosis and receive genetic counseling and assistance in coordinating agency help for their child. Counseling must occur on an individual basis, since the organ systems involved will determine the severity and extent of the disease. Consistent and early antibiotic therapy during infectious periods, and aggressive utilization of respiratory physiotherapy to drain purulent secretions are necessary to relieve pulmonary involvement. At times, long-term oral antibiotic treatment to suppress infection is somewhat effective in maintaining good health. Hospitalization and intensive treatment with intravenous antibiotics may be needed for advanced pulmonary cases. The adolescent patient may resist continued dependence on his or her parents, and the physician may need to assist the family in assigning responsibility to the patient for his or her own treatment. Emotional factors that can severely obstruct temporary recovery must be eliminated if treatment is to be effective. The eventual death of most patients with cystic fibrosis is generally caused by the progression of pulmonary disease.

School programs may accommodate the individual with cystic fibrosis during periods when chronic illness symptoms are in abeyance. Information about pulmonary problems, mucous congestion, and general stamina must be provided to the teacher to assist in developing an individualized education and management program. The teacher must keep abreast of medication needs, heart and chest function, and the level of activity permitted for the youngster. At the same time, the individual with cystic fibrosis must be assisted in developing self-esteem and independence in order to encourage his or her competency in the classroom.

Muscular Dystrophy

Description Muscular dystrophy is a degenerative disease of the skeletal muscles characterized by weakness and wasting of the muscles. In congenital muscular dystrophy, the onset is *in utero*. The most severe cases die of respiratory failure prior to the age of 1 year, but milder cases survive for prolonged periods. Congenital muscular dystrophy is characterized by depressed tendon reflexes, involvement of respiratory muscles, and somewhat elevated serum enzymes.

Pseudohypertrophic muscular dystrophy (Duchenne form) is the commonest of the three major groups. In this form of the disease, there is slow motor development with a delay in the progress of sitting, walking, and running skills. The disease is characterized by a waddling gait, difficulty in climbing, and hypertrophy of calf muscles. Other muscles, such as the tongue, may become bulky and weak due to fatty infiltration. Toe walking and contractures of the heel cords may occur when anterior leg muscles are weaker than calf muscles. Weakness in the pelvic girdle muscles results in a waddling gait and problems in rising from the floor to a standing position. Weakness of the shoulder muscles leads to problems in lifting the arms over the head. By age 12 ambulation may become a problem. Death occurs prior to age 20 in 75% of patients.

Pseudohypertrophic muscular dystrophy is rapidly progressive and usually begins in early childhood. It occurs predominately in males and is transmitted by a sex-linked recessive trait. There is slowness, clumsiness, and a tendency to fall. Muscular weakness begins in the pelvic girdle, with shoulder girdle involvement at 3 to 5 years. In 80% of cases the calf muscles are affected; atrophy and deformity of the skeleton frequently is complicated by obesity and its resultant immobility. There may be mental retardation in about 25% of cases, with a general 20-point deficit in IQ for the total group. Serum enzymes may be ten times higher than normal in infancy, even prior to the appearance of physical weakness.

Facioscapulohumeral muscular dystrophy is a slowly progressive myopathy and begins at any age from childhood into adulthood. It affects males and females equally. Characteristics include the inability to close the eyes completely, pouting, and an immobile facial expression. Drooping shoulders and difficulty in raising the arms are characteristics that occur between 6 and 20 years of age. Deep-tendon reflexes may be depressed or absent, while weakness in the lower limbs may not occur for 20 years. Contractures and physical deformities develop less frequently and are not as prominent as in the Duchenne form. This form may be arrested for long periods, and many patients remain active with a normal life expectancy.

Limb girdle muscular dystrophy has an onset at close to 10 years of age, or in the second or third decade. There may be muscular weakness in the shoulder girdle or pelvic girdle (where thigh muscles are weakened). Though the disease progresses slowly, severe disablement and a shortened life span are expected.

Incidence Pseudohypertrophic muscular dystrophy is the most common form, with an incidence of .14 individuals in 1,000 children. It occurs most commonly in boys and has sex-linked inheritance in about 50% of these cases. As stated, the IQ is generally about 20 points lower than the norm in this form of muscular dystrophy. Seventy-five percent of these patients die prior to age 20 (Rudolph, 1977). Duchenne muscular dystrophy has an incidence of about .2 in 1,000 individuals (Dubowitz, 1978).

Etiology Duchenne muscular dystrophy is inherited as a sex-linked disorder and affects only males. Facioscapulohumeral and limb girdle muscular dystrophy are generally transmitted as autosomal recessive traits.

Treatment The patient is encouraged to maintain frequent movement for as long as possible. Attendance at school or an occupation is suggested, with an avoidance of confinement in bed. Physical therapy may help to maintain the function of limbs, but too strenuous exercise causes a breakdown of muscle fibers. The prevention of contractures through full range of motion must be generated through active or passive exercise. Mental retardation or mental health problems must be a consideration when working with muscular dystrophy students. Treatment of some forms of muscular dystrophy may also include procainamide or quinine when functional impairment is due to myotonia.

Chronic Renal Disease

Description Chronic renal failure is caused by a permanent reduction in kidney function. There is a decreased glomerular filtration rate that may eventually result in uremia. The functional pattern during the progression of renal insufficiency is said to be relatively uniform. As uremia progresses, the ability to maintain a balance of water and electrolytes is decreased. The decreased rate of glomerular filtration and tubular secretion tends to cause various end products of metabolism to accumulate. Substances excreted into the urine by tabular secretion must be maintained through homeostatic nephron secretion. The demand, however, for nephron secretion eventually exceeds the working capacity of the nephrons, and filtration capacity is insufficient.

The products of nitrogen metabolism are said to cause many of the problems associated with uremia. The onset of renal disease is gradual, with vague and nonspecific symptoms that may include fatigue, headache, anorexia, nausea, and dull pain in the back area. As the disease progresses, other symptoms may occur, such as growth retardation, facial puffiness, bone or joint pain, dry and itchy skin, and muscle cramps. The primary symptoms become more pronounced as the disease progresses, and there may be vomiting, diarrhea (sometimes bloody), a tendency to bruise, less frequent urination, and confusion. Hypertension, fluid retention, and anemia may cause cardiac failure in the later stages. There may be shortness of breath, tenderness in the liver and abdomen, and headache, with some incidence of seizures.

The physical symptoms are dependent upon the severity and stage of renal failure. There may be muscle weakness; edema; dry, bruised skin; a sallow, brownish complexion; uremic "bad breath"; a coated tongue; decreased muscle strength; and a loss of deep-tendon reflexes. Signs of overload of the circulatory system may manifest outwardly in pulmonary edema, tachycardia, systolic murmur, jugulovenous distention, vascular narrowing, and possible hemorrhages. Children experiencing kidney infection may have an elevated temperature and experience painful urination. The passageways to the kidneys from the bladder are easily infected if there is obstruction to urine flow. When children have frequent kidney infection, hospitalization and eventual dialysis may be required.

Incidence Incidence of renal disease is fairly common. Congenital renal disease is frequently the result of a developmental defect and is generally not hereditary. Inherited renal diseases manifest functional problems similar to those due to accident or embryologic development.

Congenital renal disease, however, is characterized by malformations of the urinary tract and occurs more commonly than inherited renal disease. When inherited renal disease occurs, the risk increases that siblings will be affected: there is a 50% increased risk for autosomal dominant defects and 25% increased risk for autosomal recessives (Holliday, 1978).

Glomerular nephropathy is the chief cause of chronic renal failure and has the highest mortality rate (except in the birth to 5 age group). Terminal renal failure is estimated at one or two cases per million a year (Royer, Habib, Mathiew, & Broyer, 1974). Accurate statistics are said to be unavailable on the incidence of different causes of renal failure. In the past 10 years the mortality rate for children suffering from hemolytic uremic syndrome (birth to 5) has dropped from 80% to 20% because of the development of therapeutic methods.

Acute urinary tract infections are common and may occur in 15% of all females at some time during their lives. Studies show that up to 20% of females experience dysuria each year but only half seek medical attention (Isselbacher et al., 1980). Acute urinary tract infections, when left untreated for an extended period of time, may lead to renal disease. Males develop infections in middle age or after. Sixty percent of all cases of acute renal failure are the result of surgery or injury, while 40% occur in the medical setting.

Etiology Chronic renal failure is due to a variety of causes, including: congenital renal and urinary tract malformation; glomerular and hereditary renal disease; and renal vascular disorders (e.g., arterial or venous thrombosis). The congenital anomalies give rise to chronic renal failure before the age of 5, with hereditary renal problems leading to a somewhat later onset of illness.

Treatment It is important to try to distinguish the underlying cause of renal failure in order to establish a treatment program. Chronic renal disease may be aggravated by heart failure, hypertension, gastrointestinal or urinary problems, infections of the urinary tract, unusual concentrations of plasma electrolytes, or drug-induced nephrotoxicity. Major congenital structural anomalies and hereditary nephropathies that are not yet understood can make treatment prescription difficult. With proper therapy, a high proportion of children may never reach a stage at which dramatic procedures are needed to maintain life. Diligent attention early in life can assist in preserving adequate renal function, enabling the child to lead a relatively normal life.

Precise diagnosis is necessary for effective treatment. Diet is the primary means of treating renal problems caused by decreased ability to absorb end products in the metabolism of particular foods. It is important to avoid unnecessary restrictions, since some foods are essential for growth. Limited protein intake must be carefully monitored and, in some instances, proteins provided in the form of essential amino acids are recommended. Arbitrary restriction of sodium is to be avoided, although sodium intake should be restricted in some patients who have decreased ability to excrete sodium. The majority of patients with renal disease may be permitted to ingest water with no limitations. A diet low in phosphate, together with the oral administration of aluminum hydroxide and calcium, may be prescribed for renal disease complicated by hypocalcemia and bone disease. Vitamin D may also be used to treat rickets caused by renal failure. The control of hypertension in renal disease patients is essential to maintain life; this can be done through an accurate dosage of drugs. Specific therapy for anemia is not recommended, since transfusions have not been successful in patients in whom vitamin deficiencies have been ruled out. Retardation of growth occurs in some renal failure patients and may be linked to poor nutrition, negative calcium balance, and acidosis. Although hormonal treatment has been used to delay growth spurt, the provision of a healthful milieu is more frequently recommended. Dialysis (even peritoneal dialysis for infants) has been used with different degrees of success for various periods of time in patients experiencing renal failure. Terminal renal failure patients have undergone transplant surgery; as successes increase, such surgery is being used more frequently.

Children with renal disease often exhibit anxiety, depression, withdrawal, and other psychological symptoms. With uremia and kidney infection the need for drug therapy may create additional side effects that contribute to a general feeling of distress. When waste products increase in the bloodstream, clouded thinking, convulsions, and even coma may result. Fatigue and pain may create problems for the home and school, and prolonged hospitalization and home programming may be necessary. Transplantation or some therapy programs may return a patient to normal function, but continued careful scrutiny is essential in any treatment plan. Complications such as cardiac insufficiency may continue to require treatment even after the successful transplant has been achieved.

Tumors

Description Childhood and adolescent brain tumors occur most frequently between the ages of 5 and 12. Tumors or neoplasms may be diagnosed as benign or malignant, and outcome and treatment vary with the diagnosis. Gliomas account for 75% of intracranial neoplasms in children, while 50% to 60% of neoplasms are located in the area of the cerebellum, fourth ventricle, or brainstem. Relatively slow-growing neoplasms that cannot be removed may not result in early death when there is no severe neurological deficit.

The diagnosis of a tumor may follow when a child exhibits an increase in intracranial pressure and focal neurological deficit. Symptoms of intracranial pressure include headache, vomiting, papilledema, enlargement of the cranium, lethargy, and sleepiness. Impaired vision or fixed gaze may be noted, while a tilting of the head may lend evidence to muscle paresis. The prominent symptom may be a personality change, with irritability, apathy, emotional lability, pallor, and fatigue symptomatic of brain tumor. Ataxia and seizures may also occur in patients where tumor growth is of long duration. The location of the tumor can frequently be determined through the impairment of functions in surrounding areas. As tumors grow, it becomes more difficult to detect their location, since symptoms become more general. Tumors can also be classified according to the types of cells of which they are composed. Thus, the terms *medulloblastomas*, *osteomas*, *gliomas*, *astrocytomas*, and *ependymomas* are used. Some tumors resemble cysts and are contained in a firm sac, while others are shapeless and may spread in unpredictable directions. A large number of tumors in children occur along the midline of the brain or in brain cavities, where obstruction of circulation of cerebrospinal fluid may take place. Hydrocephaly may be a result of this obstruction.

Tumors of the spinal cord are found less frequently than are brain tumors (1 to 5 ratio). Meningiomas and neurofibromas are relatively common in adults, while lipomas and dermoids are more common in children. Early diagnosis is essential to prevent irreversible neurological deficit. Symptoms include pain in about 50% of children. A limp or weakness may be present, and a change in reflexes may be noted with some impairment of bladder or bowel function.

Incidence Brain tumors are second only to leukemia as a cause of neoplasia in children. Although they are rare in the first year of life, their frequency is fairly constant with each succeeding year. Brain tumors are more common in children than previously recognized because of improvements in diagnostic procedures. Fifteen percent to 20% of brain tumors occur during childhood between the ages of 5 and 12 years. Sex of the child does not appear to be a factor.

Etiology The cause of tumors is not known, and research continues to determine how they grow. There is some evidence to suggest that certain cells in the embryo display a potential for developing other kinds of cells. The examination of types of cells found in tumors supports the speculation that these cells can become tumor material. Genetic predisposition, virus infections, and toxic substances may be agents that initiate abnormal cell growth resulting in tumors.

Treatment Skull radiography, electroencephalography, echoencephalography, brain scanning by radioisotope, cerebrospinal fluid analysis, and computerized transverse axial tomography are used to detect tumors. Therapy may include surgery, chemotherapy, and drugs to reduce intracranial pressure. Adrenocorticosteriods may be used for relief of pressure in some cases of brain tumors in children. Surgical extirpation is indicated in some cases, with at least partial removal of the tumor. Brain biopsy is a surgical procedure often used for diagnostic procedures and involves the insertion of a hypodermic needle into the skull. Some tumors in the brain stem area cannot be readily removed, since destruction of areas that control breathing or heart function may occur in reaching the tumors. When excision is not feasible, rerouting (shunting) of the spinal fluid may be necessary to avoid obstructed areas. Radiation therapy may be administered in some cases, but the effects are temporary at best and may prolong life for a brief period. Further research is needed in the use of drugs for treatment, as little work has been done in this area.

CARDIAC DISORDERS

Description A wide range of cardiac disorders has been identified, and a variety of treatment programs exist. A heart abnormally placed in the thorax is said to show malposition. Hearts in malposition may have improperly localized chambers, septal defects, valve anomalies, and obstructions in blood flow. Cyanosis, malrotation of bowel, pulmonic stenosis, and congestive heart failure may accompany the various types of malpositioned heart defects. The treatment of heart defects and their complications is individualized according to the presenting problem.

In congenital heart defects, there may be abnormal shunting of the blood between pulmonary and systemic circulation. A heart murmur may occur when there is a small left-to-right shunting of the blood, while a large aortopulmonary shunting will cause enlargement and hyperactivity of the ventricle. The pulmonary circulation may be affected during the immediate postnatal period and for up to 6 weeks thereafter, when systemic and pulmonary arterial pressures do not undergo normal postnatal maturational changes. Abnormal shunting has been classified anatomically according to the numerous combinations of circulatory components affected.

Regurgitant lesions occur when there is a return of ejected blood to the chamber because of an incompetent valve. Any of the four valves may be involved, and occasionally more than one may be regurgitant. Rheumatic carditis is a frequent cause of acquired lesions and more commonly causes valve lesions than congenital defects or malformations. Mitral valve lesions are often the result of rheumatic fever, while tricuspid valve regurgitation may be the result of infective endocarditis resulting from foreign agents (e.g., contaminated drugs).

Congestive heart failure is a syndrome in which the heart is not able to supply sufficient blood flow to tissues. It may result from excessive pressure loads, valvular regurgitation, or outside factors that cause a large increase in cardiac output. Obstructions in circulation and impairment of muscle function may contribute to congestive heart failure. A structural abnormality is the most frequent cause of congestive heart failure, and surgical correction may be necessary when heart failure is controlled.

Incidence Congenital heart disease occurs in 8% to 10% of 1,000 live born children. Cardiac disorders may be caused by chromosomal abnormalities, genetic factors, or environmental elements. Because of the availability of antibiotics in the past two decades, the incidence of chronic heart disease due to rheumatic fever has decreased sharply (Myers, 1975).

Etiology Congenital heart defects are fairly common and occur early in embryonic life. The heart is formed during the first to third month of pregnancy and is susceptible to rubella and other viral diseases. Chromosomal aberrations such as Down's syndrome (formerly known as mongolism) and hereditary factors are also responsible for congenital heart defects. The fetal environment contributes to the incidence of heart defects when the mother ingests drugs such as lithium salts or progesterone, or has a chronic illness such as diabetes. Alcoholic or drug addicted mothers also have an increased risk of delivering babies with congenital heart disorders. It is estimated that single mutant genes contribute to at least 2% of heart defects in babies, while 4% are due to gross chromosomal aberrations.

Treatment Treatment of heart disorders has undergone considerable growth and change in the 20th century. Antibiotics have altered the length and type of recuperation, and surgical procedures have decreased life-threatening cardiac disorders. Malaise, fatigue, decreased appetite, weak pulse, pallor, coldness in extremities, and increased activity of the sympathetic nervous system may be symptoms of heart disease. Packed red cells may be given for severe anemia, while blood may be removed in cases of hypervolemia. Drugs may be used for the treatment of rheumatic fever or other infections. Oxygen may be administered, and a vast array of surgical procedures exist. Caution must be exercised and antibiotic prophylaxis provided to prevent infectious endocarditis preceding dental treatment or surgery. Children affected by rheumatic fever may require penicillin prophylaxis for a lengthy period to prevent recurrence. It may be necessary to restrict exercise based upon the degree and type of cardiac problem. Chest pain due to exertion, hyperventilation, anxiety, or pericarditis occurs occasionally. Identifying the cause or antecedent of chest pain is essential as an important preventive step, rather than utilizing a purely medicinal approach.

Anxiety creates additional stress for cardiac patients, since parents, siblings, and patient are constantly aware of the consequences of heart disease. Restrictions cause patients to view themselves differently from their peers, and the fear of death may be pervasive. Concerns about self-sufficiency, marriageability, childbearing, employment, and solvency create added tensions. For these reasons, treatment of heart disease may include psychological counseling, since anxiety is a contributing factor in cardiac disease.

The school program must have up-to-date information on the status of the cardiac patient so that appropriate programming can be provided. Activity, food, and drug restrictions must be recorded and adhered to. The program staff should be aware of the patient's need for medication or periods of rest, and a record should be kept of the child's symptoms of stress; therapeutic activities should also be outlined in the child's record. The combined expertise of program staff and medical personnel as well as the use of agency and hospital records may all help in the preparation of an effective individualized education plan (IEP). Many cardiac patients remain in regular programs, while also observing restrictions, whereas those incapacitated by motor or intellectual problems may require placement in special programs for handicapped persons.

BLOOD DISORDERS

Hemophilia

Description Hemophilia is an inherited, sex-linked disease of the blood, which affects males and is characterized by deficiency of the specific factors in the blood plasma that produce clotting. Due to this lack, coagulation is abnormally delayed in both internal and external bleeding. Hemorrhaging may occur throughout the life of the affected male and may arise either spontaneously or from bruises, bumps, and blows. Acute bleeding episodes are most often manifested as bleeding into a closed space such as a joint, or as bleeding into soft tissues. Hemarthrosis is the hallmark of hemophilia. If bleeding episodes occur repeatedly or are inadequately treated, degenerative changes, deformity, and, ultimately, a fixed, unusable joint may result.

Patients are classified based on the amount of clotting factor that is present. Individuals who are mildly affected (25% to 50% of the normal amount of the factor is present) or moderately affected (5% to 25% of the factor is present) often go undiagnosed until they undergo a surgical procedure, during which bleeding cannot be readily controlled. Mildly and moderately affected individuals are not considered severely handicapped. Patients in the moderate-severe range (1% to 5% of the factor is present) are found to bleed profusely after minor injury, although they rarely hemorrhage spontaneously. The severely affected have less than 1% of the normal clotting factor in their blood. In this group, diagnosis is most often made at the time of circumcision, when excessive bleeding is noted from that procedure. These individuals will experience spontaneous hemorrhage all their lives.

Incidence One out of every 4,000 American males, in every racial and socioeconomic group, is affected. The total number of cases is about 100,000. Of these, about 25,500 cases are considered moderate or severe.

Etiology Hemophilia is a sex-linked, recessive trait. Seventy percent to 80% of the cases are caused by a gene on the X chromosome that results in a profound depression of the level of clotting factor activity in the plasma. The family history for hemophilia is positive in 70% to 80% of the cases. For these individuals, the severity of the disease remains static throughout their lifetimes, and the disease is similar within the same family.

Hemophilia is usually transmitted by asymptomatic female carriers to affected sons. Each of the sons of a carrier has a 50% chance of being a hemophiliac. Each daughter of a carrier has a 50% chance of being a carrier. When a hemophiliac has children, his sons are normal and his daughters are carriers (Inman, 1980). Hemophilia has the highest known mutation rate of a genetic disease, with up to one-third of the new cases occurring without prior family history. These mutant cases tend to be more severe. There is presently no standard, reliable laboratory test available for detecting new carriers. Preventive efforts usually consist of genetic counseling, prenatal detection, and family planning. Where there is a pregnancy, amniocentesis may be performed to determine the sex of the fetus. If it is male, the parents then must consider the options, including terminating the pregnancy.

Treatment An intravenous infusion of the clotting factor, extracted from plasma, is the primary treatment of acute bleeding episodes. The infusion temporarily replaces the missing factor and converts the clotting status of the blood to normal. It can halt bleeding already in progress or can prevent it from occurring. Prophylactic administration of clotting factor concentrates, consisting of injections every 2 or 3 days, is relatively new. The patient or his family may be trained to administer it at home, thus freeing the individual from constant clinic checkups. This type of home therapy improves school attendance and may increase the individual's self-sufficiency. Severe hemophiliacs need to have special precautions taken in routine dental care and during simple medical procedures such as vaccinations and innoculations.

Most hemophiliacs should and do attend a regular school program. The teacher and school nurse will require information regarding the management of the individual. School personnel should be provided with a full record of the diagnosis and the severity of the disease and should be prepared to cope with emergency bleeding episodes. Although some activities may need to be restricted (e.g., contact sports) physical exercise is crucial. Being in good physical condition reduces the frequency and severity of the bleeding episodes and aids the muscles and joints in resisting permanent damage. Following routine bleeding episodes, walking, running, and swimming may be contraindicated. As soon as the specific joint has recovered, however, usual activities may be resumed. Too much protection and over-restrictiveness may result in the child rebelling (e.g., by participating in dangerous or "forbidden" activities). Parents and teachers need to be sensitive to the fine distinction between the amount of restriction necessary to prevent injury and the amount of restriction that represents over-protection.

Present costs for infusion preclude the use of this treatment as a prophylactic therapy for many individuals with hemophilia. Thus, the development of a synthetic clotting factor that will make treatment available to all who need it is a significant focus of current research efforts.

Sickle Cell Anemia

Description Sickle cell anemia is an inherited blood disorder characterized by a distinctive malformation of the red blood cells (hemoglobin) that carry oxygen to the body's organs and tissues. Anemia refers to an abnormally low amount of hemoglobin. In sickle cell anemia, the red blood cells are highly sensitive to decreases in oxygen and become distorted from their normally round shape. The distorted cells are usually sickle-shaped, from which the name of the disease is derived. The sickled cells do not flow as easily through the blood vessels, especially the smaller vessels or capillaries. If the delivery of oxygen is blocked by red blood cells unable to pass through the circulatory system, the oxygen-deprived tissues and organs become excruciatingly painful. These episodes or "crises" may affect all organ systems, can last for several days, and may be fatal. When the obstruction occurs in the brain, it can cause brain damage, which may affect the cognitive and motor abilities of the child. Afflicted adults may experience an average of 2 to 4 of these crises a year, in a pattern of periods of remission and exacerbation. Until age 10, children commonly have 5 to 10 crises a year. Some persons are so mildly affected that they cannot be termed severely physically handicapped.

The disease is usually recognizable in early childhood, but is not generally manifested in children under 4 years of age. Symptoms may include anemia, pallor, stunted growth, and enlargement of organs such as the heart, liver, and spleen. Young children may experience hand-foot syndrome, i.e., a painful swelling of the fingers and toes. Affected children are frequently described as having barrel-shaped chests, enlarged protruding abdomens, and thin extremities. They tend to be shorter and weigh less than their peers. Later, symptoms may affect any body parts or organ systems, including the eyes, back, and the central nervous system (Graham, 1980). Persons with sickle cell anemia are likely to have lowered resistance to infectious disease, with increased susceptibility to complications such as pneumonia.

Laboratory tests for detecting sickle cell anemia involve a solubility test and electrophoresis. Tests on other family members may be used to confirm the diagnosis.

Incidence   In the United States, it is estimated that 1 in 400 to 500 Blacks is afflicted with sickle cell anemia. Approximately 50,000 people in the United States have the disease at present. Fifty percent of the victims of sickle cell disease do not live beyond 20 years of age (Abramson, Bertles, & Wethers, 1978). Ten percent of North American blacks have one of four forms of sickle cell disease (Graham, 1980).

Etiology   Sickle cell anemia is clearly a genetically transmitted disease, affecting primarily those with black ancestry. In this group in the United States, an estimated 8% to 13% carry the sickle cell trait (Myers, 1975). The blood cells of those individuals contain both normal hemoglobin and the sickling variety. If both parents carry the trait, the probability is that one in four children may be born with sickle cell anemia, two may be carriers; and one may be normal (neither diseased nor a carrier). When one parent carries the trait, each child will either be a carrier or normal, with a 50/50 chance of being normal. Although sickle cell anemia is incurable, its clear-cut pattern of inheritance makes it preventable through genetic counseling. Carriers are told of the risks of having children with sickle cell anemia if they marry another carrier. Detection programs, including mass screenings, are carried out in most states.

Treatment   It is generally recognized that as long as the child is comfortable and able to carry out normal daily routines, including school, no special medical measures are necessary. Crises are treated as they occur, depending on type and severity. Treatment is supportive and aimed at the reduction of symptoms. Mild crises, characterized by pain and lassitude, may be treated in the home by bed rest, oral intake of fluids (particularly water) to relieve dehydration, and analgesics to relieve pain. Severe cases manifesting partial or complete immobilization due to involvement of the joints may be treated by drugs (e.g., indomethacin). In severe cases in which red cells are destroyed or hemoglobin is rapidly and severely decreased (hemolytic and aplastic crises), hospitalization is likely. Transfusions are generally reserved for extreme indications, as they may produce other types of complications.

During the winter and spring months, when respiratory infections are more frequent, affected children may be placed on a prophylactic antibiotic regime, because intercurrent infections play a large part in precipitating crises. Children should also be protected against unnecessary exposure to chicken pox because of the possibility of precipitating a crisis period. School attendance may be substantially disrupted by crisis periods requiring home rest or hospitalization. Efforts to avoid infection may result in the need for home tutelage by a visiting teacher. One study of 18 children over a 2-year period reported that each child was absent an average of 14 days per semester. Although the number of crises may be reduced if the patient takes care to avoid significant physical stress, children should not be overly restricted because of the potential psychological damage this may cause. High school or prevocational students should be guided to select occupations appropriate to their physical capabilities. Sickle cell anemia does not significantly affect intellectual functioning.

ORTHOPAEDIC HANDICAPS

Legg-Calvé-Perthes Disease

Description Legg-Calvé-Perthes disease (named for the three physicians who identified the disease) is a self-limiting illness producing a change in bone structure at the head of the femur, which forms part of the hip joint. There is an accompanying disturbance of the blood vessels that supply the bone tissue; as a result, the cells are unable to produce the material necessary to reinforce the bone. During the full course of the disease, the changes of bony tissue range from normal to abnormal and then return to a normal state again. Legg-Calvé-Perthes disease can result in a variable degree of deformity of the femoral head and in restricted motion of the joint. With the interruption of the blood supply to the femoral capital epiphysis, the bone in the growth center dies. As new bone replaces it, the epiphysis is remodeled and proceeds through this process of regrowth and healing for about 2 years. This generally occurs between 4 to 11 years of age. The disease is also known as cora plana.

Symptoms become evident about age 4 to 5, when the child may develop a limp and complain of hip pain. The disease spans an average period of 4 years, although it may vary in length from 2 to 8 years. There are two types of Legg-Calvé-Perthes disease. The most frequent and severe type is *whole head*, in which the entire femur head is affected, and in which 15% of these cases present bilateral involvement. The type involving a partial head affects only one-third to one-half of the femoral head. X rays, along with the history of symptoms, confirm the presence and scope of the disease.

Incidence The incidence of Legg-Calvé-Perthes disease is 1 in 1,200 persons. Occurrence in boys is 1 in 750 and in girls is 1 in 3,700. The disease is rare among blacks, Indians, and Polynesians (Nelson, 1979).

Etiology The exact etiology of the disease remains unknown, although some cases have been traced to initial inflammation of the synovium or lining of the hip joint. It may be that the disease is a circulatory disturbance caused by injury or strain. There is no known means of prevention.

Treatment Treatment of Legg-Calvé-Perthes has changed from maintenance of the joint in leg traction to placing the legs in braces or casts, allowing ambulation when the disease begins. A third approach may include the surgical enclosure of the head of the femur by altering the position of the acetabulum or by cutting the femur and tilting it closer to the acetabulum. Physicians feel that the healing process is considerably shortened by this latter method.

If Legg-Calvé-Perthes is neglected, joint disintegration is likely to occur. The only alternative then remaining is joint replacement after completion of the growth period. Therapeutic efforts are aimed at protecting the bone until it is strong enough to bear stress placed on the hip joint. The hip joint must not be permitted to feel the full weight of the body during this period. Formerly, treatment prescribed to relieve weight in this area resulted in the continuous confinement of the child in a hospital bed or institution for several years. The current treatment regime may consist of preliminary traction and bracing. Specially designed orthopaedic appliances may be used to achieve the restoration and protection of the affected hip while permitting ambulation. Bracing is generally discontinued after approximately 20 months. A fully functional though slightly deformed femoral head can be achieved spontaneously on occasion, with the avoidance of weight bearing for up to 24 months. Children who have recovered from Legg-Calvé-Perthes are almost always asymptomatic, with almost normal or normal range of motion.

Surgical intervention may be required for older children or for those with severe forms of the disease. Young children with only partial head involvement may require the avoidance of vigorous activity for improvement to occur. The school-age child who is undergoing bracing will generally be able to return to school. The teacher must be knowledgeable regarding the use, fit, and care of the child's braces. Because of the bracing, the child cannot assume a normal sitting position and may require environmental adaptations for writing and other desk tasks. In addition, the teacher may need to provide a supportive and understanding milieu for the child, who may react negatively to the treatment program.

Slipped Femoral Capital Epiphysis

Description Slipped femoral capital epiphysis is the sudden slipping off of the cartilaginous head of the femur. It generally occurs during the rapid growth period of adolescence (10 to 17 years) and affects males predominantly. The immediate result is a sudden limp and accompanying pain. The condition occurs more frequently in the obese, prepubertal, hypogonadal male or in asthenic females. A complication of this condition is the development of avascular necrosis of the femoral head similar to Legg-Calvé-Perthes disease.

Many characteristics are similar to Legg-Calvé-Perthes disease; a limp and pain in the knee area or thigh are common complaints. An acute, sudden pain in the groin area may indicate a traumatic slip of the epiphysis and may be corrected by gentle manipulation under anesthesia. The disease generally is accompanied by arthritis of the involved hip. The affected patient presents an intractable, painful, stiff hip, with the left hip affected more frequently. Both hips are involved in 25% of all cases. X rays will confirm a downward or backward displacement of the capital epiphysis.

Incidence Capital femoral epiphysis is more common in youngsters 10 to 13 years old. Since capital femoral epiphysis can be the result of many different problems, incidence figures are not available.

Etiology The actual cause of the disease is unknown. It may be caused by a hormonal effect at the growth plate of the femoral capital epiphysis that weakens the bone and permits the head to slip off the neck of the femur.

Treatment Abstinence from weight bearing through bed rest, crutches, slings, casting, or bracing is not effective in treatment. Surgery is indicated for all types of the disease once a diagnosis has been made. Under anesthesia, the capital epiphysis is gently manipulated and internally fixed by the insertion of several pins. After surgery, weight bearing is forbidden for several months. If untreated, joint disintegration is likely, resulting in the need for joint replacement. Homebound instruction or a regular school program with modifications of physical activity may be necessary during the postsurgical recovery period, until full healing has occurred.

Scoliosis

Description Scoliosis is a lateral curvature of the spine, usually in the thoracic area, resulting in one side of the body being out of alignment with the other side. In addition to body disfigurement, severe uncorrected deformity may displace and compress internal organs, impairing their functioning and reducing life expectancy. The curve may involve any part of the spine and be of varying length. Some curves will straighten when the body is bent, while others are rigid and remain distorted. The curves are generally noticeable upon observation of the patient's back. The first signs are frequently a slight unevenness of height, unevenness of the shoulder or pelvis, or a slight kyphosis. X rays are used to confirm a diagnosis. Differential diagnosis of the type of scoliosis is essential for appropriate management. Scoliosis may be categorized as follows:

Functional Scoliosis In this type, the child can correct the curve at will (referred to as postural scoliosis). This type is usually noted between ages 7 and 10. The curve is always mild and disappears when the child is lying down. Functional scoliosis does *not* constitute a severe handicap.

Compensatory Scoliosis This type involves the dipping down of the pelvis to the short side when one leg is longer than the other. The consequences of this type of scoliosis include the possibility of secondary osteoarthritis, due to the abnormal wearing of the vertebral joint, complicated by constant pain.

Structural Scoliosis This type of scoliosis is more serious; the younger the child, the worse the outlook. The child cannot voluntarily straighten the spine. The structural category includes scoliosis that is congenital, neuromuscular, and traumatic in origin as well as idiopathic scoliosis (also called genetic or developmental). Idiopathic scoliosis is the most common type and accounts for 70% of all scoliosis. It occurs approximately eight times more often in adolescent girls than in boys, especially in girls who undergo rapid and early growth. It may appear at any one of three well-defined growth periods, as follows: 1) Infantile scoliosis develops between birth and 3 years of age and is usually noted in the first year, predominantly among males. Most often, the curve is to the left, and the problem may resolve itself spontaneously. Those patients who do not improve become more severely handicapped and have a poor prognosis. This type is more common in England than in the United States; 2) Juvenile scoliosis occurs between 3 to 10 years of age (usually after age 6). The curve is to the right and both sexes are equally affected; 3) Adolescent scoliosis occurs between 10 years of age and maturity. The curve may have been present before the child reached age 10, but is first recognized when it becomes more pronounced during the adolescent growth spurt.

Incidence A small degree of curvature (5 degrees to 15 degrees) is present in 10% to 15% of the adolescent population. Some of the small curves progress (increase), while others stay the same or disappear. One to two per 1,000 adolescents will eventually have a curve of greater than 20 degrees, which may require bracing. The ratio is generally three to five females to one affected male. Of 50,000 X-rayed persons over age 14, 1.5% had curves of more than 10 degrees (from recent records at the Eastern Maine Medical Center [Shipman, 1979]).

Etiology As previously noted, structural scoliosis may be classified according to its various etiologies. About 90% of all idiopathic scoliosis curves are probably genetic in origin, and idiopathic scoliosis accounts for 70% of all cases of scoliosis. The scoliotic trait is not always passed on to every generation and may result in mild to severe curvature in children born to the same parents. Congenital scoliosis is probably not genetic but may accompany a number of congenital problems (e.g., spina bifida and lateral dislocation of the spine). Scoliosis may be associated with neuromuscular imbalances caused by cerebral palsy, muscular dystrophy, or polio. It may be found secondary to neurofibromatosis ("elephant man's disease" or Recklinghausen's disease) or to juvenile rheumatoid arthritis. There is no way to prevent scoliosis. All children and adolescents should be examined at intervals for the existence of a curve, so that timely intervention may be assured.

Treatment Skeletal maturation must be determined in order to provide appropriate treatment for scoliosis. Boys generally mature skeletally at approximately 18 years, while girls complete skeletal growth 15 to 18 months earlier. Review of X rays on the degree of iliac crest excursion may be helpful in determining maturation. Determination of bone age is done by X-ray film of the left hand for comparison with Greulich and Pyle atlas figures for chronological age.

Early detection and referral to a center providing complete scoliosis care is the best route to improvement. Many doctors providing exercise programs for young scoliosis patients fail to intervene in the formation of severe curves.

However, spinal bracing, along with exercises and surgical procedures, have proven somewhat effective in the treatment of scoliosis. The Milwaukee brace can successfully halt curve progression in 70% of cases (Keim, 1978). (The malignant curve, however, is only slightly controlled by bracing.) The Milwaukee brace must be carefully prescribed. It consists of a plastic pelvic mold with rigid front and back projections attached to a high metal collar that fits at the base of the skull and is high under the chin. The spine is thus held rigidly upright for the remainder of the growth period. The brace may be worn for all or part of the time, day and night, for 2 to 4 years. When it is worn around the clock (23 hours) and an exercise program is provided, there is a much greater likelihood of improvement.

Plaster casts of various shapes and sizes have been used in treating scoliosis. A localizer cast designed by Risser and the surcingle technique originated by William Von Lackum provide two alternatives (Keim, 1978). The surcingle is a broad strap used for training horses. These straps were used by Von Lackum on the apexes of the patient with scoliosis to effect dramatic correction. The technique now includes the application of traction and the use of muslin surcingle straps that are then pulled out. The patient is able to walk after the plaster hardens. Traction has also been used as an adjunct to surgical procedure. Halofemoral traction with an electric rotating bed is achieved with a halo around the head, which is screwed into the skull. Screws in the skull cause no discomfort; femoral pins are inserted into the distal portion of each femur. Weights are added to intensify the treatment, and fairly dramatic curve correction may be affected through use of this treatment.

Surgical procedures may be considered more desirable than long-term bracing or casts. Dwyer of Australia has developed a procedure in which bolts are inserted through each vertebral body, using an anterior approach (Keim, 1978). The intervertebral discs are removed between adjacent vertebrae, and the vertebrae are pulled together. Another surgical method is a posterior approach involving fusion of rotated vertebrae and bone grafting (Keim, 1978). The Harrington technique, a surgical procedure, involves the use of a distraction rod that jacks the spine into a straight line. At times the costotransverse ligaments on the concave side of the curve are released, allowing the ribs on that side to hinge forward on the ligaments, reducing the hump. As an example of a yet-to-be perfected technique, in 1973, the first electrospinal instrument was inserted by a team at Columbia-Presbyterian Medical Center in New York (Keim, 1978). This procedure involves the implantation of a small radio under the skin on the convex side of the curvature, allowing electrical impulses to be transmitted to the implanted electrodes while the patient is asleep. Electronic correction of scoliosis is a treatment of the future that requires additional research for perfection.

Operative treatment is indicated for patients with rapidly progressing curves, for those who do not respond to more conservative therapy such as bracing, for those with severe curves that present a deformity that is cosmetically unacceptable, or for those with severe curves that result in deterioration of cardiopulmonary functioning. The surgical treatment for these severe cases consists of spinal fusion and insertion of stainless steel rods to straighten and strengthen the spinal column. Postoperative treatment is followed by immobilization in a body cast from head to pelvis, worn for an average of 9 months, with the patient placed in a prone position on a bed or cart. In scoliosis associated with neuromuscular imbalance, medical intervention is frequently *not* helpful, however.

The child who undergoes surgery for scoliosis may spend frequent and prolonged periods in the hospital and may need to have special schooling provided in that setting. During the postoperative period of prone immobilization, special services may also be helpful to maintain educational programming. For example, talking books, page turners, and optical aids to make reading easier from a prone position may be obtained through the Library for The Blind and Physically Handicapped in Washington, D.C. Home-bound instruction or a home-to-school telephone hookup to provide actual participation in classroom learning may be valuable.

When the curve is mild, treatment may consist of exercises to keep the back strong and supple. Close observation, as well as ongoing periodic X-ray evaluations, are indicated to assess whether the curve is progressing. If the curve does progress from mild to moderate or was significant upon initial assessment, bracing may be used. For flexible curves of less than 45 degrees in growing children, the Milwaukee brace is the preferred treatment.

Kyphosis

Description Kyphosis refers to a rounding of the back in the thoracic region. It may be secondary to congenital deformity, tumor, trauma, infection, and other syndromes and diseases (congenital kyphosis). Kyphosis may be acquired, insidiously developing in otherwise normal, healthy, individuals about the period of puberty (juvenile kyphosis or juvenile roundback).

Juvenile kyphosis is symptomatic for 1 to 2 years, usually in the 11 to 16 age group. Often a history exists of indulgence in unusually strenuous physical activity or participation in sports followed by the development of vague pain in the lower back. Over subsequent months, the pain diminishes, while at the same time the spine develops a gradual rounding or kyphotic deformity that is rigid. On attempting to bend forward, the rigidity is at once apparent. The formation of the kyphotic rounding leads to the development of other, compensatory changes in the spine to maintain the center of weight bearing. This eventually produces bone and muscle stress and cramping of internal organs and may result in degenerative changes later in life.

Incidence Incidence figures on kyphosis are not available, since manifestations vary. The degree of curvature makes a difference in diagnosis, compounding the problem of determining incidence.

Etiology The actual causal factor is unknown, although several theories have been advanced to explain the disease. One theory suggests that a loss of the disc tissue that cushions the spine against shocks of normal weight bearing causes a transfer of maximum pressure anteriorly and a subsequent restriction of growth.

The loss may be due to various causes, including nutritional and endocrinal. Another explanation is that reduction in circulatory flow in the spine results in a temporary softening of the bones. A third theory holds that endocrine imbalances delay normal cessation of growth in certain areas.

Treatment   During the active stage of the disease, when bone growth is not completed, the deformity can be corrected by a Milwaukee brace (described in the treatment for scoliosis), which is used until maturity. Unlike a cast, the brace may be removed at intervals. Congenital kyphosis, however, is difficult to contain with a brace, and rapid progression is the rule. More severe curves may require the use of a body cast, in which the body is held in hyperextension while the area is fused surgically. Early intervention utilizing a spinal fusion also eliminates symptoms of degenerative arthritis in later life. The teacher may expect some physical fragility and discomfort in students with this condition. The teacher should check periodically to make sure the child does not become fatigued, especially after long intervals of sitting in classroom chairs. Strenuous physical activity may need to be curtailed if the youngster experiences pain.

Juvenile Rheumatoid Arthritis

Description   Juvenile rheumatoid arthritis (JRA) is a serious, painful, and often crippling inflammatory disorder that can affect the entire body and is sometimes fatal. Also known as Still's disease, JRA is characterized by joint pain, swelling, and stiffness; later characteristics may include muscle atrophy and joint deformity, severe weakness, and fatigue. Onset is prior to age 16, usually between 18 months and 4 years of age. Accurate medical diagnosis is necessary to distinguish JRA from other conditions that produce aches and pains. This diagnostic procedure may include blood and urine tests, joint fluid tests, tissue biopsies, and X-ray examinations. To facilitate differential diagnosis, various syndromes have been identified.

Monarticular arthritis affects only one or a few joints. Children may also develop chronic inflammatory eye disease, which may lead to glaucoma, cataracts, and other eye changes. *Polyarticular* arthritis involves many joints and is associated with acute, inflammatory eye difficulties and a later age of onset. The most common symptoms are frequent fevers, marked morning stiffness, joint swelling, pain, rash, subcutaneous nodules, and enlargement of the spleen and liver.

JRA is usually self-limiting, with an average duration of 3 years, although the range is from 1 to 10 years. About half of the children will have complete abatement with some residual crippling. The remaining one-fourth of the children with JRA will have sustained active symptoms such as difficulty in joint movement and pain. Less than 5% of afflicted children die of the disease itself.

Incidence   Estimates of children afflicted with juvenile rheumatoid arthritis in the United States range from 250,000 to 500,000 cases. JRA appears in 3 in 100,000 children each year, with three times as many girls as boys afflicted.

Etiology   The actual cause of JRA is unclear. The two major causal theories are: 1) it is caused by a virus; 2) the body's defense system has been disrupted, producing antibodies that attack its own joints and tissues. Emotional stress is acknowledged as a possible factor in aggravating the disease. It has been noted that many children with JRA had developed a respiratory infection just prior to onset.

Treatment The major objectives of treatment are relief of inflammatory response, to relieve pain, and to control fever. Corticosteroids are one pharmacological treatment component used to reduce fever and swelling of joints. Corticosteroids must be used with great caution, however, as steroid therapy may result in impaired growth and development of limbs, as well as delayed sexual development. In fact, the greatest risk of death in those with juvenile rheumatoid arthritis is from the secondary effects of corticosteroid treatment.

Since movement is painful, children may tend to hold themselves in fixed positions, which leads to permanent deformities. Therefore, adequate physical and occupational therapy and a sufficient level of general physical activity are crucial in preventing deformity. The maintenance of function during the early stages leads to better results than attempts to regain function once it is lost.

Other components of treatment may include periods of rest scheduled throughout the day, massage, moist heat therapy, and a well-balanced diet. Biannual ophthalmological examinations are recommended to decrease the chances of severe eye damage and vision loss.

The active disease stages usually necessitate occasional home programming. During periods of absence, teachers should maintain communication with their students. Nearly all children with JRA can be kept in the classroom in regular schools. Teachers should permit the child to move about the room fairly frequently so that he or she will not become stiff after maintaining one position for a prolonged period. The child should also be allowed extra time to move from class to class if his or her gait is slow. Periods of rest may need to be scheduled during the course of the school day.

Because of the possible disfiguring aspects of JRA and the limitations on physical activities such as contact sports, children with JRA may tend to avoid contact with others and may have a poor self-image. Personality characteristics of children with JRA include excessive anger, depression, and mood swings. They may be inhibited and uncommunicative. Both parents and teachers of children with JRA need to be careful of being overprotective and avoid developing undue dependency. Children with JRA may benefit from professional counseling or psychotherapy.

RESIDUA OF ACCIDENTS

In the United States, the most common cause of death is accidents. From the end of infancy through the teenage years, accidents kill more children than any single disease. In fact, in the age range of 1 to 4 years, accidents kill 5 times as many children as any illness, and in the age range of 5 to 14, 20 times as many. Some accident victims are fortunate to survive, but are left with residual injuries, which may include burn scars, amputations, and brain damage.

Burns

Descriptions Burns are classified according to the depth of penetration. *Superficial*, or first-degree, burns, are confined to the skin's outer layer. Because this layer does not contain blood vessels, circulation is not affected. Local symptoms include warmth, tingling sensation, and pain. The area may be red or pink, with some swelling and, later, peeling. *Partial thickness*, or second-degree, burns involve the interior, thick layer of the skin that contains blood vessels and nerve endings. If a deep second-degree burn occurs, the skin will be white, tan, or red, with dark streaks of coagulated capillaries. Blisters will have clear fluid; if they contain milky or grayish fluid, infection is probably present. *Full thickness*, or third-degree, burns penetrate through the upper two layers of the skin into the subcutaneous area or deeper. Circulation is not intact, and all skin cells (epithelial cells) are destroyed. Nerve endings have also been destroyed, so there will be no pain. The affected area appears leathery, dusky, or blackened. *Char*, or fourth-degree, burns indicate that the burn has penetrated fibrous tissues and muscle and may have damaged the bone.

Incidence In the United States, 300,000 people are seriously burned each year, with 100,000 of these requiring hospitalization and 50,000 left with disfigurement. Approximately 50% of those seriously burned are children under age 16.

Etiology The majority of burns are the result of scalds incurred by infants 6 months to 2 years of age. As the child grows older, the number of accidents involving playing with the kitchen stove or matches increases. From age 10 on, boys predominate as burn victims, with injuries frequently due to explosive ignition of flammable liquids and contact with high-tension electrical wires. Eighty percent of burns occur within the home. Burns occur most frequently when children are unattended—for example, in the early morning hours and on weekends and holidays when parents are sleeping. The likelihood of burn injuries increases in proportion to the number of children in the family, occurs more frequently in households of lower economic status, and is highly associated with marital discord. Burn prevention has recently focused on the design of flameproof children's nightwear. Widespread public education aimed at self-help measures to be taken by victims and first-aid procedures to be followed by those on the scene may greatly help to prevent the residual effects of burns.

Treatment The major treatment aspects of burn-related problems involve establishing and improving specialized treatment techniques and facilities, improving medical educational programs for emergency personnel (e.g., paramedic and rescue teams), and developing effective burn prevention programs for the public.

The first consideration in treating a burn is to stop progressive thermal injury, through administering first aid on-the-spot. The preferred means is dousing or immersion of the area in cool water or other nonflammable liquid. For serious burns, treatment in a hospital emergency room is recommended and may consist of cleaning, administration of topical antibacterials, fluid therapy, and tetanus immunization. If 20% of the total body surface is involved in second- or third-degree burns (10% for small children), hospitalization is indicated in order to provide for: frequent administration of antibiotics, monitoring of vital signs, the use of special equipment and nursing procedures, and prevention of infection. The seriously burned individual is also at risk for complications such as renal shutdown and pneumonia, which must be detected early if death is to be avoided. Grafting procedures may also be needed to protect the wound from external infection.

Burns subject a child to a horrifying experience, which may include prolonged pain, helplessness, removal from home for treatment, and fearful wounds that, even after plastic surgery, may be permanently disfiguring. Special efforts are required by family, medical, and school personnel to prevent long-lasting psychological disability after medical recovery. While the child is hospitalized, parents should be allowed and encouraged to visit the child frequently. As the child's condition improves, he or she should be placed with others more advanced in recovery and rehabilitation for social and emotional reasons. Photographs may be used to prepare siblings, students, and teachers for the child's return to home and school. Parents and teachers generally overestimate the degree of disability resulting from a healed burn injury and often make unnecessary arrangements for a home tutor, thus delaying the child's reentry into a normal life routine. Children who survive serious burns often fail to return to school; however, arrangements should be made for them to return to school if at all possible.

Amputation

Description Amputation refers to the removal of any projecting portion of the body, but usually refers to the arms or legs. Amputations are described by the area of loss (e.g., below or above the elbow) or, by the amputation's occurrence at the limb joint, as a disarticulation (e.g., shoulder disarticulation). The surgical removal of a limb or a portion of a limb may be a life-saving procedure.

Incidence In 1971, a survey by the [then] U.S. Department of Health, Education and Welfare reported approximately 274,000 persons with absence of major extremities (leg, foot, arm, or hand) in the civilian noninstitutionalized population. There are an estimated 4,000 accident-caused amputations a year. Approximately 11% to 13% of the individuals undergoing amputation of the extremities are under 21, with 5% under 11 years of age (Goldenson, 1978).

Etiology The predominant cause of amputation in children is trauma, accounting for 70% of the cases. The relative frequency and type of childhood trauma is usually related to geographic area. Common causes of accidents that result in amputation include those involving cars, railroads, farm equipment, hunting, chemicals, fireworks, and home and recreational accidents. Increased knowledge and application of known and available safety and preventive measures are essential to preventing trauma-related amputations.

Treatment The four thrusts of treatment are:

1. Surgery—the preparation of the stump of the amputated limb for greatest possible use of a prosthesis.
2. Physical therapy—an exercise regime to strengthen muscles and develop stamina, so the amputee will be able to accommodate to new ways of functioning with minimum strain.
3. Prosthesis identification and fitting—the selection of a prosthetic type and its components on an individual basis according to the child's deficit, weight, and size. The prosthesis may change in complexity as well as size, as the child grows. A new prosthesis will be required every year until the child is 5, every 2 years until age 12, and then every 3 to 4 years.
4. Education to use the prosthesis and other self-help devices (orthoses)—the introduction of a prosthesis, if prescribed, as early as possible, in order for the child to become acclimated to managing without the lost limb and to increase the likelihood that the child will accept the prosthesis and use it functionally. If there is to be no artificial device, extensive training will be needed in using other parts of the body (e.g., teeth and feet) and/or adaptive devices to preserve independent functioning. Careful monitoring of the adaptations in the performance of activities of daily living is recommended, as atypical use of the body may contribute to muscle, joint, and postural aberrations.

Amputation is likely to have an initial impact on the school-age child, with both parents and the child fearing peer curiosity and ridicule. The child must adapt to his or her loss and accept a new body image. Child amputees are best prepared for a full life if they attend regular school. The teacher should know the child's range of functioning and requirements for assistance and should be able to respond to questions from the other students and their parents. Some children, due to their level of disability and functioning, may require education in schools that are free of architectural barriers and that provide physical and occupational therapy.

Research is being conducted in the area of limb replantation, a process whereby a limb that has been completely or partially separated from the body is reattached. Limb replantation generally requires a 2- to 3-year rehabilitation program and may not result in as much functioning as a prosthetic device.

Brain Damage

Description Brain damage is a temporary or long-term change in consciousness, motor ability, sensation, intelligence, and/or emotion as a result of an injury or disease process that affects the tissues of the brain. Trauma, either a direct-closed or penetrating head injury, may cause direct tissue destruction. Brain cells may be affected indirectly by the interruption of the flow of blood to the brain. Lasting effects of brain damage from accidents may range from extremely mild to profound (prolonged comatose state).

The child may be unconscious immediately after a blow to the head and remain unconscious, or he or she may regain consciousness and be lucid and then become confused and experience severe headache and vomiting. Bleeding or swelling of the skull, causing pressure on the brain, may occur up to 2 weeks after the initial blow. In a closed head injury or when the patient is unable to give a history, X rays of the skull may give evidence of injury. Angiography (injection of a radiopaque dye into an artery) and the observation of its progress through the cerebral vessels via X ray may be used to detect a stoppage of blood flow to the brain. Computerized axial tomography (CAT) is a recent technique in which an X-ray beam scans the brain at six to eight levels to produce cross-sectional images that can reveal a problem.

Incidence Incidence varies according to population and locale. The leading cause of injury to all school children is falls, and the head is most often involved.

Etiology Head trauma in children results from falls, automobile accidents, and numerous other types of accidental injury. Accident prevention (e.g., automobile seat belts) may be the most effective method to prevent brain injury secondary to head trauma.

Treatment Head injuries are medically treated according to the symptoms. Residual effects of brain injury are extremely varied. Impairment of muscle power and coordination should receive treatment to prevent contractures and preserve range of motion. The individual may require gait training, learning of new motor patterns, increased strength in new muscle groups, and/or adaptive equipment to execute self-care and activities of daily living. If there are sensory changes, the individual may need training to accommodate or compensate for this. Speech therapy and language retraining may be necessary. Children may require complete educational reevaluation and interdisciplinary planning to program for the child's changed status (according to the range of severity of the residual brain damage and affected domains).

SUMMARY

While not all severely physically handicapping conditions have been covered in this chapter, it is hoped that the descriptions of the more common problems presented here will aid the reader in developing educational programs for this population. Severely physically handicapped individuals require long-term guidance to develop maximal self-care skills. Many such students create special problems for educators because of long periods of hospitalization and of illness-induced dependency which can seriously impair a child's self-image, social skills, and motivation for learning and achievement. Thus, important elements of any rehabilitation program must be the socialization of the disabled person and the instillation of a positive attitude toward learning. For example, it may be very difficult to motivate children who are aware that they have a possibly fatal illness. The need of severely physically handicapped students in general to accept challenges, take risks, and overcome the barriers that they daily face can seem overwhelming to the involved students and can only be accomplished by a positive outlook on the part of the individual and by a strong support system. Obviously, teachers, medical personnel, and parents play major roles in such a support system and in helping handicapped individuals to accept themselves.

Home instruction, bedside instruction, hospital-based educational programs, segregated settings with special equipment, and mainstreaming are some of the program alternatives for severely physically handicapped children. Program provision is determined by the student's functioning levels in skill areas, intellectual ability, severity of handicapping conditions, and the length and frequency of hospitalization. As the major facilitator of the child's program, the child's family has an important influence on his or her ability to adapt socially and physically to the environment. Parental involvement in a child's program may include a parent training experience, provision of information on handicapping conditions, and therapy, counseling, or group meetings. Physicians, educators, and agency personnel also need to develop sensitivity to family stress factors involving the physically handicapped child. In addition, they must be familiar with the services available for handicapped children in order to provide parents with a continuum of agency services and to augment educational facilities as necessary. Families facing years of medical intervention and ongoing contact with professionals require the support of a united agency network.

REFERENCES

Abramson, H., Bertles, J.F., & Wethers, D.C. *Sickle cell disease*. St. Louis: C.V. Mosby Co., 1978.

Anastasiow, N. Early childhood education for the handicapped in the 1980's: Recommendations. *Exceptional Children*, 1981, *47*, 276–282.

Apter, S. Applications of ecological theory: Toward a community special education model. *Exceptional Children*, 1977, *44*, 366–375.

Baker, D. Severely handicapped: Toward an inclusive definition. *AAESPH Review*, 1979, *4*, 52–65.

Baker, D. Applications of environmental psychology in programming for severely handicapped persons. *JASH*, 1980, *5*, 234–249.

Barnett, H.L., & Einhorn, A.H. (eds.). *Pediatrics* (15th ed.). New York: Appleton-Century-Crofts, 1972.

Bayes, K., & Francklin, S. (eds.). *Designing for the handicapped*. London: George Godwin, 1971.

Bender, M., & Valletutti, P.J. *Teaching functional academics: A curriculum guide for adolescents and adults with learning problems*. Baltimore: University Park Press, 1982.

Bennett, F. The pediatrician and the interdisciplinary process. *Exceptional Children*, 1982, *48*, 306–314.

Bobath, B. *Abnormal postural reflex activity caused by brain lesions.* London: William Heinemann Medical Books Limited, 1971.

Bobath, K., & Bobath, B. Cerebral palsy. In: P.H. Pearson & C.E. Williams (eds.), *Physical therapy services in the developmental disabilities.* Springfield, IL: Charles C Thomas, 1972.

Brown, L., Wilcox, B., Sontag, E., Vincent, B., Dodd, N., & Gruenewald, L. Toward the realization of the least restrictive educational environment for severely handicapped students. *AAESPH Review,* 1977, *4,* 195–201.

Davis, G.T., & Hill, P.M. Cerebral palsy. In: D.B. McElroy & G.T. Davis (eds.), *The nursing clinics of North America.* Philadelphia: W.B. Saunders Co., 1980.

Dubowitz, V. *Muscle disorders in childhood.* Philadelphia: W.B. Saunders Co., 1978.

Eastman, N.J. The obstetrical background of 753 cases of cerebral palsy. *Obstetrics and Gynecology Survey,* 1962, *17,* 457–460.

Elder, J.O., & Magrab, P.R. Administration of special facilities. In: P.J. Valletutti & F. Christoplos (eds.), *Preventing physical and mental disabilities.* Baltimore: University Park Press, 1979.

Federal Register, 1977, *42,* pp. 42474–42518. (a)

Federal Register, 1977, *42,* pp. 15063–15064. (b)

Federal Register, 1981, *46,* p. 3865.

Freund, J., Casey, P., & Bradley, R. A special education course with pediatric components. *Exceptional Children,* 1982, *48,* 348–351.

Goldenson, R.M. (ed.). *Disability and rehabilitation handbook.* New York: McGraw Hill Book Co., 1978.

Gordon-Davis, K., & Strasser, J. Nursing. In: P.J. Valletutti & F. Christoplos (eds.), *Interdisciplinary approaches to human services.* Baltimore: University Park Press, 1977.

Graham, S.J. Sickle cell retinopathy. *Journal of American Optometry Association,* 1980, *51,* 575–580.

Hankerson, H. Developing, implementing and disseminating the educational model. In: E. Jackson & J. Kark (eds.), *Program strategies for cultural diversity.* Seattle, WA: Western States Technical Assistance Resource, University of Washington, 1980.

Haring, N. Measurement and evaluation procedures for programming with the severely and profoundly handicapped. In: E. Sontag, J. Smith, & N. Certo (eds.), *Educational programming for the severely and profoundly handicapped.* Reston, VA: The Council for Exceptional Children, 1977.

Holliday, M. Developmental abnormalities of the kidney in children. *Hospital Practice,* 1978, *13,* 101–112.

Howard, J. The role of the pediatrician with young exceptional children. *Exceptional Children,* 1982, *48,* 316–322.

Inman, M. Hemophilia: Information for school personnel. *Journal of School Health,* 1980, *50,* 137–140.

Isselbacher, K., Adams, R., Braunwald, E., Petersdorf, R., & Wilson, J. (eds.). *Harrison's principles of internal medicine* (9th ed.). New York: McGraw-Hill Book Co., 1980.

Karnes, M. Evaluation and implications of research with young handicapped and low income children. In: J.C. Stanley (ed.), *Compensatory education for children ages 2 to 8.* Baltimore: The Johns Hopkins University Press, 1973.

Keim, H. Scoliosis. *Clinical Symposia,* 1978, *30,* 2–30.

Kirk, S.A., & Gallagher, J.J. *Educating exceptional children* (4th ed.). Boston: Houghton Mifflin Co., 1983.

Lathey, J. Assessing classroom environments and prioritizing goals for the severely retarded. *Exceptional Children,* 1978, *44,* 190–196.

Lauder, C., Kanthor, H., Myers, G., & Resnick, J. Educational placement of children with spina bifida. *Exceptional Children*, 1979, *45*, 432–437.

Levine, M.D. The child with school problems: An analysis of physician participation. *Exceptional Children*, 1982, *48*, 296–303.

Lyon, S., & Lyon, G. Team functioning and staff development: A role release approach to providing integrated services for severely handicapped students. *JASH*, 1980, *5*, 250–263.

McCormick, L., & Goldman, R. The transdisciplinary model: Implications for service delivery and personnel preparation for the severely and profoundly handicapped. *AAESPH Review*, 1979, *4*, 152–161.

Menolascino, F., & Egger, M. *Medical dimensions of mental retardation*. Lincoln: University of Nebraska Press, 1978.

Myers, B.A. The child with a chronic illness. In: R.H.A. Haslam & P.J. Valletutti (eds.), *Medical problems in the classroom*. Baltimore: University Park Press, 1975.

Nelson, W.E. (ed.). *Nelson textbook of pediatrics*. Philadelphia: W.B. Saunders Co., 1979.

Orelove, F., & Hanley, C. Modifying school buildings for the severely handicapped. *AAESPH Review*, 1979, *4*, 219–236.

Orlansky, M. Sam's day: A simulated observation of a severely handicapped child's educational program. *AAESPH Review*, 1979, *4*, 251–258.

Royer, P., Habib, R., Mathiew, H., & Broyer, M. *Pediatric nephrology*. Philadelphia: W.B. Saunders Co., 1974.

Ruben, I.W., Plovnick, M.S., & Fry, R.E. *Improving the coordination of care: A program for health team development*. Cambridge, MA: Bullinger Publishing, 1975.

Rudolph, A.M. (ed.). *Pediatrics* (16th ed.). New York: Appleton-Century-Crofts, 1977.

Scheuerman, N. A teacher's perspective. In: A. Thomas (ed.), *Hey, don't forget about me!* Reston, VA: The Council for Exceptional Children, 1976.

Shipman, C.F. Screening criteria and idiopathic adolescent scoliosis. *The Journal of Family Practice*, 1979, *8*, 477–482.

Silberstein, C.E. Orthopedic problems in the classroom. In: R.H.A. Haslam & P.J. Valletutti (eds.), *Medical problems in the classroom*. Baltimore: University Park Press, 1975.

Snyder, L., Apolloni, T., & Cooke, T. Integrated settings at the early childhood levels: The role of non-retarded peers. *Exceptional Children*, 1977, *43*, 262–266.

Sontag, E., Smith, J., & Sailor, W. The severely/profoundly handicapped: Who are they? Where are we? *Journal of Special Education*, 1977, *11*, 5–11.

Stickney, S.B. Schools are our community health centers. *American Journal of Psychiatry*, 1968, *124*, 101–108.

Swap, S.M. Disturbing classroom behaviors: A developmental and ecological view. *Exceptional Children*, 1974, *41*, 163–172.

Thomas, E., & Marshall, M. Clinical evaluation and coordination of services: An ecological model. *Exceptional Children*, 1977, *43*, 16–22.

Thomas, J.P. Seven cost effective models for treating spinal cord injuries. In: J.P. Quirk (ed.), *Readings in physically handicapped education*. Guilford, CT: Special Learning Corporation, 1974.

Thomason, J., & Arkell, C. Educating the severely/profoundly handicapped in the public schools: A side-by-side approach. *Exceptional Children*, 1980, *46*, 114–122.

Valletutti, P.J., & Bender, M. *Teaching interpersonal and community living skills: A curriculum model for handicapped adolescents and adults*. Baltimore: University Park Press, 1982.

Valletutti, P.J., & Christoplos, F. Interdisciplinary approaches to human services: An introduction and overview. In: P.J. Valletutti & F. Christoplos, (eds.), *Interdisciplinary approaches to human services*. Baltimore: University Park Press, 1977.

Weikert, D., Epstein, A., Schweinhart, L., & Bond, J. The Ypsilanti preschool curriculum demonstration project: Preschool years and longitudinal results. *Monographs of the High Scope Educational Research Foundation*. Ypsilanti, MI: High Scope Press, 1978.

Williams, W., Brown, L., & Certo, N. Basic components of instructional programs. In: R. Anderson & J.G. Greer (eds.), *Educating the severely and profoundly retarded*. Baltimore: University Park Press, 1976.

Wolraich, M. Communication between physicians and parents of handicapped children. *Exceptional Children*, 1982, *48*, 324–329.

SUGGESTED READINGS

Bigge, G.L., & O'Donnell, P.A. *Teaching individuals with physical and multiple disabilities*. Columbus, OH: Charles C. Merrill Publishing Co., 1979.

Bleck, E. Integrating the physically handicapped child. *Journal of School Health*, 1979, *49*, 141–146.

Bricker, D. Educational synthesizer. In: A. Thomas (ed.), *Hey, don't forget about me!* Reston, VA: The Council for Exceptional Children, 1976.

Brown, L.M., & Robson, M.J. The pathophysiology of arthrogryposis multiplex congenita neurologica. *Journal of Bone Joint Surgery*, 1980, *62*, 291–296.

Gellis, S.S., & Kagan, B.M. *Current pediatric therapy*. Philadelphia: W.B. Saunders Co., 1976.

Gluckman, S., & Barling, J. Effects of a remedial program on visual motor perception in spina bifida children. *Journal of Genetic Psychology*, 1980, *136*, 195–202.

Guralnick, M., Richardson, H., Jr., & Herser, K. A curriculum in handicapping conditions for pediatric residents. *Exceptional Children*, 1982, *48*, 338–346.

Holroyd, D., & Guthrie, D. Stress in families with neuromuscular disease. *Journal of Clinical Psychology*, 1979, *35*, 734–739.

Kempe, C.H. *Current pediatric diagnosis and treatment*. Los Altos, CA: Lang Medical Publications, 1978.

Lucas, J.T., & Ducker, T.B. Motor classification of spinal cord injuries with mobility, morbidity, and recovery indices. *American Surgeon*, 1979, *45*, 151–158.

Luckey, R., & Addison, M. The profoundly retarded: A new challenge for public education. In: R. Anderson & J.G. Greer (eds.), *Educating the severely and profoundly retarded*. Baltimore: University Park Press, 1976.

Miller, J.J. Prolonged use of large intravenous steroid pulses in the rheumatic diseases of children. *Pediatrics*, 1980, *65*, 989–994.

Moorefield, W.G., Jr., & Miller, G.R. Aftermath of oseteogenesis imperfecta: The disease in adulthood. *Journal of Bone Joint Surgery*, 1980, *62*, 113–119.

Mullins, G.B. *A teacher's guide to management of physically handicapped students*. Springfield, IL: Charles C Thomas, 1979.

Naeye, R. Causes of fetal and neonatal mortality by race in a selected U.S. population. *American Journal of Public Health*, 1979, *69*, 857–861.

Nagy, E.C., Khan, S., & Sturgess, J.M. Serum factor in cystic fibrosis: Correlation with clinical parameters. *Pediatric Research*, 1979, *13*, 729–732.

Nathanson, I., & Riddlesberger, M. Pulmonary hypertrophic osteoarthropathy in cystic fibrosis. *Radiology*, 1980, *135*, 649–651.

Newman, I., & Piazza, R. (eds.). *Severely and profoundly handicapped education*. Guilford, CT: Special Learning Corporation, 1978.

Powers, J., & Hedy, A. Inservice training for physicians serving handicapped children. *Exceptional Children,* 1982, *48,* 332–336.

Quirk, J. (ed.). *Readings in physically handicapped education.* Guilford, CT: Special Learning Corporation, 1978.

Robertson, A.M., & Schulzer, M. Neurological, psychological and educational sequelae of low birth weight. *Brain Development,* 1980, *2,* 57–67.

Sillence, D.O., Senn, A., & Danks, D.M. Genetic heterogeneity in osteogenesis imperfecta. *Journal of Medical Genetics,* 1979, *16,* 101–116.

Sirvis, B. Developing IEPs for physically handicapped children: A transdisciplinary viewpoint. *Teaching Exceptional Children,* 1978, *10,* 78–82.

Sontag, E., Burke, P., & York, R. Considerations for serving the severely handicapped in the public schools. In: R. Anderson & J.G. Greer (eds.), *Educating the severely and profoundly retarded.* Baltimore: University Park Press, 1976.

Sontag, E., Certo, N., & Burton, J. On a distinction between the education of severely and profoundly handicapped and a doctrine of limitations. *Exceptional Children,* 1979, *45,* 604–616.

Staheli, L.T. Spinal deformity. *Journal of Family Practice,* 1980, *10,* 1071–1075.

Stahlman, J. *How to start your program for special infants.* Butler, PA: United Cerebral Palsy Association, 1980.

Trahms, C., Affleck, J., Lowenbraun, S., & Scranton, T. The special educator's role on the health service team. *Exceptional Children,* 1977, *43,* 344–349.

Turek, S.L. *Orthopaedics.* Philadelphia: J.B. Lippincott Co., 1977.

Valletutti, P.J. The teacher's role in the diagnosis and management of students with medical problems. In: R.H.A. Haslam & P.J. Valletutti (eds.), *Medical problems in the classroom.* Baltimore: University Park Press, 1975.

Visconti, E.B., & Hilgartner, M.W. Recognition and management of central nervous system hemorrhage in hemophilia. *Paediatrician,* 1980, *9,* 127–137.

DISCUSSION QUESTIONS

1. How does D. Baker's definition of severely handicapped individuals help to delimit this term while making it distinct from less severe conditions?
2. What are some of the advantages of a transdisciplinary approach that do not accrue from other approaches to evaluation and treatment?
3. What are some of the reasons why it is important that the philosophical framework of a curriculum be thoroughly understood?
4. What curricular elements are appropriate to the total education of severely physically handicapped students?
5. What are examples of model programs for severely physically handicapped students? What are their distinctive elements?
6. What are the multiple handicapping conditions typically found in arthrogryposis? How do these symptoms shape treatment and educational management?
7. What are some of the manifestations of spina bifida and what is their impact on educational management and programming?
8. What are some of the diagnostic signs that point to the presence of congenital dysplasia?
9. What are some of the associated abnormalities of osteogenesis imperfecta? How do these influence treatment and educational interventions?
10. What are the various subgroups of cerebral palsy? How do they differ in their clinical expression? How do they influence the nature of educational and therapeutic interventions?

11. What is the conceptual framework of the Bobath method and what are its primary goals?
12. How do the several types of epilepsy differ in their external manifestations? What are the implications for diagnosis, management, and treatment?
13. What are the most etiologically significant factors in spinal cord injuries in childhood? In adulthood?
14. What are the ethnic and genetic factors related to the incidence and etiology of cystic fibrosis, muscular dystrophy, sickle cell anemia, and hemophilia?
15. What are the implications of the presence of a life-threatening and fatal illness in the educational management of children so afflicted?
16. What are the medically-oriented diagnostic devices and procedures that help to detect the presence of severe and profound physical handicaps?
17. What role does teacher and parent anxiety play in the management of children with severe and profound physical handicaps?
18. What are some of the most commonly occurring orthopaedic handicaps? How may they be differentially diagnosed, and how are they differentially treated?
19. What are the most frequently occurring results of serious accidents to children? How do the residua of accidents affect educational programming and the application of therapeutic procedures?
20. How can school programs aid in the socialization of severely and profoundly physically handicapped individuals?

GLOSSARY

Abduction   Movement away from the median axis or from another part of the body.
Acetabulum   The cup-shaped socket of the hip bone into which the head of the femur fits.
Acetabular fossa   A furrow or shallow depression in the cup-shaped socket of the hip bone.
Acidosis   Disturbance of the acid-base balance of the body.
Adduction   Movement toward the median axis or toward another part of the body.
Allele   One of a pair of genes that occupy the same locus in homologous chromosomes and control the heredity of a particular characteristic.
Amniocentesis   The process through which the amniotic fluid that surrounds and protects the developing fetus is sampled.
Ankylosed   Denoting fixation of a joint.
Ankylosis   Abnormal immobility and consolidation of a joint.
Anteversion   Displacement of an organ in a position that is farther forward than normal.
Aphasia   Loss of the ability for expressive or receptive language.
Apraxia   The inability to perform certain purposive movements without loss of motor power, sensation, or coordination.
Asthenic   Referring to being weak; type of physique characterized by slender build and slight muscular development.
Astrocytoma   A tumor formed from the star-shaped cells that form the nervous system.
Atrophic   Marked by a wasting away.
Autosomal dominant   A genetic trait carried on the autosomes; the disorder appears when one of a pair of chromosomes contains the abnormal gene.
Autosomal recessive   A genetic trait carried on the autosomes; both asymptomatic parents must carry the trait to produce an affected child.
Autosome   Any of the first 22 pairs of chromosomes.
Avascular necrosis   Referring to the death of blood vessels.

Brachioradialis   Muscle located in the wrist.
Breech birth   Presentation of buttocks first instead of head in childbirth.
Bronchiolitis   The inflammation of the bronchioles.

Capsulectomy   The removal of the fibrous tissues enclosing a joint.
Cataract   A disease of the eye involving opacity of the lens of the eye or its capsule or both.
Cerebrospinal fluid   A water cushion protecting the spinal cord and brain from shock.
Cephalic delivery   Presentation of head first in childbirth.
Circumduction   The action of a limb to move in such a way that it describes a cone-shaped figure.
Clonus   Spasmodic alternation of contraction and relaxation of muscles.
Contracture   Permanent shortening of muscles due to spasm or paralysis.
Coracoid process   The beak-like projection of the scapula (shoulder blade).
Cyanosis   Slightly bluish, grayish, slatelike, or dark purple discoloration of the skin.

Dermoid   A nonmalignant tumor.
Dysarthric   Difficulty in articulation due to central neurological damage.
Dysuria   Painful or difficult urination.

Echoencephalography   The use of ultrasound in examining and measuring internal structures of the skull and in diagnosing abnormalities.

Ectoderm The outer layer of cells in a developing embryo from which develops the skin, the nervous system, sense organs, as well as the pineal and part of the pituitary and suprarenal glands.
Edema A condition in which the body tissues contain an excessive amount of fluid.
Electrophoresis The migration of ions through a membrane by the action of an electric current.
Ependymoma A tumor arising from the elements of the membrane lining the cerebral ventricles and the central canal of the spinal cord.
Epiphysis A juvenile piece of bone separated from a parent bone in early life by cartilage, but later becoming part of the parent bone; a center for ossification at each extremity of long bones.
Epithelium The layer of cells forming the epidermis of the skin.
Extension Straightening of an extremity.

Fascial Referring to the fibrous membrane covering, supporting, and separating muscles.
Femur Thigh bone.
Fibrosis Abnormal formation of fibrous tissue.
Fibula The long thin bone of the leg below the knee.
Flaccid Having defective or absent muscle tone.
Flexion The bending of a joint.

Glaucoma A disease of the eye characterized by an increase in intraocular pressure.
Glioma A sarcoma of the tissue that forms the interstitial or supporting elements of the nervous system.
Glomerular Referring to the small structures in the Malpighian body of the kidney.
Gluteus maximus One of the three muscles that form the buttocks.

Hemarthrosis A condition that involves bleeding into the joints.
Humerus The upper bone of the arm.
Hydrocephalus The enlargement of the head caused by accumulation of cerebrospinal fluid in the ventricles of the brain.
Hyperflexia A condition in which there is excessive flexion of a limb.
Hypertrophy An increase in the size of an organ or structure.
Hypervolemia An overabundance of blood.
Hypocalcemia Abnormally low blood calcium.
Hypogonadal Referring to the defective production of hormonal secretion by the gonads.
Hypoplasia Defective tissue development.

Ileal Referring to the lower portion of the small intestine.
Ileus Obstruction of the small intestine.
Iliac Relating to the hip bone.
Infectious endocarditis Inflammation of the lining and membrane of the heart.
Intercostal Between the ribs.
Ischial tuberosity An elevated round process of the posterior and inferior parts of the hip bone.

Jugulovenous Referring to the veins in the neck.

Kernicterus A condition in which excessive serum levels of bilirubin result in brain damage (bilirubin refers to bile pigment formed by disintegration of red blood cells).

Lipoma A fatty tumor.

Meconium   The first feces of a newborn infant.
Medulloblastoma   A malignant, soft, infiltrating tumor of the roof of the fourth ventricle and cerebellum.
Meninges   Three membranes investing the spinal cord and brain.
Meningioma   A tumor of the three membranes that invest the spinal cord and brain.
Microcephaly   A condition in which the head has an abnormally small circumference, more than two standard deviations smaller than the average size.
Myopathy   Any diseased condition of a muscle.
Myotonia   A tonic spasm of a muscle or temporary rigidity.

Neoplasia   The development of neoplasms.
Neoplasm   A new formation of tissue that is abnormal, as a tumor or growth.
Nephron   The structural and functional unit of the kidney.
Nephropathy   Kidney disease.
Neurofibroma   A tumor of the connective tissue of a nerve.
Nuchal   Pertaining to the neck or nape of the neck.

Occiput   The back part of the skull or head.
Occlusion   Closure or state of being closed, of a passage.
Osteoma   A bony tumor.

Papilledema   Edema and inflammation of the optic nerve at its point of entrance into the eyeball.
Paresis   Partial or incomplete paralysis.
Pericarditis   Inflammation of the fibroserous sac enclosing the heart and the roots of the great blood vessels.
Perinatal   During the birth process.
Periosteal   Referring to the membrane of tough, fibrous, connective tissue covering all bones except at the joints.
Plexus   A network of nerves or blood vessels.
Polyp   A tumor with a stem.
Prolapse   The dropping of an internal part of the body.
Pseudobulbar palsy   Paralysis that resembles bulbar palsy due to lesions of cortical centers.
Pulmonic stenosis   Narrowing of the blood vessels of the lungs.

Rheumatic carditis   Inflammation of the heart muscles.

Sacrum   A thick, triangular bone at the lower end of the spinal column.
Sclera   The tough, white, fibrous membrane covering all of the eyeball except the area covered by the cornea.
Septal defect   A defect in the dividing wall of an organ.
Sphincter   The circular muscle that closes the anus.
Spinal epidural   Located over or upon the outer membrane covering the spinal cord.
Stenosis   The constriction or narrowing of a canal or passage.
Strabismus   Imbalance of the muscles of the eyeball, resulting in a squint.
Supination   A position of the hand and arm in which the palm faces upward; a corresponding position of the foot and leg.

Tachycardia   Abnormally rapid heart beat.
Thrombosis   A blood clot that forms at the site of occlusion.

Tomography A diagnostic technique using X-ray photographs, enabling a three-dimensional evaluation of body tissue, usually the lung.
Transection A cutting made across a long axis.
Trochanter Either of the two bony processes below the neck of the femur; the greater is located at the lateral side; the lesser trochanter at the medial.

Uremia Toxic condition from urinary constituents in the blood.
Ureterostomy The surgical formation of a permanent passage for the draining of a ureter (one of the two tubes carrying urine from the kidney to the bladder).

Vas deferens The excretory duct of the testes.

Chapter 4

Severely and Profoundly Emotionally Disturbed and Autistic Students

Kate E. Grosman

CHAPTER OBJECTIVES

After reading this chapter, you should be able to:

1. Present diverse definitions of *emotional disturbance* and *autism*.
2. Describe how the different definitions provide a global view of the emotionally disturbed child.
3. Distinguish severely emotionally disturbed children from mildly and moderately disturbed children.
4. Identify popular screening devices that are used to detect children with mild and moderate behavioral disorders/deficiencies.
5. Discuss why screening for severely emotionally disturbed individuals has focused on the neonatal period, and also identify devices and techniques that may facilitate the screening process for emotionally disturbed and autistic students.
6. Enumerate and explicate the symptoms typically demonstrated by children diagnosed as being autistic.

7. Describe, discuss, and differentiate the five major theoretical positions relevant to the etiology of emotional disturbance.
8. Describe and discuss the major symptom categories that are considered to be characteristic of severely emotionally disturbed children.
9. Discuss and elaborate on various schema developed for the classification of emotional disturbance in children.
10. Differentiate among the subcategories of childhood psychosis.
11. Describe possible programs and strategies that might be instrumental in preventing emotional disturbance in children.
12. Describe commonly utilized intervention programs pertinent to the treatment of emotional disturbance in children and discuss, in addition, model educational programs currently available.

DEFINITIONS

Children and adolescents who manifest grossly deviant behaviors have long puzzled parents, physicians, and educators. A litany of labels to describe these young persons has evolved over the years; such labels have become even more pervasive in recent times with the increased interest that has been displayed in understanding and analyzing these individuals (Shea, 1978). Common labels, past and present, include: *behaviorally disordered, mentally ill, emotionally handicapped, socially maladjusted, severely emotionally disturbed, children in conflict, childhood psychosis,* and *children with pervasive disorders*. The two terms most frequently used are *emotionally disturbed* and *behaviorally disordered*. While the term *behaviorally disordered* is not as threatening or as stigmatizing as *emotionally disturbed*, the term *emotionally disturbed* is currently the more favored. This selection of terms results primarily from the wording of PL 94-142 (*Federal Register,* 1977) and from use of the term in professional research and by school programs (Hewett & Taylor, 1980).

Despite the increased efforts being made to study children so labeled, psychologists as well as psychiatrists and other physicians still are able to offer few clear-cut explanations or treatments, and teachers can point to only limited educational solutions and successes.

Reinert (1972) has stated that the term *emotional disturbance* has been used to describe a variety of specific problems. Many professionals working with children who display emotional disorders have attempted to define these behaviors (Armstrong, 1976). None of these definitions, however, has found universal acceptance. As Reinert (1980) has stated:

> The clarity of definition we have so long assumed seems to have disappeared in recent years to the extent that we can no longer state a definition of emotional disturbance with any clarity or unity. Rhodes and Paul (1978) suggest that clarity has disappeared in the definition of emotional disturbance as it has in many areas of knowledge. This has occurred as a result of the "explosion" of ideas, viewpoints, and nuances by professionals and lay persons (p. 3).

Whelan (1978) has argued that definitions are intended as "descriptors of behavior" and not, as is too often the case, explanations of causation. Difficulties arise when a teacher constructs or adopts specific educational programming based strictly upon a label or a definition; a medically or etiologically based definition rarely implies specific educational or management methodology.

The definitions of emotional disturbance that are presented below describe various aspects of the total picture of emotional disturbance, including psychiatric, educational, and legal components of the problem. While none of these definitions is sufficiently comprehensive to speak for the whole, together they serve to present an overall view of the emotionally disturbed child.

In addition, the reader is offered two definitions of autism. Autistic students are a widely studied subgroup of the severely handicapped population. Although autism is legally classified under the category of "other health impaired" in PL 94-142 (*Federal Register*, 1981), its discussion in this book is presented along with that of severe emotional disturbance. This juxtaposition is based upon historical precedent (Bender, 1947; Kanner, 1943, 1973; Mahler, 1952) and upon similarities in educational programming between autistic and emotionally disturbed students (Paluszny, 1979; Ritvo, 1976; Sailor, Wilcox, & Brown, 1980; Simonson, 1979; Wing, 1980).

It should be noted, however, that there are dangers to assuming too much similarity between autistic and emotionally disturbed children relevant to educational programming. The need to emphasize language and communication development when working with autistic children makes their educational programs in many respects more closely resemble those designed for aphasic children (see Chapter 5). Indeed, the incredible range of symptoms found in the severely emotionally disturbed group suggests that educational programming for autistic children may be more different than similar. Further, given the early history of autism and the psychodynamic attitude held by many toward serious emotional disturbance, too much emphasis has been placed in the past on parental therapy rather than on developing effective parent support and interactions.

Early infantile autism was first identified as a diagnostic entity in 1943 by Leo Kanner who diagnosed 11 children with the following common characteristics: social withdrawal and an inability to establish affective relationships, mutism or abnormal language, obsessive desire to maintain sameness in the environment, bizarre mannerisms, monotonous and repetitive play habits, lack of anticipatory posture in preparation for being picked up, and wild, undirected behavior. Kanner suggested the name *early infantile autism* because social withdrawal was the most distinguishing feature. Autism is derived from the Greek *autos* meaning "self" and was first used in psychiatry in the early 1900s to describe the withdrawal from the outside world manifested by adult schizophrenics. Wing (1980) suggested that autistic children have always been present by hypothesizing that the legends of changeling children (especially those who were remarkably beautiful but strange and remote) arose as a response to the presence of autistic children. She also posited that Victor, "the Wild Boy of Aveyron," rather than being severely mentally retarded was autistic. Victor demonstrated many signs of autism. He did not play with toys. He never looked at people but showed a remarkable memory for the position of objects in his room and resisted any change of these objects (Paluszny, 1979; Wing, 1980).

Over the years, different clinicians used various labels to diagnose autistic children relevant to specific aspects of the condition. *Childhood schizophrenia* was used by Lauretta Bender (1947), who believed that infantile autism was an early expression of adult schizophrenia. Margaret Mahler (1952), based on her interest in mother-child interactions, used the term *symbiotic psychosis* to indicate a pathologic relationship.

The exact age of onset of autism is unknown, but symptoms have been observed during the first several months. The National Society for Children and Adults with Autism views autism as a developmental physical disability arising from an unknown dysfunction in the central nervous system (Ritvo & Freeman, 1977).

Until 1981, autism was legally classified as a form of serious emotional disturbance (*Federal Register*, 1977), as many of the distinguishing symptoms displayed by autistic children were viewed as indicative of childhood psychosis. Even though autism is now recognized as a health impairment or developmental disability by a significant number of professionals, many medically oriented professionals still classify it as a psychiatric disorder. Many of the educational techniques and methods employed with severely emotionally disturbed students are still often used with autistic children and youth (Hewett & Taylor, 1980).

Psychiatric Definitions

The Joint Commission on Mental Health of Children (1969) has suggested the following definition of emotional disturbance for psychiatric use:

> An emotionally disturbed child is one whose progressive personality development is interfered with or arrested by a variety of factors so that he shows impairment in the capacity expected of him for his age and endowment: (1) for reasonably accurate perception of the world around him; (2) for impulse control; (3) for satisfying and satisfactory relations with others; (4) for learning; or (5) any combination of these (p. 253).

This definition is, in this author's view, sufficiently general to include all classes and types of severe emotional disturbance. Little if any difference exists between this psychiatric definition and educational definitions of emotional disturbance.

Two other classification systems that are more detailed and broader in scope are frequently used by psychologists and psychiatrists when referring to children with long-term severe emotional disabilities. The first system, the *Diagnostic and Statistical Manual of Mental Disorders: DSM-III* (American Psychiatric Association, 1980), defines approximately 30 childhood disorders in a section entitled,

"Disorders Usually First Evident in Infancy, Childhood or Adolescence." The manual also presents a broad definition of, and diagnostic criteria for, each disorder. The second system, designed in 1969 by the Group for the Advancement of Psychiatry (GAP), includes 10 general categories (e.g., psychotic disorders, personality disorders) that are used to classify the various psychiatric disturbances of childhood.

In Epanchin's (1982) view, the GAP system is more sensitive to the changing nature of children's behavior than the DSM-III system. For example, in describing psychotic disorders in children, the GAP definition states that childhood psychosis is a chronic disorder often characterized by aloofness, tantrum-like outbursts, impaired interpersonal relationships, fixation on inanimate objects, stereotypic behavior patterns, sensory disturbances, abnormal intellectual development, and sensory disorders. Critics, however, comment on the "lack of specificity" of the broad GAP descriptions of diagnostic criteria. This lack of specificity may be responsible, in part, for the low inter-rater reliability measure found by Freeman (1971) when he arranged for a number of diagnosticians to classify children using the major GAP categories.

In contrast to the GAP system, three major psychotic disorders of childhood are listed in the DSM-III system. They are: 1) infantile autism, 2) childhood onset pervasive developmental disorders, and 3) atypical pervasive developmental disorders. These disorders, termed *pervasive developmental disorders,* are:

> characterized by distortion in the development of multiple basic psychological functions that are involved in the development of social skills and language, such as attention, perception, reality testing, and motor movement. . . . many basic areas are affected at the same time and to a severe degree (American Psychiatric Association, 1980, p. 86).

Specific definitions, symptoms, age of onset, course, complications, prevalence, sex ratio, familial pattern, differential diagnosis, and diagnostic criteria are then offered for the psychotic disorders of autism, childhood onset pervasive developmental disorders, and atypical pervasive developmental disorders.

The GAP is oriented to the fluidity and developmental nature of children's behavior. The DSM-III is specific in overt symptomatic behaviors, using operational definitions and a cross-referenced "multi-axial" approach to final classification.

Educational Definitions

Educators have offered numerous definitions of the emotionally disturbed child. Most of these contain a reference to the child's deviant or inappropriate behaviors. Often the child's history of negative interference with the normal routines of persons in his or her environment is mentioned, as is the child's apparent lack of self-control.

The definitions included below represent the thinking of educators and psychologists over the past two decades, and are presented chronologically to provide a historical perspective on the changing perceptions of emotional disturbance.

1. The emotionally handicapped child is defined as having moderate to marked reduction in behavioral freedom, which in turn reduces his ability to function effectively in learning and working with others. In the classroom this loss of freedom affects the child's educative and social experiences and results in a noticeable susceptibility to one or more of these five patterns of behavior:

    An inability to learn which cannot be adequately explained by intellectual, sensory, neuro-physiological, or general health factors

    An inability to build or maintain satisfactory interpersonal relationships with peers and teachers

    Inappropriate or immature types of behavior or feelings under normal conditions

    A general pervasive mood of unhappiness or depression

    A tendency to develop physical symptoms, such as speech problems, pains or fears, associated with personal or school problems (Lambert, 1963, pp. 3–4; Lambert & Bower, 1961, p. 2)

2. Emotionally disturbed children are children who have more or less serious problems with other people—peers and authority figures such as parents and teachers—or who are unhappy and unable to apply themselves in a manner commensurate with their abilities and interests. In general, one might say that an emotionally disturbed child is one who has a sizeable "failure pattern" in living instead of a "success pattern" (Haring & Phillips, 1962, p. 1).

3. A child is disturbed when his behavior is so inappropriate that regular class attendance would be disrupting for the rest of the class, would place undue pressure on the teacher, or further the disturbance of the pupil.... thus, disturbed children are viewed as having limited patterns of behavior and lacking flexibility to govern and modify their behavior (Pate, 1963, p. 242).

4. The person whose behavior is maladaptive does not fully live up to the expectations for one in his role, does not respond to all the stimuli actually present and does not obtain the typical or maximum forms of reinforcement available to one of his status (Ullmann & Krasner, 1965, p. 20).

5. The emotionally disturbed child is a socialization failure. Underlying all of the specialized terms and complex diagnostic labels used to describe him is the implication that his behavior, for whatever reason, is maladaptive according to the expectations of the society in which he lives.... At each age level, certain behaviors, capabilities, knowledge, beliefs and customs must be acquired if successful adaptation to the environment is to occur. As an individual's behavior deviates from what is expected for his age, sex, and status it is *maladaptive* and he may experience serious difficulties in getting along (Hewett, 1968, p. 3).

6. A behavior disorder [is] a deviation from age-appropriate behavior which significantly interferes with: the child's own growth and development and/or the lives of others (Kirk, 1972, p. 389).

7. Fundamentally, children who exhibit emotionally disturbed behaviors are excessively aggressive, withdrawn or both. Their central problem usually is not violation of social rules or the mores and folkways of culture: they are, however, very unhappy people (Smith & Neisworth, 1975, p. 27).

8. Children with behavior disorders are those who chronically and markedly respond to their environment in socially unacceptable and personally gratifying behavior (Kauffman, 1977, p. 23).

9. These children, either because of intrapsychic conflicts or social learning handicaps, have difficulty:

    Accepting themselves as individuals worthy of respect

    Interacting with peers in a consistently acceptable and personally productive manner

    Interacting with authority figures such as... teachers, instructors and parents in a consistently acceptable and personally productive manner

    Engaging in "normal" affective, psychomotor and cognitive learning activities without inordinate frustration and conflict (Shea, 1977, p. 6)

10. Those students whose educational programs require a high degree of control from special personnel outside of regular education and whose intervention programs are extremely intense (Grosenick & Huntze, 1979, p. 7).

11. [Emotional disturbance] is the categorical term used to refer to deviations in the normal course of psychosocial development that are related to impaired interactions between the individual and the environment (Wyne & O'Connor, 1979, p. 520).

12. Wyne and O'Connor (1979) also offer these theoretically based definitions:

    Psychodynamic: Impairment of emotional growth during one or more of the stages of ego development resulting in feelings of inadequacy, distrust of others, and hostility or withdrawal in reaction to anxiety.

    Behavioral: Inadequate, inappropriate, or undesirable behaviors that are learned and that can be changed or eliminated by the use of applied behavioral analysis.

    Developmental/Ecological: All forms and degrees of behavioral deviance, irrespective of etiology, which result in behavioral-environmental maladaption and personal-social alienation (p. 316).

13. A broad term used to describe individuals whose major difficulty is managing their emotions and maintaining them within the range of acceptability (Gearheart, 1980, p. 480).

14. Emotional disturbance is a complex problem of childhood [that may be] manifested in problems of inappropriate behavior, faulty thinking, excessive variations of mood, depressed intellectual functioning, symptoms of physical illness, developmental lag in social and emotional maturity or underachievement. The ways in which emotionally disturbed children are noticeably different from their peers may be social, behavioral, psycho-organic or educational. *Emotional disturbance* is a label applied to many different patterns of characteristics (Paul, 1982, p. 4).

Finally, two separate definitions frequently used by educators of autistic children are provided:

1. Autism is a syndrome of childhood characterized by a lack of social relationship, a lack of communication abilities, persistent compulsive rituals, and resistance to change... The syndrome's outset is usually in infancy—sometimes reported from birth, but certainly evident in the first three years of life (Paluszny, 1979, p. 1).

2. According to the National Society for Children and Adults with Autism, autism is a "behaviorally defined syndrome." The essential features are typically manifested prior to 30 months of age and include disturbances of: (1) developmental rates and/or sequences, (2) responses to sensory stimuli, (3) speech, language and cognitive capacities, and (4) capacities to relate to people, events, and objects (Ritvo & Freeman, 1977, p. 1).

Legal Definitions

With the introduction in the 1970s of legislation protecting and providing for handicapped children's rights, the necessity of developing a legal definition for emotional disturbance became apparent.

The Bureau of Education for the Handicapped (currently Special Education Programs) took Bower's (1969) revised version of Lambert and Bower's (1961) definition, added a statement excluding "socially maladjusted" children, and proposed it for use in Public Law 91-230. The subsequent definition in PL 91-230, the Elementary and Secondary Education Assistance Programs, 1970, reads as follows:

> Seriously emotionally disturbed children does not include children who are socially maladjusted but not emotionally disturbed. In distinguishing between such children, the following criteria may be used to determine those children who are seriously emotionally disturbed: those children who exhibit one or more of the following characteristics over a long period of time and to a marked degree:
> a. an inability to learn which cannot be explained by intellectual, sensory, or health factors;
> b. an inability to build or maintain satisfactory interpersonal relationships with peers and teachers;
> c. inappropriate types of behavior or feelings under normal circumstances;
> d. general pervasive mood of unhappiness or depression; or
> e. a tendency to develop physical symptoms, pains or fears associated with personal or school problems (Cullinan & Epstein, 1982, p. 19).

In 1977, the [then] U. S. Department of Health, Education and Welfare (HEW) further modified the definition of serious emotional disturbance used in PL 91-230. The HEW regulations written to implement the Education for All Handicapped Children Act (PL 94-142), while retaining the essence of material in the earlier definition, made several textual changes. The first was a revision of the opening paragraph, to emphasize the educational impact of serious emotional disturbance. The paragraph now reads: "The term [seriously emotionally disturbed] means a condition of exhibiting one or more of the following characteristics over a long period of time and to a marked degree, which adversely affects educational performance" (*Federal Register,* 1977). The "characteristics" that then follow are identical to those delineated in PL 91-230.

Another major addition to the definition of severe emotional disturbance was the inclusion of autism in the initial sentence of the final paragraph of PL 94-142, Sec.121a5. This sentence has caused much controversy in the years following its publication:

The term includes children who are schizophrenic or autistic. The term does not include children who are socially maladjusted, unless it is determined that they are seriously emotionally disturbed *(Federal Register, 1977)*.

Professionals and groups, especially the National Society for Children and Adults with Autism and the National Institute for Neurological and Communicative Disorders and Stroke, disagreed with the inclusion of autism as a serious emotional disturbance and supported the contention that the autistic syndrome is primarily a language or developmental disability (Schopler & Reichler, 1976). In 1981, their collective pressure prompted Terrence Bell, the Secretary of the U.S. Department of Education, to issue the following regulation that amends Part B of PL 94-142.

(1) The reference to "autistic" children is deleted from the disability category of "seriously emotionally disturbed" under the definition of "handicapped children"; and
(2) A reference to "autistic" children is added under the disability category of "other health impaired" under the definition of "handicapped children" *(Federal Register, 1981, p. 3865)*.

Issues concerning the nature and needs of autistic children are presented later in this chapter.

Epstein, Cullinan, and Sabatino (1977) surveyed the definitions of emotional disturbance of all 50 states and the District of Columbia and identified 11 specific components that appeared in one or more of the definitions. *Disorders of emotion/behavior* was the prominent component in all definitions. Forty-nine of the responding agencies' definitions included discussion of "Emotions or behaviors [that] are improper, immature, or [represent] a specific [type of] disturbance" (Epstein et al., 1977, p. 21). The mention of *interpersonal problems* appeared in 34 of the 51 responses. *Learning/achievement problems* caused by, or existing because of, emotional disorders was contained in 27 of the definitions. In addition, 21 definitions spoke about the problem of *length* of existence *(chronicity)* of the disability.

Three components primarily of legal, not psychiatric or educational, concern appeared in 31, 18, and 17 of the responses respectively, as follows: The first was a statement that *special education services are legally indicated* for the child under requirements of federal and state laws. The second was the requirement of *certification* of the disorder, specifying that the behaviorally disordered child must be labeled. The third component, which Epstein et al. (1977) entitled *exclusions*, discussed who is *not* to be considered behaviorally disordered and should not, therefore, receive services. Four other remaining components of legal definitions of emotional disturbance that appeared in state definitions concerned the child's display of behaviors that clearly deviate from the norm, as well as the etiology, severity, and prognosis of the problem.

Cullinan and Epstein (1982) offer the following as a typical state definition of emotional disturbance:

> Emotionally disturbed shall mean children with behavioral disorders variously designated as neurotic, psychotic, or character disordered, and whose inabilities may manifest themselves in school accomplishment, social relationships or feelings of self adequacy and may result both from experience or biological limitations (p. 21).

A recurring element of psychiatric, educational, and legal definitions is the indication that the disturbed individual interferes with normal routine or exerts "undue pressure" on family, teachers, and peers. Thus, the way persons in the child's environment perceive him or her is the diagnostic key in determining if the child is emotionally disturbed. The state definitions furthermore underscore that the behavior exhibited by the child must interfere with his or her ability to develop intellectually, academically, and socially—for example, such children may routinely involve themselves in inappropriate interpersonal interactions, engage in isolative, antisocial activities, aggressive behaviors, and/or other nonconforming social practices. A final indicator of emotional disturbance is the child's immature or unrealistic self-concept. Whelan and Gallagher (1972) succinctly characterize emotional disturbance as typified, fundamentally, by behavioral excesses and deficits.

Severely Emotionally Disturbed vs. Moderately or Mildly Disturbed Behavior Disordered Children

Children displaying mild behavior disorders and situational adjustment problems must be differentiated from those who manifest severe emotional disturbance. Children may, at one time or another, display mildly or moderately inappropriate behaviors or adjustment problems. These problems, while if they occurred in the classroom might be severe enough to merit intervention on an interim, crisis, or resource basis, are rarely pronounced enough prior to school entry to receive undue attention or to be of concern to parents. Nevertheless, professionals who work with mildly and moderately emotionally handicapped children are often able to analyze situations in which abnormal behavior is displayed and identify causative agents. This is typically not the case, however, with severely emotionally disturbed children, whose deviant or bizarre behavior is frequently cloaked in mystery. Parents of severely disturbed young children complain of the unpredictability of deviant behavior episodes and indicate that these abnormal episodes occur early in childhood. For example, severely disturbed children will often engage in stereotypic or bizarre behaviors, fixating on a repetitive arm movement or producing nonsensical vocalization for hours. Kauffman (1974) has offered a definition of severe emotional disturbance that clearly distinguishes severely emotionally disturbed children from their normal and mildly/moderately disturbed peers. Kauffman's definition fulfills the need for an operational and functional definition of the severely emotionally disturbed child.

> Traditionally, emotionally disturbed children have been defined in psychiatric terms or categories which emphasize underlying "pathology" and disturbance of thought and affect. Psychiatric terms commonly used to describe severely disturbed children

include: childhood psychosis, childhood schizophrenia, symbiotic psychosis and infantile autism. Many severely disturbed are multiply handicapped in that they are also mentally retarded, brain injured, or sensory handicapped.... However, the distinguishing feature of severely disturbed children is their extreme deviance in overt behaviors. Educationally, severely disturbed children are those whose behavior is consistently so debilitating, self-destructive, or disturbing to others that they cannot be educated with their normal peers (p. 380).

The implications of Kauffman's definition are that if a disturbance is great enough to warrant special class or special school placement, then the person is severely handicapped since he or she must be segregated from his or her same-age peers. The use of the term "serious" in the PL 94-142 definition refers to all handicapped children who are emotionally disturbed, differentiating them from those students who are either not disturbed or whose emotional disturbance is not an educational problem because it does not interfere with their education. The problem then is to differentiate among subcategories of the seriously emotionally disturbed for treatment and research purposes.

Given the need to operate under the legal definition of PL 94-142, one is faced with a semantic problem of major proportions. For instance, a classification system that emphasizes degree of disability requires one to recognize a subcategory with the absurd rubric: *mildly seriously emotionally disturbed*. This vagueness and confusion of terminology has a major impact on the state of the art and knowledge base. No one can really be sure about whom he or she is talking when discussing the category of severely emotionally disturbed since the speaker is attempting to describe a classification with the unlikely designation: *severely seriously emotionally disturbed*.

The author accepts the premise that for educational purposes, noncategorical degree of disability designations are the most productive since they suggest specific organizational and treatment approaches and strategies. Mildly and moderately emotionally disturbed students, because of the relative mildness of their symptoms, can be educated in the least of the least restrictive environments, i.e., the regular classroom, where they are educated in the educational mainstream while receiving varying amounts of diverse related services, including the help of resource specialists (Hewett & Taylor, 1980). Severely and profoundly emotionally disturbed students, on the other hand, are viewed as those who are so greatly impaired that they must be educated in segregated settings, i.e., the most restrictive of education environments, because they require extraordinary and comprehensive education and/or therapeutic interventions.

Limiting the term *severely and/or profoundly disturbed* to only psychotic conditions as suggested by Hewett and Taylor (1980) excludes all those severely disturbed students who are so dysfunctional (yet not classifiable medically or psychiatrically as psychotic) that they require exceptional educational practices and strategies in segregated settings. The problem of educational classification is further compounded if one accepts the position that autism is not a form of childhood psychosis but rather a developmental disability. If so, then childhood schizophrenia may be the only form of severe emotional disturbance that is generally recognized. The author, however, believes it is nonproductive for instructional programming and classroom organization purposes to accept the medical label of psychosis as the sole determining factor in establishing severity because the nature of the student's behavior should be the educational focus, and, therefore, the diagnostic emphasis.

INCIDENCE

Figures on the incidence of severe emotional disturbance vary greatly, a reflection, in part, of the fact that estimates of the number of children with severe emotional disabilities often make no distinctions between mild and more severe impairments. In 1975, Morse reviewed existing data and found that incidence figures of emotional disturbance in school-age children had been estimated to be between 0.1% and 30%. Reinert (1980) has offered several reasons for this wide discrepancy. Definitions and incidence figures, he explains, vary between agencies and individuals because of their differing philosophical orientations and purposes for estimating the incidence of emotional disturbance. In addition, the specific instruments and techniques used for collecting incidence information may partially account for the variation.

Reinert (1980) has established a 2% figure for serious emotional disturbance in children in the United States. This figure is consistent with 1% to 3% population estimates offered by Hewett and Taylor, (1980); Kauffman (1981); Kelley, Bullock, and Dykes (1977); and Morse and Coopchik (1979). Disagreement centers mainly on the proportion of school-age children with mild and moderate emotional problems. Bower (1969) has suggested a 10% rate for children needing some intervention during their school careers; however, less than 1% of these are seriously disturbed enough to require long-term, intensive help. The Joint Commission on Mental Health of Children (1969) has delineated three degrees of emotional disturbance: severe, moderate, and mild. Of the total school-age population, the committee reported that approximately 35% of children display some characteristics of emotional disturbance. Mildly disordered children represent 20% of this figure, moderately disturbed children 10%, and severely emotionally disturbed children 3.6%. There have been few estimates of the incidence of severe emotional disturbance, and when they are available, it is unclear to whom they are referring given the ambiguity of degree-oriented boundaries. Koegel, Egel, and Dunlap (1980) report that "one child in every 2,500 births is likely to be labeled autistic" (p. 259).

Morse and Coopchik (1979) have suggested that children whose primary handicaps include mental retardation or physical disabilities account for 13% of the population labeled as seriously emotionally disturbed. They offer four classifications to describe the remaining 87% of children, whose primary handicaps they label as "socio-emotional." These are children with mild to moderate attachment, temperament, affect, and emotional problems (Anastasiow, 1981). Children who are *reactive* constitute 26% of the total seriously emotionally disturbed population and are children who are severely affected by chronic stressful situations usually occurring outside the school environment. Another 25% are considered *neurotic*, displaying impulse/control disorders. *Inadequately socialized* children (27%) have character disorders that conflict with prevailing culture mores. Finally, 8% of the population falls into the category of *psychotic*; these children exhibit severe difficulties in identifying reality and appropriately interacting with their environment. Autism is included by Morse and Coopchik (1979) as one of the severe psychotic disturbances.

Regarding autism, studies in the United States, Denmark, and Britain, and investigations by numerous researchers, including Lotter (1966), Treffert (1970), and Wing (1976) have established incidence figures for the syndrome of autism. It is indeed a rare disability, with incidence estimates ranging from 3 to 4 children per 10,000 children (Paluszny, 1979). Ritvo and Freeman (1977) indicate that autism is found throughout the world with an incidence of 4 to 5 per 10,000 births. They also report a 4–5 time male to female ratio. (See discussion of autism in the Screening, Identification, and Diagnosis section of this chapter.)

Although severe emotional disturbance affects children of both sexes, the incidence of disability is appreciably higher in boys than girls. Estimates vary from seven males per one female (Lyons & Powers, 1963) to three males per one female (Clarizio & McCoy, 1976). This general sex pattern is also true of autism. Figures show a ratio of between two to five males to every female affected (Hington & Bryson, 1972; Morse, 1975; Paluszny, 1979). However, as Paluszny (1979) pointed out:

> A word of caution should be inserted at this point regarding the male to female ratio. This higher incidence in males should not give voice to speculations about etiology. It is well-known that more disorders, whether physical, mental or emotional, affect the male child more than the female. For example, in children with minimal brain damage . . . the ratio of males to females has been estimated to be anywhere from 25:1 to 15:1 (Cruickshank, 1977). It is generally accepted that the male infant is more delicate and vulnerable to illness and injury. Furthermore, the usually large size of the male infant may make the baby more susceptible to injury during the birth process (p. 18).

SCREENING, IDENTIFICATION, AND DIAGNOSIS

In screening, the first questions are related to student selection and classification, i.e., is the student emotionally disturbed and, if so, what is the nature and severity of the handicap? Hallahan and Kauffman (1982) point out that most disturbed children do not usually escape notice and are identified and referred without a formal screening process. They point out that disturbed children, especially those with conduct disorders, are so readily identified by school personnel that few schools use systematic screening procedures. Most severely emotionally disturbed children, because of their degree of deviation, are likely to be identified long before they come to the attention of public school personnel. It has been pointed out that as many as 50% of severely handicapped children can be identified at 1 month of age (Haring, Hayden, & Beck, 1976). Certainly, the more severe the handicap, the earlier it is likely to be identified because of the individual's obvious departure from normal expectations. In many cases, as with serious physical anomalies, the handicap is clearly demonstrated during the neonatal period. The problem, usually, is not whether a handicap exists but what type of problem is being manifested.

The identification puzzle is one of differential diagnosis since many severely handicapped children resemble each other in their behaviors, and differentiating among them becomes a complex and time-consuming task. Severely mentally retarded, severely emotionally disturbed, autistic, profoundly deaf, and markedly aphasic children often behave in similar ways, mandating comprehensive and multidisciplinary evaluation.

Diagnosis, of course, if it stops at the assignment of a label, is educationally and therapeutically unsound. It must lead to the identification of those relevant factors that may be causing and maintaining the problem (Erickson, 1978) as well as to the development of a total educational and therapeutic plan that will eliminate, control, or diminish the problem (Samuels, 1981).

Early Life Screening

Because severe emotional disturbance is frequently manifested in infancy, early life screening assumes major importance in the identification process. Normative-referenced scales appropriate for total developmental evaluation are the Bayley Scales of Infant Development (Bayley, 1969) and the Gesell Development Schedule (Gesell & Amatruda, 1941). Norm-referenced tests are based on the performance of large numbers of children of the same chronological age of the child to be tested whose own performance is then compared with that of his or her same-age peers (Salvia & Ysseldyke, 1978). Criterion-referenced tests, on the other hand, are employed to compare the child's skills to a set of standards rather than to other children and to measure competency, i.e., what a person does rather than what a person can do (Tyler, 1978). Criterion-referenced tests for infants include the Albert Einstein Scale of Sensorimotor Intelligence and the Ordinal Scales of Psychological Development (Samuels, 1981).

High-Risk Screening of Infants The identification of severe emotional disorders has recently been directed at the newborn population, and is a rapidly expanding field today. Infant screening requires a portfolio of techniques previously not available. Clark (1980) initiated birth certificate screening in the state of Utah to locate infants at risk for hearing loss. Other states have established high-risk registers to identify infants at birth who may be handicapped. Criteria for placement on a register vary, but qualifying information generally includes hereditary history of abnormality, intrauterine fetal infection, observable physical abnormality, low birth weight, and high bilirubin levels. Several of these factors are implicated as etiologies of severe emotional disturbance (Tanguay, 1980).

In addition to the registers, hospitals nationwide have established high-risk nurseries. Newborn infants who fall below criteria for healthy development are housed in separate quarters, where they are monitored and observed closely. Children who are severely handicapped from birth in areas such as intellectual functioning, visual acuity, and neurological involvement often are commonly found on high-risk registers and in high-risk nurseries.

Case History Screening One of the more commonly utilized screening procedures in exceptional education is the case history form. Parents or guardians of the child are asked to answer a number of questions relating to history of pregnancy, family history of disease and mental disorder, behavior of child, developmental landmarks of child, and, if applicable, the reason(s) for referral. Review of this information helps to identify children who may need to be evaluated at greater length. A sample case history form appears in Figure 1.

Child-Find The location, identification, and diagnosis of handicapped children are high-priority concerns of special educators. Public Law 94-142 focuses national attention on these issues by mandating that any agency serving children and receiving federal monies must initiate Child-Find components of programming in order to find handicapped people as early as possible, preferably from birth to 3 years of age. To fulfill this requirement, many agencies have developed comprehensive screening programs to differentiate children who may need special services from those who do not. These services may be medical, therapeutic, psychological, or educational, and often are provided by a combination of two or more disciplines. Blake (1981) described the three stages of Child-Find: awareness, screening, and referral. Awareness involves the use of various media to educate the public to the kinds of problems exceptional children have, the services available to them, and the need to put them in contact with service programs. The screening phase examines the individual to determine whether a problem exists, while the referral phase involves an indepth study of the person to ascertain his or her eligibility for special education and related services and to compile information for judging how best to meet his or her educational and service needs.

Formal Screening Instruments

Teacher Rating Scales A rating scale or checklist allows for the systematic observation and evaluation of another's behavior. Rating scales have problems in both reliability and validity (Hallahan & Kauffman, 1982; Samuels, 1981). Some scales that have been used to screen emotionally disturbed children are:

1. Quay–Peterson Behavior Problem Checklist
2. Walker Problem Behavior Identification Checklist
3. The Early School Personality Questionnaire
4. The Early Detection Inventory
5. The Referral Form Checklist of Problem Behaviors
6. Burks Behavioral Rating Scale

Case History Form

Date _____

I. Biographical Information
   Name: _____   Date of birth: _____
   Address   Sex: _____
   of child: _____   Age: _____

   Phone: _____
   Parents'/guardians' name (circle one): _____

   Address of parents'/guardians' (if different from above): _____

   Phone (if different from above): _____
   Person supplying information for this form: _____

   Relationship to child: _____
   Referral source (if applicable): _____

II. Information on Family
   Mother's age: _____   Marital status:
   Father's age: _____   Living together _____
                                              Separated   _____
                                              Divorced   _____
   Occupation
      Mother: _____
      Father: _____
   Education
      Mother: _____
      Father: _____
   Age of siblings (indicate sex): _____

   Is there anyone in the child's family who has:
      Hearing loss? _____
      History of mental illness? _____
      Severe visual impairment? _____
      Mental retardation? _____
      Emotional problems? _____
      Learning disabilities? _____
   If the answer to any of the above is "yes," please elaborate:
   _____
   _____
   _____

Figure 1. Sample case history form.

Case History Form
(continued)

III. Health History
1. Was this the first pregnancy of mother? _____
   If not, what number is the child? _____
2. Were there any irregularities about the pregnancy (i.e., German measles, rash, false labor, anemia, bleeding, and others)?
   _____
   _____
3. What medications, if any, were taken during pregnancy?
   _____
4. What was the length of pregnancy? _____
   Of labor? _____
5. What was the type of delivery? _____
6. What was the birth weight? _____
7. How old was child when released from hospital? (If older than 3 days, explain why) _____
   _____
   _____
8. Were there problems in feeding? _____
9. Which childhood illnesses has the child had?
   (Indicate at what age) _____
   _____
   _____
10. Has the child been hospitalized at any time since birth? _____
    If so, why and at what age? _____
    _____
11. Does the child routinely take medicine? _____
    If so, what kind and dosage? _____
    _____
12. What allergies, if any, does the child have?
    _____
    _____
    _____

IV. Developmental Milestones
   Please fill in approximate ages for the activities outlined below. Place an *N* next to the activities that the child does/did not perform.
   _____ turned over in crib
   _____ sat up alone
   _____ crawled
   _____ said first word
   _____ ate baby foods
   _____ ate solid foods
   _____ walked
   _____ used short sentences
   _____ toilet trained

Figure 1. *(continued)*

Case History Form
(continued)

V. Social/Emotional Development
Describe the child by marking only the appropriate terms below:

Sad	Happy	Hard to discipline
Moody	Even-tempered	Has temper tantrums
Friendly	Prefers to be alone	Is affectionate
Leader	Follower	Is usually fearful
Quiet	Very active	Has trouble sleeping
Independent	Dependent	Sucks thumb

Does the child have any behavior problem? If so, please elaborate: _____
_____
_____

Figure 1. *(continued)*

7. The Devereux Elementary School Behavior Rating Scale
8. Behavior Rating of Pupils Section of A Process for In-School Screening of Emotionally Handicapped Children
9. The Bristol Social Adjustment Guides

(Hallahan & Kauffman, 1982; Samuels, 1981; Swanson & Watson, 1982)

It should be noted that teachers are often as accurate as psychiatric tests in evaluating emotional disturbance (Bower, 1974; Hallahan & Kauffman, 1982). Numerous studies have been conducted comparing teachers' ratings of children with other measures, including children's self-ratings, direct observational data, mother's ratings, and ratings of psychiatrists, psychologists, and counselors. According to Epanchin (1982), all have concluded that the use of teacher ratings in screening and identification is a valid practice. She cautioned, however, about teacher bias. Davis (1978) found that teachers perceived that only 12% of girls are in need of help while 33% of the girls perceived themselves as requiring help. Teachers do not appear to perceive social withdrawal as a critical sign and do not seek professional help or seek assistance in managing and instructing students who are socially withdrawn (Cooke & Apolloni, 1976).

Peer Ratings Peers frequently have greater insights about disturbed classmates than do adults, including teachers (Hammill & Bartel, 1978). Peer evaluation can be accomplished through sociometric procedures in which pupils are asked to identify classmates whom they would most like and least like to work with on a project. Examples of peer rating scales include: A Class Play (Bower, 1961a), The Class Picture (Bower, 1961b), and The Minnesota Sociometric Status Test (Moore & Updegraff, 1971).

Screening for Autism and Autistic-Like Disorders The majority of autistic children exhibit symptoms of the disorder at a very early age. Parents of autistic children can usually trace the onset of abnormal behavioral patterns to the period before 30 months of age (Ornitz & Ritvo, 1976). Many parents of autistic children, especially those with normal older children, notice subtle indicators at or soon after birth. For example, the child fails to look up when the mother approaches and, when held, becomes rigid, refusing to snuggle as most infants do. Other severely disturbed children may respond in ways similar to those of autistic children, but in a less pronounced manner. Autistic children play in inappropriate ways and do not display acceptable social behaviors. Some cognitive abilities will be unexpectedly well developed for children of their age, while other abilities will lag severely behind (Rimland, 1978). Often it is the existence of the above inappropriate behaviors compounded by the absence of normal language development during the second and third years that prompts parents to seek professional attention for their severely disturbed child.

Formal diagnosis of autism requires an interdisciplinary team approach. Bricker and Campbell (1980) strongly support the use of cross-disciplinary evaluation. It has also been suggested that medical professionals, including neurologists, are crucial representatives on the interdisciplinary team (Ornitz & Ritvo, 1976). Representatives of the medical field, for example, may help identify syndromes with behavioral manifestations that could be mistaken for autism. Screening procedures, however, aimed at identifying an autistic population for further assessment have also been constructed that can be administered by educational personnel alone.

The earliest instruments used for identification of autistic populations were questionnaires (Rendle-Short, 1969; Rimland, 1964; Wing, 1980). Rimland (1964) requested information from parents on social interactions, affect, speech, manipulative ability, intelligence, reaction to sensory stimuli, family characteristics, illness, development, and physiological data. (See also Freeman & Ritvo, 1981.)

The Behavior Rating Instrument for Autistic and Other Atypical Children (Ruttenberg, Kalish, Wenar, & Wolfe, 1974) samples behaviors in eight categories: 1) relationship, 2) communication, 3) drive for mastery, 4) vocalization and expressive speech, 5) sound and speech reception, 6) social functioning, 7) body movement, and 8) psychosocial development. Direct observation (as required for this instrument), rather than informant interview, is seen by some as a more productive and accurate approach to evaluation. One drawback to the above Behavior Rating Instrument seems to be its scoring criteria, which have been criticized as being complicated and vague (Freeman & Ritvo, 1981).

Recognizing the need for an educational screening device, Krug, Arick, and Almond (1981) developed the Autism Screening Instrument for Educational Planning (ASIEP). Four subtests, plus an Autism Behavior Checklist, are used to screen the areas of vocal behavior, interaction skills, functional skills of education (in-seat behavior, receptive and expressive language, speech imitation, and body concept), and learning rate. In addition, a checklist comprised of weighted items provides data upon which to plot a behavioral profile. The standardization process of the ASIEP involved 3,000 autistic and severely handicapped children. The authors report that content and criterion-reference validity have been established on all subtests. Split-half reliability and interrater reliability were achieved on all subtests, and all but one subtest showed test-retest reliability (Krug, Rosenblum, Almond, & Arick, 1981). (See further discussion of autism in the Diagnosis section of this chapter.)

Direct Observation

Blake (1981) described three principal types of seriously emotionally disturbed pupils: acting-out, withdrawing, and psychotic pupils. She identified those behaviors that alert teachers to the possibility that a serious emotional problem may exist. The acting-out child may evidence poor self-control, verbal and physical attacks on other pupils, resistance to adults, destruction of property, and inappropriate group behavior. The withdrawing child may demonstrate excessive quietness and shyness, extreme self-consciousness, excessive anxiety, low approach, depression, low interest, frequent illness, and serious social misperception. The psychotic pupil may evidence social insulation, excessively immature behavior, self-injurious behavior, unusual physical habits, delusions, and unusual speech or language patterns.

The teacher is the ideal person to screen children because she or he spends a substantial amount of time with the pupil and can observe the entire range of the student's skills in a natural setting. Informal observation allows for the examination of behavior that may not be easily measured by formal instruments and allows for focusing on specific behaviors. Direct observations may take the form of a diary (running record) or an anecdotal record. Running records focus on behavior for a specific event. Behaviorists suggest that teachers should create their own direct observation checklists, composed of explicitly defined observable behaviors, to serve as a focused screening device. Their principal diagnostic technique is direct behavioral observation and behavior checklists for recording their observations (Kauffman, 1981; Kauffman & Kneedler, 1981; Strain, Shores, & Kerr, 1976).

The first step in the systematic observation process is to get a baseline assessment of each behavior. This baseline provides a base from which behavior is measured and the need for intervention is assessed (Fallen & McGovern, 1978). The baseline is assessed through various recordings relevant to the presence of the behavior: frequency counting (the counting of a behavioral action within a defined period), duration counting (the measurement of how long a behavior continues), interval recording (the counting of the presence or absence of a behavior during specified time units), or time recording or sampling (the measurement of the presence or absence of a behavior during alternate time intervals).

Behavioral rating systems with explicitly defined descriptors are available for measuring maladaptive behavior. The Werry & Quay Observational Procedure

(Werry & Quay, 1969) is available for measuring the deviant behaviors, attending behavior, and teacher-pupil contacts at the elementary school level.

Direct observation from an ecological perspective involves not only examining a behavior but identifying its antecedents, consequences, time, place, and frequency (Prieto & Rutherford, 1980). Wallace and Larson (1978) suggested following the child for an entire day, relating each behavior to each environment in which it occurred.

Diagnosis

After the identification of a handicapping condition is made, the next logical step is the establishment of a diagnosis. Diagnosis for the sake of labeling a child is a nonproductive exercise unless it leads directly to prescriptive action (Kauffman, 1974). The diagnosis of severe emotional disturbances or of autism is frequently restricted to assigning a diagnostic classification after differentiating the labeled condition from other conditions or syndromes that resemble it. Many severely emotionally disturbed children are untestable when traditional psychological instruments are used (Kauffman, 1974). As a result, often the only diagnosis developed is a medical one, a label placed on a child who displays a catalog of specific symptoms.

Autism Autism, a syndrome first described by Kanner in 1943, is most probably the diagnosis when a child exhibits the following symptoms or characteristics:

1. Disturbance of developmental rates and sequences
2. Disturbances of responses to sensory stimuli
3. Disturbances of language and speech, including echolalia
4. Disturbances of the capacity to relate appropriately to people, events, and objects
5. High level of activity
6. Self-stimulation
7. Isolated areas of high-level functioning

In addition, there is evidence that the:

1. Home environment is usually stable
2. Parents are employed in professional areas.
3. Family history does not include a significant incidence of psychosis

(Koegel et al., 1980; Rimland, 1964, 1978; Ritvo & Freeman, 1978, 1981; Webster, 1980; Wing, 1980).

The Neuropsychiatric Institute (NPI) of the Department of Psychiatry at the University of California, Los Angeles, developed the Evaluation and Prescription for Exceptional Children (EPEC) procedure (Flaharty, 1976) for use in diagnosing a population of children thought to be autistic. The EPEC, which is an example of a developmental scale of skills, samples 15 skill areas. Among the skills evaluated are fine motor, socialization and play, matching, receptive and expressive language, and body image skills. Flaharty (1976, p. 37) noted that the instrument was developed "because no previously devised method of educational or psychological assessment fully met the needs of our program." The Childhood Rating Scale (CARS) has been used to distinguish autistic children from other developmentally disabled children (Schopler, Reichler, DeVellis, & Daly, 1980).

Childhood Schizophrenia Children with schizophrenia usually develop normally and do not manifest signs until after the age of 6 (Samuels, 1981). Symptoms such as withdrawal of environmental interest, the lack of emotional rapport but greater responsiveness than found in autistic children, thought and language disturbances, vocal stereotyping, poor motor skills, bizarre movements, occasional hallucinations and delusions that increase as the condition progresses, and abnormal EEGs are sometimes present (Blake, 1981; Samuels, 1981).

Psychodynamic methods of diagnosis may be used on a portion of the population of severely disturbed children who are not included in Kauffman's "untestable" group (mentioned above). Personality assessment instruments (the most widely known is the Rorschach Inkblot Test) are used with children who possess the verbal skills to appropriately interact with an examiner. Other examples of assessments of personality are the Thematic Apperception Test (TAT) and the Children's Apperception Test (CAT), which employ more highly structured stimuli than the inkblot tests (Samuels, 1981). Projective measures such as Jung's Word Association Test and the Rosenzweig Picture-Frustration Test are also valuable personality tests.

Finally, some attempt to develop standardized diagnostic instruments useful in planning educational programming has been made. Preschool children with severe behavioral disturbances may be administered, for example, the Psychiatric Behavior Scale (PBS) (Barker, Sandler, Borneman, Knight, Humphrys, & Risan, 1973), a useful screening device that takes only 7 to 8 minutes to administer. However, the PBS was originally intended to assess the emotional development of disturbed children on a longitudinal basis. Subtests in the areas of expression of aggression, relationships, independence-dependence, impulse control, reaction to stress, need for communication, appropriate coordination, appropriate feeling, and bizarre behaviors assess emotional-social development (Cross & Johnston, 1977). A second example of an educational instrument used for diagnostic/prescriptive purposes is The Adaptive Behavior Scales (Nihira, Foster, Shellhaus, & Leland, 1974), a two-part informant scale that explores the child's behavioral functioning. Part one concerns appropriate behavioral and learning areas; part two encompasses maladaptive behavioral attributes. Other diagnostic instruments (Preschool Attainment Record [Doll, 1966]; Vineland Social Maturity Scale [Doll, 1965]) offer assessments of behavioral functioning within their testing packages.

Screening for children with severe emotional disturbance has focused on the neonatal period, primarily because older children display aberrant behaviors so deviant that they alert adults in their environments to a problem, and therefore, there is little need for screening. Diagnostic measures approach emotional disturbance from several perspectives: medical, psychological and psychiatric, developmental, and educational. Treatment, prescribed from the results of diagnostic measures, is therefore affected by the background and perspective of the screener and by the professional orientation and/or the type of facility/agency performing the assessment.

ETIOLOGY

The causes of severe emotional disturbance are not clearly understood. Seventeenth- and 18th-century religious leaders ascribed severely deviant behavior to satanic influences and tried to purge evil from the bodies of affected individuals (Sue, Sue, & Sue, 1981). Kanner (1962) translated a passage from the autobiography of the writer Gottfried Keller that describes the death of a 7-year-old emotionally disturbed child in his German village in 1713. Custody of the child had been given to the local minister, who was directed to rid the girl of the demonic elements within her. The town's population believed that after this purging, she would enjoy a normal childhood. For several months the minister exposed the child to a ritual of beatings, starvation, and isolation; when she died (apparently from the treatment), the town and her parents rejoiced.

Fortunately, society's treatment of severely emotionally disturbed individuals improved dramatically in the 1900s under the guidance of physicians, including psychiatrists, as well as psychologists, educators, and sociologists. Investigation into the causes of emotional disorders has provided the impetus for treatment modifications that are both more humane and more scientific.

Five theories of causation—1) the psychodynamic/psychoeducational, 2) the organic, 3) the behavioral, 4) the ecological, and 5) the sociological—constitute the major suggested etiological bases of emotional disturbance. These five theories differ significantly from one another reflecting, in large part, the training and personal philosophies of the foremost proponents of each.

The Psychodynamic/Psychoeducational View

The terms *psychodynamic* and *psychoeducational* are often used interchangeably in the literature. McDowell, Adamson, and Wood (1982) suggest, however, that there is a slight difference between them and that the difference focuses on a therapeutic (psychodynamic) or an educational (psychoeducational) treatment strategy. Furthermore, these authors state, "changes in the terminology associated with this model parallel the changes in programs themselves... as early efforts were primarily associated with analytic treatment... and more recent efforts (on) educational aspects of programming" (p. 48).

Although there is no empirically validated evidence connecting severe emotional disturbance with the failure of students to progress satisfactorily through psychoanalytic developmental stages, a number of psychoeducational intervention programs with severely emotionally disturbed and autistic children have their roots in psychoanalytic theory (Knoblock, 1983).

Psychodynamic theory is, in reality, a group of related theories. Its various definitions and formulations hold that emotional disturbances are a manifestation of one or more uncompleted emotional/psychological tasks of maturation. Advocates of the theory, who subscribe to the Freudian interpretation of emotional development, discuss behavior deviances in terms of arrested stages of personality growth or regression to more infantile or immature stages of ego development.

Also contributing to psychodynamic theory are the humanistic psychological tenets of Alfred Adler, Abraham Maslow, Carl Rogers, Albert Ellis, and William Glasser. These tenets are more holistic and socially oriented than those of Freud. Humanist psychologists believe that abnormal behaviors may be attributed to an individual's inability to fulfill his or her potential. Potential is seen to be both personally and socially determined. When a gap occurs between an individual's potential for experiencing and his or her actual experience, distorted emotions, human isolation, and apathy may result. In addition, humanist psychologists discuss the possible conflict between collective (societal) consciousness and the conscious self. They advocate therapy using open systems of thought that are oriented toward self-discovery rather than using more direct, goal-oriented systems aimed at achieving specific ends (Darley, Glucksberg, Kamm, & Kinchla, 1981; Gleitman, 1981; Mahrer, 1978; Nevill, 1977). Humanist psychologists subscribe to a belief in people's basic goodness, and their theories are considered less sexist than Freudian theory (Mosak & Dreikurs, 1973). They feel, as do followers of Freud, that behavioral outbursts are to be treated as symptoms of deep-seated problems that originate from abnormal emotional development.

Clinical settings are most often the preferred environment for implementing psychodynamic treatment techniques. The process of psychological healing, as dictated by proponents of psychodynamic theory, is usually lengthy, with immediate positive behavior changes seldom occurring. Psychodynamicists regard negative behaviors as symptoms of long-standing emotional problems, and that permanent change must, therefore, take time. Disturbed individuals are guided through exploration of their past and present feelings and actions. By helping individuals to gradually understand their motivation for inappropriate behavior, and thus to change those behavioral motivators, it is hoped that new symptoms will not appear and that old ones will disappear.

Opponents of the psychodynamic approach criticize the typically lengthy time required before results are seen. In a classroom situation, such critics contend that continued severe behavioral deviations cannot be tolerated and, therefore, demand more immediate techniques of behavior change. Often, too, teachers opt for "more simplistic" techniques that do not require the direct cooperation of the disturbed child. Reinert (1980) cautions:

> The abandonment of psychodynamic theories for more simplistic forms of intervention has not been as productive as it originally appeared. In order to capitalize on

the psychological developments of recent years, teachers should become familiar with the array of psychodynamic thought so available to us (p. 41).

Interested readers are directed to reviews of theoretical systems by Munroe (1955), Fine (1973), McDowell, Adamson, & Wood (1982), and Rezmierski & Kotre (1972).

The Organic View

Organic theories, also termed *biophysical, biogenic,* or *biological* theories, are based on the belief that severe emotional disturbance has physical determinants. Some organic theorists suggest that through positive manipulation of causative agents, emotional disturbance can be reversed. Others investigate and speculate on the source of the problem but offer no cure or treatment process. All support the contention that some biophysical deficits, either genetically or environmentally determined, have probably affected the child's central nervous system (CNS) in such a way as to cause a severe emotional disorder. Rimland (1969), a major supporter of organic theory, predicted that "research will ultimately show psychosocial factors to have minor, if any, relevance in causing a severe disorder known as psychosis" (p. 704). Though many who espouse the biological position would not take as strong a stand as Rimland, they would nevertheless concur that an organic etiology is one of the major determinants of emotional disturbance.

Genetic Theories One group of researchers investigating possible organic causes of disturbance has directed its attention at genetic factors. Several difficulties, however, are inherent in performing genetic research: First, the process is time consuming; second, environmental influences cannot be precisely gauged; and, third, not all families wish to participate in genetic research. This last factor has had an exceedingly negative effect upon the progress of research into low-incidence handicaps (Reinert, 1980), owing to the fact that when a family refuses to participate, a researcher may be unable to gather a large enough sample of handicapped individuals to produce results for generalization to the rest of the population of persons with that disability.

Genetic investigation, because of these and other limitations, has proceeded in other directions. Studies of twins, one or both affected by schizophrenia, have been particularly productive. Rates of concordance of the disease appear to be higher in identical than in fraternal twins (Buss, 1966; Pollin, 1972; Ritvo, Ritvo, & Brothers, 1982). In a review of over 10 investigations of schizophrenia in populations of twins, Pollin (1972) found percentages of concordance in identical (monozygotic) twins to range between 61% and 86%, with the majority of studies reporting a mean of approximately 50%. In contrast, research suggests that there is less than a 20% concordance rate among fraternal (dizygotic) twins. Pollin cautioned against assuming simple genetic etiology from these figures. Prenatal environment, intrauterine position, and other less-explored factors may also affect the unborn child, and, in turn, may be the cause of schizophrenia at a later age.

A second method employed by geneticists to study the relationship between heredity and severe emotional disturbance is observation of disease incidence rates in family groupings. As with the research on twins, conclusive results have not been produced; however, there is some indication of a positive relationship between family history of schizophrenia and the likelihood of becoming schizophrenic (Reinert, 1980).

Physical Environmental Theories Some biophysical theorists suggest a link between environment and emotional disturbance. For example, diet, air pollutants, and fluorescent lighting are among a list of items that have been implicated in triggering emotional outbursts and in creating maladaptive/abnormal behaviors. The relationship between food additives and behavioral disorders has received much attention in the media. The Feingold or Kaiser-Permanente (K-P) diet recommends elimination of foods containing additives as well as salicylates (e.g., almonds, cherries, apples, tomatoes, and grapes) from the diets of children with behavioral and learning disabilities (Feingold, 1975; Fine, 1980). Often, improvements are reported in children's overt behavior once they follow the Feingold diet (Brenner, 1977; Williams, Cram, Tausig, & Webster, 1978). Since the use of food additives in the U. S. is pervasive (Paul, 1982), their elimination entails drastic dietary alterations. Feingold speculated that some children are more sensitive to the effects of chemical additives than others. These are actually allergic reactions, and this susceptibility, he suggested, is inborn. An elimination diet, with slow and programmed additions of new foods, is prescribed for emotionally disturbed children in order to identify those substances that seem to precipitate observable behavioral incidents. "At present, it appears that a multitude of different additives may precipitate hyperkinesis and learning problems in children with an altered ability to tolerate chemicals" (Brenner, 1979).

A second viewpoint on diet suggests that food allergies are the precipitating factor in some cases of emotional disturbance. The natural elements of some foods may cause adverse reactions.

> Richard, the 6-year-old son of a friend, displayed behavior typical of children with emotional problems. He appeared unhappy and cried very easily; temper tantrums were frequent. Physicians had on several occasions diagnosed Richard as mentally retarded, hearing impaired, partially sighted, and severely emotionally disturbed. Two years ago, in desperation, his mother took him to an allergy clinic one hundred miles from her home. A diet restricting Richard's intake of wheat, milk, and other foods with several specific additives was prescribed. Today Richard's temperament and behavior have improved to the point where they resemble those of a normal 6-year-old. Richard is now enrolled in a first grade classroom for gifted children, and his occasional outbursts invariably can be traced to the consumption of forbidden food (personal communication, child's mother, May 2, 1983).

It should be noted, however, that dietary treatment research has not produced sufficient or conclusive evidence linking emotional disturbances to particular foods or food additives.

Vitamin Theories Vitamin deficiencies have also been proposed as a probable cause of emotional disturbance (Cott, 1971; Rimland, Callaway, & Dreyfus, 1978). In a study of 16 autistic children, Rimland et al. (1978) reported positive effects from treating the children with large doses of vitamin B_6. Lelord, Muh, Barthelemy, Martineau, Garreau, & Callaway (1981) suggested that "a positive clinical response to B_6 and magnesium occurs in children with autistic symptoms" (p. 229), and presented evidence to encourage other researchers to examine this phenomenon. Megavitamin therapy is championed by some as the solution to a variety of emotional disorders including severe chronic depression and frequent lapses in memory. Although preliminary investigation into the use of megavitamin therapy with severely disturbed and autistic children has been encouraging, Sankar (1979) postulated that its successes are not due to existing decreased levels of vitamins but rather because of the positive effects of heavy vitamin intake on metabolic processes. The American Academy of Pediatrics in a 1976 article in *Pediatrics* found no valid base for suspecting vitamin deficiencies as causing emotional disturbance.

Neuropsychopharmacologic Theory Chemical imbalance within the neurologic system is another area of interest to those concerned with the causes of severe emotional disturbance. Neuropsychopharmacologic theories explore the chemical interactions of the neural pathways. Antipsychotic drugs (e.g., haloperidol, chlorpromazine, and thiothixene) have been prescribed in hopes of restoring normal chemical function to the pathways. In suggesting a possible biochemical basis for minimal brain dysfunction (MBD), Wender (1975) remarked on the impressive effects stimulant and antidepressant drugs have had on some children with the disorder. He described children diagnosed as having MBD and who were undergoing drug therapy as having displayed immediate improvement in behavioral, cognitive, and social functioning. The question still remains, however, whether a positive response to drugs necessarily indicates that a biochemical deficit exists in children with MBD. Wender stated:

> I am aware of [this argument's] pitfalls. The response to cortisone does not imply a lack of adequate adrenal function in arthritis, and the response of pneumoccocal pneumonia to penicillin does not imply a defect in the enzymes of the penicillin-synthesizing gland. Nonetheless, the response of some children with MBD to stimulant and, more rarely, to antidepressant medication does suggest that in these children a specific deficit is being reversed . . . . The drugs produce changes in behavior at levels far more complex and important than simple motor activity (p. 21).

Initial research in this area and in-depth experimental drug manipulation have been performed on animal subjects, and while results have been illuminating, one must acknowledge that animal psychosis is not identical to human psychosis (Schroeder & Schroeder, 1982). Continued investigation with humans is warranted.

Theories on Disease and Brain Damage Brain injury caused by disease processes has attracted the attention of investigators interested in the causes of severe emotional disturbance. Figures on intellectual functioning in autistic children have prompted researchers to suspect that a range of diseases previously etiologically implicated in mental retardation also cause autism and other psychotic states of childhood. Tanguay (1980) reported that 72% of all autistic children score in the retarded range when tested by qualified examiners. In addition, he cited findings that suggest that the etiologies of mental retardation and autism may be similar. Congenital rubella, tuberous sclerosis, phenylketonuria, and postnatal encephalitis have been linked to the syndrome of autism and to mental retardation.

The Behavioral View[1]

The focus of the behavioral view is on defined, observable, and measurable indicators of emotional disturbance. Neither introspection nor drug therapy are procedures appropriate to behavioral theory. The premise of the behavioral approach to emotional disturbance is that all behaviors are learned and, therefore, can be unlearned.

The behavioral view that psychology should address observable responses has been around for a long time, but it is only recently that this view has emerged as a distinct therapeutic orientation (Eysenck, 1959; Skinner, 1953a). While terms like *behavior management* or *behavior modification* may be more familiar, *behavior therapy* is more accurate in that it encompasses all therapies that share the basic elements of the behavioral view. There are a variety of techniques typically used by behavior therapists, but the behavioral approach is not defined by the techniques behaviorists use. Instead, it is defined by the characteristics described below:

1. The focus of treatment is on specific observable behavior(s). Behavior therapists are not interested in changing an individual's personality, supposed traits, neuroses, or deep-seated complexes. Rather, the focus is on developing adaptive behavior and eliminating specific maladaptive ways of behaving.
2. Learning is assumed to play a critical role in both the development of maladaptive behaviors and in the acquisition of new adaptive behaviors. That is, maladaptive behaviors are learned in the same ways that desirable or adaptive behaviors are learned.
3. While behavior is acknowledged to be determined by physiologic factors, learning history, and current environmental conditions (Ross, 1974), behavior therapists focus on current behavior and current environmental conditions. That is, treatment is very much oriented to the present, as opposed to dealing with historical and therefore unobservable interactions with parents, siblings, and other influential caregivers.
4. Because of its historical ties to the scientific study of behavior, behavior therapy places a greater emphasis than do other therapies on scientific validation of techniques. In everyday language, that means behavior therapists are concerned with measuring whether a particular intervention produces changes and whether it regularly produces change in a variety of individuals.

---

[1]This section on the behavioral view was prepared by Jon P. Ziarnik and Gail S. Bernstein. Portions of this material were adapted from Bernstein, Ziarnik, Rudrud, and Czajkowski (1981).

Two distinct types of learned behavior are focused on here: operant and respondent. Operants are those behaviors that operate on the environment to produce certain consequences (Skinner, 1953a), while respondent behavior is influenced by events that occur just before the behavior (Gardner, 1978).

Operant Behaviors   B. F. Skinner (1953b) is probably as responsible as any individual for the suggestion that the principles of operant conditioning could be applied to human learning problems. The operant model is usually characterized as an A–B–C model in which A refers to antecedents, B to behaviors, and C to consequences. Events that occur immediately before a behavior are called antecedents, and events that immediately follow a behavior are called consequences. Antecedents may set the occasion for the occurrence of a behavior, and consequences serve to either increase, maintain, or decrease a behavior.

Antecedents   Antecedents that consistently occur just before a behavior is reinforced may become signals that reinforcement is likely to occur. Other antecedents that consistently occur just before a behavior is not reinforced can become signals that reinforcement is not likely to occur (Kazdin, 1975). Both these types of antecedents are called discriminative stimuli. They allow the individual to discriminate between situations where the probability of reinforcement is high and those where it is not high.

There are two types of discriminative stimuli: an S^D, which signals that a behavior will likely be reinforced, and an S^Δ (read "S delta"), which signals that a response is not likely to be reinforced. For example, the telephone ringing can be an S^D since the probability of the response (answering and saying "hello") being reinforced (pleasant conversation with the caller) is high. On the other hand, if a bill collector has called an individual five times in a row, the phone ringing a sixth time is an S^Δ because the probability of the response being reinforced is low.

Consequences   Consequences, the events that follow behavior, serve to increase, decrease, or maintain behavior (Powers & Osborne, 1976). In order to modify a behavior, consequences must be systematically delivered contingent upon the immediate occurrence of that behavior (Sulzer-Azaroff & Mayer, 1977). Behaviors will not be altered unless they are consistently followed by effective consequences. For instance, if it is desired that a withdrawn child increase the frequency of interactions with others, positive consequences must be the result of such interactions.

There are two types of consequences: reinforcers and punishers. A reinforcer is any stimulus that, when presented contingent upon the occurrence of the behavior, increases the probability that the behavior will occur again (Powers & Osborne, 1976). A punisher is any stimulus that, when presented contingent upon the occurrence of the behavior, will decrease the probability of that behavior occurring again (Powers & Osborne, 1976). The most important thing about these definitions is that they are functional. Something is only a reinforcer for a particular individual if it strengthens that individual's behavior when presented contingently. If a given consequence does not strengthen a particular individual's behavior, it is not a reinforcer for that person. The definition of a punisher is also

	1	2
Increase responding	Present reinforcer	Remove punisher
Decrease responding	Present punisher	Remove reinforcer

Figure 2. Effects on behavior of the presentation or removal of the two types of consequences: reinforcers and punishers. (Adapted from Powers and Osborne, 1976; reprinted by permission from Bernstein, Ziarnik, Rudrud, & Czajkowski, 1981.)

functional in that if a person's behavior is not decreased contingent upon presentation of the consequence, that consequence cannot be considered a punisher.

Reinforcers and punishers can either be presented or removed. Figure 2 shows the effects of the presentation or removal of the two types of consequences on behavior. In general, behavior can be increased by either presenting a reinforcer or removing a punisher. Behavior can be decreased by either applying a punisher or removing a reinforcer.

Respondent Respondent or classically conditioned behavior is influenced by the events which occur just prior to the behavior. The application of therapeutic interventions to respondent behaviors was pioneered by Joseph Wolpe (1958). Respondent behavior includes most instances of irrational fears or inappropriate feelings. This type of learning is particularly important when analyzing the behavior of emotionally disturbed children because much of what we call emotional behavior is learned via respondent conditioning. The basic rule of emotional learning is "neutral events come to control emotional reactions both pleasant and unpleasant after being associated on numerous occasions with other events that produce those reactions" (Gardner, 1978, p. 271). For instance, one early type of respondent learning occurs when a child associates the positive feelings that come with being fed with the sound of his or her mother's voice. This type of learning, of course, can also occur with unpleasant or negative events. For instance, the child who associates walking in the door of his or her home after school with being hit by a parent is likely to develop the same negative emotional reactions to coming home as he or she initially had to being hit.

While both Skinner and Wolpe have been singled out in this section for their contributions in the application of the behavioral view to human problems, many others have made substantial contributions to the field. For more detailed descriptions of the behavioral view, interested readers should consult texts such as Kanfer and Phillips (1970), Rimm and Masters (1974), or Ullmann and Krasner (1975).

The Ecological View

The ecological position views the individual as being part of a larger whole, that being the surroundings and culture that comprise the individual's environment.

Theoretically, the individual acts on and reacts to both human and physical aspects of his or her environment, just as the environment acts on or reacts to the individual. These interacting elements are collectively referred to as the person's ecosystem.

According to Bronfenbrenner (1979), the ecosystem can be viewed as four separate systems: the microsystem, the mesosystem, the exosystem, and the macrosystem.

1. A *microsystem* is a pattern of activities, roles, and interpersonal relations experienced by the developing person in a given setting with particular physical and material characteristics (p. 22).
2. A *mesosystem* comprises the interrelations among two or more settings in which the developing person actively participates, such as, for a child, the relations among home, school, and neighborhood peer group; for an adult, among family, work, and social life (p. 25).
3. An *exosystem* refers to one or more settings that do not involve the developing person as an active participant, but in which events occur that affect, or are affected by, what happens in the setting containing the developing person (p. 25).
4. The *macrosystem* refers to consistencies, in the form and content of lower-order systems (micro, meso, and exo) that exist, or could exist, at the level of the subculture or the culture as a whole, along with any belief systems or ideology underlying such consistencies (p. 26).

When there is harmony within the ecosystem, a state of mental health exists. When there is discord, emotional disturbance is present. According to the ecological perspective, emotional disturbance in children is caused by a negative interaction between the child and his or her ecosystem (Swap, 1978). Salzinger, Antrobus, and Glick (1980) state that "Disturbed behavior, within an ecological framework...is largely defined by the society itself as behavior that is unacceptable in the situations in which it occurs in its present forms and this is selected for modification" (p. 4).

Another approach to understanding the development of a behavior disorder that is congruent with the ecological viewpoint may be seen in the work of Thomas, Chess, and Birch (1969) and Thomas and Chess (1977). This approach focuses on the temperament or behavioral style of a child and his or her interaction with the environment; temperamental individuality is considered to be well established by the time the child is 3 months old. Therefore, unlike orthodox psychodynamic/psychoeducational, behavioral, and organic positions, deviance and normalcy, in the ecological view, are defined by the community, and, depending upon the community's current values, a child may or may not be labeled emotionally disturbed.

Since, according to ecological theorists, the problems causing deviant behavior do not stem solely from the child but from a combination of the child and his or her ecosystem, intervention strategies are focused upon understanding and positively altering the child's nonproductive interactions with his or her environment (Knoblock, 1983). Swap, Prieto, and Harth (1982) delineate five assumptions basic to the ecological view concerning the interaction between a child and the environment. These are:

1. The child is not disturbed. The environment may present conditions that elicit disturbing behaviors or may inconsistently label a behavior as disturbing.
2. Interventions must alter the ecological system. They must address the total system rather than focusing solely on altering the child's behavior.
3. Ecological interventions are eclectic; they borrow from many disciplines when planning interventions.
4. Interventions in a complex system may have unanticipated consequences. The ecosystem is an interdependent system and includes all aspects of the child's environment: his or her family, school, classmates, friends, the neighborhood, the community, and society. Any alteration of an element in the system may produce unintended effects to another element.
5. Each interaction between the child and setting is unique. The need to treat each episode of disturbance as unique makes it inappropriate to make predictions about which variable should be assessed, to evaluate the efficacy of specific interventions, or to generalize results.

Rhodes and Paul (1978) state:

However, we still treat the variant individual as distinctive, unique and independent of the whole. We treat him or her as an isolated unit, without a function or place in the whole.

For all we know, the variant condition of the individual may be a very necessary part of our own psychological and physical balance and survival. Although we may not comprehend his or her part in the general scheme of things, we could be creating grave harm to our whole system by our extensive campaigns to change such individuals one by one. Perhaps there is a need to consider the whole social unit as maladaptive and, instead of interfering with the processes of the single individual, perhaps we should try to examine and intervene in the comprehensive, holistic system (Rhodes & Paul, 1978, pp. 198–199).

The Sociological View

Several sociological theories of deviance can be applied to the issues of emotional disturbance and mental health. By far the most popular of these is *labeling theory*, which was developed during the early 1960s and has gained substantial support in the intervening years (Des Jarlais & Paul, 1978).

Labeling theory is based on the premise that all individuals are rule breakers to some extent. Whether individuals are labeled deviant, however, depends on the answers to a series of questions, as outlined by Des Jarlais and Paul (1978). First, does the community have a need for the deviant role to be filled? And, depending on the answer to this first question: Is the power held by the rule breaker high or low compared to others in the community? Do particular persons or groups have a special interest in seeing that penalties are given to rule breakers and that labeling then occurs? What is the level of conflict between the rule breaker and the agents of social control? Finally, how great a degree of rule breaking is the community prepared to accept?

Rule breaking behavior in children is viewed differently than the violation of rules by adults. Childhood is a period of testing the social rules of the system, whereas adults are expected to possess this knowledge and, therefore, to adhere to society's rules. Deviance in the child is diagnosed when rule-learning behavior is unusual, not just when adult rules are violated. During a child's developmental years, rules are added periodically that the child is expected to follow. If, for example, a 2-year-old refuses to wear clothes and removes them when out of view of an adult supervisor, we might call his or her actions "cute." On the other hand, if a 10-year-old behaves in the same manner, we view him or her as a deviant who has not properly learned and internalized the accepted rules of behavior for children of that age. A child risks being labeled as deviant when rules in this growing repertoire are ignored, unknown, or purposefully disobeyed.

According to labeling theory, the agents of social control hold pivotal positions in a child's life. These individuals may be the child's parents, teachers, members of the clergy, relatives, or any person or institution implicitly or directly responsible for enforcing social rules, such as police officers, court officials, and employers. These persons determine when rules have been broken by an individual and whether one of the many labels of deviance should be assigned.

> Labels affect the way persons behave toward each other. The behavior of individuals as well as the performance expectations of organizations contribute to the labeling process. *Emotionally disturbed* is a label applied to individuals who at some level threaten our shared view of the social nature of man (Schlechty & Paul, 1982, p. 244).

The use of labels to identify handicapped children has been discouraged in the past decade (Algozzine, 1981; Algozzine, Mercer, & Countermine, 1977) by those who believe that once children are labeled as deviant they carry the label forever. In addition, opponents of labeling stress that the label encourages continued deviant behavior, in that the child may strive to fulfill the role that has been created for him or her. To counteract the negative effects of labeling, many states require schools to reevaluate children labeled as handicapped on a 1–3-year schedule (Mississippi State Department of Education, 1982). Broader, less definitive categories, such as those referring to mildly, severely, and profoundly handicapped individuals, are also seen more often in the nation's school systems.

Four sociological theories—anomie, cultural transmission, social disorganization, and functionalism—have been proposed in addition to labeling theory to explain deviance in society. The word *anomie* is used to describe a condition in an individual that is characterized by disorientation, anxiety, and isolation. The theory of anomie, advocated by E. Durkheim, states that deviance is often the consequence of a rate of societal change that exceeds the rate of personal change (Reinert, 1980). In such a condition, demands are placed upon an individual that he or she cannot handle. *Cultural transmission theory* perceives of deviance as a learned behavior; in other words, a person may be classified as deviant if he or she associates with persons previously designated as deviant. The *social disorganization theory* of deviance holds that prevalence of deviance in a society is directly related to the level of organization in the community. A highly organized society produces fewer individuals classified as deviant than a loosely organized society. Finally, *functionalism* stresses the dynamic equilibrium maintained by society. Thus, rule breakers and enforcers are vital elements of a properly functioning social system (Rhodes & Paul, 1978; Shea, 1978).

CLASSIFICATION SYSTEMS

The classification of severely emotionally disturbed children is controversial. As knowledge grows in the field and theoretical postures change, so do classification systems. Another factor influencing the organization of the numerous labels of emotional disturbance is the particular theory of causation employed. Five theories of etiology, the psychodynamic, the organic, the behavioral, the ecological, and the sociological, have been discussed previously. Several of these theories offer schemata for classifying conditions of emotional disturbance.

Behavioral Approaches to Classification

As stated, behaviorists believe that emotional disturbance has been learned and, therefore, can be unlearned. The focus is away from labeling and toward the objective description of behavior. In fact, many supporters of the behavioral position avoid using the term *emotional disturbance* altogether. Identifying the original cause of the behavioral disorder is seen as both a time-consuming and fruitless endeavor. Instead, energy is directed toward discerning agents or situations that maintain undesirable behavior. For example, a child classified as autistic by a system based on the medical model might be described by behaviorists as "displaying the following self-stimulatory behaviors: finger wagging, eye blinking, and monotonous repetition of the sound, 'mees'." Behaviors, not types of children, are classified by proponents of behavior theory.

Sociological Approaches to Classification

Kauffman (1982) offered a prototype of a classification system of emotional disturbance based on Bandura's social learning theory, which includes elements of both the behavioral and sociological viewpoints. Three components, the person's observable behavior, the person's environment, and the person's cognition are, in Bandura's words "reciprocal determinants" (interactive elements) of the theory. Again, the focus is not on labeling groups of similar individuals but on describing types of behavior. In Bandura's model, the individual's observable behavior is coded with a *B*, his or her environment *E*, and cognition *P*. Interactions are illustrated with three overlapping circles forming a triangular-shaped structure. In one area of the model the individual is shown to be affected exclusively by cognition, in another, environment, and in the third, his or her observable behavior. The model has three areas that display two-element interactions and a final area that combines all elements in a three-way relationship (Bandura, 1977, 1978; Kauffman, 1982). For example, a 3-year-old boy wants the candy he sees in a grocery store. He grabs for it and begins to eat it (B). He does not know that the rules of his society specify that the candy be purchased before it is consumed (C). The grocer asks the boy's mother to pay for the candy, which she does (E). The mother in turn scolds the child for *his* actions, and he begins to learn an important rule of the society. Thus, his cognition (P) is altered. This example illustrates interaction of all three components of the social learning theory. A summary of the components and their interactions is presented in Table 1.

It would be misleading to view either the borders between the elements or the amount of influence one element exerts on another as steadfast; however, the model is conceptually an adequate representation of the social learning theory.

> The unreliability of current "diagnostic" categories and the little value they have in selecting intervention strategies has been commented on earlier in my paper and in many other sources. The conceptualization I have suggested implies that exceptionality should be classified according to behaviors, cognitions, environments and reciprocal influences . . . . It is possible to mention some types of exceptionality that fit into the schematic drawing . . . . Because appropriate responses do not occur, cognitions and environments are left in a two way interaction which exacerbates "neurotic" withdrawal or inhibition. In the area labeled B—P one might locate what have traditionally been called "psychotic" reactions. Here behavior and ideas are caught up in reciprocal influence with little or no influence over either being exerted by

Table 1. Summary of Bandura's social learning theory

Single element affecting social learning	Two-element combinations affecting social learning	Three-element combinations affecting social learning
Behavior (B)	Behavior Cognition (B↔P)	
Environment (E)	Behavior Environment (B↔E)	Cognition ↔ Environment ↘ ↗ Behavior
Cognition (P)	Cognition Environment (P↔E)	$\begin{pmatrix} P \leftrightarrow E \\ \searrow B \nearrow \end{pmatrix}$

Source: Bandura (1977, 1978) and Kauffman (1982).

the environment . . . . The advantages of the suggested conceptualization over those currently employed include the possibility of devising classifications that are empirically derived and related to intervention strategies (Kauffman, 1982, pp. 66–67).

Psychodynamic Approaches to Classification

Psychodynamic theorists offer a different system for classifying emotional disturbance. They rely heavily on medical labels. Psychiatrists dealing with mental disorders of children before the 1940s regarded the problem as a childhood manifestation of adult mental illness. Kanner (1948) discussed an earlier text on child psychiatry by T. Ziehen that elaborated on the symptoms and course of various disorders but made no mention of age of onset, developmental patterns, or the child's environment. "On the whole," wrote Kanner, "the book was an almost literal translation of adult psychiatry into terms of how much of it one might find in children" (p. 18). A historic 1943 article by Kanner documented the first cases of a disorder specific to childhood, for which he suggested the use of the term *early infantile autism*. Infantile autism became one of the first mental disorders considered by psychiatrists to have specifically originated in the period of childhood. This awareness prompted a movement aimed at differentiating between mental illness in children and in adults.

DSM-III The *Diagnostic and Statistical Manual of Mental Disorders: DSM-III* (American Psychiatric Association, 1980) lists five groups of emotional disturbances displayed by children, and is a guide for practitioners working with emotionally disturbed adults and children. The five disability groups are: 1) disorders of the intellect, 2) disorders of behavior, 3) emotional disturbances, 4) physical disturbances, and 5) pervasive developmental disorders.

Disorders of the Intellect The first category deals with mental retardation and the characteristics of the several subgroups (mild to profound). Prevalence figures, complications, course, etiologic factors, and familial patterns, as well as sex ratio and associated features, are described.

Disorders of Behavior Attention deficit disorder (minimal brain dysfunction) is the first topic in the behavioral disturbances section. Conduct disorders are also discussed, including four subtypes of conduct disorders. Their common feature is the existence of a persistent pattern of nonacceptable conduct. The manual presents diagnostic criteria on unsocialized, socialized, aggressive, and nonaggressive types of conduct disorder.

Emotional Disturbance Separation anxiety and avoidant disorder in childhood or adolescence are presented in this section. Five separate disorders—elective mutism, identity disorder, reactive attachment disorder of infancy, schizoid disorder of childhood or adolescence, and oppositional disorder—are discussed.

Physical Disturbance This section includes various physical disorders of eating. Pica, the craving for and ingestion of non-eatable materials; bulimia, a continuous and abnormal hunger; and anorexia nervosa, an abnormal pursuit of extreme weight loss, are presented in this section (Millican, Dublin, & Lourie,

1979; Sours, 1979). Also included under physical disturbances are abnormal rumination and atypical eating disorders. Motor tics and Tourette's syndrome (a repetitive, uncontrollable movement of a particular muscle or muscle groups, including uncontrolled vocal outbursts) (Lucas, 1979), as well as stereotypic behaviors (e.g., rocking and head banging) are presented under the heading *"Stereotyped Movement Disorders."* Finally, this section presents a discussion of the disorders of enuresis (uncontrolled urination that is caused by emotional rather than physiological disorders [Anders & Freeman, 1979]), encopresis (uncontrolled elimination of feces by children over the age of 4 years [Fisher, 1979]) stuttering, and sleep walking.

Pervasive Developmental Disorders   The last section of the *DSM-III* discusses primary disorders in infancy, childhood, and adolescence and relates directly to severely emotionally disturbed populations. The category, *pervasive developmental disorders*, is used to replace the terms, *atypical children, symbiotic psychotic children, childhood schizophrenia,* and other medically based terms used extensively in the past. The manual states:

> Since these disorders apparently bear little resemblance to the psychotic disorders of adult life, the term 'psychosis' has not been used . . . in the name of the group of conditions. The term *pervasive developmental disorder* has been selected because it describes most accurately the core clinical disturbance: many basic areas of psychological development are affected at the same time and to a severe degree (American Psychiatric Association, 1980, p. 86).

Table 2 presents information on pervasive developmental disorders included in the DSM-III classifications. It can be used to compare and contrast the disorders of infantile autism and childhood schizophrenia.

Other Psychodynamic Approaches to Classification   Though not part of an organized system of classification, other terms are used in the literature to label severely emotionally disturbed children (Kanner, 1973; Quay & Werry, 1979; Samuels, 1981; Wing, 1976). For example, the heading preferred by many diagnosticians for the various conditions of severe and emotional disturbances is *childhood psychosis.*

Among the conditions classified under childhood psychosis by many professionals, despite changes in its legal status and the advocacy of the National Society for Children and Adults with Autism, is *autism*. (Diagnostic criteria for autism are those presented in Table 2.) The differentiation between autism and schizophrenia has been a disputed topic in psychiatry since the syndrome of early infantile autism was first described. Kanner (1973) posed the question:

> Must we assume that early infantile autism represents a syndrome which is not in any way related to the known psychopathological patterns, or are we justified in correlating the essential features of the syndrome with the essential features of a condition which it most closely resembles, namely, schizophrenia? (p. 54).

In responding to his own inquiry, Kanner pointed out that he believes that autism may be considered the earliest manifestation of schizophrenia and he referred

Table 2. Diagnostic criteria for the pervasive developmental disorders

Disorder:	Infantile autism	Childhood onset pervasive developmental disorder
Previous label:	—	Childhood schizophrenia
Diagnostic criteria:	1. Onset before 30 months of age. 2. Pervasive lack of responsiveness to other people. 3. Gross deficits in language development. 4. If speech is present, peculiar speech patterns such as immediate and delayed echolalia, metaphorical language, and pronominal reversal. 5. Bizarre responses to the various aspects of the environment, e.g., resistance to change, peculiar interest in or attachments to animate or inanimate objects. 6. Absence of delusions, hallucinations, loosening of associations, and incoherence as in schizophrenia.	1. Gross and sustained impairment in social relationships, e.g., lack of appropriate affective responsivity, inappropriate clinging, asociality, and lack of empathy. 2. At least three of the following: —sudden excessive anxiety —constrained or inappropriate anxiety —resistance to change in environment —oddities of motor movement —abnormalities of speech (or voice) —hyper- or hyposensitivity to sensory stimuli —self-mutilation 3. Onset of the full syndrome after 30 months of age and before 12 years of age. 4. Absence of delusions, hallucinations, incoherence, or marked loosening of association.

Table developed by K. Grosman using material in American Psychiatric Association (1980, pp. 89–91).

readers to a chapter discussing schizophrenia and early infantile autism in his book, *Child Psychiatry* (1948).

Symbiotic psychosis is considered another of the conditions of childhood psychosis. Briefly, it is assumed that an infant directs his or her attention inwardly until the age of 3 months. At that time the infant's mother becomes the focus of attention, and is perceived by the infant as an extension of himself or herself. The normal child moves through this stage to a point at which mental separation from the mother begins. The child displaying symptoms of symbiotic psychosis, however, does not attempt separation and, therefore, is not able to build a personal identity image. As a result, separation anxiety ensues. Whereas the autistic child ignores the presence of his or her mother, the child with symbiotic psychosis panics when physically separated or at the suggestion of physical separation. External and internal stress produce severe emotional problems in some children. These conditions have been labeled *borderline states*, characterized by fears and fantasies of bigger-than-life enemies. Separation from the mother is difficult and, in time, develops into a dependency that may cause the school-phobia problems many of these children exhibit. This dependency prevents maturation toward adult independence.

A final classification of childhood psychosis is *schizophrenia*. Childhood schizophrenia can be differentiated from early infantile autism in several ways. First, the age of onset is later in life, occurring after a period of normal childhood development. Physicians, when questioning parents of schizophrenic children, usually find the first years of the child's life to be medically unremarkable. The child appears to the parents as healthy in all respects. However, electro-encephalographic readings (EEG) from schizophrenic youngsters are frequently abnormal, while readings from autistic children appear normal (Rimland, 1964). Schizophrenic children often come from families with a history of the disorder. As the schizophrenic child matures, physical illness becomes a common problem. Autistic children, on the other hand, are usually healthy individuals.

SYMPTOMATOLOGY

A Case Study

Paula [not her real name], a 13-year-old child, routinely arrives at school in a taxicab each morning, 1 hour before school begins. An instructional aide meets the cab and watches Paula for a half hour until her teacher arrives. During this time, Paula paces the hallway: 15 steps down and 17 back. She smiles on the way down the hall and sticks her tongue out on the way back. Each time she turns, she turns to the right; never to the left. When the classroom is opened, she is taken by the hand and led inside. Within 30 seconds she returns to the exact spot she left in the hall and resumes pacing. Again, she is taken to her classroom, where she remains with the door closed. She sits down by herself and begins to rock back and forth. (If left alone, Paula usually completes over 700 full rocking cycles per hour.) Suddenly she stops rocking, jerks her head to the right, and an exaggerated smile slowly creeps onto her face. When all facial muscles are stretched to their limit, she quickly relaxes them and begins another slow smile cycle. Her attention is directed by her teacher to the work in front of her, which she completes effortlessly but without apparent interest. Later, when Paula is moved to the front of the room for individual work, she refuses to go. She holds tightly to her chair as if it is part of her, and she cannot be moved without it. The teacher pushes Paula and her chair to the new instructional area. Paula resists, and awkwardly runs back to the spot she has left, her chair tightly held to her buttocks. (It is as if Paula has become fixated in a particular time/space and will not allow anyone to oust her from it.) Finally, Paula begins to violently beat her fingertips against her chin. She stands up and dives onto the floor, upsetting a nearby desk. For 10 minutes, with the teacher and aide attending to her to ensure she does as little damage to herself as possible, Paula rigidly pounds her body against the floor. After the incident is over, she collapses in a puddle of sweat and begins to hum softly.

Paula has a history of displaying bizarre behaviors. Her mother reports that she does not sleep well and wanders the house late at night. One morning Paula's mother awoke to a perfectly frosted cake, popcorn in a bowl, and all the laundry ironed. One day during the first week of attending a new school, 16 miles from her home, Paula jumped out of the taxi cab and disappeared. She had seen the neighborhood only once before during the ride to school on the previous day. Police searched the area for Paula but did not locate her. Two hours later, she walked up the steps of her house and opened the front door.

Symptoms like those exhibited by Paula, a student with whom the author worked during the years 1975–1977, in the above case study are characteristic of severely emotionally disturbed children. Behavioral variations abound in these children (Kauffman, 1974), but most bizarre behaviors can be grouped into several major categories or behavior types.

1. *Perseverative or stereotypic behaviors.* These are usually repetitive motor or vocal acts. Many severely disturbed children take delight in repeatedly waving a hand, tapping a desk, or flicking a switch.
2. *Ritualistic and obsessive-compulsive behaviors.* Ritualistic behaviors are ones that the child performs in a set pattern. When a ritual is interrupted, the child often begins again, attempting to perform the ritual until completion. (For example, a child may walk in a repeated rhythmic pattern—1 hop, 2 jumps, 3 hops, a skip. If interrupted at any point, the child will begin the ritual walk again.) Obsessive-compulsive behaviors are those that the child apparently is self-driven to perform (for example, a child may wash his or her hands every time he or she touches food).
3. *Inappropriate behaviors.* These are behaviors exhibited at a socially inappropriate time or place (e.g., lying down to sleep in the middle of a sidewalk, overt masturbation in public, and sexual exhibitionism and aberrations).
4. *Object fixation.* In object fixation an object assumes unparalleled importance to the child, to the point that the desire to obtain the object overrides all other desires. Often, the child would rather play with the object than eat or sleep, and, if it is taken away from him or her, a temper tantrum invariably results.
5. *Self-abusive behavior.* Violent behaviors that are self-directed are symptoms of severe emotional disorder. Head banging, hitting or biting oneself, and drawing blood by scratching are examples of self-abusive behaviors.
6. *Self-stimulating behavior.* These behaviors may be perseverative and ritualistic in nature; the child performs these behaviors apparently in an unconscious attempt to stimulate his or her body. Severely disturbed children often engage in self-stimulating acts such as finger manipulation, spinning, eye blinking, mouth movement, and incessant humming.
7. *Violent aggressiveness.* Outwardly directed behaviors that are violent in nature fall under this classification. These acts occur apparently without perceptible provocation. The child frequently attacks classmates, siblings,

parents, and teachers by punching, biting, scratching, or throwing objects at these people. Additionally, because material possessions have little meaning for the child, he or she may destroy them in outbursts of anger. Setting fires, sexual assaults on others, and cruelty to animals and people are highly indicative of pathological aggression.

8. *Disorders of activity.* Movement patterns deemed inappropriately slow (hypoactivity) or fast (hyperactivity) are common characteristics of severely disturbed children. Teachers of hyperactive children often describe incidents in which a child appears to be in two distinct places at one moment. Conversely, teachers of hypoactive children complain they can find nothing that will motivate these children to action.

9. *Communication disturbances.* Numerous communication difficulties arise in severely disturbed children. Problems range from the complete lack of speech (elective mutism) to minor impairments in articulation. In elective mutism the child can speak, as demonstrated in conversations with stuffed toys or animals, but refuses to speak to some or all people. Deviant language patterns are often exhibited by disturbed children in the form of neologistic phrase repetition (e.g., "Sin sa ma by new-sin sa ma by new; yab na na own she-yab na na own she"). Unusual voice, breathing, and pitch fluxuation frequently appear in the speech of severely disturbed children. Some children refrain from using the personal pronoun, referring to themselves in the third-person singular as "he" or "she."

10. *Functional physiological disorders.* Activities such as eating, sleeping, muscle control, urination, and defecation may be abnormal in severely disturbed children. When eating, they may do so too rapidly or stuff their cheeks until they resemble a chipmunk, carrying food around all day in this manner. They may have limited bowel or bladder control, may refuse to void or evacuate, or be overly interested in, and concerned with, their urine or feces.

11. *Social interaction disorders.* Some severely disturbed children rebuke human contact and rarely initiate it on their own. These children may scream, turn away from others, and fail to demonstrate any affective responses when approached. Other children may react inappropriately or inconsistently to social interactions (e.g., a child may cry when given a present or may laugh when hurt).

12. *Idea fixation.* This behavior often manifests itself in excessive concern with death, destruction, and macabre aspects of stories, pictures, and occurrences. Children who are idea-fixated will often see death, warfare, and evil in innocuous and even joyous events and situations. Also, this symptom may be expressed in the form of fixed ideas that, at least on the surface, are emotionally neutral or emotionally positive.

Two additional areas must be discussed when the symptomatology of emotional disorders is presented: onset and chronicity of disability. The time at which severe emotional disturbance begins in childhood is of interest to educators, psychologists, and the medical community, because it has a significant impact on educational programming and medical treatment plans. Although many of the symptoms of childhood schizophrenia appear similar to those of autism, childhood schizophrenia, unlike autism, is diagnosed only if behavioral symptoms surface after the age of 30 months and before the age of 12 years (American Psychiatric Association, 1980). Therefore, age of onset may be of medical interest. Educators and psychologists using behavioral approaches with severely emotionally disturbed children may also find information on onset age informative when constructing behavior modification programs. The longer behaviors have been established, the harder it may be to modify them.

Regarding chronicity, behavioral abnormalities in the severely disturbed child differ from those exhibited by his or her moderately and mildly emotionally disordered peers because they are chronically displayed and are often independent or unrelated to a particular environment or situation. Such abnormalities are long-term disorders that require extensive intervention. Clarizio and McCoy (1976) stated that 70% to 75% of children with severe emotional disorders carry these problems into adulthood. The more chronic an inappropriate behavioral display, the more difficult it may be to alter. Another consideration is that some children may on occasion react to situational cues in a manner that educators and parents consider severely deviant, but, because their responses are not chronic, total special education would not be deemed necessary.

PREVENTION AND TREATMENT PROGRAMS

Prevention

Prevention may be distinguished as primary (direct) or secondary prevention. *Primary prevention* refers to efforts to decrease the incidence of new cases of a particular disease or disability. It includes efforts to change actions and values relevant to behaviors and situations that foster unmanageable conditions. *Secondary prevention* refers to efforts to prevent diseases or disabilities that arise directly from an existing primary condition. It requires broad social actions, including the application of procedures designed to increase the acceptance of handicapped individuals by their normal peers and their institutions (Valletutti & Christoplos, 1979).

The prevention of severe emotional disturbance in children and adolescents continues to be primarily a medical concern. While ecological, behavioral, and sociological theorists focus on altering the environment for both prevention and treatment, organic theorists search for biophysical determinants of mental illness that may be altered through the application of scientific and medical treatment. Orthomolecular physicians, for example, believe that some emotional disorders can be prevented by supplying the brain with optimal amounts of nutrients, especially in the case of vitamin-dependent genetic disorders (Brenner, 1979).

Currently, genetic counseling and anticipatory guidance is the primary avenue for biological prevention of severe multiply handicapping disorders. However, research positively linking severe emotional disturbance and autism to genetic etiologies is limited, therefore making genetic counseling for the prevention of severe emotional disturbance a highly speculative procedure. Nevertheless, interest in the relationship between genetic factors and severe emotional disturbance remains high (Buschbaum, Coursey, & Murphy, 1976; Connaughton, 1979; Hunter, 1977; Kety, 1976; Winokur, Clayton, & Reich, 1969). For example, as mentioned earlier, researchers suggest that schizophrenia, in part, may be determined by heredity (Algozzine, 1981; Buss, 1966; Fish & Ritvo, 1977; Gottesman & Shields, 1976). A child whose fraternal twin has schizophrenia is 3 to 17 times more likely to show schizophrenic symptoms than a child without a familial history of the disorder (Buss, 1966). Disorders known to be specifically linked to genetic factors, such as sickle cell anemia, Down's syndrome, phenylketonuria (PKU), and Klinefelter's syndrome, have been implicated in causing behavioral disorders. PKU, for example, often has autism as part of its clinical picture (Knobloch & Pasamanick, 1975).

Couples with reason to suspect the presence of a genetically transmitted defect are often referred for genetic counseling. A genetic workup may include blood tests of the potential parents as well as collection of case histories. Questions asked by genetic counselors concern family origin, presence of disorders in the family, and the age of potential parents. From this information, a risk level for the possibility of an affected child being born with a condition that has severe emotional disturbance or autism as part of its features may then be calculated. Genetic counseling may provide valuable information to couples contemplating pregnancy. There are, however, many genetic disorders that cannot be detected prior to conception.

> Genetic counseling by its very nature, represents the very essence of primary disease prevention. It can and will play a vital role toward this goal, provided that it continues and further improves its efforts to communicate clearly, accurately, and with sympathy and that it continues to safeguard the public's right to privacy and the right for each family member to make individual decisions on the basis of all the information the science of genetics can provide (Moser, 1979, p. 162).

Connaughton (1979) points out that genetic factors molded by biological and psychosocial factors influence the developing infant from conception throughout his or her life. Rahe and Ransom (1978) have commented on the necessity of thinking in terms of the complex interaction of social, psychological, and physiological variables as they relate to the development of illness.

The prevention of emotional disturbance, therefore, must not be viewed as solely the province of organic theorists. Certainly, the development of strategies such as comprehensive child care programs can do much to support the family unit since the stable family is considered by many to be the most effective unit in which to promote the healthy development of children (Connaughton, 1979). The children of disorganized families fail to develop adequate cognitive skills and manifest serious behavioral difficulties suggesting that parental skill training may prove to be the most effective means of preventing severe emotional disturbance. Programs that attempt to rehabilitate parents who are physically abusive to their children may significantly decrease the number of children who are so psychologically damaged that they are unable to function in school and other social settings.

A related problem is the presence of psychiatric disorders in parents and their impact on the emotional development of their children. Psychiatric disturbances in parents are highly correlated with disturbed functioning in their offspring (Graham, 1978; Lewis & Shanok, 1978). Thus, the effective psychiatric treatment of parents with serious emotional difficulties and the close scrutiny of children being raised in households with markedly disturbed parents offer approaches that promise to contribute to the prevention of severe emotional disturbance in children and adolescents.

Treatment Programs and Services

Medical Intervention   An area commanding much attention in the study of severely emotionally disturbed children is psychoactive drug treatment. The relationships between specific drugs and the reduction of specific disturbing behaviors continue to be the focus of medical researchers as the data supporting such links are inconclusive. The primary focus of pharmacologic intervention in severe emotional disturbance and autism is to suppress the symptoms of the disorder rather than cure the problem.

Several groups of drugs have been employed for the purpose of altering behavior.

Stimulants   The use of stimulants has been studied mainly in terms of their effects on children diagnosed as emotionally disturbed and displaying extreme hyperkinetic behavior (Barkley, 1976; Bradley, 1937; Bradley & Bowen, 1941; Greenberg, Yellin, Spring, & Metcalf, 1975). Bradley (1937) noted significant decreases in mood swings and increases in productivity of school assignments when children deemed hyperactive were given stimulant drugs. In particular, performance in mathematics seemed greatly improved. Most children, though not all, displayed a decrease in extraneous motion and became calmer. These initial findings have been supported by subsequent research, which has found stimulant drugs to have positive effects on emotionally disturbed children displaying impulsive and uncontrolled behaviors (Conners & Werry, 1979). However, in a review of research efforts concerning stimulant drug treatment studies with autistic, mentally retarded, hyperactive, and normal children, Aman (1982) found that while hyperactive and normal children respond beneficially to stimulant medication, autistic and mentally retarded children do not.

Antipsychotics   Because of their tendency to slow intellectual functioning, antipsychotic drugs are usually not prescribed in cases of hyperactivity. The major tranquilizers have been employed, however, with greater success in children such as autistic and schizophrenic children whose behavioral attributes tend to be more bizarre and less reality-based than those of hyperkinetic children. Suppression of intellectual functioning is less of a drawback when used with psychotic children than with hyperactive ones because the severity of the handicap makes behavior change more of a priority consideration. Campbell (1975) suggested that treatment of psychotic children with tranquilizers is most successful in preschool children: "At a later age or stage of the illness, such a child may no longer be so responsive to drugs as he was in the first years of his life" (p. 249). Durand (1982) suggested that the use of antipsychotics (haloperidol) was most effective when combined with behavioral intervention.

Antidepressants Psychotic drugs falling into the category of antidepressants have been prescribed for a variety of childhood disorders. Children displaying depression, enuresis, conduct disorders, hyperkinesis, or school phobia have been targeted for the administration of antidepressants. The effectiveness of antidepressants is not clear at this time.

Sedative and Anxiolytics Sleep disorders and anxiety in children are often treated with sedative and anxiolytic drugs. Prescription of these drugs for such disorders is commonplace; however, little has been reported in the literature to support their usage with children affected by either disorder (Conners & Werry, 1979). Many drugs included in this classification have been tried in the treatment of hyperactivity. Initial reports suggest the use of sedatives and anxiolytics is nonproductive for the treatment of hyperactivity.

Megavitamin Therapy Rimland (1973) and Rimland et al. (1978) administered large dosages of vitamins to a group of psychotic children. Improvements were noted in the behaviors of many of the children, with the most impressive gains made by children with early infantile autism. The results, however, were not conclusive, suggesting that vitamin therapy is an area that demands continued research.

Major side effects or treatment emergent symptoms (TES) have been associated with the use of psychotropic drugs. These side effects may be even more harmful to the child than the conditions being treated. Weight loss, growth suppression, elevation in blood pressure, reduced intellectual functioning, and possible decrease in rapid-eye movement (REM) sleep are among the most frequently noted effects (Safer & Allen, 1975). When prescribing a particular drug for long-term use with a severely disturbed child, physicians must carefully weigh the drug's possible side effects against potential benefits.

The Behavioral Approach to Treatment[2]   The scientific roots of the behavioral approach and its continuing reliance on scientific validation of treatment procedures distinguish it from other approaches to treatment. Behavioral inter-

---

[2]This section on the behavioral approach to treatment was prepared by Gail S. Bernstein and Jon P. Ziarnik.

vention in a particular case resembles a small experiment in which the target is identified and a functional analysis is undertaken. The analysis is used to generate hypotheses about what is maintaining the present troublesome behavior and what might work to change it. Then, the hypothesis is tested and data are kept to determine whether the intervention confirms the hypothesis and therefore is effective. That is, treatment decisions are based on data collected by directly observing what the child does (Rimm & Masters, 1974).

Functional analysis is the heart of any behavioral therapy. A functional analysis looks for relationships between environmental events and behavior. That is, it seeks to determine what events regularly precede behavior, called antecedents, and what events regularly follow behavior, called consequences. This is not a causal analysis and does not consider how behaviors were learned in the past. Often the way in which a particular behavior was learned originally is not the same as the way in which the behavior is maintained in the present. Rather, it is a functional analysis in which the therapist seeks to answer the following questions:

1. What are the problem behaviors and what adaptive behaviors can replace them? It is assumed that there is no such thing as an absolute definition of psychological disorder or emotional disturbance. Instead, the assumption is that all deviance is relative and is defined according to standards set by the culture and specific environment in which the individual is behaving (Ross, 1974). Therefore, disturbing behaviors, emotional disturbances, or whatever child behavior problems are called can be redefined as either deficits in or excesses of behavior. When the child does not engage in as much of a certain behavior as is expected (this includes not engaging in the behavior at all), there is a deficit. Excessive behavior occurs when the child engages in more of a behavior than is expected under a given set of circumstances (Gardner, 1978). The goal of treatment thus becomes to change the child's behaviors, so that if there is a deficit, more of the desired behavior is produced, and/or if there is an excess, less of the undesirable behavior is produced.
2. Under what current conditions (i.e., who, what, where, when) do the maladaptive behaviors occur? Can these conditions be changed? The consequences of a child's maladaptive behaviors are of particular importance. The behavior therapist is interested in providing positive consequences for desirable behaviors and removing consequences that support undesirable behaviors.
3. Given the answers to questions 1 and 2, what changes in environmental conditions appear most likely to result in behavior change? Note that the answers to this question are different for each child and therefore treatment is individualized (Rimm & Masters, 1974). This is because behavior is a function of the environmental conditions under which it occurs, and those conditions are never exactly the same for two different individuals. Thus, each child's environment must be functionally analyzed in order to identify factors that may be maintaining undesirable behavior.

Some of the basic techniques of *behavioral intervention* utilized by behavior therapists are reviewed below. This is intended only as an overview to provide some familiarity with the terminology and to provide a rough idea of the terms' meaning. As with any approach, the effective use of behavior therapy requires intensive study and supervised experience.

Respondent Learning Based Interventions

1. *Systematic desensitization*—also called counterconditioning. This technique, pioneered by Joseph Wolpe (1958), is based on the assumption that stimuli that once were cues for irrational fears must be reconditioned. In this process an alternative, adaptive response such as relaxation is substituted for the anxious response. The individual is taught to relax in the face of increasingly intense stimuli that previously produced the anxious response. This may be done when possible in live situations or when more practical through guided imagery. For example, a child with a school phobia might be first taught to relax and then brought increasingly closer to his or her school.
2. *Flooding or implosion.* This technique suggests that if fears are irrational there is no really bad consequence for the feared events other than the person's anxiety. Therefore, fearful events that are even *worse* than the individual's irrational fears are repeatedly presented until the child learns no harm will come if he or she exercises normal caution.
3. *Aversive conditioning.* In this technique, a noxious or unpleasant stimulus is paired with a formerly pleasant stimulus in order to condition a fear response. A wide variety of behaviors such as smoking, overeating, and drinking have been treated with this method. Perhaps most familiar to readers is drinking in which the alcoholic is given drugs that, when alcohol is swallowed, produce vomiting. However, one must be alert to the serious risks of aversive conditioning such as discomfort, anger, or increased anxiety, which have caused most professionals to seriously question the utility of this procedure.

Interventions Based on Operant Learning   There are far more behavior change strategies based on the operant learning model than can be adequately covered in this section. As a result, a number of the more commonly used techniques are briefly defined here and examples for a selected few are provided. Common interventions are:

1. *Positive reinforcement*—the increase in the probability of desirable behavior by the contingent use of stimuli, things, or events the person likes
2. *Shaping*—reinforcement of successively closer approximations of a desired behavior
3. *Prompting*—providing guides (such as a demonstration or physical assistance) before the behavior occurs to help in learning
4. *Self-control*—teaching a person to guide his or her own behavior rather than it being controlled by a therapist or other external source

5. *Token economy*—the use of tokens (such as poker chips) as reinforcers for adaptive behavior which can be later exchanged for items desired by the child
6. *Extinction*—withholding or removing reinforcement following a previously reinforced excessive behavior
7. *Response cost*—withdrawing a specified amount of reinforcers contingent upon the occurrence of an excessive behavior
8. *Timeout*—removing the opportunity to earn reinforcement for a specified amount of time following the occurrence of the excessive behavior
9. *Reinforcement of alternative behavior*—reinforcing an alternative, adaptive behavior that is incompatible with the undesirable behavior

(Bernstein et al., 1981)

Examples

1. *Reinforcement of alternative behaviors.* This procedure is positive and quite effective in both reducing the occurrence of undesirable behavior and in teaching the child what is desirable. The first step is to pick a behavior that is incompatible with the undesirable response. For example, sitting and working are incompatible with running around; talking softly is incompatible with screaming; and following instructions is incompatible with tantrumming. Next, it is important to reinforce the person for the desired behavior. Basarich, Ferrara, and Rudrud (1980) utilized this procedure with severely emotionally disturbed adolescents in a classroom to increase on-task behavior, which is incompatible with not working.
2. *Extinction*. Extinction has been used effectively with a variety of behaviors including aggression (Scott, Burton, & Yarrow, 1967), tantrums (Carlson, Arnold, Becker, & Madsen, 1968), and disruptive classroom behavior (O' Leary & Becker, 1967). However, in order for this procedure to be maximally effective it should be used in conjunction with positive reinforcement for desirable behavior. In order to use extinction effectively one must be able to first identify and then control the reinforcer(s) maintaining the undesirable behavior.

Ignoring is one of the most frequently used forms of extinction. Pinkston, Reese, LeBlanc, and Baer (1974) showed that teacher attention maintained a preschool child's aggression toward his peers. The child's aggressive behavior was reduced when the teacher was instructed to ignore the child and attend to the peer or peers who were the target of the aggressive behavior. Teachers often assume that their commands to behave appropriately are punishing rather than reinforcing. Madsen, Becker, and Thomas (1968) investigated the effects of "sit down" commands on out-of-seat behavior. The more the teacher told out-of-seat students to sit down, the more often out-of-seat behavior occurred. Ignoring out-of-seat behavior resulted in its decrease. Thus, ignoring inappropriate behavior while showing approval for desired behavior was an effective method for controlling classroom behavior.

3. *Self-management.* Every child who becomes an independent adult learns to manage his or her own behavior. Self-management is a particularly important skill to teach children with problems in emotional control. Otherwise, successful treatment remains effective only when the child is in the treatment setting. Self-management can be used in any setting and thus increases independence.

Goodwin and Mahoney (1975) reported on the teaching of hyperactive, impulsive 6- to 11-year-old boys to manage verbal aggression from peers. The boys were exposed to models using coping self-instructions such as "I won't get mad" and "I'm not going to let them bug me." The models' behaviors were discussed by the teacher, with emphasis on coping behaviors. Another use of self-management has been reported by Meichenbaum and Goodman (1971), who used it to teach impulsive children to use planned approaches to problem solving.

There are a number of excellent books available that can give interested readers a more in-depth view of behavior therapy, including Beth Sulzer-Azaroff and Roy Mayer, *Applying Behavior Procedures with Children and Youth* (1977), William Gardner, *Learning and Behavior Characteristics of Exceptional Children and Youth* (1977), and Gerald Patterson, *Living with Children* (1980).

Psychodynamic Treatment *Milieu therapy* and *life-space interview* are two treatment approaches popularized by Redl (1959a,b). Milieu therapy is most often used in inpatient programs and involves manipulating the total environment in a manner that eliminates most possibilities for expressing deviant behaviors. All staff, not just educators and therapists, must be trained in order for milieu therapy to achieve optimal success. The life-space interview approach is often used in the environment created by milieu therapy. Because the life-space interview involves verbal reconstruction of a behavioral crisis, use of this approach is limited to only some severely disturbed children. The interview has two major components, emotional first aid and clinical exploitation of life events. Following a behavioral crisis, the child is either calmed by the teacher, who then quickly works through the events of the crisis, or time is spent in slowly reconstructing the situation in order to determine precipitating events, to discuss the child's feelings, and to discover coping techniques.

Several other forms of psychodynamic therapy, *play, art, music,* and *dance therapies,* have been used as treatment modes for severely disturbed children (Gantt, 1979; Landreth, 1982), with both nonverbal and verbal youngsters responding positively to these approaches. Play therapy, a form of psychotherapy, was introduced by Virginia Axline in 1947. It is conducted in a clinical setting in which the child is permitted to progress at his or her own pace by interacting with various toys provided to him or her. The therapist creates a safe atmosphere in which the child can express himself or herself. Aggressive use of the props (toys) is not denied or limited by the therapist. As a warm relationship between child and therapist develops, the child may begin to express fears, doubts, and other feelings through play and in speech. Eventually, the child may allow the therapist to help identify solutions to problems that the child has been unwilling or unable to share.

Dance and art therapy provide the child with creative outlets to vent emotions inappropriate elsewhere. In addition, the child's use of the medium, (e.g., movement, paint, or clay) helps the therapist make clinical judgments about the nature of the child's problem (Kramer, 1979). Many children, having expressed negative aspects of personality through dance or art, find little need to do so in daily interactions, thus reducing the number of aberrant behaviors displayed.

The aim in music therapy is twofold. For the verbal child, music is provided as a background for guided fantasy that later becomes the topic of conversation between the therapist and the child. For the nonverbal child, music can be used to stimulate the hypoactive child or to calm the hyperactive child and may be used as a means of self-expression for an otherwise nonverbal youngster.

EDUCATIONAL PROGRAMS AND SERVICES

Severely emotionally disturbed children and adolescents have frequently had their instructional needs met outside of the realm of the public school system. Owing to the determination and energies of parents, educators, and mental health workers, several outstanding facilities have emerged within the past 30 years. Some of these facilities' programs are structured along the lines of a particular etiological philosophy of emotional disorders, while others are eclectic in educational approach. A review of nine facilities (each offering a different approach) is presented in this section. These are certainly not the only noteworthy programs, but are merely a sample of the better-known facilities.

Linwood Children's Center Located in Ellicott City, Maryland, the Linwood Children's Center was founded in 1955 to serve psychotic children unable to receive education in more traditional programs. Linwood offers both day treatment and residential care, depending on the status of the child and the judgments of the staff and family. Residential placement is flexible and is usually recommended when a child has been referred to Linwood for crisis intervention. Programming for psychotic children is based on meeting individual needs. Most instruction occurs in one-to-one interactions within a group rather than in a separate, isolated room. Techniques of instruction and the experiences structured for the child are concrete, using the child's natural tendency to think in a concrete versus an abstract manner. Employees do not review children's records prior to admission, as a means to ensuring unbiased interaction with the child. The staff receives training in the application of instructional techniques aimed at the characteristically compulsive behavior of these children. Speech and language, at least during the initial stages of placement at Linwood, are not a target of remediation. The center's philosophy is that speech and language development in nonverbal psychotic children will occur once a child has developed a basic trust in other human beings. Therefore, communication is seen as a behavior that develops within the context of interaction with others (Kanner, 1973).

The Rutland Center Central to the development therapy program at the Rutland Center in Athens, Georgia, is the conviction that autistic children need exposure to normal models. To provide this interaction, the children are involved daily in both specialized programming and classes serving nonautistic children. The curricular goals of the development therapy program are to improve the child's communicative, behavioral, social, and preacademic functioning. Each of these curriculum areas has been divided into five stages that move the child from acquisition of skills in the initial stage to generalization of skills in the final stage. The development therapy program is highly individualized, as are the majority of educational programs for autistic children (Paluszny, 1979).

The Judevine Center The approach at the Judevine Center is a highly structured, behavioral one. Judevine, located in St. Louis, requires extensive parental participation. Parent-child and parent-teacher interactions are carefully analyzed, with attention directed to the behavioral outcomes of these interactions. Behavior modification programs are then developed to modify interactions that do not produce desirable results. The child, in the meantime, undergoes a 4-week series of instructional sessions varying in duration from a few minutes at the beginning of instruction to up to 5 hours toward the end. Three program areas—physical manipulation, social relationships, and intellectual development—are emphasized. The Judevine program is built on five progressively more demanding levels of treatment. At level one, treatment is often initiated on a one-to-one basis for compliance training. By the time the child reaches the last level of instruction, the child is expected to interact in a group situation with other children on his or her level. During the 4-week period, parents receive training in educational and behavioral techniques for use in the home environment with their children (Paluszny, 1979).

The Neuropsychiatric Institute (NPI) The Department of Psychiatry, University of California at Los Angeles, operates the NPI for children diagnosed as seriously emotionally disturbed. The school program is based on behavior theory and utilizes an operant conditioning approach to remediation. Baseline data is carefully recorded and subsequent improvements mapped in the areas of behavior, academic skills, and language. School days typically consist of three, 1-hour sessions. Directed play comprises half of each session and specific instruction the other half. Children are assigned primary teachers who accompany them through the entire program sequence from initial evaluation to discharge. Both the NPI curriculum and language program are based on a developmental sequence of skills. For example, the child progresses developmentally through the sequential milestones attained by normal children (i.e., training in receptive language precedes training in the expressive use of language). The institute takes the position that "creative communicative language cannot be taught" (Richey,

1976, p. 206). Although reinforcers are used to modify behaviors, primary reinforcers are used only as a last resort. Physical punishment procedures are not employed at NPI (Graham, 1976).

The Language Development Program The Language Development Program, located in the Los Angeles area, focuses on the acquisition of language skills through the application of operant conditioning principles. The program's developers contend that language is produced when a listener hears certain cues or stimuli that alert him or her to an expected response. These stimuli may be either internal or external in origin, and, according to Lovaas (1977), are not perceived by the autistic child. It is the autistic child's inability to detect cues for verbal interaction that interferes with his or her language performance. Through the systematic application of behavior therapy, in particular positive reinforcement and adversive stimuli presentation, autistic children are taught language. A series of eight language programs are presented sequentially to the child. The eight levels are: 1) *building vocal responses*—often echolalic and without intentional meaning; 2) *labeling* common objects and persons in the environment; 3) *acquiring* a vocabulary of words that describe *relationships,* such as ''on'' and ''under; 4) stimulating simple *conversations*—the child asks and responds to basic questions; 5) encouraging the acquisition of *information*—the child uses language to gain information; 6) facilitating *grammatical rules*—the child learns grammatical rules of sentence structure; 7) enhancing *recall*—the child shares experiences from the past through language, and 8) motivating *spontaneous production*—the child initiates conversation (Paluszny, 1979).

Treatment and Education of Autistic and Related Communications Handicapped Children Program (TEACCH) The TEACCH program was implemented in North Carolina in 1972 when, by legislative action, centers to serve autistic children were established across the state. TEACCH is a parent-centered program that regards parents as the primary contacts in the autistic child's life. Autism is seen as a biogenic disorder, not one caused by cold, ungiving parents. After initial assessments are made, autistic children are placed in TEACCH classrooms located in public-school settings. Although the classroom functions as a self-contained unit for the autistic children, other communicatively disordered children in the school receive resource help in the room. Parents are considered cotherapists and are trained by the TEACCH staff. The TEACCH staff is comprised of persons who are hired not simply on the basis of educational background or training but because of their sensitivity and interest in helping autistic children and their parents (Morgan, 1981). All staff receive inservice training in TEACCH methods and in techniques of being parent trainers. The aim of this program is to maintain autistic children in their own homes with parents who are comfortable with and capable of participating directly in their child's education (Morgan, 1981; Paluszny, 1979).

The Children's Guild, Inc. The Children's Guild located in Baltimore, Maryland, is a preschool and primary program for emotionally disturbed and/or learning disabled children that offers a multidisciplinary range of mental health services to children and their families, and day programs for children from 3 years of age to the second grade. The program is an eclectic one in which behavioral management techniques are employed, where ecological approaches are emphasized through parental and family counseling and education, and where psychoeducational insights are encouraged through the interpretation of behavior. The psychodynamic emphasis is evident in the school's self-description as a therapeutic-educational facility and in its characterization of its instructional staff as therapeutic teachers (Lewis, 1979; M. Lewis, personal communication, July 3, 1983).

Benhaven School The Benhaven School Community for Autistic and Neurologically Impaired Individuals is located in New Haven, Connecticut. Benhaven's curriculum is based on a behavioral approach to teaching and combines prevocational and vocational training with behavior management. A priority consideration at Benhaven is the elimination of those behaviors that interfere with the performance of activities important to the learning process. The format and design of the curriculum are also behavioral. Each unit of the curriculum identifies a work activity expressed in functional, task-centered terms, as well as the activity's related language, reading, number, and fine motor skills. Each work activity is task analyzed into relatively small steps and emphasis is placed on the teacher's need to evaluate the level at which instruction should begin (Simonson, 1979).

The League School The League School for the Seriously Disturbed in Brooklyn, New York, was established as a psychoeducationally oriented day-school alternative to institutional schools for schizophrenic, autistic, psychotic, and prepsychotic children. The basic conceptual framework emphasized that special educational techniques in a therapeutic setting can affect behavioral change without individual psychotherapy. At the beginning of the program, it was felt that teachers should play an unstructured role that permitted children to freely ventilate feelings and primitive drives. Experience, however, soon changed this orientation, and it was recognized that disturbed, disorganized children needed a highly organized program of education and training with exceptions made for fearful, inhibited, and submissive children.

> It has taken a long time for many child therapists and authorities in the field of early childhood education to discover that a child can derive pleasure not only by satisfying the primitive impulses of the id but by developing an ego that can control these impulses and that can function autonomously and effectively within the realm of reality. It is becoming quite evident that most disturbed children not only find satisfaction by assuming responsibilities, following directions, completing difficult tasks, and mastering new skills—but they grow and thrive in the process (Fenichel, 1971, p. 344).

SUMMARY

Various definitions have been offered in an attempt to clarify the nature and needs of severely and profoundly emotionally disturbed and autistic children. These definitions are presented from psychiatric, educational, and legal perspectives, while the position is taken that autism is a severe/profound developmental disability in accordance with revised PL 94-142 definitions that reflect the opinion of the National Society for Children and Adults with Autism. Severe and profound emotional disturbance was distinguished from milder forms of serious emotional disturbance by its behavioral impact on the education of individual students rather than limiting it to the psychiatrically oriented label of *psychotic* or *prepsychotic*. Incidence figures also were presented, with the disproportionately high male to female ratio for all categories of severe/profound emotional disturbance stressed. Attention was then directed toward the screening and identification of this population of students with particular emphasis on the role of early identification because severe pathology is usually obvious to most lay as well as professional observers. A discussion of observation techniques and teacher and pupil rating scales preceded a clarification of the prescriptive requirements of the diagnostic process with the characteristics of autism and childhood schizophrenia briefly reviewed. Etiologic speculations were examined from the five principal theories of causation: psychodynamic/psychoeducational, organic, behavioral, ecological, and sociological. Diverse classification systems, including the DSM-III, psychodynamic, behavioral, and sociological were presented, as were major behavioral symptoms that characterize this population of students, regardless of classification or label. Finally, prevention and treatment programs and services were examined and educational program models were provided.

REFERENCES

Algozzine, R. Biophysical perspective of emotional disturbance. In: R. Algozzine, R. Schmid, & C. Mercer (eds.), *Childhood behavior disorders: Applied research and educational practice*. Rockville, MD: Aspen Publications, 1981.

Algozzine, B., Mercer, C., & Countermine, T. The effects of labeling handicapped children. *Exceptional Children*, 1977, 44, 131–132.

Aman, M. Stimulant drug effects in developmental disorders and hyperactivity—toward a resolution of disparate findings. *Journal of Autism and Developmental Disorders*, 1982, 12, 385–398.

American Academy of Pediatrics, Committee on Nutrition. Megavitamin therapy for childhood psychosis and learning disabilities. *Pediatrics*, 1976, 58, 910–911.

American Psychiatric Association. *Diagnostic and statistical manual of mental disorders: DSM-III* (3rd ed.). Washington, DC: American Psychiatric Association, 1980.

Anastasiow, N. Socioemotional development. The state of the art. In: N. Anastasiow (ed.), *Socioemotional development*. San Francisco: Jossey-Bass, 1981.

Anders, T., & Freeman, E. Enuresis. In: J. Noshpitz (ed.), *Basic handbook of child psychiatry. Vol. II: Disturbances of development*. New York: Basic Books, 1979.

Armstrong, J. Taxonomies in special education. In: L. Mann & D. Sabatino (eds.), *The third review of special education*. New York: Grune & Stratton, 1976.

Axline, V. *Play therapy*. Boston: Houghton Mifflin Co., 1947.

Bandura, A. *Social learning theory*. Englewood Cliffs, NJ: Prentice-Hall, 1977.

Bandura, A. The self system in reciprocal determination. *American Psychologist*, 1978, 33, 344–358.

Barker, W., Sandler, L., Borneman, A., Knight, G., Humphrys, F., & Risan, S. *The Psychiatric Behavior Scale*. Philadelphia: The Franklin Institute Research Laboratories, 1973.

Barkley, R. Predicting the response of hyperkinetic children to stimulant drugs: A review. *Journal of Abnormal Child Psychology*, 1976, *4*, 327–348.

Basarich, T., Ferrara, J., & Rudrud, E. *Validation of the PSMP with severely emotionally disturbed adolescents*. Unpublished manuscript, University of South Dakota, Vermillon, 1980.

Bayley, N. *Bayley Scales of Infant Development: Birth to two years*. New York: The Psychological Corporation, 1969.

Bender, L. Childhood schizophrenia, clinical study of one hundred schizophrenic children. *American Journal of Orthopsychiatry*, 1947, *17*, 40–56.

Bernstein, G.S., Ziarnik, J.P., Rudrud, E.H., & Czajkowski, L.A. *Behavioral habilitation through proactive programming*. Baltimore: Paul H. Brookes Publishing Co., 1981.

Blake, K.A. *Educating exceptional pupils*. Reading, MA: Addison-Wesley Publishing Co., 1981

Bower, E.M. *A class play*. Princeton: Educational Testing Service, 1961. (a)

Bower, E.M. *The class picture*. Princeton: Educational Testing Service, 1961. (b)

Bower, E. *Early identification of emotionally handicapped children in school* (2nd ed.). Springfield, IL: Charles C Thomas, 1974.

Bradley, C. The behavior of children receiving benzedrine. *American Journal of Psychiatry*, 1937, *94*, 577–585.

Bradley, C., & Bowen, M. Amphetamine (benzedrine) therapy of children's behavior disorders. *American Journal of Orthopsychiatry*, 1941, *11*, 92–103.

Brenner, A. A study of the efficacy of the Feingold diet on hyperactive children: Some favorable personal observations. *Clinical Pediatrics*, 1977, *16*, 652–656.

Brenner, A. Nutrition. In: P. Valletutti & F. Christoplos (eds.), *Preventing physical and mental disabilities: Multidisciplinary approaches*. Baltimore: University Park Press, 1979.

Bricker, W., & Campbell, P. Interdisciplinary assessment and programming for multihandicapped students. In: W. Sailor, B. Wilcox, & L. Brown (eds.), *Methods of instruction for severely handicapped students*. Baltimore: Paul H. Brookes Publishing Co., 1980.

Bronfenbrenner, U. *The eulogy of human development: Experiments by nature and design*. Cambridge, MA: Harvard University Press, 1979.

Buschbaum, M.S., Coursey, R.D., & Murphy, D.L. The biochemical high risk paradigm. Behavioral and familial correlates of low allet monomine oxidase activity. *Science*, 1976, *194*, 330–341.

Buss, A. *Psychopathology*. New York: John Wiley & Sons, 1966.

Campbell, M. Psychopharmacology in childhood psychosis. In: R. Gittelman-Klein (ed.), *Recent advances in child psychopharmacology*. New York: Human Sciences Press, 1975.

Carlson, C.S., Arnold, C.R., Becker, W.C., & Madsen, G.H. The elimination of tantrum behavior in a child in an elementary classroom. *Behavior Research and Therapy*, 1968, *6*, 117–120.

Clarizio, H., & McCoy, G. *Behavior disorders in children* (2nd ed.). New York: Thomas Y. Crowell Co., 1976.

Clark, T. Workshop presented at the Annual SKI-HI Outreach Summer Training Institute. Utah State University, Logan, July, 1980.

Connaughton, J.P. Psychiatry. In: P.J. Valletutti & F. Christoplos (eds.), *Preventing physical and mental disabilities: Multidisciplinary approaches*. Baltimore: University Park Press, 1979.

Conners, C., & Werry, J. Pharmacotherapy. In: H. Quay & J. Werry (eds.), *Psychopathological disorders in children* (2nd ed.). New York: John Wiley & Sons, 1979.

Cooke, T.P., & Apolloni, T. Developing positive emotional behaviors: A study in training and generalization effects. *Journal of Applied Behavior Analysis*, 1976, *9*, 65–78.

Cott, A. Orthomolecular approach to the treatment of learning disabilities. *Schizophrenia*, 1971, *3*, 95–107.

Cross, L., & Johnson, S. The bibliography. In: L. Cross & K. Goin (eds.), *Identifying handicapped children: A guide to casefinding, screening, diagnosis, assessment and evaluation*. New York: Walker and Co., 1977.

Cullinan, D., & Epstein, M. Administrative definitions of behavior disorders: Status and directions. In: F. Wood & K. Lakin (eds.), *Disturbing, disordered or disturbed?* Reston, VA: The Council for Exceptional Children, 1982.

Darley, J., Glucksburg, S., Kamm, L., & Kinchla, R. *Psychology*. Englewood Cliffs, NJ: Prentice-Hall, 1981.

Davis, W.E. A comparison of teacher referral and pupil self-referral measures relative to perceived school adjustment. *Psychology in the Schools*, 1978, *15*, 22–26.

Des Jarlais, D., & Paul, J. Labeling theory: Sociological views and approaches. In: W. Rhodes & J. Paul (eds.), *Emotionally disturbed and deviant children: New views and approaches*. Englewood Cliffs, NJ: Prentice-Hall, 1978.

Doll, E. *Vineland Social Maturity Scale*. Circle Pines, MN: American Guidance Service, 1965.

Doll, E. *Preschool Attainment Record*. Circle Pines, MN: American Guidance Service, 1966.

Durand, V. A behavioral/pharmacological intervention for the treatment of severe self-injurious behavior. *Journal of Autism and Developmental Disorders*, 1982, *12*, 243–251.

Epanchin, B. Screening, identification and diagnosis. In: J. Paul & B. Epanchin (eds.), *Emotional disturbance in children*. Columbus, OH: Charles E. Merrill Publishing Co., 1982.

Epstein, M., Cullinan, D., & Sabatino, D. State definitions of behavior disorders. *Journal of Special Education*, 1977, *11*, 417–425.

Erickson, M.T. *Child psychopathology: Assessment, etiology and treatment*. Englewood Cliffs, NJ: Prentice-Hall, 1978.

Eysenck, H.J. Learning theory and behavior therapy. *Journal of Mental Science*, 1959, *105*, 61–67.

Fallen, N.H., & McGovern, J.E. *Young children with special needs*. Columbus, OH: Charles E. Merrill Publishing Co., 1978.

Federal Register. Assistance to states for education of handicapped children. Washington, DC: *Federal Register (46)* 3865, January 16, 1981.

Federal Register. Education of handicapped children. Washington, DC: *Federal Register (42)*, 42474–42518, August 23, 1977.

Feingold, B. *Why your child is hyperactive*. New York: Random House, 1975.

Fenichel, C. Psycho-educational approaches for seriously disturbed children in the classroom. In: N.J. Long, W.C. Morse, & R.G. Newman (eds.), *Conflict in the classroom: The education of children with problems* (2nd ed.). Belmont, CA: Wadsworth, 1971.

Fine, M. *Intervention with hyperactive children: A case study approach*. Jamaica, NY: Spectrum Press Medical and Scientific Books, 1980.

Fine, R. Psychoanalysis. In: R. Corsini (ed.), *Current psychotherapies*. Itasca, IL: F. E. Peacock Publishers, 1973.

Fish, B., & Ritvo, E. Psychoses of childhood. In: J. Noshpitz (ed.), *Basic handbook of child psychiatry. Vol. II: Disturbances of development*. New York: Basic Books, 1977.

Fisher, S. Encopresis. In: J. Noshpitz (ed.), *Basic handbook of child psychiatry. Vol. II: Disturbances of development*. New York: Basic Books, 1979.

Flaharty, R. EPEC: Evaluation and Prescription for Exceptional Children. In: E. Ritvo, B. Freeman, E. Ornitz, & P. Tanguay (eds.), *Autism: Diagnosis, current research and management.* New York: Spectrum Publications, 1976.

Freeman, M. Reliability study of psychiatric diagnosis in childhood and adolescence. *The Journal of Childhood Psychology and Psychiatry and Allied Disciplines,* 1971, *12,* 43–54.

Freeman, B., & Ritvo, E. The syndrome of autism. A critical review of diagnostic systems, follow-up studies, and the theoretical background of the Behavior Observation Scale. In: J. Gilliam (ed.), *Autism: Diagnosis, instruction, management and research.* Springfield, IL: Charles C Thomas, 1981.

Gantt, L. Art therapy. In: P. Valletutti & F. Christoplos (eds.), *Preventing physical and mental disabilities: Multidisciplinary approaches.* Baltimore: University Park Press, 1979.

Gardner, W.I. *Learning and behavior characteristics of exceptional children and youth.* Boston: Allyn and Bacon, 1977.

Gardner, W.I. *Children with learning and behavior problems.* Boston: Allyn and Bacon, 1978.

Gearheart, B. *Special education for the 80's.* St. Louis: C. V. Mosby Co., 1980.

Gesell, A., & Amatruda, C. *Developmental diagnosis: Normal and abnormal child development.* New York: Hoeber, 1941.

Gleitman, H. *Psychology.* New York: W. W. Norton & Co. 1981.

Goodwin, S.E., & Mahoney, M.J. Modification of aggression through modeling: An experimental probe. *Journal of Behavior Therapy and Experimental Psychiatry,* 1975, *6,* 200–202.

Gottesman, I., & Shields, J. A critical review of recent adoption twin and family studies of schizophrenia: Behavioral genetic perspectives. *Schizophrenia Bulletin,* 1976, *2,* 360–401.

Graham, P.J. Epidemiological perspectives in maladaption in children. Neurological, familial, and social factors. *Journal of Child Psychology,* 1978, *17,* 196–207.

Graham, V. Educational approaches at the N.P.I. School: The general program. In: E. Ritvo, B. Freeman, E. Ornitz, & P. Tanguay (eds.), *Autism: Diagnosis, current research and management.* New York: Spectrum Publications, 1976.

Greenberg, L., Yellin, A., Spring, C., & Metcalf, M. Clinical effects of imipramine and methlphenidate in hyperactive children. In: R. Gittelman-Klein (ed.), *Recent advances in child psychopharmacology.* New York: Human Sciences Press, 1975.

Grosenick, S., & Huntze, J. *National needs analysis in behavioral disorders: Human issues in behavior disorders.* Columbia, OH: Department of Special Education, University of Missouri-Columbia, 1979.

Group for the Advancement of Psychiatry. *Psychopathological disorders in childhood: Theoretical considerations and a proposed classification.* New York: Group for the Advancement of Psychiatry, 1969.

Hall, R. *Managing behavior* (3 vols). Lawrence, KS: H & H Enterprises, Inc. 1971.

Hallahan, D.P., & Kauffman, J.M. *Exceptional children* (2nd ed.). Englewood Cliffs, NJ: Prentice-Hall, 1982.

Hammill, D.D., & Bartel, N.R. *Teaching children with learning and behavior problems.* Boston: Allyn and Bacon, 1978.

Haring, N., Hayden, A., & Beck, R. General principles and guidelines in programming for severely handicapped children and young adults. *Focus on Exceptional Children,* 1976, *8,* 1–14.

Haring, N., & Phillips, J. *Educating emotionally disturbed children.* New York: McGraw-Hill Book Co., 1962.

Hewett, F. *The emotionally disturbed child in the classroom: A developmental strategy for educating children with maladaptive behavior.* Boston: Allyn and Bacon, 1968.

Hewett, F.M., & Taylor, F.D. *The emotionally disturbed child in the classroom. The orchestration of success*. Boston: Allyn and Bacon, 1980.

Hington, J., & Bryson, C. Recent developments in the study of early childhood psychoses: Infantile autism, childhood schizophrenia, and related disorders. *Schizophrenia Bulletin*, 1972, 5, 8–54.

Hunter, H. XXY males: Some clinical and psychiatric aspects deriving from a survey of 1,811 males in hospitals for the mentally handicapped. *British Journal of Psychiatry*, 1977, *131*, 468–477.

Joint Commission on Mental Health of Children. *Crisis in mental health: Challenge for the 1970's*. New York: Harper & Row, 1969.

Kanfer, F.H., & Phillips, J.S. *Learning foundations of behavior therapy*. New York: John Wiley & Sons, 1970.

Kanner, L. Autistic disturbance of affective contact. *Nervous Child*, 1943, *2*, 217–250.

Kanner, L. *Child psychiatry*. Springfield, IL: Charles C Thomas, 1948.

Kanner, L. Emotionally disturbed children: A historical review. *Child Development*, 1962, *33*, 97–102.

Kanner, L. Early infantile autism revisited. In: L. Kanner (ed.), *Childhood psychosis: Initial studies and new insights*. Washington, DC: V. H. Winston and Sons, 1973.

Kauffman, J. Severely emotionally disturbed. In: N. Haring (ed.), *Behavior of exceptional children: An introduction to special education*. Columbus, OH: Charles E. Merrill Publishing Co., 1974.

Kauffman, J. *Characteristics of children's behavior disorders*. Columbus, OH: Charles E. Merrill Publishing Co., 1977.

Kauffman, J. *Characteristics of children's behavior disorders* (2nd ed.). Columbus, OH: Charles E. Merrill Publishing Co., 1981.

Kauffman, J. A historical perspective on disordered behavior and an alternative conceptualization of exceptionality. In: F. Wood & K. Lakin (eds.), *Disturbing, disordered or disturbed?* Reston, VA: The Council for Exceptional Children, 1982.

Kauffman, J.M., & Kneedler, R.D. Behavior disorders. In: J.M. Kauffman & D.P. Hallahan (eds.), *Handbook of special education*. Englewood Cliffs, NJ: Prentice-Hall, 1981.

Kazdin, A.E. *Behavior modification in applied settings*. Homewood, IL: Dorsey, 1975.

Kelley, T., Bullock, L., & Dykes, M. Behavioral disorders: Teacher's perceptions. *Exceptional Children*, 1977, *43*, 316–318.

Kety, S.S. Genetic aspects of schizophrenia. *Psychiatry Annal*, 1976, *6*, 15–32.

Kirk, S. *Educating exceptional children*. Boston: Houghton-Mifflin Co., 1972.

Knobloch, H., & Pasamanick, B. Some etiologic and prognostic factors in early infantile autism and psychosis. *Pediatrics*, 1975, *55*, 182–191.

Knoblock, P. *Teaching emotionally disturbed children*. Boston: Houghton-Mifflin Co., 1983.

Koegel, R., Egel, A., & Dunlap, G. Learning characteristics of autistic children. In: W. Sailor, B. Wilcox, & L. Brown (eds.), *Methods of instruction for severely handicapped students*. Baltimore: Paul H. Brookes Publishing Co., 1980.

Kramer, E. *Childhood and art therapy: Notes on theory and application*. New York: Schocken Books, 1979.

Krug, D., Arick, J., & Almond, P. The autism screening instrument for educational programming: Background and development. In: J. Gilliam (ed.), *Autism: Diagnosis, instruction, management and research*. Springfield, IL: Charles C Thomas, 1981.

Krug, D., Rosenblum, J., Almond, P., & Arick, J. *Autistic and severely handicapped in the classroom: Assessment, behavior, management, and communication training*. Portland, OR: ASIEP Education Co., 1981.

Lambert, N. *The development and validation of a process for screening emotionally handicapped children in school.* Sacramento: California State Department of Education, 1963.

Lambert, N., & Bower, E. *A process for in-school screening of children with emotional handicaps: Manual for school administrators and teachers.* Sacramento: California State Department of Education, 1961.

Landreth, G. *Play therapy: Dynamics of the process of counseling with children.* Springfield, IL: Charles C Thomas, 1982.

Lelord, G., Muh, J., Barthelemy, C., Martineau, J., Garreau, B., & Callaway, E. Effects of pyridoxine and magnesium on autistic symptoms. Initial observations. *Journal of Autism and Developmental Disorders,* 1981, *11,* 219–230.

Lewis, D.O., & Shanok, S.S. Delinquency and the schizophrenic spectrum of disorders. *Journal of Child Psychiatry,* 1978, *17,* 263–277.

Lewis, M. Psychology. In: P.J. Valletutti & F. Christoplos (eds.), *Preventing physical and mental disabilities: Multidisciplinary approaches.* Baltimore: University Park Press, 1979.

Lotter, V. Epidemiology of autistic conditions in young children. I-Prevalence. *Social Psychiatry,* 1966, *1,* 124–137.

Lovaas, O. *The autistic child. Language development through behavior modification.* Irvington, NY: Irvington Publishers, 1977.

Lucas, A. Tics. In: J. Noshpitz (ed.), *Basic handbook of child psychiatry. Vol II: Disturbances of development.* New York: Basic Books, 1979.

Lyons, D., & Powers, V. Study of children exempted from Los Angeles Schools. *Exceptional Schools,* 1963, *30,* 155–162.

Madsen, C.H., Becker, W.C., & Thomas, D.R. Rules, praise, and ignoring: Elements of elementary classroom control. *Journal of Applied Behavior Analysis,* 1968, *1*(2), 139–150.

McDowell, R., Adamson, G., & Wood, F. *Teaching emotionally disturbed children.* Boston: Little, Brown, & Co., 1982.

Mahler, M.S. On child psychosis and schizophrenia, autistic and symbiotic infantile psychosis. *Psychoanalytic Study of the Child,* 1952, *7,* 286–305.

Mahrer, A. *Experiencing: A humanistic theory of psychology and psychiatry.* New York: Brunner/Mazel, 1978.

Meichenbaum, D., & Goodman, J. Training impulsive children to talk to themselves: A means of developing self-control. *Journal of Abnormal Psychology,* 1971, *77,* 115–125.

Mercer, C., & Mercer, A. *Teaching students with learning problems.* Columbus, OH: Charles E. Merrill Publishing Co., 1981.

Millican, F., Dublin, C., & Lourie, R. Pica. In: J. Noshpitz (ed.). *Basic handbook of child psychiatry. Vol. II: Disturbances of development.* New York: Basic Books, 1979.

Mississippi State Department of Education. *Referral to placement process.* Jackson, MS: Mississippi State Department of Education, July 1982.

Moore, S., & Updegraff, R. Minnesota Sociometric Status Test. In: P.D. Guthrie (ed.), *Headstart test collection report measures of social skills.* Princeton: Educational Testing Service, 1971.

Morgan, S. *The unreachable child: An introduction to early childhood autism.* Memphis, TN: Memphis State University Press, 1981.

Morse, W., The education of socially maladjusted and emotionally disturbed children. In: W. Cruickshank & G. Johnson (eds.), *Education of exceptional children and youth* (3rd ed.). Englewood Cliffs, NJ: Prentice-Hall, 1975.

Morse, W., & Coopchik, H. Socioemotional impairment. In: W. Morse (ed.), *Humanistic teaching for exceptional children: An introduction to special education.* Syracuse, NY: Syracuse University Press, 1979.

Mosak, H., & Dreikurs, R. Adlerian psychotherapy. In: R. Corsini (ed.), *Current psychotherapies*. Itasca, IL: F. E. Peacock Publishers, 1973.

Moser, H.W. Genetic counseling. In: P.J. Valletutti & F. Christoplos (eds.), *Preventing physical and mental disabilities: Multidisciplinary approaches*. Baltimore: University Park Press, 1979.

Munroe, R. *School of psychoanalytic thought: An exposition, critique and attempt at integration*. New York: Holt, Rinehart & Winston, 1955.

Nevill, D. *Humanistic psychology: New frontiers*. New York: Gardner Press, 1977.

Nihira, N., Foster, R., Shellhaus, M., & Leland, H. *Adaptive Behavior Scales*. Washington, DC: American Association on Mental Deficiency, 1974.

O'Leary, K.D., & Becker, W.C. Behavior modification of an adjustment class. A token reinforcement program. *Exceptional Children*, 1967, *33*, 637–642.

Ornitz, E., & Ritvo, E. The syndrome of autism: A critical review. *American Journal of Psychiatry*, 1976, *133*, 609–621.

Paluszny, M. *Autism: A practical guide for parents and professionals*. Syracuse, NY: Syracuse University Press, 1979.

Pate, J. Emotionally disturbed and socially maladjusted children. In: L. Dunn (ed.), *Exceptional children in the schools*. New York: Holt, Rinehart & Winston, 1963.

Patterson, G.R. *Living with children* (rev. ed.). Champaign, IL: Research Press, 1980.

Paul, J. Emotional disturbance in children. In: J. Paul & B. Epanchin (eds.), *Emotional disturbance in children*. Columbus, OH: Charles E. Merrill Publishing Co., 1982.

Peterson, D.R., & Quay, H.C. *Behavior Problem Checklist*. New Brunswick, NJ: School of Professional Psychology, Rutgers University, 1979.

Pinkston, E.M., Reese, N.M., LeBlanc, J.M., & Baer, D.M. Independent control of a preschool child's aggression and peer interaction by contingent teacher attention. *Journal of Applied Behavior Analysis*, 1974, *7*, 313–325.

Pollin, W. The pathogenesis of schizophrenia. *Archives of General Psychiatry*, 1972, *27*, 29–37.

Powers, R.B., & Osborne, J.G. *Fundamentals of behavior*. New York: West Publishing Co., 1976.

Prieto, A.G., & Rutherford, R.B., Jr. An ecological assessment technique for behaviorally disordered and learning disabled children. In: N.L. Long, W.C. Morse, & R.G. Newman (eds.), *Conflict in the classroom: The education of emotionally disturbed children* (4th ed.). Belmont, CA: Wadsworth Publishing, 1980.

Quay, H., & Werry, J. *Psychopathological disorders of childhood* (2nd ed.). New York: John Wiley & Sons, 1979.

Rahe, R.H., & Ransom, J.A. Life change and illness studies. Past history and future directions. *Journal of Human Stress*, 1978, *4*, 3–13.

Redl, F. The concept of the therapeutic milieu. *American Journal of Orthopsychiatry*, 1959, *29*, 721–734. (a)

Redl, F. The concept of the life space interview. *American Journal of Orthopsychiatry*, 1959, *29*, 1–18. (b)

Reinert, H. The emotionally disturbed. In: B. Gearheart (ed.), *Education of the exceptional child*. San Francisco: Intext Educational Publishers, 1972.

Reinert, H. *Children in conflict: Educational strategies for the emotionally disturbed and behaviorally disordered*. St. Louis, MO: C. V. Mosby Co., 1980.

Rendle-Short, J. Infantile autism in Australia. *Medical Journal of Australia*, 1969, *2*, 245–249.

Rezmierski, V., & Kotre, J. A limited literature review of the pychodynamic model. In: W. Rhodes & M. Tracy (eds.), *A study of child variance: Conceptual project in emotional disturbance*. Ann Arbor: The University of Michigan, 1972.

Rhodes, W., & Paul, J. *Emotionally disturbed and deviant children: New views and approaches*. Englewood Cliffs, NJ: Prentice-Hall, 1978.

Richey, E. The language program. In: E. Ritvo, B. Freeman, E. Ornitz, & P. Tanguay (eds.), *Autism: Diagnosis, current research and management*. New York: Spectrum Publications, 1976.

Rimland, B. *Infantile autism*. New York: Meredith Publishing Co., 1964.

Rimland, B. Psychogenesis versus biogenesis. The issues and evidence. In: S. Ploy & R. Edgerton (eds.), *Changing perspectives in mental illness*. New York: Holt, Rinehart & Winston, 1969.

Rimland, B. Height-dosage levels of certain vitamins in the treatment of children with severe mental disorders. In: D. Hawkins & L. Pauling (eds.), *Orthomolecular psychiatry*. San Francisco: W. H. Freeman & Co., 1973.

Rimland, B. Inside the mind of an autistic savant. *Psychology Today*, 1978, *12*, 68–80.

Rimland, B., Callaway, B., & Dreyfus, P. The effect of high doses of Vitamin B_6 on autistic children: A double blind crossover study. *American Journal of Psychiatry*, 1978, *135*, 472–475.

Rimm, D.C., & Masters, J.C. *Behavior therapy: Techniques and empirical findings*. New York: Academic Press, 1974.

Ritvo, E.R. (ed.). *Autism: Diagnosis, current research and management*. New York: Spectrum Publications, 1976.

Ritvo, E.R., & Freeman, B.J. *Definition of the syndrome of autism*. Washington, DC: National Society for Autistic Children, 1977.

Ritvo, E., & Freeman, B. National society for autistic children: Definition of the syndrome of autism. *Journal of Autism and Childhood Schizophrenia*, 1978, *8*, 162–167.

Ritvo, E., & Freeman, B. Current research on the syndrome of autism. In: J. Gilliam (ed.), *Autism: Diagnosis, management, and research*. Springfield, IL: Charles C Thomas, 1981.

Ritvo, E.R., Ritvo, E.C., & Brothers, A. Genetic and immunohematologic factors in autism. *Journal of Autism and Developmental Disorders*, 1982, *12*, 109–110.

Ross, A.O. *Psychological disorders of children: A behavioral approach to theory research and therapy*. New York: McGraw-Hill Book Co., 1974.

Ruttenberg, B., Kalish, B., Wenar, C., & Wolfe, E. *Behavior Rating Instrument for Autistic and Other Atypical Children*. Philadelphia: Developmental Center for Autistic Children, 1974.

Rutter, M. A children's behavior questionnaire for completion by teachers: Preliminary findings. *Journal of Child Psychology and Psychiatry*, 1967, *8*, 1–11.

Safer, D., & Allen, R. Side effects from long-term use of stimulants in children. In: R. Gittelman-Klein (ed.), *Recent advances in child psychopharmacology*. New York: Human Sciences Press, 1975.

Sailor, W., Wilcox, B., & Brown, L. *Methods of instruction for severely handicapped students*. Baltimore: Paul H. Brookes Publishing Co., 1980.

Salvia, J., & Ysseldyke, J.E. *Assessment in special and remedial education*. Boston: Houghton Mifflin Co., 1978.

Salzinger, S., Antrobus, J., & Glick, J. *The ecosystem of the "sick" kid*. New York: Academic Press, 1980.

Samuels, S. *Disturbed exceptional children: An integrated approach*. New York: Human Sciences Press, 1981.

Sankar, D. Plasma levels of polates, riboflavin, Vitamin B_6, and ascorbate in severely disturbed children. *Journal of Autism and Developmental Disorders*, 1979, *9*, 73–82.

Schlechty, P., & Paul, J. Sociological theory and practice. In: J. Paul & B. Epanchin (eds.), *Emotional disturbance in children*. Columbus, OH: Charles E. Merrill Publishing Co., 1982.

Schopler, E., & Reichler, R. (eds.). *Psychopathology and child development: Research and treatment*. New York: Plenum Publishing Corp., 1976.

Schopler, E., Reichler, R.J., DeVellis, R.F., & Daly, K. Toward objective classification of childhood autism: Childhood Rating Scale (CARS). *Journal of Autism and Developmental Disorders,* 1980, *10,* 91–103.

Schroeder, S., & Schroeder, C. Organic theories. In: J. Paul & B. Epanchin (eds.), *Emotional disturbance in children.* Columbus, OH: Charles E. Merrill Publishing Co., 1982.

Scott, P.M., Burton, R.V., & Yarrow, M.R. Social reinforcement under natural conditions. *Child Development,* 1967, *38,* 53–63.

Shea, T. *Camping for special children.* St. Louis: C. V. Mosby Co., 1977.

Shea, T. *Teaching children and youth with behavior disorders.* St. Louis: C. V. Mosby Co., 1978.

Simonson, L.R. *A curriculum model for individuals with severe learning and behavior disorders.* Baltimore: University Park Press, 1979.

Skinner, B.F. *Science and human behavior.* New York: Macmillan, 1953. (a)

Skinner, B.F. *Studies in behavior therapy, Metropolitan State Hospital, Mass.* Status Report I: Preliminary report on the study of psychotic behavior, Office of Naval Research, U.S. Navy, 1953. (b)

Smith, R., & Neisworth, J. *The exceptional child: A functional approach.* New York: McGraw-Hill Book Co., 1975.

Sours, J. The primary anorexic nervosa syndrome. In: J. Noshpitz (ed.), *Basic handbook of child psychiatry. Vol. II: Disturbances of development.* New York: Basic Books, 1979.

Strain, P.S., Shores, R.E., & Kerr, M.M. An experimental analysis of "spillover" effects on the social interaction of behaviorally handicapped preschool children. *Journal of Applied Behavior Analysis,* 1976, *9,* 31–40.

Sue, D., Sue, D. W., & Sue, S. *Understanding abnormal behavior.* Boston: Houghton Mifflin Co., 1981.

Sulzer-Azaroff, B., & Mayer, R.G. *Applying behavior procedures with children and youth.* New York: Holt, Rinehart, & Winston, 1977.

Swanson, H.L., & Watson, B.L. *Educational and psychological assessment of exceptional children: Theories, strategies, and applications.* St. Louis, MO: C.V. Mosby Co., 1982.

Swap, S. The ecological model of emotional disturbance in children: A status report and proposed synthesis. *Behavioral Disorders,* 1978, *3,* 186–196.

Swap, S., Prieto, A., & Harth, R. Ecological perspectives of the emotionally disturbed child. In: R. McDowell, G. Adamson, & F. Wood (eds.), *Teaching emotionally disturbed children.* Boston: Little, Brown, & Co., 1982.

Tanguay, P. Autism and mental retardation. In: L. Szymanski & P. Tanguay (eds.), *Emotional disorders of mentally retarded persons.* Baltimore: University Park Press, 1980.

Thomas, A., & Chess, S. *Temperament and development.* New York: Brunner/Mazel, 1977.

Thomas, A., Chess, S., & Birch, H. *Temperament and behavior disorders in children.* New York: New York University Press, 1969.

Treffert, D. Epidemiology of infantile autism. *Archives of General Psychiatry,* 1970, *22,* 431–438.

Tyler, L.E. *Individuality.* San Francisco: Jossey-Bass, 1978.

Ullmann, L., & Krasner, L. *Case studies in behavior modification.* New York: Holt, Rinehart & Winston, 1965.

Ullmann, L., & Krasner, L. *A psychological approach to abnormal behavior.* Englewood Cliffs, NJ: Prentice-Hall, 1975.

Valletutti, P.J., & Christoplos, F. Introduction and overview. In: P.J. Valletutti & F. Christoplos (eds.), *Preventing physical and mental disabilities: Multidisciplinary approaches.* Baltimore: University Park Press, 1979.

Vitamin B$_6$ helps autistic children. *Science News*, 1978, *1*, 308–309.

Walker, H.M. *Walker Problem Behavior Identification Checklist:* Los Angeles: Western Psychological Services, 1970.

Wallace, G., & Larson, S.C. *Educational assessment of learning problems: Testing for teaching*. Boston: Allyn and Bacon, 1978.

Webster, C. The characteristics of autism. In: C. Webster, M. Konstantareas, J. Oxman, & J. Mack (eds.), *Autism: New directions in research and education*. New York: Pergamon Press, 1980.

Wender, P. Speculations concerning a possible biochemical basis of minimal brain dysfunction. In: R. Gittleman-Klein (ed.), *Recent advances in child psychopharmacology*. New York: Human Sciences Press, 1975.

Werry, J.S., & Quay, H.C. Observing the classroom behavior of elementary school children. *Exceptional Children*, 1969, *35*, 461–470.

Whelan, R. The emotionally disturbed. In: E. Meyen (ed.), *Exceptional children and youth: An introduction* (1st ed.). Denver: Love Publishing Co., 1978.

Whelan, R., & Gallagher, P. Effective teaching of children with behavior disorders. In: N. Haring & A. Hayden (eds.), *The improvement of instruction*. Seattle, WA: Special Child Publications, 1972.

Williams, J., Cram, D., Tausig, F., & Webster, E. Relative effects of drugs and diet on hyperactive behaviors: An experimental study. *Pediatrics*, 1978, *61*, 611–817.

Wing, L. The handicaps of autistic children: A comparative study. *Journal of Child Psychology and Psychiatry*, 1969, *10*, 1–40.

Wing, L. (ed.). *Early childhood autism*. New York: Pergamon Press, 1980.

Winokur, G., Clayton, P.J., & Reich, T. *Manic depressive illness*. St. Louis: C.V. Mosby Co., 1969.

Wolpe, J. *Psychotherapy by reciprocal inhibition*. Stanford, CA: Stanford University Press, 1958.

Wyne, M., & O'Connor, P. *Exceptional children: A developmental view*. Lexington, MA: D. C. Heath and Co., 1979.

SUGGESTED READINGS

General References

Paul, J., & Epanchin, B. *Emotional disturbance in children*. Columbus, OH: Charles E. Merrill Publishing Co., 1982.

Reinert, H. *Children in conflict*. St. Louis: C. V. Mosby Co., 1980.

Rhodes, W., & Paul, J. *Emotionally disturbed and deviant children: New views and approaches*. Englewood Cliffs, NJ: Prentice-Hall, 1978.

Rutter, M., & Schopler, E. *Autism: A reappraisal of concepts and treatments*. New York: Plenum Publishing Corp., 1978.

Definitions

Wood, F., & Taken, K. *Disturbing, disordered or disturbed?* Minneapolis: Department of Psychoeducational Studies, University of Minnesota, 1979.

Screening, Identification, and Diagnosis

Cross, L., & Goin, K. (eds.). *Identifying handicapped children: A guide to casefinding, screening, diagnosis, assessment and evaluation*. New York: Walker and Co., 1977.

Sloan, J., & Marcus, L. Some findings on the use of the adaptive behavior scale with autistic children. *Journal of Autism and Developmental Disorders*, 1981, *2*, 191–199.

Classification Systems and Symptomatology

American Psychiatric Association. *Diagnostic and statistical manual of mental disorders: DSM-III* (3rd ed.). Washington, DC: American Psychiatric Association, 1980.

Fann, W. W., & Cohen, C. E. *The language of mental health.* St. Louis: C. V. Mosby Co., 1973.

Kanner, L. *Child psychiatry.* Springfield, IL: Charles C Thomas, 1948.

Theories of Causation, Treatment and Educational Programs

Gittelman-Klein, R. (ed.). *Recent advances in child psychopharmacology.* New York: Human Sciences Press, 1975.

Majorski, L., & Oettinger, L. Neuropsychological and treatment aspects of learning and behavior disorders in children. *Behavioral Disorders,* 1979, *1,* 30–40.

Quay, H., & Werry, J. *Psychopathological disorders of childhood.* New York: John Wiley & Sons, 1979.

Scholevan, G., Denson, R., & Blinder, B. *Emotional disorders in children and adolescents: Medical and psychological approaches to treatment.* New York: SP Medical and Scientific Books, 1980.

DISCUSSION QUESTIONS

1. What are some of the definitions of emotional disturbance? When combined and assimilated, how do they provide a global view of the emotionally disturbed child?
2. How may severely emotionally disturbed children be distinguished from those who are mildly and moderately disturbed?
3. What are some of the popular screening devices that are used to detect children with mild and moderate behavioral disorders/deficiencies?
4. Why has screening for the severely emotionally disturbed child focused on the neonatal period? Describe the possible role of birth certificate screening, high-risk nurseries, high-risk registers, and the case history approach in the identification of children with severe emotional disturbance.
5. What are the symptoms or characteristics typically demonstrated by a child diagnosed as being autistic?
6. What are the five major theoretical positions relevant to the etiology of emotional disturbance? In what ways do they differ from each other? What are their major tenets?
7. What are the several major symptom categories or behavior types considered to be characteristic of severely emotionally disturbed children? How do these behaviors manifest themselves?
8. What are several of the schemata that have been suggested for the classification of emotional disturbance in children?
9. What are the subcategories of childhood psychosis? In what ways do they differ from each other?
10. What are some strategies that may be followed in the prevention of emotional disturbance in children?
11. What are the most commonly utilized treatment programs suggested by medical, behavioral, and psychodynamic intervention orientations?
12. Discuss the nature and scope of seven program models for the education and treatment of emotionally disturbed children.

Chapter 5

Severely and Profoundly Language Impaired Students
Developmental Dysphasia

Audrey S. Hoffnung

CHAPTER OBJECTIVES

After reading this chapter, you should be able to:

1. Differentiate between adult aphasia and developmental dysphasia.
2. Discuss some of the terms previously used to describe severely and profoundly language impaired children.
3. Differentiate between speech and language and discuss the nature of phonology and syntax.
4. Discuss the reasons for the problems inherent in determining the incidence of developmental aphasia, and cite current incidence figures.
5. Describe the relationship to developmental dysphasia of hearing acuity, auditory processing, emotional stability, intelligence, diverse perceptual deficiencies, and articulation disorders.
6. Define *percentile, stanine,* and *linguistic age.*
7. Discuss the nature, purpose, and dimensions of commonly used formal tests of linguistic ability.

Copyright © 1984 by Audrey S. Hoffnung.

8. Discuss the hypothesized neurological bases for the presence of developmental dysphasia.
9. Discuss the nature of several typical approaches recommended for therapeutic interventions with children who have developmental dysphasia.
10. Discuss steps and procedures to be used in providing educational programs and services as well as therapy programs for children with developmental dysphasia.

The severely and profoundly language impaired child may be found in a number of categories of handicapped persons, including mentally retarded (cognitively impaired) persons, hard-of-hearing and deaf (sensorially impaired) persons, autistic (health impaired) persons (Ritvo, 1976), and dysphasic individuals. This chapter is devoted to the last group: the dysphasic child.

DEFINITIONS

Terminology

Children with severe and profound language disorders have been described in the literature by the terms: *aphasoid* (Lowe & Campbell, 1965), *audimutes* (Ajuriaguerra, 1966), *childhood aphasia* (Cromer, 1978), *congenital auditory imperception* (Ajuriaguerra, 1966), *developmental aphasia* (Benton, 1964; Tallal & Piercy, 1973a,b, 1974, 1975), *developmental dysphasia* (Benton, 1978), *developmental language disorder* (Aram & Nation, 1975), *functionally deviant language* (Menyuk, 1964), *infantile speech* (Menyuk, 1964), *language disorder* (Menyuk & Looney, 1972a,b), *linguistically retarded* (Ewing, 1967), *sensory aphasia* (Furth, 1964), *severe oral language handicap* (Luick, Agranowitz, Kirk, & Busby, 1982), and *specific language disorders* (Aram & Nation, 1975; Menyuk & Looney, 1972a). This list is by no means complete.

The problem with terminology has been compounded for three major reasons. First because many researchers have indicated that language disordered children were subjects in their studies, yet they have not explicitly defined their experimental population (Menyuk, 1964; Wolfus, Moscovitch, & Kinsbourne, 1980). Second, children in many studies either were diagnosed by speech-language pathologists as having language disorders or were receiving therapy for language disorders (Aram & Nation, 1975; Leonard, 1972; Stark & Tallal, 1981; Tallal, 1975). Third, many authors use Benton's (1964) method of classification, which is based more on negative than positive evidence. Benton (1964) suggested that the developmental aphasic child was one who had a "specific" language disability that could not be explained by mental retardation, hearing loss, emotional factors, or motor disability. Hardy (1965) concurred, explaining that negative evidence or circular reasoning was used when diagnosing a child. He stated that a child can be said to have childhood aphasia if the child's language problem cannot be directly related to the above-mentioned factors. Benton's classification of dysphasia is arrived at, therefore, by a process of elimination. Recently, children have been classified as being aphasic if they scored two standard deviations below the mean on the auditory verbal scale on one or more standardized language assessment tests or subtests (Luick et al., 1982).

Though the term *developmental aphasia* has been used in the past to describe the severely and profoundly language impaired child (Benton, 1964; Eisenson, 1968a, 1972), the term *developmental dysphasia* is found with greater frequency in recent literature (Tallal & Piercy, 1978; Wyke, 1978). Therefore, *dysphasia* is used in this chapter, except when referring to a specific label used by another researcher. (Note that the prefix "dys-," means "impaired," the prefix "a-," means "without" [Webster, 1969]). Wood (1971), in defining terms used by speech-language pathologists, states that the term *dysphasia* is the "same as aphasia" (p. 11). In clinical situations, the term "aphasia" has been used more consistently when referring to adults, though very few aphasic adults are totally without language.

The dysphasic child has difficulty developing language, while the aphasic adult at one time had a previously functioning language system, i.e., a well-established sound system, a wide functional vocabulary, and a complex syntactic system. The aphasic adult was formerly able to form all the sounds of the language, was able to use a variety of words and, without necessarily being able to recite the rules of grammar, could produce complex sentences. For example, the aphasic adult could vary his or her verbal expression by alternately utilizing the passive sentence, "The apple was eaten by the man," the past progressive sentence, "The man was eating the apple," a relative clause, "The apple, which was red and juicy, was eaten by the man," or a simple declarative sentence in the present tense, "The man eats the apple." Adults who formerly had a developed language system can, when neurologically damaged, become fluent aphasic individuals (Geschwind, 1968). A fluent aphasic person speaks easily (without any struggle behavior) and uses good prosody (melody, stress, rate), but may substitute one sound for another (literal paraphasia—"kable" for "table") or one word for another (verbal paraphasia—"table" for "chair"). The fluent aphasic individual is therefore not communicating, though sounds and perhaps words of the language are being used. (See Goodglass and Kaplan, 1976, for excellent examples of the language of a fluent aphasic.)

A developmental dysphasic child could never become a fluent aphasic or dysphasic adult, because the child does not have an established phonological, semantic, or syntactic system. The dysphasic child may be mute, may have a faulty sound system though the articulators are not paralyzed, may use some words though the number of words that comprise the lexicon (vocabulary) may be limited, and may string one or two words together but is not able to form complex utterances.

Speech vs. Language

During a child's first year, the child produces vocalizations (cooing and babbling) with his or her articulators—tongue, lips, teeth, and velum. At this time, the movements of the articulators may be used for what is considered prelanguage vocalization, i.e., the vocalizations may not refer to any specific referent (Winitz, 1969). Vocalizations, at this age, are not part of a "lexicosemantic" system (Halliday, 1975, p.9), in that the sounds do not have the meanings of words but belong to the child's semantic system, i.e., a consistent and systematic system that has been devised by the child to express his or her own meaning through the sounds of adult language (Halliday, 1975). At this stage, the child is believed to be producing the phones or sounds of all the world's languages. Bever (1961, in McNeill, 1970) noted that the child has a quiet period at age 11 or 12 months, when there is a total collapse of babbling before the start of true linguistic development. When the child uses sounds to differentiate meaning in actual words ("pen–men," "pen–pan," "pen–pet"), the child is capable of using the phonemes of the language.

The development of speech, or the sound structure of language (phonology), when combined with syntax and semantics, forms oral language. "Oral language is a code with structural properties characterized by a set of rules for producing and comprehending spoken utterances" (Rees, 1980, p.3). Phonemes develop through the systematic use of a series of rules, and are the sounds that, at this point, are part of a child's language (Perkins, 1977). To illustrate, let us consider one of the earliest meaningful sounds that may be produced by a child: "ma" (Jakobson, 1968). This utterance is formed by the joining together of /m/ and /a/. Each sound is formed by a set of rules.

The /m/ is a voiced sound (the vocal cords vibrate to form the sound), a nasal sound (the air travels from the lungs into the nasal cavity [nose] because the soft palate does not elevate to separate the oral cavity [mouth] from the nasal cavity), and an anterior sound (formed in the front part of the mouth). Therefore, the /m/ carries, in addition to other distinctive features, the features of + voice, + nasal, and + anterior. The + or − symbols belong to a binary system indicating that either a feature is present (+) or absent (−). In order to form a new consonant, for example /p/, for the meaningful word "papa," the child must add new rules to the ones already possessed. To form the phoneme /p/, the child must prevent phonation by maintaining the vocal cords in an open position, for the /p/ is a voiceless sound; must close the passageway into the nasal cavity, for the /p/ is an oral sound; and must momentarily halt or interrupt the escape of air to build up air pressure for an explosive release, for the /p/ is a stop (plosive or interrupted) sound. The /p/ is then formed by a combination of the features: − voice, − nasal (or + oral), + interrupted, in addition to other distinctive features (McReynolds & Engmann, 1975).

The acquisition of the distinctive features to form new sounds occurs slowly and systematically, i.e., in a specific order, though the timing may differ for each child (Jakobson, 1968), based on the child's individual developmental schedule. To achieve new sounds the child must maintain control over his or her articulators, while utilizing cognitive and linguistic skills to formulate new feature rules. These sounds (phonemes) are performing a linguistic function, in that they differentiate meaning. For instance, if a child babbles "ba, ba, da, da, pa, pa," only phones are being formed; the sounds are present but they provide no meaning. However, if "ba" is a call for a "bottle," in contrast to "da," which is a request for a "doll," /b/ and /d/ are now phonemes because they differentiate one meaningful word from the other. As a phoneme, a sound is based on a rule system, i.e., on an orderly combination of distinctive features (e.g., + voice, + interrupted, + oral). If the child has an interdental /s/ lisp (the /s/ is formed between the teeth) or a hypernasal /s/ (the /s/ is formed with nasal emission of air) because of a structural defect such as a cleft palate, the child has dyslalia (Wood, 1971). These errors are not based on a faulty rule system. The child with dyslalia has defective articulation that is not considered to be caused by a lesion of the central nervous system, but rather the etiology is said to be a defect of the speech organs or faulty learning of the sounds of the language (Wood, 1971). If the child produces /z/ for /s/, /b/ for /p/, and /d/ for /t/ because the child cannot produce the − voice distinctive feature (s/p/t/ are all voiceless), the child has a problem with the rule system of sounds. Thus, the acquisition of a distinctive feature may affect all sounds that have that feature (McReynolds & Engmann, 1975). In addition to accurately producing sounds when forming a word, the sounds must be correctly sequenced or ordered. The English language relies heavily on order; to violate the rules of order would affect not only words, but the sequence of words.

Syntax, the ordering of the words of the language, is also based on a rule system, the mastery of which is essential to language ability. For example, a declarative sentence is formed by combining a noun phrase (NP) with a verb phrase (VP) (Chomsky, 1965). A declarative sentence might be: "The boy (NP) + is eating a cookie (VP)." If a native speaker of the language were asked to state the rule to form a "Yes/No" question, he or she might not be able to do so. If that person, however, were asked to form a question from the above sentence that could be answered by a "Yes/No" response, the immediate reply would be, "Is the boy eating the cookie?" To produce this sentence, a permutation rule was employed transposing the auxiliary verb "is" and the NP "the boy." A question using a "Wh" interrogative pronoun (what, where, when or why) would require an additional interrogative rule. Children with dysphasia seem to have difficulty in forming the complex rule systems that are required for the formation of the phonemes and syntactic structures.

INCIDENCE

The determination of the incidence of childhood dysphasia has encountered major problems because of: 1) the lack of established criteria that could definitely identify the dysphasic child, 2) the degree of impairment that must be present before a child is considered to be language impaired (Leske, 1981), and 3) the omission of the dysphasic category by researchers conducting studies on the prevalence of speech-language disorders (Milisen, 1971).

Stevenson and Richman (1976) found that 2%–3% of preschool children have delayed language. Marge (1972), in an analysis of the 1969 U.S. Bureau of the Census, presented figures showing that an estimated 6.2% of all children in the 4–17-year age range (55,932,000 children) experienced problems in language acquisition. This classification does not allow a separate breakdown of categories but includes the mentally retarded, deaf, hard-of-hearing, emotionally disturbed, learning disabled, and speech impaired who were not part of any of the preceding categories. Fein (1983) reported that in 1980 the U.S. Bureau of the Census numbered the population of the United States at 226,504,825 persons. The National Center for Health Statistics (1981) reported that of the approximately 16 million children in the 0–5-year age group, 9% were speech impaired and 1% were hearing impaired; of the approximately 16 million children in the 6–12-year age group, 19% were speech impaired and 2% were hearing impaired. According to various other research reports, the school population of childhood dysphasia varies from 0% to 0.6%, with no mention of childhood dysphasia in high school or college (Milisen, 1971). Milisen believes that many of the incidence reports are "best guesses" (p. 630).

SCREENING, IDENTIFICATION, AND DIAGNOSIS

As noted previously, the dysphasic child has been diagnosed by negative evidence (Benton, 1964; Hardy, 1965) rather than by positive evidence; i.e., dysphasic children have difficulty with comprehension and expression of oral language in the absence of mental retardation, hearing impairment, or emotional disorders. In an effort to find a definite method of discriminating a group of children with developmental dysphasia or with "specific language deficits" (p. 114) as Stark and Tallal (1981) refer to this population, they examined a population of 132 subjects, ages 4–8½ years, who were receiving therapy and who were referred to them as children with language problems. Clinically, these children were considered to have normal hearing, normal intelligence, to be free of neurological difficulties, and to be socially adjusted. Children were excluded from the group who the researchers believed did not have the criteria required to meet the diagnosis of specific language deficits. The criteria were:

1. Emotional stability. One child was eliminated because of emotional difficulties that required professional treatment.
2. Hearing. Three children were eliminated: two children did not pass a hearing screening at 25 dB; one child had a history of recurrent otitis media.
3. Intelligence. Fifty children failed to meet the criterion of a performance IQ of 85 on the Wechsler Intelligence Scale for Children (WISC–R) (Wechsler, 1974) or the Wechsler Preschool and Primary Scale of Intelligence (WPPSI) (Wechsler, 1963).
4. Neurological status. One child was eliminated because of a medical history of neurofibromatosis.

5. Articulation disorders. Nine children were excluded because their articulation ability as determined by the Templin-Darley Test of Articulation (Templin & Darley, 1960) was "more than six months below the estimated expressive language age" (p. 117). These children were considered to have mixed disorders.
6. Reading level. One child was excluded because his reading age was 6 months below his language age on the Gates-MacGinitie Comprehension and Vocabulary Tests (Gates & MacGinitie, 1972), which were administered to children who were 7 years or older. This, too, was suggestive of a mixed disorder.
7. Language disorder. Thirty-three children were rejected because their language age (LA) was not sufficiently below their chronological age (CA). In order to be selected for the study, the receptive language age (LAR) was required to be at least 6 months lower than the mental performance age (MAP). Twenty-six of the 33 children were thus excluded because their scores were too high. In addition, the expressive language age (LAE) had to be at least 12 months lower than the MAP. Seven of the 33 children were thus excluded because of a score that was too high.

Stark and Tallal reported that only 39 children of the original 132 children were selected as having a specific language impairment. They concluded that there may be many subgroups within the population of children with specific language deficits, even when mentally retarded, moderately or severely hard-of-hearing or deaf, or emotionally disturbed children are excluded from this classification. For example, mixed disorders of cognitive deficits and language disorders, hearing loss and language disorders, and articulatory difficulties and language disorders were in evidence in the group of children classified as having specific language deficits. Greater heterogeneity within the population exists than had been hypothesized.

Each criterion that was utilized by Stark and Tallal has been examined by other researchers. A review of some of those findings follows.

Hearing

Hearing Acuity Ewing (1967), who observed and tested "aphasic" children, wrote that the major discovery of his research was the finding that 6 of his 10 aphasic subjects had a "high-frequency deafness" (p. 37). The children could hear the lower frequencies (64 Hz, 128 Hz, and 256 Hz) but had a loss of 55 dB or more for the higher frequencies (512 Hz, 1024 Hz, 2048 Hz, and 4096 Hz). The reception of high-frequency sounds is crucial for the reception of consonant sounds.

Lowe and Campbell (1965) suggested that their aphasoid subjects may have had some minimal peripheral hearing losses. Goldstein, Landau, and Kleffner (1960) stated that few aphasics have normal hearing. Johnson and Myklebust (1967) and McGinnis (1963) stated that soft sounds may be too abstract, with sounds below 30 dB being difficult to perceive. Yet, severe language disorders have been attributed to auditory difficulties other than hearing acuity.

Auditory Processing Children with "congenital auditory imperception" as classified by Ajuriaguerra (1966), may hear differently and may be more disturbed by "hearing differently than by not hearing at all" (p. 120). Sounds may not be interpreted correctly, and the child may develop a defensive and rejective attitude toward the world. Reichstein (1964) tested the hearing acuity of three groups of children (normal, hearing loss, and aphasic) with complex stimuli: the bark of a dog, a warbled pure tone of 350 Hz, a verbalized word "baby," and a short piano selection. The aphasic group presented a wide range of variances in their responses to these auditory stimuli. Reichstein (1964) and Myklebust (1954) reported inconsistent responses in their aphasic group, responses that are not present in the normal child or in the child with a hearing loss. Reichstein reported that the data on aphasic hearing acuity is neither consistent nor conclusive. Time of response was not a factor in his experiment.

Johnson and Myklebust (1967) found a time lag existed in some of their dysphasic children, in that the dysphasic children required a greater amount of time than did the normal children between the reception of the auditory stimulus and their response to it. Other researchers have found a delay in responses in other modalities.

Morehead and Ingram (1973) reported an unpublished research project of N. Grandstaff, N. Mackworth, A. de la Pena, and K. Pribram, in which children with deviant language took twice as long as the normal group to indicate their choice of a visually matched symbol, after the symbol had been located. The problem was not in selecting the correct visual match but in the time required to point to it. Thus, dysphasic children may be slower in their responses in more than just the auditory modality.

Variability of performance may be a factor in the behavior of brain-injured children. Strauss and Lehtinen (1947) cautioned teachers to be aware of the variability in the academic performance of their students. For example, they said, material mastered one day may be perceived as new material on the succeeding day. This may be another area where storage, memory, recall, and response are unstable.

Behavior crosses modalities. Strauss and Lehtinen (1947), for example, noted the importance of figure-ground relationships in many of our daily activities. The visual and auditory foreground stimuli must be attended to for reading and listening. To develop language, a child has to listen as well as hear. A dysphasic child may have difficulty selecting the sounds of language from a background of traffic, conversation, running water, or television. If the words of the mother cannot be separated from, e.g., the broadcaster on the radio and/or the water splashing in the sink, the child may not follow basic instructions. If the comments of the teacher cannot be separated from, e.g., other children's footsteps or chattering in the hall, the child, on an advanced level, may not focus on the homework assignment that may be called out during the last minutes of the class session.

While the average clinician does not have the equipment or time necessary for elaborate testing of auditory processing, the work of researchers is an invaluable reference when considering methods and techniques of therapy. Research and discussions supporting and rejecting auditory processing as the major underlying problem in the language disorders of dysphasic children can be found in the professional literature. Many such studies relating to auditory processing are concerned with succession, sequencing, and same and different discrimination tasks. Tests of succession, for instance, ask the listener to determine whether one or two sounds are being presented. Tests of sequence require that the listener determine which of the presented sounds came first and which last. Same or different tasks require that the listener determine whether two sounds are different or identical. Stimuli are provided of tones of varying frequency (Efron, 1963; Lowe & Campbell, 1965), of isolated sounds, or of sound embedded in a phonetic context (McReynolds, 1967; Rosenthal, 1970 [in Eisenson, 1972]; Tallal, Stark, & Curtiss, 1976).

Lowe and Campbell (1965) used pure tones to test the ability of eight "aphasoid" children, ages 7 to 14 years, to determine succession of tones (one tone or two) and order of tones. A nonsignificant difference between normal and aphasoid children was found on the succession test, though the normal group had better scores. The times between two tones, sometimes called the intersound interval (ISI) or the interstimulus interval, had a mean of 18.5 msec for the normal group and a mean of 35.8 msec for the aphasoid group. A statistical difference at the .005 level was found between the two groups on the order task. The groups were asked to sequence two 15 msec pulses at 2200 Hz and 400 Hz. The normal group scores ranged from 15 msec to 80 msec, with a mean of 36.1 msec, while the aphasoid group scores ranged from 55 msec to 700 msec, with a mean of 357 msec. These findings were in agreement with Efron's (1963) study of aphasic adults. The aphasic population, on the nonverbal sound stimuli (pure tones), required a statistically significant longer time between tones presented in order to place them in the proper sequence.

In 1970, Rosenthal used six different types of stimuli, ranging from differentiation of nonspeech tones (pure tone and noise, high tone, and low tone) to differentiation of speech sounds (vowels "ah" and "ee," vowel "ah" and affricate "ch," fricative "s" and fricative "sh," and fricative "sh" and affricative "ch"). He, too, concluded that the basic condition for the reduction of error in dysphasic children was the length of the ISI. The performance of the normal children was always superior to that of the dysphasic child. The dysphasic children invariably required significantly longer ISI than the normal group to discriminate between two different types of stimuli. Proper temporal order of phonemes or timing is necessary to maintain the proper linguistic sequence of sounds, i.e., to maintain the sounds of a word in the correct order. An example of this in actual words might be "steak-skate."

Through a series of studies, Tallal and Piercy, (1973a, 1974, 1978), continued the examination of the auditory processes of the dysphasic child. In their 1973a study, a difference was found in the sequencing ability of the dysphasic and the normal child. In 1974, they noted that the dysphasic child was able to discriminate vowels better than stop consonants such as /b/ and /d/. Tallal and Piercy hypothesized that the rate of change (transition) from one sound to another may be the cause of the difficulty. Speech scientists are able to synthesize (create) sounds that can be presented to the listener. The sounds used in these experiments were created (synthesized) by Tallal and Piercy. The stops /b/ and /d/ can be differentiated by their formant transitions. (A formant transition is an energy change that alters the acoustic signal [Borden & Harris, 1980].) An energy change would normally occur when the articulators are placed in a different position in the vocal tract. For example, the elevation of the tongue for /d/ causes a different resonance pattern in the vocal tract than a sound that does not require tongue-tip elevation, as is the case with the /b/ sound. Tallal and Piercy found that if the formant transition that differentiates the /b/ and /d/ were lengthened, the dysphasic children's performance improved to the point that there was no longer a statistically significant difference between the dysphasic children and the normal children. The speed of the presentation of sounds was the crucial factor. Based on these findings, the dysphasic children were said to have a rate-specific auditory perceptual deficit that was believed to be the primary disorder underlying the children's language disorder, i.e., the children were unable to process rapidly changing acoustic signals (Tallal & Piercy, 1978).

Tallal and Piercy (1978) also discussed the relationship between auditory memory and the rate of auditory processing. The stimuli used to test the memory of dysphasic children were a number of sounds of 250 msec in length, with a large ISI (428 msec). (Dysphasic children in previous studies were able to sequence elements with this ISI.) In the 1978 study, the dysphasic children were able to remember two or three elements but performed more poorly with four elements; there was a significant drop in performance with five elements. It was thus concluded that the language problems of *some* dysphasic children occurred "as the direct consequence of defective processing of rapidly changing acoustic information and an associated, possibly consequential reduced memory span for auditory sequence" (Tallal and Piercy, 1978, p. 82).

According to Tallal (1978), a memory deficit may be present along with a problem in rapid processing. Aten and Davis (1968) pointed out that auditory memory and auditory temporal disorders are not unique to children with developmental dysphasia but exist also in children with normal language development in the presence of brain damage. No definitive statement of primary causation can be made at this time concerning the area of auditory processing in dysphasia, despite the number of controlled and carefully executed research projects.

Emotional Stability

Dysphasia has been associated with neurological damage (Benton, 1964; Rapin & Wilson, 1978). Emotional lability and a number of unusual or disruptive behaviors may be evident (Strauss & Lehtinen, 1947). The children may display the phenomena of: a) distractibility, either as "undue fixation upon irrelevant stimuli" (p. 25) or as a fluctuation of attention from one object to another, b) hyperactivity or disinhibition, with mood swings from silliness or joy to one of tears or depression, c) catastrophic reactions or tears when presented with a difficult problem, and d) perseveration or the maintenance of behavior patterns or verbal utterances when such behavior or utterances are no longer relevant. Emotional problems can be accompanying problems, but they are not considered to be the primary cause of dysphasia.

Intelligence

The intellectual functioning of dysphasic children is an unresolved issue. One group of researchers has found that children with dysphasia generally have normal intelligence, while a second group believes that dysphasic children have some cognitive impairment. Among studies in the first group, Menyuk and Looney (1972a) noted that dysphasic children attain average or above-average performance IQ scores on standardized intelligence tests; Luick et al. (1982) stated that a child with dysphasia can be considered to have normal intellectual potential as shown on tests requiring no oral directions or verbal expression. Leonard (1972) also suggested that dysphasic children cannot be considered mentally retarded.

Stark and Tallal (1981), who, as previously mentioned, studied children with specific language deficits, are among those researchers who believe dysphasic children display cognitive impairment. They accepted 50 dysphasic children for their study who were referred by their classroom teachers as having normal intelligence (a clinical judgment on the part of the teachers). These children were later disqualified from the study, however, because of their low scores on standardized performance tests. Benton (1978) suggested that there is a greater variability in the general intelligence of dysphasic children than in the normal child, and that there is a trend toward a lower IQ than had been previously expected.

Benton (1978) offered two major reasons for the diminished intellectual functioning of dysphasic children. One reason, termed the "concurrence hypothesis," suggests that the cerebral abnormality of the dysphasic child may be extensive enough to retard both intellectual and linguistic development. The second reason, labeled the "cultural deprivation" factor, reasons that a child's language handicap may restrict his or her experiences and, because of factors such as rejection and/or diminished stimulation, the child (like other handicapped persons) presents a picture of "pseudo-retardation." In Benton's 1978 study, language training was found to have improved one child's intelligence quotient from a score of 78 to 97. Benton (1978) further stated that "Dysphasia is not an independent disorder but a particular expression of a more basic cognitive impairment influencing non-verbal as well as verbal behavior'' (p. 50). In 1974, Yvan Lebrun and Richard Hoops (Kertesz, 1976) wrote that the same anatomical location in the left cerebral hemisphere causes language and non-verbal intelligence to be "independently vulnerable" (p. 335). This suggests similar causation for disorders in language development and for nonverbal abilities. Morehead and Ingram (1973) hypothesized that there may be a relationship between the delayed acquisition of language and an underlying aspect of cognitive development. A subtle cognitive difference may occur because perceptual deficiencies relate to general representation development.

Perceptual abilities (e.g., visual and auditory) of dysphasic children have been scrutinized over the years. Auditory perception was mentioned earlier in this section. The results concerning visual perception have been subjected to discussions similar to those for auditory perception. Furth (1964) noted that aphasic children scored above the mean on the Block Design Test, but scored poorly on a speed test of Coding and on a Picture Arrangement task requiring temporal sequencing. The dysphasic children's overall mean IQ performance score was 100.7. Furth, therefore, maintained that the aphasic children do not have a general perceptual or learning problem that would differentiate them from a deaf population, but suggested that their temporal sequencing abilities should be tested. Luick et al. (1982) tested 237 subjects with "severe language disorders" using the Illinois Test of Psycholinguistic Abilities (Kirk, McCarthy, & Kirk, 1968), and found that they performed better with the visual motor channel (i.e., visual reception, visual association, visual closure, visual sequential memory, and manual expression) than with the auditory-vocal channel. Tallal (1978) mentioned that the children in her study were more adept in the visual modality than in the auditory modality, but cautioned the reader that her groups were matched for IQ on the Ravens Progressive Matrices Test (Ravens, 1960) and that a subgroup with visual perceptual difficulties might have been eliminated as a result. (The Ravens Test is a performance test based on the creation of designs.)

It should be noted that conclusions such as the above, even when based on examination of the same modality, may depend on the methods used. Doehring (1960), using a totally different method, noted that aphasic children were significantly different from normal and deaf children on overall errors in visual memory tasks. The performance of the aphasic group was equal to children of the deaf and normal groups who were chronologically 2 years younger. It was noted though, that the aphasic group's score was 10 points lower on the IQ test than either of the two other groups, not unusual among deaf and aphasic children. Delayed recall and recall after interference did not retard the responses of the aphasic group.

No great concurrence of opinion has emerged, therefore, from the above-reported studies, perhaps, because of 1) a difference in the methods of testing and selecting the population and/or 2) the fact that there are many subgroups in the dysphasic population.

As stated previously, delay in a child's representational development may be based on subtle cognitive impairments that result from perceptual deficiencies (Morehead & Ingram, 1973). Representational is defined as ". . . having reference. Linguistically, a word or utterance that stands for or represents something else" (Muma, 1978, p. 375). Ajuriaguerra (1966) believed that thought is made flexible by the development of speech. The children in his report showed a deficit in the representational and figurative (graphic) dimensions of language; they were deficient in imagery, drawing, symbolic play (make-believe), dreaming, and language. Symbolic play involves the use of symbols to substitute one item for another, e.g., a block is a make-believe truck. The connection between verbal language and symbolic play is supported by Lovell, Hoyle, and Siddall (1968). The children in their study who used fewer morphemes per utterance (uninflected words or words plus inflections, e.g., eat + s (plural) = 2 morphemes; work + s (3rd person singular) = 2 morphemes) spent less time in symbolic play than those whose utterances contained more morphemes. The language disordered children used fewer morphemes and spent less time in symbolic play, demonstrating a diminution of symbolic use in both verbal and nonverbal expression. An example of a normal child's utterance might be, "The man worked quickly." This utterance has 6 morphemes in 4 words, as compared with 4 morphemes in 3 words, "Man work quick." in a possible utterance of a language disordered child. Benton (1978) reported great variability in the use of gestures and pantomime by dysphasic children; some used them liberally and others not at all.

Menyuk (1978) suggested that there are other areas in which dysphasic children may have difficulty functioning, specifically, those in which processing abilities are necessary to 1) categorize, i.e., to establish certain identities of properties (all types of chairs belong to one category); or 2) develop the idea of relationships, e.g., actor (an animate who does the action), action (that which is performed), object (e.g., that which receives the action of the verb), as in "The cat (actor) pushes (action) the ball (object)." Problems may occur in both areas, because the same process used to interpret linguistic material may be pertinent in the processing of nonlinguistic material (Menyuk, 1978; Tallal, 1978). Further research is necessary to determine the exact areas of cognitive differences and their causation.

Denckla and Rudel (1976) found that dyslexic children with minimal brain dysfunction (MBD) in their population were "subtly dysphasic" (p. 12). The MBD children presented soft neurological signs such as slow or dysrhythmic coordination. These children were compared with a normal population and with a population of MBD nondyslexic children. The dyslexic children performed at least at an average intellectual level on the visual-spatial subtests of Block Design and Object Assembly (Wechsler, 1974). Denckla and Rudel noted that "there is increasing evidence against 'visual perceptual impairment' as a major neuropsychological source of reading failure" (p.2). Rather, they believe, the dyslexic difficulty stems from a language problem. Using the Newcombe, Oldfield,

Ratcliff, and Wingfield (1971) modification of the Oldfield and Wingfield (1965) picture naming test, they found that dyslexic children had linguistic retrieval difficulties. The children had difficulty recalling the names of objects presented in pictures, using instead circumlocutions (a description of the objects), pantomimed demonstrations or associative paraphasic responses (usually a different work in the same category, e.g., "baghorn" for "bagpipe" or "telescope" or "stethoscope" (p.9). Some children also displayed phonetic errors. Therefore, they concluded from the results of the study that ". . . dyslexic MBD children resembled dysphasics in that they have linguistic retrieval problems" (p.14).

Articulation Disorders

Speech Perception and Articulation Disorders   Tallal et al. (1976) studied the relationship between speech perception and production impairments in a population of 12 dysphasic children. The children were asked to discriminate between /ba/ and /da/ and between / ɛ / and /æ/. Five of the 12 children reached criterion and were classified as perceptually unimpaired, while the other 7 children were classified as perceptually impaired. The authors hypothesized that there would be differences in the speech production tasks between perceptually impaired dysphasic children who failed to perceive the speech sounds and the other children in the experiment.

As hypothesized, the perceptually impaired dysphasic children had greater difficulty in producing all speech sound categories than both the perceptually unimpaired dysphasic children and the normal control group. The consonant clusters (e.g., blɛ, brɛ, plɛ, and prɛ) were the most difficult, followed by the stop consonants in nonsense syllables (e.g., tɛ , gɛ , dɛg, and gɛd), isolated vowels (e.g., u, i, ɛ, and ɪ), and the nasal consonants (m,n). The last two categories, though, were significantly less impaired than the former two. The dysphasic children also had much greater difficulty producing the vowels in context than in isolation than the normal children. In normal children, stops (b,d) are perceived categorically, i.e., there is an abrupt perception for a stop; the /b/ is perceived as /b/, or it is not. The vowels are perceived along a continuum when the formants change rate or direction. (Formants are energy bands or changes of resonance in the vocal tract.) The dysphasic children, however, were not able to use the categorical information of the stop consonant to aid them in producing the correct vowel. As expected, the children in the study who had fewer errors in perception had fewer errors in production, leading the authors to conclude that there is a clear relationship between perception and production: "speech production deficits in dysphasic children mirror their defects in speech perception" (Tallal & Piercy, 1978, p. 75).

Menyuk (1978) distinguished three different patterns of phonological processing in a group of 27 language disordered children who ranged in age from 4.1 (4 years, 1 month) to 10.10 years. The children were asked to discriminate and produce selected stops /p,t,k/b,d,g/, semivowels /w/r/l/, and fricatives /s,f/sh/.

One group of dysphasic children had significantly greater difficulty (as did the control group) in perception than in production; a second group had significantly greater difficulty in production, while a third group had difficulty in both. Menyuk's finding supports the suggestion that there is a heterogeneous population within the deceptively homogeneous-appearing population of dysphasic children.

Most of the studies in the literature have used tones or sounds that are nonmeaningful stimuli. Dysphasic children have been found to differ in their ability to process and produce meaningful versus nonmeaningful material. Menyuk and Looney (1972b) reported that the meaningful sequences of phonemes (words) were recalled with greater accuracy than nonmeaningful sequences of sounds (nonsense syllables) in both the language disordered child and the normal child, despite the fact that the nonsense syllable stimuli did not exceed three elements, e.g., /abi, aba, abu/.

Blumstein (1978) suggested that different strategies are employed when processing meaningful and nonmeaningful material. Prelinguistic phonological processing requires only sensitivity to certain acoustic signals (Blumstein, 1978). For example, a normal 4-month-old infant can discriminate the acoustic signals of /ba/ and /pa/ (Eimas, Siqueland, Jusczyk, & Vigorito, 1971) or /ba/ and /da/ (Moffitt, 1971), but these sounds are not linguistic signals because they do not communicate meaning. Children at this age are at the feature detection stage (Lubert, 1981). Blumstein suggested that the prelinguistic (involving perception) and linguistic (involving meaning) levels need to be integrated in order for language development to proceed normally. A similar developmental pattern appears to exist for production as for perception.

Articulation and Linguistic Rules Children babble the sounds of the language. Such sounds do not convey meaning, nor are they created by the systematic use of distinctive features. As stated earlier, McNeill (1970) contends that babbling abruptly stops before the onset of speech. Verbalizations occurring after that period are no longer random productions of sounds as observed in babbling but are articulations based on a phonological rule system. The ability to form a sound (babble) or to repeat a sound does not indicate that this sound can be utilized in meaningful production. Stimulability, or the ability to imitate sound, is a phonetic production and differs from the use of sounds (phonemes) to differentiate meaning (Rees, 1973, 1975). Phonemes are constructed, using a system of distinctive features. Acceptance of these premises supports the view that language is based on a hierarchial rule system.

Articulation problems may result from diverse factors, including structural abnormalities (cleft palate); inaccurate placement of articulators (an /s/ lisp); or, a wholly separate problem, the faulty acquisition of a phonological rule system. In the latter instance, the foundation for developing sounds may be defective, causing the subsequent development of syntax and semantics to be distorted.

Hoffnung (1974) compared the imitation, comprehension, and production of 30 children who had severe articulation problems with a matched group of normal children. Each child who was considered to have an articulation problem scored over 30 errors on the Photo Articulation Test (Pendergast, Dickey, Selmar, & Soder, 1969), a test that uses colored pictures of actual objects and in which all the stimuli in the test therefore are meaningful. A test of language was devised to examine the syntactic development of the children in the areas of *negatives* ("The boy cannot pick the apple"), *questions* ("Where are they hiding?"), *copulas* ("He is a policeman"), and *auxiliaries* ("She is talking on the telephone"). The production scores of the experimental population were significantly lower than the normal population, who were matched for age, sex, IQ, and socioeconomic level. Based on these results, Hoffnung suggested that a relationship exists between the phonological and the syntactic levels of language. If a severe phonological problem exists based on the individual's inability to form rules relating to the development of sounds (Chomsky & Halle, 1968; Jakobson, Fant, & Halle, 1952), then a problem in syntax will exist (Hoffnung, 1974; Menyuk, 1978).

Faulty production of sound may also affect surrounding sounds. Analysis-by-synthesis allows one to anticipate the future production of sounds. Through analysis-by-synthesis, a listener's knowledge of language, based on his or her experiences, enables the listener to form internal expectancies about the language being spoken; thus, the person anticipates or predicts the completion of a word or a sentence ("I'll have pie and ___ for ___"). This type of processing may exist when producing sounds.

Daniloff and Moll (1968) suggested that anticipatory programming or co-articulation exist when producing a sound. This theory bears some similarity to analysis-by-synthesis. Through their research, Daniloff and Moll discovered that the formation of a sound may be initiated a number of phonemes prior to the actual production of the sound i.e., the rounding of the lips for /u/ in "construe" may be started on the /n/, four sounds before the actual production of the sound: . . . *n s t r u*. Based on this factor of coarticulation, a child's inconsistent or defective articulation may prevent him or her from anticipating and planning the use of future phonemes. It is possible, therefore, that a defect in one sound will affect the accurate production of other sounds in the word or utterance. Moreover, the child's defective articulation may affect the sound he or she receives as a listener.

Lieberman (1967) contended that by the process of analysis-by-synthesis the listener makes use of the knowledge of articulatory formations to understand speech. Liberman, Cooper, Harris, and MacNeilage (1963) had stated a similar hypothesis. In their motor theory of speech perception, Liberman et al. (1963) hypothesized that knowledge of articulatory gestures (the way in which articulators move to form a sound) aids the listener in decoding (understanding) the production of speech. Marquardt and Saxman (1972) found that children who have a number of misarticulations also have a lower level of language comprehension. The researchers believed that interference was also likely to occur in other language areas if one or more language skills did not remain within the normal range of development. Martin and Caramazza (1982), when studying short-term memory in aphasic adults, noted that the adults' comprehension was improved if they were allowed to rehearse or say the utterances to themselves. Martin and Caramazza stated that "comprehension of an entire sentence is impaired by inhibiting phonological encoding" (p. 67).

Since the development of speech and language precedes the development of reading, problems in articulation and in applying linguistic rules can forecast reading difficulties. Carroll (1976) noted that both slow and skilled readers use slight articulatory movements when reading, as if they were trying to produce the words subvocally. He suggested that "the child must know the language he is going to learn to read" (p. 5). The development of the sounds, semantics, and syntax of a language requires auditory, temporal, spatial, classificatory, and conceptual abilities. An inability to generate linguistic rules can thus cause reading failure (Menyuk, 1969).

Wiig and Semel (1976) suggested that the language problems of learning disabled children are multifaceted, involving auditory perception, linguistic processing and cognitive processing. Each of these three major categories has subdivisions. For example, Chalfant and Scheffelin (1969) indicated that children with poor auditory perception (or poor central processing of auditory stimuli) have difficulty with the identification of the source of sounds, discrimination of sounds and words, reproduction of the prosodic features of the language, selection of foreground stimuli or important stimuli from background noise, synthesis of sounds into words, and comprehension of environmental sounds.

Regarding linguistic processing, Critchley (1970) and Klasen (1972) suggested that speech disorders are present in many cases of reading-writing disorders. Klasen (1972) reported that of the 500 dyslexic children in her study, 112 or 22.4% (almost one-fourth) had speech impediments described predominantly as stuttering and articulation errors or defects; of 414 children with dyslexia, 164 or 39.6% did not speak words until after the age of 18 months, some started to use words at their second birthday and some not until kindergarten. Critchley (1970) noted that 41 of the 125 children with dyslexia in his population were late in the development of speech. He stated that there is a relationship between the proper formation of sounds and reading. Klasen (1972) emphasized the interdependence of the auditory and visual modalities.

In terms of an older population of children, linguistic deficits were found in a large majority of the 6%-15% of the children who failed reading in the first or second grades. Wiig, Semel, and Crouse (1973) found that the children with learning disabilities in their study used a fewer number of morphological rules on a test similar in design to the one created by Berko (1958). Vogel (1974), studying a dyslexic population of elementary school level found that they demonstrated significantly poorer performances on oral syntax tests that included the recognition of grammaticality, repetition of sentences with increasing complexity, oral cloze procedures, and application of morphological rules for nonsense syllables. Moran and Byrne (1977), after studying the use of past tense markers in 60 learning disabled children, suggested that learning disabled children use different rules when forming the past tense. There is a general agreement in the field that many children who are learning disabled have linguistic deficits.

On the other hand, many performances of learning disabled children are attributed to cognitive processing. It envelopes areas such as: memory, acquisition and generalization of distinctive features, and development of semantic units (Wiig & Semel, 1976). Leonard, Bolders, & Miller (1976) examined the semantic relations used by 20 children with language disorders and 20 children with normal language development. The children in both the 3- and 5-year-old normal groups produced semantic relations of greater complexity than did the language disordered group of the same age, but if the normal and language disordered groups were matched by mean length of utterance or ". . . general stage of linguistic development , . ." (p. 383) both groups ". . . seemed to be using utterances reflecting the same semantic relation utterances types . . ." (p. 383). Faulty linguistic processing and its effects on the myriad of skills dependent upon or related to it is still a fertile area for investigation.

The material presented in this section of the chapter has indicated children with dysphasia have a primary problem in language that may include difficulty in rapid auditory processing, lessened auditory acuity, and faulty phonological and syntactical development of a rule system. No definitive statement can be made as to whether the intellectual problems are primary or secondary to the language problems, or whether they exist in each child with dysphasia. There seem to be differing criteria and many subgroups within the general group classified as dysphasia. Standardized tests may be used to substantiate clinical impressions or informal evaluations.

Tests

Before discussing some of the available tests and their applications, a caution to the reader is in order. A test is only meaningful if it is interpreted with knowledge and understanding. Test scores can provide a student's percentile ranking, stanine, and linguistic age, among other information, but it is only through analyzing such information, together with qualitative knowledge of the student, that a student's abilities can be characterized. A *percentile* score indicates how the client would rank in a group of 100 people, i.e., it indicates that the client has scored better than or poorer than a specific part of the population. For example, if a client has a percentile of 88, it means that 87% of the population scored lower than the client. More people achieve a score in the 50th percentile than at either of the two extremes. A *stanine* score provides a general comparison of a client's test score relative to the scores of the rest of the test population. The units of a stanine score are divided into 9 bands or units, with 5 as the mean. The score the client received on the test is ranked according to his or her stanine. A stanine of 3, for example, would mean that the client has achieved a low score in comparison to the rest of the population tested; 4 would indicate low-average, and 5 would be an average score.

Stanine scores are based on standardized scores but are not as sensitive to minor score differences as are standardized scores or percentile rank differences. A *linguistic age* score does not mean the child is using the same type of language as a child of that chronological age; rather it means that the child has scored as many points as did the average child of that chronological age. For instance, when scoring spontaneous utterances (Lee & Canter, 1971), a child of 4 and a child of 7 each may receive a score of 5 points for their particular utterance. For example, the normally developing 4 year old may say, "I am good." The child receives 1 point for "I," 3 points for "am," and 1 point for a complete, syntactically correct sentence. On the other hand, a 7-year-old child with deviant linguistic production may say, "Why he come?" The child receives 4 points for "Why" and one point for "he." The child has not formed a syntactically correct sentence, but he or she has used cognitive knowledge of causation ("Why") to use an advanced interrogative term. The two children may earn the same number of points but for different reasons. Of course, the linguistic differences between the two children will be further differentiated because 100 utterances would have to be analyzed for each child. The corpus of utterances is then used to determine a test score and a linguistic age. This corpus should be analyzed in great detail before starting a program of intervention.

During the administration of formal tests, the examiner should informally try to answer the questions:

1. What type of language is the child using for expression?
2. Where does the child's problem lie, i.e., what areas are involved?
3. Are there patterns to the child's articulatory, syntactic, semantic, or pragmatic difficulties?
4. What does the child understand?
5. What behavior patterns are present?

Table 1 lists just a few of the many commercially available tests that might be of help in an evaluation. In these tests, the scores of linguistically handicapped children can be contrasted with the scores of linguistically normal children. A short discussion of the tests, under the headings of the ability measured, follows. It should be emphasized here that an audiological examination (a hearing test for acuity) is mandatory. Because of the age and/or behavior of the child, it may not be possible to complete the test in one session. Testing that occurs over a period of time should be continued until the therapist can say with confidence that the speech and language problems are not based on a loss of hearing acuity or solely on the loss of hearing, i.e., there is a normal threshold for hearing sounds.

Expression

1. The Developmental Sentence Scoring (DSS) method (Lee & Canter, 1971) is easy to administer but difficult to mark the responses. The speech-language pathologist (SLP) tapes 100 spontaneous utterances of the child, elicited

Table 1. Sample list of standardized language tests

Tests[a]	Age range of standardization scores
A. Expression	
1. Developmental Sentence Scoring (child uses spontaneous utterances [Lee & Canter, 1971])	3.0–6.11 (3 years, 0 months to 6 years, 11 months)
2. Carrow Elicited Language Inventory (child imitates the language of the examiner [Carrow, 1974])	3.0–7.11
3. Goldman-Fristoe Test of Articulation (child names pictures [Goldman & Fristoe, 1969])	6.0–16+ years
4. The Fletcher Time-by-Count Test of Diadochokinetic Syllable Rate (child uses articulators rhythmically and sequentially as quickly as possible [Fletcher, 1978])	6.0–13 years
B. Reception	
5. Peabody Picture Vocabulary Test—Revised (child points to a picture in response to the verbal stimulus of the examiner [Dunn & Dunn, 1981])	2.6–18.11 years
6. Test for Auditory Comprehension of Language (child points to a picture in response to a verbal stimulus by the tester [Carrow, 1973])	2.10–7.9 years
C. General Linguistic Abilities (These tests may require the child's reception and expression in a number of modalities: auditory, visual, and gestural.)	
7. Illinois Test of Psycholinguistic Abilities (Kirk et al., 1968)	2–10 years
8. Clinical Evaluation of Language Functions (Semel & Wiig, 1980)	5 years–adult (grades K–12)
9. Detroit Tests of Learning Aptitude (Baker & Leland, 1967)	3–adult
10. The Test of Language Development (Newcomer & Hammill, 1977)	4.0–8.11

[a]See chapter text for explanation of individual tests.

through conversation with the child concerning books, games, or any items in the environment. The SLP then listens to the tape and transcribes the child's exact utterances, e.g., "He no go" (d/g) "to the (d/ð) park" /hi no do tu də pa/. Points are given for specific parts of speech and for the use of syntactically correct sentences. The total number of points received by the linguistically handicapped child is then compared to scores (provided by Lee and Canter) of the normal population to determine the child's linguistic age. The information transcribed for this test can also be used by the tester to perform a personal evaluation. The

Treatment section of this chapter provides a method for analyzing patterns of errors in the child's corpus of utterances.

2. The Carrow Elicited Language Inventory judges a child's syntactic usage by his or her ability to imitate. Developed by Carrow (1974), the test requires that the child repeat 52 sentence structures ranging from the very simple to the complex. Examples of simple structures are, "Big girl" (adjective + noun) and "Cats jump" (plural subject + verb). An example of a complex structure would be "If it rains, we won't go to the beach," a sentence composed of a subordinate clause and a main clause. The subordinate conditional clause contains the subordinate conjunction "If" plus the pronoun "it" and a verb "rains" inflected for third-person singular. The main clause is a declarative sentence containing a plural nominative pronoun "we," a modal "will," a negative "not," a contraction rule involving "will" + "not" = "won't," a verb "go," a prepositional phrase containing a preposition "to," plus a noun phrase containing a definite article "the" and a noun "beach."

Vygotsky (1962) stated that imitation occurs only within the limits of the child's development. Ervin-Tripp (1970) and Lenneberg (1969) suggested that imitation implies the use of phonological, semantic, and syntactic rules. Lenneberg (1969) declared that children can only repeat linguistic structures correctly when they have learned the rules of grammar. He earlier pointed out (1964) that the child's use of imitation implies that the child is using grammatical rules both receptively and expressively. Ervin (1964) stated that imitation is not grammatically progressive; rather it is slightly more advanced grammatically than is spontaneous production. Hoffnung (1974, 1977) studied the comprehension, imitation, and production of negative structures and found the comprehension scores for 30 linguistically handicapped children to be the highest (234 of 300), imitation scores were second (141 of 300), and production scores, while the lowest (107 of 300), were not markedly different from those of imitation. Fraser, Bellugi, and Brown (1963) administered a test to 12 normal children involving grammatical contrasts, e.g., singular-plurals, present progressive-future, and found that imitation was easier than comprehension, which was easier than production. The differences in the findings of these last two studies may be due to the type of populations and/or stimuli used. Slobin (1968) suggested that an imitated structure, if not currently used by the child, will be used in spontaneous speech in the immediate future. Care must be taken, when utilizing imitation as a test of grammatical competence, to present stimuli just above the child's short-term auditory memory span; otherwise, the child's responses will be based on short-term memory and not on linguistic knowledge.

3. The Goldman-Fristoe Test of Articulation (Goldman & Fristoe, 1969) consists of a spiral book containing large colorful pictures, one picture per page, plus a set of situation pictures that can be used to elicit spontaneous speech, e.g., a child accidentally knocking over a lamp. The pictured items are usually within the vocabulary of a 4½- or 5-year-old child. For example, "hand" is listed at the

2½–3-year level in the Peabody Picture Vocabulary Test (Dunn & Dunn, 1981) while "feather," one of the more difficult words, is listed as the 4-year level. The child is asked to tell the examiner what he or she sees. The form accompanying the test has color-coded columns for marking the child's production of sounds. Other columns are available for noting stimulability. The test is easy to administer because a distractible child seems to enjoy being the "helper", i.e., flipping the cards over for the examiner. A score can be computed, but the examiner is responsible for interpreting the responses.

4. The Fletcher-Time-by-Count Test of Diadochokinetic Syllable Rate (Fletcher, 1978) requires a test form and a stop watch. The child is asked to produce, for example, "pʌ, pʌ, ...," "tʌ, tʌ, ...," "kʌ, kʌ, ..." as fast as possible. The time that it takes the child to produce 20 "tʌ, tʌ, tʌ, ..." sounds, for example, is then computed and compared against the scores of the statistical norms presented on the test form. In addition, the examiner should note the child's volitional and rhythmical movements, the accuracy of articulatory placement, and the control of breath. Later items in the test are more complex, requiring accurate sequencing of different sounds, e.g.," pʌ tə kə ." The test is easy to administer, can be fun for the child, and can provide a number of important items of information for the sophisticated observer.

Reception

5. The Peabody Picture Vocabulary Test (Dunn & Dunn, 1981) can be used to test the child's comprehension of isolated words. Using black and white line drawings throughout the test (displayed four to a page), the examiner asks the child to select, e.g., "bus" (2½–3-year-old level), "empty" (4-year level), "dripping" (6-year level), "ceremony" (9-year level), and "transparent" (16-year level). The test is simple to administer and mark. The raw score can be computed for a linguistic age, percentile, and stanine, enabling the examiner to gain some estimation of the child's auditory comprehension of isolated words.

6. In the Test for Auditory Comprehension of Language (TACL) (Carrow, 1973), the child is required to point to one of three horizontally placed pictures. Initially, the child is asked to select simple nouns, but as the test progresses the stimuli are used to gain information concerning more advanced linguistic and cognitive concepts. For Question (Q) 7, for example, the child is asked to point to "hand"; Q.8 "man"; Q.11 "red"; Q.15 "fast"; Q.21 "two"; Q.67 "balls"; Q.44 "on"; Q.45 "under"; and for the last question, Q.101, the child is asked to select the picture that fits the directive, "Look at the third picture and point to the baby of this animal."

The stimuli in this test can be judged linguistically, e.g., "hand" and "man" are nouns; "red," "fast," and "two" are adjectives; "balls" is a plural noun; "on" and "under" are prepositions. The same stimuli can be judged cognitively: "hand"—part of the body; "man"—animate, human, male; "red"—color; "fast"—time; "two," "balls"—quantity; "on," "under"—spatial relationships.

The test is easy to administer and mark. The age norms are listed for each item, and the linguistic age and percentile can be computed. Again, the examiner must be knowledgeable when evaluating the results.

General Linguistic Abilities

7. The Illinois Test of Psycholinguistic Abilities (ITPA) (Kirk et al., 1968) can be used to test the child's ability to decode (comprehend), encode (produce), and associate material. The test is organized both on a representational level (in which the individual's ability to use symbols is judged) and on an automatic level (in which the highly organized linguistic habits of the individual are rated). Twelve subtests utilize the auditory-vocal and visual-motor channels of communication. Indicated after each title listed below are the specific skills required to perform each test, e.g., auditory reception, association, retention, and sequencing, but the tests can be evaluated and interpreted to include other abilities. Hoffnung (1981) analyzed the Auditory Reception Subtest of the ITPA and determined that, in addition to auditory reception, accurate responses required an understanding of many concepts. For example, the ability to differentiate +human from +animate was necessary to succeed on the demonstration question II.b, "Do ponies shave?" and on Q. 14, "Do eagles paint?" The subtests of the ITPA include:

The Auditory Reception Test, requiring understanding of language (e.g., Q. 5, "Do babies cry?"; Q. 50, "Do mute musicians vocalize?").

The Auditory Association Test, requiring auditory reception of words and an understanding of the relationship between two items (e.g., "Daddy is big; baby is ____").

The Auditory Sequential Memory Test, requiring digit retention of progressively longer sequences of numbers.

The Auditory Closure Test, requiring the filling in of the missing parts of a word (e.g., Q.4, "tele__one").

The Visual Reception Test, requiring an understanding of the significance of the visual stimuli (e.g., Q.12, "Match a little girl mopping with a mop to a little girl sweeping with a broom").

The Visual Sequential Test, requiring retention of a sequence of visually presented nonmeaningful geometric designs.

The Visual Association Test, requiring an understanding of the relationship between two pictures (e.g., Q.4, "table and chair").

The Visual Closure Test, requiring the recognition of a visual form from an incomplete presentation of the form (e.g., the child is asked to find all the fish in a picture; parts of the fish may be hidden by other objects in the picture such as seaweed).

The Verbal Expression Test, requiring the use of language to convey ideas (e.g., Q. 1, "Tell me all about the ball").

The Grammatic Closure Test, requiring the child to produce correct syntactic responses (e.g., Q. 1, "Here is a dog. Here are two ____").

The Sound Blending Test, requiring the blending of two or more sounds into a whole word (e.g., Q.2, "m'–an" and Q. 19, "d–i–nn–er").

The Manual Expression Test, requiring the expression of ideas by the use of gestures (e.g., Q. 1, "Show me what you do with a guitar").

A psycholinguistic age can be obtained and a comparison of the standard scores for each of the above tests can be visually displayed to reveal the areas of strength and weakness.

8. The purpose of the Clinical Evaluation of Language Functions (CELF) test (Semel & Wiig, 1980) is to differentiate "measures of language functions in phonology, syntax, semantics, memory, word finding and retrieval" (p. 1). The CELF is an excellent test for a child of kindergarten age or older, but is a little too advanced to be used with the average preschool population. The first six tests and Test 12 require the child to process or understand material. Tests 7 through 11 and Test 13 are used to test the child's production. Following is a brief description of each:

Test 1 Test 1 asks the child to choose the correct picture, e.g., Q. 5, "The boy is eating an ice cream sundae," from four presented pictures. This requires that the child differentiate gender (boy and girl) and the time reference of the verb. Question 11, "The girl has a big spotted, black and white dog," requires the child to select the big dog in contrast to a little dog and the spotted dog in contrast to one-color dogs.

Test 2 Test 2 requires the child to select two items that are related in some way, e.g., Q. 1, "Shoes, sock, and bread"; Q. 14, "run, sleep, night, and winter"; Q. 22," truth, success, fear, and failure."

Test 3 and Test 5 Tests 3 and 5 require processing of linguistic concepts and oral directions. Both tests require that the child point to an item. Test 3, Q. 1 asks the child to, "Point to the line that is *not* yellow"; Q. 22, "Before you point to a blue line, but after I point to a red line, you point to a yellow line." Test 5 asks the child to, Q. 1, "Point to the last circle"; Q. 25, "Point to the last small black circle to the left of the big black square."

Test 4 and Test 6 Tests 4 and 6 require comprehension of the type of language that would occur in a more spontaneous setting. Test 4 requires that the child understand relationships and ambiguities, e.g., Q. 1, "Are parents older than their children?"; Q. 32, "Still waters run deep. Does it mean: The water is deep in some places?". Test 6 requires the child to answer questions about paragraphs that are read to him or her.

Test 12 Test 12 is designed to test the ability of a child to judge whether two words are the same or different, e.g., Q. 1, "pie–pie" and Q. 21, "leaf–leave."

Test 7 Test 7, the first test that is used to examine production, requires the use of automatic serial speech. The child is asked to name the days of the week and the months of the year.

Test 8 and Test 9 Tests 8 and 9 require the ability to name. Test 8 requires that the child name colors, forms, and color plus form items as they are visually presented. Test 9 requires that the child retrieve the names of food and animals from his or her own knowledge and language corpus.

Test 10 and Test 11 Tests 10 and 11 require the production of sentences. Test 10 requires that the child imitate the utterances of the examiner, e.g., Q. 1, "The dog chased the cat," while Test 11 requires that the child make up sentences using specific words, e.g., Q. 1, "car" and Q. 12, "if."

Test 13 Test 13 is an indirect test of articulation in which the child is required to complete the sentence, and his or her articulatory ability is based on that completion. For example, in Q. 1, the target sound is the /kw/; the child is asked to complete "Once upon a time there was a king and a ____."

The CELF test is detailed, comprehensive, and well organized. Each subtest can be given a total score, and standard scores of the individual tests can be compared. In addition, items missed by the child can be easily analyzed according to specific categories. If a total score is not required, parts of the test can be selected for administration based on the information desired.

9. The Detroit Tests of Learning Aptitude (Baker & Leland, 1967) is a comprehensive test that can be used from the age of 3 to an adult level. Seven major categories of abilities, as listed below, are required to successfully complete the 19 subtests of the test. Some, but not all, of the subtests are cited below under the major categories.

Verbal Ability can be judged informally from the child's responses to the various tests and specifically from the Free Association Test.

Reasoning and Comprehension Abilities can be analyzed through the Pictorial Absurdities, Verbal Absurdities, and Social Adjustment tests.

Time and Space Relationships can be judged through the Orientation Test.

Practical Judgment can be judged through the Pictorial Opposites Test.

Auditory Attentive Ability can be judged through the Auditory Attention Span for Unrelated Words Test.

Motor Ability can be judged through the Motor Speech and Precision Test.

Number Ability can be judged through a test of the same name.

A minimum of 9 tests and a maximum of 13 tests is suggested when the Detroit Tests of Learning Ability is used for diagnosing the problem of a child. One test should be selected under each of the major categories. Some of the tests are suggested for all children (e.g., Visual Attention Span for Objects) and some are restricted to students under the ages of 9 years or 14 years, or over the age of 3.6 years.

The test scores can be totaled to find the mental age of the child and ranked to develop a profile of the child.

10. The Test of Language Development (TOLD) (Newcomer & Hammill, 1977) consists of seven subtests designed to measure the language ability of children ages 4–8 years. The test includes items that are similar in design to other tests but the items are grouped together so as to measure a number of linguistic abilities. The test includes items of:

Word Discrimination (e.g., Q. 1, "red-dead" and Q. 20, "conical-comical")
Picture Vocabulary or single word reception (e.g., Q. 1, "mirror" and Q. 25, "infantry")
Grammatic Completion or sentence completion (e.g., Q. 1, "Mary has a dress and Joan has a dress. They have two ____" ; and Q. 30, "Jeff ate the candy quickly and when Bill came, it had all been ____ .")
Word Articulation (e.g., Q. 1, "tree" and Q. 20 "birthday")
Sentence Imitation (e.g., Q. 1, "Her friends walked to school" and Q. 30, "They gave the lion who had become very dangerous to the zoo.")
Oral Vocabulary or Word Definition (e.g., Q. 1, "bird" and Q. 20 "north")
Grammatic Understanding (e.g., Q. 1, "She went quickly" and Q. 25, "The bicycle had been stolen.")

A language quotient can be determined, and the scaled scores permit comparison among the various subtests.

Many of the tests mentioned above and other commercially available tests have items that overlap or that test the same abilities in a slightly different way or at a slightly different level. A speech-language pathologist may have a limited amount of time that can be used for testing. Therefore, familiarity with available tests is recommended. Care must be taken to determine exactly what information is desired, and the best way to ferret out this information.

It is a good idea to test early in the term, as the results of testing can provide a direction for therapy. A pretherapy evaluation can also be used later to determine how successful the therapy program has been. Though testing is advised, practitioners should not ignore their own clinical judgment, clinical observations, and clinical intuition. Qualitative interpretation of the client's actual behavior can be more important than quantitative scoring. When retesting at the end of a semester, do not wait until the last session, as the student's attention span and the lesson's time restriction may limit the number of tests that can be completed in one session. In addition, unexpected illness, family problems, or vehicle breakdowns may cause unplanned absences. Therefore, try to allow extra sessions to accommodate for last-minute emergencies.

Testing should not be continued if the test is too difficult, if the practitioner believes the test results are invalid because the testing time has exceeded the child's attention span, or if the child is not responding as well as the practitioner knows he or she can. Scores should not be sent to other agencies when their validity is in doubt. Test scores are likely to follow that child permanently.

ETIOLOGY

Childhood aphasia can be classified as acquired or developmental. Acquired childhood aphasia is said to occur when there is a known focal lesion that occurred after birth (Tallal, 1978). The processing of language occurs in the left hemisphere (dominant hemisphere) in most right-handed people. Anatomical differences are present at birth between the right and left temporal lobes, yet Rapin and Wilson (1978) have stated that either the right or the left hemisphere may be removed in a child without interfering with the child's development of speech and language. This development will not occur if bilateral damage of the hemispheres is present, however. In acquired aphasia, the child may be mute initially but may later acquire speech and language because of the development of the right hemisphere.

The etiology of developmental aphasia has not been determined definitively. Chase (1972) noted the term "developmental aphasia" is applied often in children who have a family history of language disabilities and who are considered to be congenitally aphasic children. It has been suggested that developmental aphasia may stem from "high level" audioperceptual impairment (Benton, 1964, 1978), from hereditary factors (Myklebust, 1971a), and from the slow maturation of the central nervous system (Rapin & Wilson, 1978).

Menyuk and Looney (1972a,b) reported that the children with specific language disorders in their study showed no obvious central nervous system damage; Stark and Tallal (1981) found no "frank" neurological deficits in their population. Benton (1964, 1978), however, stated that evidence is being amassed to support the claim of early central nervous system damage as the causative factor of developmental dysphasia. Extensive lesions of the left posterior temporal lobe produce greater disturbances of language function the older the child is at the time of damage. Recovery is expected until the age of 10 or 12 years because "during the first decade, the nondominant hemisphere (right) is capable of mediating normal language function" (Chase, 1972, p. 108).

Recent pneumoencephalograms were taken of 87 language disabled children (Rapin & Wilson, 1978). Twenty-six of the children were found to have an enlargement of the left temporal horn, 6 of the right temporal horn, and 14 of both horns, i.e., a little over 50% of the children were discovered to have a neurological problem. Similarly, Goldstein, Landau, & Kleffner (1958) reported that 40% of their population of 69 aphasic children had abnormal electroencephalograms, making it possible, then, to have a normal encephalogram and a deviant developmental pattern of language. Eisenson (1972) stated that 30% of the children in his study with developmental aphasia were neurologically impaired.

Minor neurological signs can be overlooked during routine examinations. These signs can be "impairment of coordinated fine movements of the hands, general clumsiness, choreiform or athetoid movements, and strabismus" (Chase, 1972, p. 117). The significant etiological factors that Chase listed were:

> hemorrhage, use of toxic drugs, and viral infections during pregnancy; toxemia of pregnancy; prolonged and complicated labor; prematurity; subdural hematoma; ceph-

alohematoma; anoxia; low birth weight; kernicterus; meningitis; encephalitis; arrested hydrocephalus; severe dehydration; lead intoxication; and head trauma (p. 117). The mildest of the deficits may be in association with the syndrome of minimal cerebral dysfunction; the most severe deficits would result in abortions, stillbirths, or neonatal deaths.

Children with developmental aphasia have severe linguistic problems and severe behavioral problems (Eisenson, 1968a). The behavior problems can be perceived as perceptual dysfunction, intellectual inefficiency, emotional instability, lack of consistent responses, perseveration, and hyperactivity. Other areas of difficulty may include problems in walking, difficulty with visuo-motor tasks, and impairment in visual memory (Rapin & Wilson, 1978). Because of the varying linguistic and behavioral problems of these children, one suspects that no single deficit is responsible for the multiple syndromes presented by the children with developmental language disability (Rapin & Wilson, 1978). Ajuriaguerra (1966), too, commented, "Even if there is only a single point of impact, the organization of this plastic function must involve more than just a single system" (p. 129). These findings support the position that different subgroups exist within what was once thought a homogeneous population of childhood aphasic individuals.

Left-handedness or lack of established laterality have been considered by some to be related to problems in speech and language. A large percentage of dysphasic (and dyslexic) children are reported to be left-handed, of mixed laterality, or from families who have not established right-handed dominance (Zangwell, 1978). This fact assumes importance when one considers that the perception of speech and language is processed in the left hemisphere (Eisenson, 1972). Kimura (1967) demonstrated a right-ear advantage (REA) for dichotically presented verbal material, i.e., when different material was presented to each ear. Superior responses were given to the stimuli presented to the right ear, indicating that the material was being processed by the left hemisphere. Cutting (1973) listed results that agree with those of Kimura, but he concluded that the left hemisphere does not process all classes of sounds equally. The stops (plosives) /b, d, g, p, t, k/ were processed with the strongest REA, while the liquids /l, r/ did not have as strong an REA, and the vowels showed no REA. The stops used in the study are known to have sharper boundaries (Liberman, Delattre, & Cooper, 1958) than do the steady-state isolated vowels. In categorical perception, "Speech sounds are perceived as belonging to groups with abrupt perceptual shifts between groups" (Borden & Harris, 1980, p. 274); either the sound is heard as a /b/ or it is not. Since consonants supply most of the intelligibility or cues for understanding language, the likelihood that they are processed differently than other sounds (vowels) is significant. If the sounds with rapid transitions (stops) (Cutting, 1973) are the sounds that the children have the most difficulty processing; if these sounds are furthermore processed with a right-ear advantage; and if the children have a laterality problem—then, perhaps, a neurological underpinning for the language problem can be assumed present. Menyuk (1978) theorized that there must be neurological substrates that are specific to verbal tasks because of the fact that the processes required for language acquisition are unique. This rapid processing for stops may be one of the neurological sequences required.

CLASSIFICATION SYSTEMS

Classification takes specific functions into consideration, e.g., the nonverbal intelligence of the child and the child's ability to hear, discriminate, recognize, sequence, comprehend, store, organize, integrate, retrieve, formulate, and motorically produce the sounds and words of the language. The child's performance of these functions must be continually reevaluated irrespective of the classification or label placed on that child.

Myklebust (1954) hypothesized three types of language disturbances: One affecting the reception of language, a second affecting the output or expression of language, and a third affecting inner language or the child's integration of language. Benton (1978) described two broad categories of language disorders: expressive dysphasia and receptive-expressive dysphasia. In expressive dysphasia, the child's comprehension is superior to his or her level of expression; in receptive-expressive dysphasia, the receptive impairments are considered to be primary and are the basis for the expressive impairment. Wolfus et al. (1980) tested 20 children with developmental language impairments and categorized the children similarly. Two subgroups were differentiated: a group with expressive difficulties and a group with expressive-receptive difficulties, where the deficits were more global in nature. The expressive group displayed normal comprehension of syntax, semantic ability, digit-span retention, and good phonological discrimination, but had difficulty with syntactic production, with the production of consonant clusters, diphthongs in words, and three-syllable words. The expressive-receptive group had poor comprehension and production of syntax, poor semantic ability, a lower digit-span retention, poor phonological discrimination, and behavior problems, e.g., impulsivity and distractibility. Wolfus et al. (1980) do not believe that an auditory-perceptual basis is primary for developmental language impairments, i.e., a perceptual deficit is not the cause of a child's inability to produce consonants. Rather, they believe a child may have difficulty in organizing verbal information. Morehead and Ingram (1973) believed the difficulty stems from subtle cognitive differences.

Aram and Nation (1975), after testing 47 children with developmental language disorders, suggested that there are hierarchial levels in the development of language. They stated, "Language is a unified system that employs multiple levels simultaneously" (p. 232) (those levels being, semantic, syntactic and phonological). They believe that if the semantic level is deficient, the syntactic and phonological levels will be defective as well; that if the syntactic level is deficient so also will be the phonological level; and that only the phonological level may be deficient without involving the other two areas. Hoffnung (1974) found that 20 severely phonologically impaired children who were screened to be included in her study could not be accepted because they did not reach the mental age criteria of the Peabody Picture Vocabulary Test (Dunn, 1965). Clinically, as in the Stark and Tallal (1981) study, these children were not judged to be retarded, but when tested, it was found that their comprehension of isolated words was below their chronological age level. This finding, coupled with the serendipitous findings of the above mentioned authors suggests that all levels of language are interrelated.

Language requires the use of rules at each level. Therefore, a child who is unable to apply linguistic rules at one level may have difficulty applying appropriate linguistic rules at another level. Children with severe phonological problems were found to have syntactic difficulties (Hoffnung, 1974; Menyuk, 1964). Because language is based on rules, a child with knowledge of syntactic rules can anticipate the next word or group of words in a sentence (Eisenson, 1972), thus, the processing of language is faster, and comprehension and production are aided.

SYMPTOMATOLOGY

No clear picture of the syndrome of childhood dysphasia has yet to emerge. Dysphasic children, in terms of their expressive language, can range from those who are totally mute to those who are able to speak but with severely impaired phonological, semantic, and syntactic systems. With respect to their receptive language, dysphasic children can range from those who fail completely to respond to speech or to environmental sounds (Chappell, 1970, 1972) to those who possess good comprehension skills for spoken language.

More specifically, with respect to their expressive language, dysphasic children may be unable to verbally formulate an idea or to form a verbal utterance using an intelligible speech pattern; they may repeat words clearly but their productive ability may deteriorate in normal conversation (Benton, 1964) in which rapid production of speech is prerequisite (i.e., rapid movement of the articulators); they may present syntactic difficulties along with their articulation defects (Hoffnung, 1974), and these same difficulties may be observed in writing (Benton, 1964) or in other ways may disrupt their total education "because the brain dysfunction affects not only auditory language behavior but the manner in which the child can best learn to read, write, tell time, understand maps, calculate...." (Myklebust, 1971a, p. 1203). At present, strong interest is being shown in studying the subgroups within the larger classification of developmental aphasia.

A major problem in classification is that the underlying neurological defect may differ from child to child. Therefore, small homogeneous groups, each comprised of persons with some underlying defect, may be identified within the larger group of developmental aphasics. Inter-study comparisons are difficult because the researchers may start with a neurologically variable population. The findings of such studies then produce children who not only differ from each other in degree or severity of language disorders but who differ from each other in the type or principal area or areas of disability.

Auditory Modality

Many studies have been designed to test the auditory modality of dysphasic children. A major question arises: Though the auditory modality is tested, does the child's response to the various tests always require the use of the same auditory processes? Weiner (1972) tested dysphasic children on a variety of tests that required auditory perceptual ability and found dysphasic children to be statistically inferior on all the auditory tests except the Wepman Auditory Discrimination Test (Wepman, 1958) (and Weiner questioned the results of that test). The auditory tests used in the Weiner study required a variety of responses, i.e., repetition, pointing, and oral-motor production. For instance, the test for assessment of oral language comprehension (Carrow, 1968) required comprehension of isolated words of varying linguistic information, and the Repetition of Sentence Test (Weiner, 1969) required that the child repeat a number of sentences. Though both tests are valuable, the reader must recognize that though the input for each test was auditory, the output required different information and different processing, making comparison of auditory ability among dysphasic children difficult.

Stark, Poppen, and May (1967) asked children in their study to depress three keys with pictures on them representing common, one-syllable words, in the order in which they were auditorily presented. Five of the eight aphasic children tended to forget the first of the three stimuli, suggesting to the authors that these five children may have auditory memory or sequencing problems.

Lowe and Campbell (1965) and Tallal and Piercy (1978) examined the time interval between sounds and the transition times of sounds in studies with dysphasic children and concluded that rapid auditory processing may be part of the dysphasic child's problem.

On the strength of these and numerous other studies, many theorists conclude that difficulties in the auditory modality are at the base of a dysphasic child's language problem. Others, however, disagree (see below, under The Linguistic Structure). Care must be given to determine exactly which auditory process(es) is/are not functioning, i.e., rapid processing of auditory material, sequencing, memory, comprehension of words, or perhaps some linguistic factor that depends on cognitive ability plus the auditory modality.

In this author's view, continued research is necessary to determine the relationship between the problem in auditory processing and the utilization of speech and language. Tallal and Piercy (1978), working with 12 dysphasic children, found that the 5 dysphasic children who were able to discriminate between single consonants /bɛ/ and /dɛ/, even though they were not able to discriminate between clusters (consonant blends), e.g., /blɛ/ and /prɛ/, were superior to the 7 dysphasic children who were unable to discriminate between consonant sounds singly or in clusters. The /ɛ/ vowel was used consistently throughout the research project in order that the phonetic environment (surrounding sounds) would remain stable. Tallal and Piercy (1978) concluded that a relationship between auditory reception and production was clearly established. If the results of future studies continue to substantiate these findings, the clinician may find it beneficial to try to improve the integrity of a child's auditory perceptual processing before introducing production, on the theoretical basis that the child's ability to discriminate between sounds will aid his or her production. The sound combinations in the Tallal and Piercy (1978) study were not true speech but were nonsense syllables. The question remains whether a person processes nonsense syllables in the same manner (i.e., neurologically, psychologically, cognitively, and linguistically) as true speech.

Liberman et al. (1963) hypothesized that knowledge of the articulatory gestures (movements of the articulators as they produce sounds) aids the listener in decoding (understanding) the production. They suggested that accurate motor production will aid perception. This theory leads to the supposition that a child's faulty production of a sound may affect his or her reception of the sound. If the clinician accepts this premise, it would then be beneficial to the client to try to achieve accurate production of these sounds as they are used in words (to differentiate meaning-phonemes) in order to assist in the auditory perception of language.

The Linguistic Structure

Some theorists are unconvinced that auditory processing is the key to the language problem. Rees (1973) stated that the concept of an auditory processing difficulty as the cause of aphasia has not been supported by strong evidence and suggested that understanding of the linguistic structure may be at the base of the difficulty. Other authors (Cromer, 1978; Wolfus et al., 1980; Zangwell, 1978) concur, postulating that the problem in dysphasia stems either from difficulties with linguistic coding or from problems with the hierarchial ordering of language.

Language is not a sequential chain but is hierarchial in nature (Cromer, 1978). Cromer uses the sentence, "The people who called and wanted to rent your house when you go away next year are from California" (p. 86) an an example of a construct that requires the ability to use a hierarchial linguistic structure in order to be understood. The "are" at the end of the sentence is related to the noun phrase (NP) "the people," which is 14 words away from it at the beginning of the sentence. Language is not just the memorization of the ordering of items; there are transformations and a generative aspect to it. It is not possible, for example, to remember 19 words in short-term memory (as in the above sentence), if they are separate strings of elements. When items are chunked together in noun phrases or verb phrases (VPs), however, more than 7 ± 2 elements (Miller, 1956) can be retained. The NP "The people" is two words in length; the VP "wanted to rent your house" is five words. By comprehending the above sentence as a series of units, including NPs, VPs, and the smaller sentence that is embedded in the larger sentence, "You go away next year," the listener is able to remember the sentence and gather meaning from it.

Speakers of a language have tacit knowledge (knowledge they cannot easily explain that enables them to perform tasks). The 19 word sentence just cited implies:

1. The people called;
2. The people wanted to rent your house; and
3. The people are from California.

It would be awkward and unnecessary to repeat the words "The people" three times. A transformational rule employing deletion thus allows the speaker to delete "the people" from the sample sentences 2 and 3. A listener who speaks the same language as the speaker has knowledge of an identical set of transformational rules, and therefore understands a spoken sentence that uses the deletion transformation. Structure and rules enable people to generate novel sentences (Chomsky, 1965). Structure and rules apply, as indicated earlier, to all levels of language.

The generation of a sentence uses words composed of sounds that are grouped into categories, e.g., plosives (stops) (p, t, k, b, d, g), fricatives (f, v, s, z, ʃ, ʒ, tʃ, dʒ, θ, ð), and others. Dysphasic children may develop general categories or groups of sounds, or a globular notion of consonant phonemes (Eisenson, 1972) but may not be able to differentiate within individual categories of speech sounds. For example, the child may produce one stop, e.g., /p/, and not be able to produce the /b/, which requires + voice; or the child may produce the /p/ and /b/ (both are anterior and formed in the front of the mouth, anterior to the /ʃ/ sound) (Chomsky and Halle, 1968) and be unable to form the /t/ or /d/, which adds the distinctive feature of +coronal, requiring the alteration of the contact of the articulators (tongue to the alveolar ridge instead of closure of both lips). The child may merge the labial and dental plosives into one labial sound, e.g., /p/. The practice of "paradeltazismus" is ". . . the merger of dentals and labials into a single series, which is represented for the most part by labial sounds (Jakobson, 1968, p. 62). The child then has a reduced number of words. Differentiation of the sounds within a category (e.g., plosives) enables the child to add new words to his or her expressive and receptive lexicon, e.g., "pie," "bye," "tie," and "die." Sound structure or the phonological aspect of language is related to syntax (Aram & Nation, 1975; Marquardt & Saxman, 1972; Menyuk & Looney, 1972b). The ability to differentiate, which is absent or present to a nonproductive degree at the phonological level, may be defective at the syntactic level. If the child's ability to differentiate within a sound category (phonological level) is nonproductive, this same limitation concerning differentiation of linguistic categories may be defective at the syntactic level, causing problems in the syntactic development of language.

250   Hoffnung

Initially, a child develops general categories of language. These are subject to differentiation. The problem of feature detection in phonology or the ability to develop subcategories can also be observed in syntax. Two major linguistic problems for dysphasic children are demonstrated in the inability to use the nominal (subject) pronoun and the auxiliary verb with a verb (to be + verb). An example of an ungrammatical utterance, "Me walking home" /mi w ɔ -ɪ ho /for "I am walking home" /aɪ æm w ɔ kɪŋ houm/ is representative of a combined problem of phonology and syntax.

The dysphasic child may develop the accusative pronouns "me" and "him" and use them appropriately in the utterances, "Give me," "Go him." Later the child may use these accusative pronouns in the nominal position, e.g., "Me eat," "Him go." Though the utterances produced were not syntactically correct, the pronouns were not being used randomly, but according to the child's present level of linguistic rule development. The use of "me" and "him" indicates that the child has a category of pronouns, in this instance accusative, but this category has not been differentiated into accusative and nominative. The dysphasic child does not usually produce the pronouns out of sequence, nor does the child use them randomly. Rather the child is using a linguistic rule "pronoun + verb," but has not differentiated the category of pronouns. Trantham and Pedersen (1976) analyzed a number of linguistically normal and a number of language impaired children and found that the pronoun "I" was mastered by the normal children between the ages of 24–30 months, while the pronoun "he" was mastered between 24–36 months. The language impaired child may start to use the "I" and "he" pronouns at 24 months but will use them only rarely.

An identical pattern is used in the development or lack of development in the verb phrase. Dysphasic children may not differentiate the VP from a simple verb "walk" to an auxiliary + verb + inflection ("is + walk + ing"), as is required in the present progressive tense. The child usually adds the "-ing" inflection (morpheme indicating continuing action), but is unable to use an auxiliary + a main verb, e.g., a form of "to be" and a verb. Again, the order is usually maintained, indicating that the child is using a set of rules but has not differentiated within the category of verbs.

More complex transformational rules are required for advanced linguistic productions. Questions and negatives require the obligatory use of the transformational rule of permutation, which necessitates the transposition of the elements in a sentence while maintaining the meaning of a sentence (Traugott & Pratt, 1980). The child employs a rising inflection "He is?" when first asking a "Yes/No" question. Later, this interrogative sentence is transformed into a more advanced linguistic structure "Is he?" by the use of a permutation transformational rule. As a child matures cognitively and linguistically, more complex utterances are formed. For example, a child may use two simple sentences to express an idea, e.g., "The man is on the corner"; "The man has red hair." By transformational rules this can be combined into a sentence containing an embedded sentence, e.g., "The man, who has red hair, is on the corner." In this instance, the duplication of the subject NP "The man" has been deleted, the relative pronoun "who" has been added, and the VP "has red hair" has been permuted. These changes of deletion, addition, and permutation are all accounted for by the transformation rules of grammar (Chomsky, 1965).

Cromer (1978) described the written narratives of deaf and aphasic children in response to a story they were told. On examination of their written productions, Cromer found that aphasic children almost exclusively used a specified sentence type with which they were familiar. An example was given of one child who used the present progressive form of the verb, i.e., verb + "ing" ("running") and who never tried to use the present, future ("will" + verb) or perfect tenses, i.e., "has-had" + verb + inflection ("has jumped" and "had eaten"). The aphasic children also did not use simple transformations that would allow the use of two adjectives in an NP, e.g., "The big, tall one" (Cromer, 1978, p. 124) or of conjoined adjectives, e.g., "He is big and strong" (Cromer, 1978, p. 124). The use of qualifying adjectives may be based on hierarchy (Cromer, 1978), for one does not reverse this order and say, e.g., "a red, tall, big one," but rather, "a big tall, red one." There were no examples of adverb-adjective strings in the dysphasic children's written productions, e.g., "the very big ball" (Cromer, 1978, p. 124), or of coordinate structures, e.g., "but" or "because." In addition, there were no instances of two embedded sentences. If one embedded sentence was produced, the dysphasic child omitted the second verb—for example, "The boy, who read the book, ___ here." No negative, question, or conjoined sentences were written.

In contrast, the deaf children in the Cromer (1978) study used seven categories of verbs, i.e., present ("walk"), past ("walked"), future ("will walk"), copulas ("is" or "are"), progressive ("walking"), perfects ("have"-"had walked"), and infinitive ("to walk"). Negatives, questions, complement clauses, and embedded or conjoined elements were also used. The structures were not always correct, but they were attempted, e.g., "Suddenly coming the duck to pick up the basket and the ball to a small basket but the two duck are frightened" (p. 125). The complement verb ("picked up ball to put..." [Cromer, 1978, p. 125]) was used by the deaf child but not by the dysphasic child.

Overall, the dysphasic children in Cromer's (1978) study made a greater number of errors than did the deaf children. Hierarchial organization needed in complex sentences requires an increased number of transformational levels of complexity, in which one level is built upon the other (Cromer, 1978). For example, dysphasic children experience difficulty in the use of conjoined verbs, e.g., "The lady is *laughing* and *crying* at the same time." They also lack the ability to use a structure that is interrupted. Interdependence of separated elements may exist in a sentence; for example, in the sentence, "*The girl,* who is pretty, *is* my sister," the second verb relates to the first NP, even though they are separated by the clause "who is pretty." The sentence elements are hierarchially structured, not merely sequenced. It has been suggested that the dysphasic child may be "using simple grammatical rules based on adjacent elements" (Cromer, 1978, p. 128). The dysphasic child may relate a word only to the word adjacent to it and thus may not connect a separated second part of the sentence with the first part of the sentence.

Leonard (1972), studying kindergarten children with a mean age of 5.3 years, found no significant difference between normal and language-deviant groups in terms of the number of children who used a structure, though significant differences occurred when the frequency of a particular structure was counted. There was a trend for normal children to use the more basic structures accurately and to use the less-frequently occurring negative and question transformations consistently. As the complexity of the sentence was increased, the language disordered children were found to omit structures they were capable of using. Leonard's examples support Cromer's (1978) description of children who have difficulty with hierarchial order and with structures that require "interruption," e.g., "Jimmy eats like a pig" (Leonard, 1972, p. 436). In this sentence, the third-person singular inflection ("eats") is produced, but in the ungrammatical structure, "That *man,* over there, *run* fast" (p. 436), the third-person singular inflection is omitted, possibly because of the embedding of "over there," which interrupts the NP and its verb. This same pattern occurred with the past tense. In the sentence, "Mommy, a doggie walked home with me" (p. 436), the past tense was well formed, but in the ungrammatical complex sentence with embedding, "The *monkey,* who fell, *jump* back up" (p. 436), the /-ed/ morpheme was omitted.

Children with articulation problems may not use morphological endings, either because they are unable to produce the sound or because of their difficulty with linguistic rules. Many children referred to speech centers are unable to use morphological inflections such as plural ("hats– hæts," "bags–bægz") or past tense ("washed–waʃt" "combed–koumd") because they are unable to use a final sound ("coat"–kou). A clinician can judge a child's linguistic knowledge of the rules for plural and past tense by noting the child's ability to say, e.g., "witches" (wɪ-ɪ/wɪtʃɪz) and "painted" (pe-ɪ/peɪntɪd). The plural and past-tense forms in these examples required the addition of the morphemes /-ɪz/ and /-ɪd/ respectively. The child's knowledge of these linguistic features can be judged by the presence or absence of two syllables in these words, even though only the vowel /ɪ/ was included, rather than vowel + consonant /-ɪz/ and /-ɪd.

Menyuk (1964), after studying normal and infant speech, found the most significant factor for accurate production "was the child's ability to determine the complete sets of rules that were used to generate and differentiate structure at any level of grammar" (p. 119). Menyuk and Looney (1972a) noted that the language disordered children in their study preserved the intention of the sentence, the word order, and the main relations, i.e., actor-action-object, but did not use transformations. There was a significant difference in the phonological and structural aspects of the sentences formed by the language disordered child, as well. The child omitted the auxiliary ("be," "do," or "have"), the modals ("can," "will," "may," "must," or "should"), and/or did not use the permutation rule in, e.g., negative sentences ("He ___ no have money" [Menyuk & Looney, 1972a, p. 274]) and interrogative sentences ("Where ___ he going? When he will come?", p. 274). On repetition, a child might produce a sentence of the same length or longer but might simplify the sentence linguistically because of difficulty in the utilization of transformations. For example, the sentence, "Can't I come?" is more complex than "I want cake and milk and candy," even though the second sentence is longer. "Can't I come?" requires a permutation transformation "I can" to "Can I," an addition of the negative "no" and the modal "can," plus the use of a contraction rule forming "can't" from "can+not." A child may say, "I no can sing" for "I can't sing." The first sentence has one more word and the same number of morphemes ("no can" and "can't" are each two morphemes), but does not use a permutation transformation.

Morehead and Ingram (1973) found there is a delay up to as much as 3½ years in the onset of language in linguistically deviant children. In their study, the linguistically deviant group required nearly 2½ years longer to go from Level I to Level V. The levels in their study were based on the use of, e.g.:

1. Specific pronouns, e.g., Level I—"I", II—"my," III—"you," IV—"we," V—"her"
2. Demonstratives, e.g., I—"that," II—"these," III—"this," IV—"those"
3. Wh forms, e.g., II—"where," III—"what," IV—"why," V—"when"
4. Prepositions, e.g., II—"in," III—"to," IV—"up," V—"down"
5. Modals, e.g., I—"want," III—"gonna," IV—"can," V—"won't."

The control population of 15 normal children might reach Level III by 3 years of age, while the linguistically deviant children might not reach Level III until 6 years of age. According to Morehead and Ingram (1973), the linguistically deviant children do not have bizarre linguistic systems, but are delayed in linguistic development in "onset and acquisition time" (p. 344), and do not produce the varied utterances that are to be found in the language of normal children. Linguistically deviant children do not seem to steadily and progressively develop language as do normal children. Based on these findings, intervention programs are strongly indicated.

Two types of extreme difficulties, agnosia and apraxia, should be mentioned here. *Agnosia* is defined as the "loss of the function of recognition of individual sensory stimuli" (Wood, 1971, p. 6). This problem may occur in the visual, tactile, or auditory modalities. A child with auditory agnosia, i.e., agnosia for nonlinguistic sounds, does not find environmental or household noises (e.g., water running or telephone ringing) meaningful. The child with extreme auditory problems (auditory agnosia) may have a period of sound rejection that is a defensive period because the sounds are not meaningful to him or her (Stein & Curry, 1968). Care must be taken not to diagnose these children as being deaf.

A child with specific auditory agnosia for verbal symbols would be considered a receptive aphasic. Words, though they can be heard, have no meaning for these children. In addition, the child's auditory ability may be erratic or inconsistent. The inability to process linguistic and nonlinguistic sounds is a problem of great severity and suggests that damage may have occurred to both the right and left cerebral hemispheres, because the child is unable to process both nonspeech and speech sounds.

Apraxia is defined as the "loss of the ability to execute simple voluntary acts" (Wood, 1971, p. 7). The problem of oral apraxia would then be the problem of producing voluntary movements of the articulators to produce sounds that are combined to form language. Myklebust (1971b) reported that in 1929, J. Ley suggested, after studying twins with congenital expressive aphasia but with excellent auditory comprehension, that their problem was a type of apraxia that was probably hereditary in nature. Children with apraxia are able to produce movements of their articulators and may form some sounds, but are unable to do this at will. A person diagnosed as having aphasia is said to have problems in all areas of language, i.e., comprehension, expression, reading, and writing (if old enough) (Schuell, Jenkins, & Jimenez-Pabon, 1967); if these children with oral apraxia have excellent auditory comprehension, should oral apraxia be considered a subdivision of aphasia or should it be considered a separate disorder? A child with oral apraxia, as determined from clinical observations of the author and from the child's scores on the Screening Test for Developmental Apraxia (Blakeley, 1980), produced test scores at or above age level on the Illinois Test of Psycholinguistic Abilities (ITPA), Peabody Picture Vocabulary Test (PPVT), and the Test for Auditory Comprehension of Language (TACL) (tests of auditory comprehension). This child could not program the production of speech sounds, nor could he produce the desired speech sounds on volition. As the child developed, he learned to produce some speech sounds in isolation or within a word, and could produce consonant blends if he proceeded at a very slow rate and elongated or separated the elements ("sss-to-p/stop").

It should be noted that phonological problems can cause what superficially seem to be syntactic problems. For example, language disordered children omit the final sounds in words. As a consequence of this, inflectional endings are not added, e.g., plural (hæ/hat$; bɛ /bed$), third person singular (gou/goe$; tɪ/tip$), or past tense endings (pɪ/pi¢k¢d; rʌ /rub¢d). In these instances, syntactic productions must be judged by other methods, i.e., by noting slight changes in the child's productions. The child's use of plurals, third person singular, and past tense must be ascertained by recognizing the added syllable attached to the stem, e.g., in one form of production of the plural (bʊ-ɪ/bushes), the third person singular (reɪ-ɪ/races), and the past tense (hʌ -ɪ/hunted) all two-syllable productions.

This can be compared to the one-syllable productions of "hats" (plural), "writes" (third person singular) and "washed" (past tense). The added vowel in the two-syllable plural, third person singular, and past tense productions provides clues to the SLP of the child's syntactic competence. The expression of this competence is hampered by the child's articulatory problems. Thus, the problems here may be due to faulty programming of articulators, not to difficulty with linguistic rules.

Weiner (1972) found that seven dysphasic children in his study were inferior to a control group of normal children on the oral-motor tests that involved either a single motor act, e.g., stick out your tongue, or a two-sequence oral motor act, e.g., lick your lips and stick out your tongue. This difference occurred with the tasks that required the movement of the tongue. Though the stimuli were non-speech oral motor acts, and the movements required were not as detailed or as rapid as those that would be required for the production of rapid, spontaneous speech, the results suggest an overlapping of expressive problems that may be more prevalent than pure defects and that may have a different etiological base.

PREVENTION AND TREATMENT PROGRAMS

McGinnis (1962) suggested that if a young child in a natural environment has not acquired speech by the age of 4, formal training is needed to develop communication skills. Intervention may be necessary for some children at age 4, for some before the age of 4, while with others the SLP may decide, after careful evaluation, to withhold therapy for a period of time. This decision is based on the level of functioning and on the special needs of the individual child. The speech-language pathologist is a key individual in the habilitation of the dysphasic child. To carry out his or her program, the SLP should have a strong theoretical background, an astute ability to assess the areas of strength and weakness in a child, a practical understanding of therapy procedures, a creative ability to use materials, a flexible attitude in accepting the child and the responses of the child, and a warm manner that fosters a friendly and trusting relationship with the child. Attention and motivation depend, to a great extent, on the therapist-child relationship and on the appropriate use of the materials chosen. Each program must be individualized for the specific child.

The goals of many programs are identical, but, depending on their theoretical approach, some programs are highly structured, proceeding from one designated level to another, while others are more informal, allowing the therapist a broader range for implementation. No previously established program is complete unto itself. The therapist must continually add, delete, and revise as appropriate for the client.

Many therapists rely on operant behavior techniques to provide procedures for therapy. Sloane and MacAulay (1968) have included several chapters in their book offering practical suggestions for utilizing this type of therapy with a severely impaired population. Operant behavior techniques follow the stimulus-response-reinforcement mode, in which a stimulus reinforcement applied after a child's response will increase or decrease that type of response. It is important to remember that the operant technique does not dictate what is to be taught, the stimuli that are to be used, or what reinforcers will be accepted or preferred by the child; rather, the approach details a very structured and highly quantifiable method of working with the child. Many therapists prefer this method because a record of exact, countable responses can be maintained that specifies the stimuli presented (verbal or visual), the prompts (verbal, gestural, or visual) used by the therapist to elicit the response, and the responses elicited. Other therapists believe the method too rigid and too structured, and prefer a more informal method. The procedure selected is not of prime importance; rather, it is the structuring of the type of therapy in the mind of the SLP that is important. The SLP must define and determine:

1. The long-term goals, e.g., over the next year
2. The short-term goals, e.g., for each lesson or set of lessons
3. The manner in which the goals will be achieved
4. The appropriateness of the materials to be used to maintain the child's interest and attention and to facilitate the growth of a child at a particular chronological age, level of maturity (both intellectual and behavioral), and with a specified problem
5. The child's ability to perform or approximate (narrow the distance from) the desired task. Books, articles, and commercially published materials are available to help the SLP to integrate and establish an individual program for a child (see discussions following). An organized, thoughtful, eclectic approach can offer the child the most beneficial aspects of each theoretical approach and therapeutic program.

EDUCATIONAL PROGRAMS AND SERVICES

Numerous books, and sections of books, include theoretical and practical suggestions for developing educational programs for children with speech and language problems. Following is a review of a few of these resources:

> Bricker and Bricker (1970, 1974) provide a program of language training for the severely language handicapped child. A diagrammed, "Language Training Lattice" (1974, p. 450), specifically devised to teach speech to a mentally retarded population, can be modified for use with a dysphasic population. The authors concentrate on how to develop a wide number of areas that include motor, cognitive, social, and language processes. The SLP is required to provide the specific materials and activities for each step of the program.

Bush and Giles (1969) include materials and suggestions for activities that follow the format of the Illinois Test of Psycholinguistic Abilities.

Eisenson (1972) includes three chapters concerning therapeutic approaches in a book that contains both theoretical and practical material. The first chapter contains specific considerations for use with the hyperactive child, i.e., the benefits of using a single modality, larger stimuli, and developing concepts. The second chapter lists levels and methods of developing representation behavior, i.e., matching, associating, and recognizing the function of various objects. The third chapter presents levels of linguistic development and suggests goals for each stage.

Gray and Ryan (1973) provide a detailed treatment of theory, program, and preparation from a behavioristic viewpoint.

Hubbell (1981) approaches intervention in terms of problem solving and consider the benefits of therapy in developing the child's "use" of language. Hubbell discusses intervention in terms of linguistic, interpersonal, and family phenomena. Children are taught to make decisions and are presented with activities during language training that stimulate responses similar to the ones they would be expected to produce in real-life situations. Hubbell believes this approach will enhance the chances of a child's generalizing these responses to the natural environment.

Johnson and Myklebust (1967) offer a broad view of children's disabilities, and include discussion of deficiencies in auditory behavior as it pertains to reception, expression, and learning. Practical educational procedures are outlined. This book is a classic in the field.

McGinnis (1963) advocates an association method in which individual phonemes are singly and accurately produced (phonetic approach), then combined or blended with other phonemes into an articulatory sequence. Later, when the child advances to cursive script (writing) an intersensorimotor association is stimulated, when the oral production of sounds is associated with the appropriate graphemes.

McReynolds (1974) edits a monograph that includes a number of systematic approaches to language training, e.g., English verbal auxiliary and copula, in the context of a behavioral-psycholinguistic approach.

McReynolds and Engmann (1975) discuss distinctive feature theory as it applies to a child's phonological development, to analysis of articulation errors, and to training for reduction of errors.

Schiefelbusch and Lloyd (1974), Schiefelbusch (1978a, 1978b), Schiefelbusch and Hollis (1979), and McLean, Yoder, and Schiefelbusch (1972) offer a series of books on language that include chapters relating to language development, assessment, nonverbal communication, language intervention strategies, and programs. Contributing authors provide diverse viewpoints in wide-ranging areas of expertise.

Wiig and Semel (1976) provide three chapters devoted to remediation, including discussion of perceptual, linguistic, and cognitive processing deficits, and language production deficits. The chapters cover basic principles and are filled with practical ideas under various category headings.

A number of publishing companies concentrate on producing instructional materials in the area of speech and language development. Some material is programmed while other material is intended for use in a particular framework, e.g., conceptual or syntactic. Most companies' materials can be modified for a number of developmental levels. *All* materials must be combined into an integrated approach by the SLP. The list of publishers that follows is by no means complete, but is offered as an initial resource list for beginning (and practicing) SLPs.

American Guidance Service
Publishers' Building
Circle Pines, MN 55014
    (Materials plus *Small Wonder Program* and *Peabody Language Development Kits*)

C.C. Publications, Inc.
P.O. Box 23699
Tigard, OR 97223
    (Materials plus *STEPS Toward Basic Concept Development*)

Charles E. Merrill Publishing Co.
1300 Alum Creek Dr.
Columbus, OH 43216
    (Materials plus *Clinical Language Intervention Program*)

Communication Skill Builders
3130 N. Dodge Blvd.
P.O. Box 42050-E, Dept. 12
Tucson, AZ 85733
    (Materials plus *Communication Competence: A Functional-Pragmatic Language Program*)

Developmental Learning Materials
P.O. Box 4000
One DLM Park
Allen, TX 75002
    (Materials plus *O/Wll–Oral/Written Language Lab*)

Frank Schaffer Publication, Inc.
1028 Via Mirabel, Dept. 34
Palos Verdes Estates, CA 90274
    (Materials plus duplicating masters)

LinguiSystems, Inc.
Suite 806
1630 Fifth Ave.
Moline, IL 61265
    (Materials plus *HELP* and *OLSIST*)

Newby Visual Language Inc.
Box #121-A
Engleville, PA 19408
(Materials with hierarchial presentation and workbooks)

Teaching Resources Corp.
50 Pond Park Rd.
Hingham, MA 02043
(Materials plus *Fokes Sentence Builder* and *Developmental Language Lessons*)

A child with a severe or profound auditory reception problem who hears the words of a language but is not able to interpret them (Johnson & Myklebust, 1967) will certainly have difficulty learning through the auditory modality. Those who have language problems that are not as severe as verbal agnosia may also have difficulty in learning for less obvious reasons, i.e., the normal rate of speech of the parent or the teacher is too rapid for them to process; their short-term auditory memory may be limited; small sound differences in words, though heard, are not perceived ("can/can't"—negative inflectional morphemes and, "back/bag"—confusion of the voicing feature); background noises (cars passing in the street below) compete for attention with foreground sounds; semantic duality is limited ("can" = ability to, "can" = a container); vocabulary is limited; recognition of temporal factors ("wash," "is washing," "was washing," and "washed") is reduced; and category differentiation ("Me go/I go"—nominal; "Him book/his book"— possessive) is not utilized.

Sounds must be related to graphemes when a child advances to the written and read aspects of the language. If sounds are not produced correctly, they may not be identified correctly for association with a particular grapheme (letter). If "two"/tu/ and "do" /du/ are produced identically as /du/ because of a voicing problem, the child will have difficulty selecting the correct grapheme to represent "two."

Learning deficiencies are both verbal and nonverbal in character. "Deficiencies in acquiring spoken, read and written language constitute the primary areas under the category of disabilities in verbal learning" (Johnson & Myklebust, 1967, p. 17). Nonverbal deficiencies will affect such areas as body orientation, comprehension of spatial directions, and learning to tell time.

SUMMARY

When devising a program of therapy, in addition to practical knowledge concerning therapy techniques, the SLP should have a strong theoretical background in the areas of cognition and normal and deviant language development. The therapist must try to recognize patterns in the child's production errors. For example, if the child says "/to/" for "coat" or "/du/" for "goose," the child is using a dental /t,d/ for a velar /k,g/, not having developed the back category and is omitting final sounds. If the child says, "I no see," "I come?" or "I riding", the child has developed neither the ability to use transformations nor the category of auxiliary verbs ("to be," "to do") and modals. It is important to look for individual patterns and to note how patterns are hierarchially built, rather than to treat each utterance or sentence as a single unit. Individual steps of therapy should be based on an analysis of patterns a child uses and on the pattern of errors. Rote learning will only help the child to communicate within a limited framework. The child must have tacit command of the rules of the language and must use those rules to generate novel sentences.

The problem of dysphasia may stem from a number of causes, e.g., differences in auditory processing, an inability to utilize the hierarchial levels of language, subtle cognitive differences, and a lack of maturation of the central nervous system. Whatever the etiology, whether genetically based or otherwise, the need for intervention exists. The SLP must endeavor to make therapy productive and fun. Language learning should be a source for establishing self-pride and self-motivation in the child. It is, afterall, the basis for a child's social adjustment, academic achievement, and vocational accomplishments—and ultimately, a fulfilled and satisfying life.

REFERENCES

Ajuriaguerra, J. De. Speech disorders in childhood. In: E. Carterett (ed.), *Brain function, Vol. III*. Los Angeles: University of California Press, 1966.

Aram, D. M., & Nation, J. E. Patterns of language behavior in children with developmental language disorder. *Journal of Speech and Hearing Research*, 1975, *18*, 229–241.

Arthur, G. *The Arthur adaptation of the Leiter International Performance Scale*. Washington, D.C.: Psychological Service Center Press, 1952.

Aten, J., & Davis, J. Disturbances in the perception of auditory sequence in children with minimal cerebral dysfunction. *Journal of Speech and Hearing Research*, 1968, *11*, 236–245.

Baker, H., & Leland, B. *Detroit Tests of Learning Aptitude*. Indianapolis, IN: Bobbs-Merrill Co., 1967.

Benton, A. Developmental aphasia and brain damage. *Cortex*, 1964, *1*, 40–52.

Benton, A. The cognitive functioning of children with developmental dysphasia. In: M. A. Wyke (ed.), *Developmental dysphasia*. New York: Academic Press, 1978.

Berko, J. The child's learning of English morphology. *Word*, 1958, *14*, 150–177.

Bever, T. *Pre-linguistic behaviour*. Unpublished honors thesis. Department of Linguistics, Harvard University, Boston, 1961.

Blakeley, R. *Screening Test for Developmental Apraxia*. Tigard, OR: C. C. Publications, 1980.

Blumstein, S. The perception of speech in pathology and ontogeny. In: A. Caramazza & E. B. Zurif (eds.), *Language acquisition and language breakdown*. Baltimore: The Johns Hopkins University Press, 1978.

Borden, G., & Harris, K. *Speech science primer*. Baltimore: Williams and Wilkins Co., 1980.

Bricker, W., & Bricker, D. A program of language training for the severely language handicapped child. *Exceptional Children*, 1970, *37*, 101–111.

Bricker, W., & Bricker D. An early language training strategy. In: R. Schiefelbusch and L.

Lloyd (eds.), *Language perspectives—acquisition, retardation, and intervention.* Baltimore: University Park Press, 1974.
Bush, W., & Giles, M. *Aids to psycholinguistic teaching.* Columbus, OH: Charles E. Merrill Publishing Co., 1969.
Carroll, J. B. *The nature of the reading process. Reading forum. No. 11,* Bethesda, MD: NINCD Monograph, No. 11, U.S. Dept. of Health, Education and Welfare, 1976.
Carrow, E. *Test for Auditory Comprehension of Language.* Austin, TX: Urban Research Test Group, 1973.
Carrow, E. *The Carrow Elicited Language Inventory.* Austin, TX: Learning Concepts, 1974.
Carrow, M. The development of auditory comprehension of language structure in children. *Journal of Speech and Hearing Disorders,* 1968, *33,* 99–111.
Chalfant, J. C., & Scheffelin, M. A. *Central processing dysfunctions in children: A review of research.* Bethesda, MD: U.S. Department of Health, Education, and Welfare, National Institute of Neurological Diseases and Stroke, 1969.
Chappell, G. Developmental aphasia revisited. *Journal of Communication Disorders,* 1970, *3,* 181–197.
Chappell, G. Language disabilities and the language clinician. *Journal of Learning Disabilities,* 1972, *5,* 611–619.
Chase, R. A. Neurological aspects of language disorders in children. In: J. V. Irwin & M. Marge (eds.), *Principles of childhood language disabilities.* Englewood Cliffs, NJ: Prentice-Hall, 1972.
Chomsky, N. *Aspects of the theory of syntax.* Cambridge, MA: The M.I.T. Press, 1965.
Chomsky, N., & Halle,M. *The sound pattern of English.* New York: Harper & Row, 1968.
Critchley, M. *The dyslexic child.* Springfield, IL: Charles C Thomas, 1970.
Cromer, R. The basis of childhood dysphasia: A linguistic approach. In: M. A. Wyke (ed.), *Developmental dysphasia.* New York: Academic Press, 1978.
Cutting, J. A parallel between encodedness and the ear advantage: Evidence from an ear-monitoring task. *Journal of the Acoustical Society of America.* 1973, *53,* 358 (A).
Daniloff, R., & Moll, K. Coarticulation of lip-rounding. *Journal of Speech and Hearing Research,* 1968, *11,* 707–721.
Denckla, M. D., & Rudel, R. G. Name of object-drawing by dyslexic and other learning disabled children. *Brain and Language,* 1976, *3,* 1–15.
Doehring, D. G. Visual spatial memory in aphasic children. *Journal of Speech and Hearing Research,* 1960, *3,* 138–149.
Dunn, L. M. *Peabody Picture Vocabulary Test.* Circle Pines, MN: American Guidance Service, 1965.
Dunn, L. M., & Dunn, L. M. *Peabody Picture Vocabulary Test—Revised.* Circle Pines, MN: American Guidance Service, 1981.
Efron, R. Temporal perception, aphasia and déja-vu. *Brain,* 1963, *86,* 403–424.
Eimas, P. D., Siqueland, E. R., Jusczyk, P., & Vigorito, J. Speech perception in infants. *Science,* 1971, *171,* 303–306.
Eisenson, J. Developmental aphasia: A speculative view with therapeutic implications. *Journal of Speech and Hearing Disorders,* 1968a, *33,* 3–13.
Eisenson, J. Developmental aphasia: A postulation of a unitary concept of the disorder. *Cortex,* 1968b, *4,* 184–200.
Eisenson, J. *Aphasia in childhood.* New York: Harper & Row, 1972.
Ervin, S. Imitation and structural change in children's language. In: E. H. Lenneberg (ed.), *New directions in the study of language.* Cambridge, MA: The M.I.T. Press, 1964.
Ervin-Tripp, S. Discourse agreement: How children answer questions. In: J. Hayes (ed.), *Cognition and the development of language.* New York: John Wiley & Sons, 1970.

Ewing, A. *Aphasia in children*. New York: Hafner Publishing Co., 1967.
Fein, D. J. Population data from the U.S. Census Bureau. *Asha*, 1983, *25*, 47.
Fletcher, S.G. *The Fletcher Time-By-Count Test of Diadochokinetic Syllable Rate*. Tigard, OR: C.C. Publications, 1978.
Fraser, C., Bellugi, U., & Brown, R. Control of grammar in imitation, comprehension and production. *Journal of Verbal Learning and Verbal Behavior*, 1963, *2*, 121–135.
Furth, H.G. Sequence learning in aphasic and deaf children. *Journal of Speech and Hearing Disorders*, 1964, *29*, 171–177.
Gates, A., & MacGinitie, W. *Gates-MacGinitie Reading Tests*. New York: Columbia University Teacher's College Press, 1972.
Geschwind, N. Neurologic foundations of language. In: H. Myklebust (ed.), *Progress in learning disabilities*. New York: Grune & Stratton, 1968.
Goldman, R., & Fristoe, M. *Goldman-Fristoe Test of Articulation*. Circle Pines, MN: American Guidance Service, Inc., 1969.
Goldstein, R., Landau, W.M., & Kleffner, F.R. Neurologic assessment of deaf and aphasic children. *Transactions of the American Otologic Society*, 1958, *46*, 122–136.
Goldstein, R., Landau, W.M., & Kleffner, F.R. Neurologic observations in a population of deaf and aphasic children. *Annals of Otology, Rhinology, and Laryngology*, 1960, *69*, 756–767.
Goodglass, H., & Kaplan, E. *The assessment of aphasia and related disorders*. Philadelphia: Lea & Febiger, 1976.
Gray, B., & Ryan, B. *A language program for the nonlanguage child*. Champaign, IL: Research Press, 1973.
Halliday, M.A.K. *Learning how to mean*. New York: Elsevier North-Holland, Inc., 1975.
Hardy, W.G. On language disorders in young children: A reorganization of thinking. *Journal of Speech and Hearing Disorders*, 1965, *30*, 3–16.
Hoffnung, A. *An analysis of the syntactic structures of children with deviant articulation*. Unpublished doctoral dissertation, City University of New York, New York, 1974.
Hoffnung, A. An analysis of the language performance of the negative structure of children with normal and deviant articulation. In: M. Burns & J. Andrews (eds.), *Selected papers in language and phonology, Vol. I. Identification and diagnosis*. Evanston, IL: Institute for Continuing Professional Education, 1977.
Hoffnung, A. Judging cognition during language assessment. *Topics in Language Disorders*, 1981, *1*, 47–58.
Hubbell, R. *Children's language disorders*. Englewood Cliffs, NJ: Prentice-Hall, 1981.
Ingram, D. The production of word-initial fricative and affricates by normal and linguistically deviant children. In: A. Caramazza & E.B. Zurif (eds.), *Language acquisition and language breakdown*. Baltimore: The Johns Hopkins University Press, 1978.
Jakobson, R. *Child language aphasia and phonological universals*. The Hague: Mouton & Co., Printers, 1968.
Jakobson, R., Fant, G., & Halle, M. *Preliminaries to speech analysis*. Cambridge, MA: The M.I.T. Press, 1952.
Johnson, D., & Myklebust, H. *Learning disabilities*. New York: Grune & Stratton, 1967.
Kertesz, A. Reviewed: Intelligence and aphasia by Lebrun, Yvan and Hoops, Richards. *Brain and Language*, 1976, *3*, 335–336.
Kimura, D. Functional asymmetry of the brain in dichotic listening. *Cortex*, 1967, *3*, 163–178.
Kirk, S.A., McCarthy, J.J., & Kirk, W.D. *Examiner's manual: Illinois Test of Psycholinguistic Abilities* (rev. ed.). Urbana, IL: University of Illinois Press, 1968.
Klasen, E. *The syndrome of specific dyslexia*. Baltimore: University Park Press, 1972.
Lee, L., & Canter, S. Developmental Sentence Scoring: A clinical procedure for estimating syntactic development in children's spontaneous speech. *Journal of Speech and Hearing Disorders*, 1971, *36*, 315–340.

Lenneberg, E. Speech as a motor skill with special reference to nonaphasic disorders. In: U. Bellugi & R. Brown (eds.), The acquisition of language. *Monograph of the Society for Research in Child Development,* 1964, *29,* 35–39.

Lenneberg, E. On explaining language. *Science,* 1969, *164,* 635–643.

Leonard, L. What is deviant language? *Journal of Speech and Hearing Disorders,* 1972, *37,* 427–446.

Leonard, L.B., Bolders, J., & Miller, J. An examination of the semantic relations reflected in the language usage of normal and language-disordered children. *Journal of Speech and Hearing Research,* 1976, *19,* 371–392.

Leske, C. Prevalence estimates of communicative disorders in the U.S. *ASHA,* 1981, *23,* 217–225.

Liberman, A.M., Cooper, F.S., Harris, K.S., & MacNeilage, P.F. A motor theory of speech perception. *Proceedings of the Speech Communication Seminar.* Stockholm: Speech Transmission Laboratory, Royal Institute of Technology, 1963.

Liberman, A.M., Cooper, F.S., Shankweiler, D.P., & Studdert-Kennedy, J. Perception of the speech code. *Psychological Review,* 1967, *74,* 431–461.

Liberman, A.M., Delattre, P.C., & Cooper, F.S. Some rules for the distinction between voiced and voiceless stops in initial position. *Language and Speech,* 1958, *1,* 153–167.

Lieberman, P. *Intonation, perception, and language.* Cambridge, MA: The M.I.T. Press, 1967.

Lovell, K., Hoyle, H., & Siddall, M. A study of some aspects of the play and language of young children with delayed speech. *Journal of Child Psychology and Psychiatry,* 1968, *9,* 41–50.

Lowe, A., & Campbell, R. Temporal discrimination in aphasoid and normal children. *Journal of Speech and Hearing Research,* 1965, *8,* 313–314.

Lubert, N. Auditory perceptual impairments in children with specific language disorders: A review of the literature. *Journal of Speech and Hearing Disorders,* 1981, *46,* 3–9.

Luick, A., Agronawitz, A., Kirk, A., & Busby, R. Profiles of children with severe oral language disorders. *Journal of Speech and Hearing Disorders,* 1982, *47,* 88–92.

McGinnis, M. Comments. In: R. West (ed.), *Childhood aphasia.* San Francisco: California Society for Crippled Children and Adults, 1962.

McGinnis, M. *Aphasic children.* Washington, D.C.; Alexander Graham Bell Association of the Deaf, 1963.

McLean, J., Yoder, B., & Schiefelbusch, R. (eds.), *Language intervention with the retarded: Development strategies.* Baltimore: University Park Press, 1972.

McNeill, D. *The acquisition of language.* New York: Harper & Row, 1970.

McReynolds, L. Verbal sequencing discrimination training for language-impaired children. *Journal of Speech and Hearing Research,* 1967, *32,* 244–256.

McReynolds, L. (ed.), Developing systematic procedures for training children's language. Danville, IL: *ASHA Monographs, No. 18,* Interstate Press, 1974.

McReynolds, L., & Engmann, D. *Distinctive feature analysis of misarticulations.* Baltimore: University Park Press, 1975.

Marge, M. The general problem of language disabilities in children. In: J.V. Irwin & M. Marge (eds.), *Principles of childhood language disorders.* New York: Appleton-Century-Crofts, 1972.

Marquardt, T., & Saxman, J. Language comprehension and auditory discrimination in articulation deficient kindergarten children. *Journal of Speech and Hearing Research,* 1972, *15,* 382–389.

Martin, R., & Caramazza, A. Short-term memory performance in the absence of phonological coding. *Brain and Cognition,* 1982, *1,* 50–70.

Menyuk, P. Comparison of grammar of children with functionally deviant and normal speech. *Journal of Speech and Hearing Research,* 1964, *7,* 109–121.

Menyuk, P. *Sentences children use.* Cambridge, MA: The M.I.T. Press, 1969.

Menyuk, P. Linguistic problems in children with developmental dysphasia. In: M.A. Wyke (ed.), *Developmental dysphasia*. New York: Academic Press, 1978.
Menyuk, P., & Looney, P. A problem of language disorder: Length versus structure. *Journal of Speech and Hearing Research*, 1972, *15*, 264–279. (a)
Menyuk, P., & Looney, P. Relationship among components of the grammar in language disorder. *Journal of Speech and Hearing Research*, 1972, *15*, 395–406. (b)
Milisen, R. The incidence of speech disorders. In: L.E. Travis (ed.), *Handbook of speech pathology and audiology*. New York: Appleton-Century-Crofts, 1971.
Miller, G.A. Magical number seven, plus or minus two. *Psychological Review*, 1956, *63*, 81–97.
Moffitt, A.R. Consonant cue perception by twenty-to twenty-four-week-old infants. *Child Development*, 1971, *42*, 717–731.
Moran, M., & Byrne, M. Mastery of verb tense markers by normal and learning-disabled children. *Journal of Speech and Hearing Research*, 1977, *20*, 529–542.
Morehead, D., & Ingram, D. The development of base syntax in normal and linguistically deviant children. *Journal of Speech and Hearing Research*, 1973, *16*, 330–352.
Muma, J. *Language handbook: Concepts, assessment, intervention*. Englewood Cliffs, NJ: Prentice-Hall, 1978.
Myklebust, H. *Auditory disorders in children: A manual for differential diagnosis*. New York: Grune & Stratton, 1954.
Myklebust, H. Childhood aphasia: An evolving concept. In: L.E. Travis (ed.), *Handbook of speech pathology and audiology*. New York: Appleton-Century-Crofts, 1971. (a)
Myklebust, H. Childhood aphasia: Indentification, diagnosis, remediation. In: L.E. Travis (ed.), *Handbook of speech pathology and audiology*. New York: Appleton-Century-Crofts, 1971. (b)
National Center for Health Statistics. *Prevalence of selected impairments, United States-1977*. Department of Health, Education and Welfare Pub. No. (PHS) 82–1562, 1981.
Newcombe, F., Oldfield, R.C., Ratcliff, G.G., & Wingfield, A. Recognition and naming of object-drawings by men with focal brain wounds. *Journal of Neurology, Neurosurgery and Psychiatry*, 1971, *34*, 329–340.
Newcomer, P., & Hammill, D. *Test of Language Development*. Austin, TX: Empiric Press, 1977.
Oldfield, R.C., & Wingfield, A. *A series of pictures for use in object-naming*. M.R.C. Psycholinguistic Research Unit Special Report No. PLU/65/19, 1965.
Pendergast, K., Dickey, S., Selmar, J., & Soder, A. *Photo Articulation Test*. Danville, IL: Interstate Printers & Publishers, 1969.
Perkins, W. *Speech pathology: An applied behavioral science*. St. Louis: C.V. Mosby Co., 1977.
Rapin, I., & Wilson, B. Children with developmental language disability: Neurological aspects and assessment. In: M.A. Wyke (ed.), *Developmental dysphasia*. New York: Academic Press, 1978.
Ravens, J. C. *Guide to using the coloured progressive matrices (sets A, Ab, B)*. London: H.K. Lewis, 1960.
Rees, N. Auditory processing factors in language disorders: The view from Procrustes' bed. *Journal of Speech and Hearing Disorders*, 1973, *38*, 304–315.
Rees, N. Imitation and language development: Issues and clinical implication. *Journal of Speech and Hearing Disorders*, 1975, *40*, 339–350.
Rees, N. Learning to talk and understand. In: T.J. Hixon, L.D. Shriberg, & J.H. Saxman (eds.), *Introduction to communication disorders*. Englewood Cliffs, NJ: Prentice-Hall, 1980.

Reichstein, J. Auditory threshold consistency in differential diagnosis of aphasia in children. *Journal of Speech and Hearing Disorders,* 1964, *29,* 147–155.
Ritvo, E. *Autism.* New York: Spectrum Publications, 1976.
Schiefelbusch, R. *Bases of language intervention.* Baltimore: University Park Press, 1978. (a)
Schiefelbusch, R. *Language intervention strategies.* Baltimore: University Park Press, 1978. (b)
Schiefelbusch, R., & Hollis, J. *Language intervention from ape to child.* Baltimore: University Park Press, 1979.
Schiefelbusch, R., & Lloyd, L. *Language perspective—acquisition, retardation, and intervention.* Baltimore: University Park Press, 1974.
Schuell, H., Jenkins, J.J., & Jimenez-Pabon, E. *Aphasia in adults.* New York: Harper & Row, 1967.
Semel, E., & Wiig, E. *Clinical Evaluation of Language Functions.* Columbus, OH: Charles E. Merrill Publishing Co., 1980.
Sloane, H., & MacAulay, B. *Operant procedures in remedial speech and language training.* New York: Houghton Mifflin Co., 1968.
Slobin, D. Imitation and grammatical development in children. In: N.S. Engler, L.R. Boulter, & H. Osser (eds.), *Contemporary issues in developmental psychology.* New York: Holt, Rinehart & Winston, 1968.
Stark, J., Poppen, R., & May, M. Effects of alterations of prosodic features on the sequencing performance of aphasic children. *Journal of Speech and Hearing Research,* 1967, *10,* 849–855.
Stark, R. E., & Tallal, P. Selection of children with specific language deficits. *Journal of Speech and Hearing Disorders,* 1981, *46,* 114–122.
Stein, L., & Curry, F. Childhood auditory agnosia. *Journal of Speech and Hearing Disorders,* 1968, *33,* 361–370.
Stevenson, J., & Richman, R. The prevalence of language delay in a population of three-year-old children and its association with general retardation. *Developmental Medicine and Child Neurology,* 1976, *18,* 431–441.
Strauss, A., & Lehtinen, L. *Psychopathology and education of the brain-injured child.* New York: Grune & Stratton, 1947.
Tallal, P. Perceptual and linguistic factors in the language impairment of developmental dysphasics: An experimental investigation with the Token Test. *Cortex,* 1975, *11,* 196–205.
Tallal, P. An experimental investigation of the role of auditory temporal processing in normal and disordered language development. In: A. Caramazza & E. Zurif (eds.), *Language acquisition and language breakdown.* Baltimore: The Johns Hopkins University Press, 1978.
Tallal, P., & Piercy, M. Defects of non-verbal auditory perception in children with developmental dysphasia. *Nature,* 1973, *241,* 468–469. (a)
Tallal, P., & Piercy, M. Developmental aphasia: Impaired rate of non-verbal processing as a factor of sensory modality. *Neuropsychologia,* 1973, *11,* 389–398. (b)
Tallal, P., & Piercy, M. Developmental aphasia: Rate of auditory processing and selective impairment of consonant perception. *Neuropsychologia,* 1974, *12,* 83–93.
Tallal, P., & Piercy, M. Developmental aphasia: The perception of brief vowels and extended stop consonants. *Neuropsychologia,* 1975, *13,* 69–74.
Tallal, P., & Piercy, M. Defects of auditory perception in children with developmental dysphasia. In: M.A. Wyke (ed.), *Developmental dysphasia.* New York: Academic Press, 1978.
Tallal, P., Stark, R., & Curtiss, B. The relation between speech perception impairment and

speech production impairment in children with developmental dysphasia. *Brain and Language,* 1976, *3,* 305–317.

Templin, M. *Certain language skills in children.* Minneapolis: The University of Minnesota Press, 1957.

Templin, M., & Darley, F. *The Templin-Darley Test of Articulation.* Iowa City, IA: University of Iowa, Iowa City Bureau of Educational Research, 1960.

Trantham, C.R., & Pedersen, J.K. *Normal language development.* Baltimore: The Williams & Wilkins Co., 1976.

Traugott, E., & Pratt, M. *Linguistics for students of literature.* New York: Harcourt Brace Jovanovich, 1980.

Vogel, S. Syntactic abilities in normal and dyslexic children. *Journal of Learning Disabilities,* 1974, *7,* 47–53.

Vygotsky, L.S. *Thought and language.* Cambridge, MA: The M.I.T. Press, 1962.

Webster's Seventh New Collegiate Dictionary. Springfield, MA: G & C Merriam Co., 1969.

Wechsler, D. *Wechsler Preschool and Primary Scale of Intelligence.* New York: The Psychological Corp., 1963.

Wechsler, D. *Wechsler Intelligence Scale for Children—Revised.* New York: The Psychological Corp., 1974.

Weiner, P. Perceptual level of functioning of dysphasic children. *Cortex,* 1969, *5,* 440–457.

Weiner, P. The perceptual level of functioning of dysphasic children: A follow-up study. *Journal of Speech and Hearing Research,* 1972, *15,* 423–438.

Wepman, J. *Auditory Discrimination Test. (Manual of directions).* Chicago: Language Research Associates, 1958.

Wiig, E., & Semel, E. *Language disabilities in children and adolescents.* Columbus, OH: Charles E. Merrill Publishing Co., 1976.

Wiig, E.H., Semel, E.M., & Crouse, M.A. The use of English morphology by high-risk and learning disabled children. *Journal of Learning Disabilities,* 1973, *6,* 457–465.

Wilson, L.F., Doehring, D.G., & Hirsh, I.J. Auditory discrimination learning by aphasic and nonaphasic children. *Journal of Speech and Hearing Research,* 1960, *2,* 130–137.

Winitz, H. *Articulatory acquisition and behavior.* New York: Appleton-Century-Crofts, 1969.

Wolfus, B., Moscovitch, M., & Kinsbourne, M. Subgroups of developmental language impairment. *Brain and Language,* 1980, *10,* 152–171.

Wood, K.S. Terminology and nomenclature. In: L.E. Travis (ed.), *Handbook of speech pathology and audiology.* New York: Appleton-Century-Crofts, 1971.

Wyke, M.A. *Developmental dysphasia.* New York: Academic Press, 1978.

Zangwell, O.L. The concept of developmental dysphasia. In: M.A. Wyke (ed.), *Developmental dysphasia.* New York: Academic Press, 1978.

DISCUSSION QUESTIONS

1. Why is it not possible for a developmental dysphasic child to become a fluent aphasic individual?
2. What are the sound rules that govern a child's earliest production: "ma"? What are the sound rules for the production of the word "papa"?
3. What are the basic elements of a language system? How do they differ from each other?
4. Why is it so difficult to determine the incidence of developmental dysphasia?
5. What are some of the commercially available tests that are frequently used to measure linguistic ability? What are the nature, purpose, and dimensions of each of these tests?

What questions should a tester ask himself or herself during the administration of formal tests?
6. What are the most frequently suggested etiological bases for developmental dysphasia?
7. How may developmental dysphasia be classified?
8. What are some of the more common symptoms associated with developmental dysphasia?
9. How may *agnosia* and *apraxia* be defined and described?
10. What are examples of typical speech and language therapy programs? How may they be described?
11. What steps should a speech and language pathologist follow in structuring a therapy program?
12. What impact does the presence of developmental dysphasia have on educational programs and services?

Chapter 6

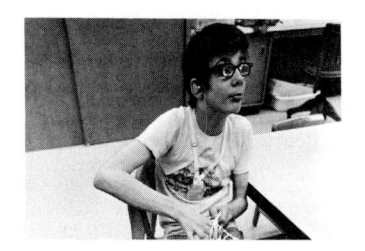

Severely and Profoundly Auditorially/Visually Impaired Students

The Deaf-Blind Population

Bernita M. Sims-Tucker and Corinne Klein Jensema

CHAPTER OBJECTIVES

After reading this chapter, you should be able to:

1. Discuss and analyze the medical and educational characteristics of deaf-blind individuals.
2. Describe the differences between severely mentally retarded deaf-blind and other multi-handicapped individuals.
3. Discuss and analyze educational progams for deaf-blind individuals, such as:
   a. Visual training
   b. Auditory training
   c. Movement programs.
4. Discuss the implications of medical and educational characteristics on educational programming.
5. Describe the anatomy of the eye and the ear and the implications of sensory deficits on educational progress.
6. Discuss and describe various diagnostic devices used for measuring intelligence, adaptive behavior, and present level of functioning.

For many years educational services for deaf-blind children were limited to a handful of facilities that catered to the intellectually elite. The first recorded education given to a deaf-blind individual took place in 1837 at the Perkins School for the Blind, in Watertown, Massachusetts, when tutorial services were provided to Laura Bridgeman. The legendary Helen Keller was later also a pupil at the Perkins School. For decades after the opening of the Perkins School, however, the educational needs of less intelligent deaf-blind students went unmet.

Gradually, services to deaf-blind children began to expand to encompass the needs of children with a variety of abilities. Due to the limited number of individuals in the deaf-blind population, most of these children were served in programs for other types of handicapped individuals. As a result, services were inadequate to meet the extensive needs of these children. In order to provide more comprehensive services and to coordinate the efforts of professionals working with deaf-blind youth, in 1967, the federal government, through the Bureau of Education for the Handicapped (BEH), now, Special Education Programs (SEP) established 10 deaf-blind regional centers. The centers were mandated under PL 91-230, Title VI-C (Education of the Handicapped Act, 1970) and were created in response to the rubella epidemic of 1963–1965, which significantly increased the number of children afflicted with this dual handicap. When the regional centers actually got under way in 1968, they were instructed by the BEH to adopt a 10-year mission to pursue the following goals:

1. Identification and assessment of deaf-blind children
2. Provision of appropriate educational services
3. Provision of inservice education for direct-service staff (teachers, aides, therapists)
4. Provision of support services to the parents or surrogate parents of these deaf-blind children (Salmon & Spar, 1977–1978, p. 413)

Over the next decade, the regional centers demonstrated they could successfully realize these goals. In 1978, in order that the states assume greater financial and programmatic responsibility, the regional centers divided into eight single-state centers and eight regional or multi-state centers. This trend was in concurrence with other federal mandates (e.g., Education for All Handicapped Children Act, PL 94-142), which placed greater responsibility for education of handicapped children at the state level. (See list of regional centers at end of this chapter under Educational Programs and Services.)

DEFINITIONS

The most difficult task of the regional centers was to create a standard for identifying the children they served. The BEH provided the following general guidelines:

[D]eaf-blind children are those who have auditory and visual handicaps, the combination of which causes such severe communication and educational problems that they cannot be properly accommodated in special education programs solely for the hearing handicapped and/or the visually handicapped child (*Federal Register*, 1975, p. 9).

Since the BEH guidelines were published, several other definitions have emerged. For example, Kramer and Rosenfeld (1975, p. 27) proposed the following definition: "Deaf-Blind persons are those who have substantial visual and hearing losses such that a combination of the two causes extreme difficulty in learning."

Although a number of other definitions have evolved, clinical interpretation continues to be a problem. For example, when severe/profound retardation exists, it is not always possible to determine if a child has physiological deafness (actual physical impairment) or functional deafness (non-use of intact hearing). Some programs will allow children who function as though they were deaf-blind persons to receive deaf-blind services. Others will accept only those with physical impairments. In addition, because so many of these children are difficult to test medically, determination cannot be made as to whether they fit precise guidelines for handicapping conditions.

The criteria used in defining multihandicapped, hearing impaired persons, as proposed by Griffing (1981, p. 5) also have implications for deaf-blind persons. These criteria stipulate that: 1) a sensory deficit is the primary handicapping condition, 2) the effect of a set of handicapping conditions is principally one of degree rather than of kind, and 3) the multiples of handicapping conditions in the child are significant in their compounded state. For deaf-blind individuals the severity of their sensory impairments is a major factor in determining their educational functioning level and the types of services they will require (Jensema, 1980). An example of a definition based upon Griffing's criteria would be: "Deaf-blindness comprises a double handicap with the implications beyond the absence of sight and hearing, creating unique problems of communication and mobility" (Helen Keller National Center, undated). In other words, congenital deaf-blindness thwarts normal development to a greater extent than the simple additive impact of visual and auditory impairments (Barraga, 1973; Kennedy, 1974; Lenneberg, 1967). Factors related to each condition affect conceptual development and interact, as well, causing impediments to normal growth to a greater extent than might be expected by analyzing each impairment separately.

INCIDENCE

In 1974, Hammer reported that approximately 3,563 (87% of the then known population) deaf-blind children were being served in public schools, private schools, and residential institutions for severely and profoundly handicapped individuals. This figure included nonrubella children as well as those not receiving federal funds for educational services. In 1980, Lockett and Rudolph reported that there were 5,982 deaf-blind children between birth and 22 years of age. This increase in numbers can be largely attributed to the work of Child Find activities that were prompted by federal legislation. Lockett and Rudolph estimated that 1,639 of these children were between the ages of 14 and 15, a population bubble attributable to the 1963–1965 rubella epidemic. The total population count for deaf-blind persons is predicted to be 6,000.

SCREENING, IDENTIFICATION, AND DIAGNOSIS

The diagnostic process should be designed to determine the causes of a child's condition, the functional manifestations of this condition, the educational prognosis, and the treatment plan (Van Etten, Arkell, & Van Etten, 1980).

The classroom teacher is directly involved in conducting educational assessments to determine instructional planning. The educational assessment process is meant to provide a way of identifying meaningful and relevant curricular goals (Collins, 1977), and helps in evaluating a child's readiness level for various activities. By pinpointing a child's present functioning level, a teacher is able to judge the tasks the child can currently perform, as well as performance goals along a developmental hierarchy toward which instruction should be targeted.

Intelligence and Adaptive Measures

For years, intelligence tests were the principal instruments used in determining classroom placement of handicapped children. The two most commonly used tests have been the Stanford-Binet Intelligence Scale and the Wechsler Intelligence Scale for Children (WISC). For hearing-impaired children specifically, the Hiskey-Nebraska Test of Learning Aptitude has been frequently used and requires no speech or verbal skills. The Leiter International Performance Scale and Arthur adaptation has also been utilized widely with hearing impaired children.

In more recent years developmental scales have provided valuable educational information. Two of the scales often used with deaf-blind children are the Cattell Infant Intelligence Scale and the Bayley Scales of Infant Development.

Adaptive scales, which ascertain a child's competence for independent survival, are also frequently used with deaf-blind children. The Maxfield-Bucholz Scale of Social Maturity for Use with Preschool Blind Children, the Vineland Social Maturity Scale, and the Balthazar Scales of Adaptive Behavior are the most popular adaptive scales used with this group.

Except for the above-mentioned Hiskey-Nebraska Test of Learning Aptitude and the Leiter Test, none of these tools were designed specifically for the deaf-blind population, nor do the tools contain deaf-blind norms. Each of these instruments must be adapted in part or in whole when administered. Because there are no specific rules for interpreting results, errors are common. The lack of qualified personnel to administer these tests and the communication barriers between deaf-blind children and test administrators further increase the likelihood of error (Vernon & Alles, 1982).

Hearing Testing

Deaf-blind children often are labeled as hard or impossible to test audiologically. Several techniques have been developed to facilitate testing the hearing acuity of these children, the two most commonly used types of testing being electrophysiological and behavioral (Cox & Lloyd, 1976).

Electrophysiological procedures involve reflexive responses and include impedance audiometry and electroencephalograph-evoked (EEG) response audiometry. Because electroencephalographic procedures are so expensive, they are used less often than impedance testing. Impedance testing does not measure the responsiveness of the cochlea or the auditory nerve, but tests the mobility of the tympanic membrane and the loudness level at which the stapedius muscle contracts. Impedance testing was one of the first successful tests used to determine presence of hearing loss in persons suspected to be deaf-blind. Impedance testing determines only presence of hearing, not level of deficit.

Behavioral testing includes behavior observation audiometry, play audiometry, and visually-reinforced audiometry (Cox & Lloyd, 1976). In behavior observation audiometry (BOA), a sound is presented while the child is in a soundproof room; the tester observes the child for any behavior change (e.g., an eye blink or a breathing pattern change). This behavior change is assumed to be a voluntary or an involuntary response to the introduction of sound. Play audiometry requires teaching a child to respond with a toy when a sound is presented. For example, a child is given blocks and shown how to drop them into a bucket while the tester pantomimes hearing a sound. Educators of severely mentally retarded deaf-blind children frequently employ this method as stated. Visually-reinforced audiometry refers to the technique of using visual stimulation combined with an auditory stimulus. For deaf-blind children the most common type of visual stimuli are large (approximately 24 inches high), lighted, plastic toys. The toys are illuminated when the sound is presented, and they provide reinforcement for the correct response. Jabaley and Brown (personal communication, September, 1975) tested many deaf-blind infants and children and found that visually-reinforced testing seems to have even more appeal when taped television commercials are used as the sound stimulus.

Vision Testing

Ophthalmological test results provide educators with information about the deaf-blind child's ocular condition. Visual acuity is one measure of ocular condition. Standard visual acuity instruments are the Snellen Chart, Tumbling E Chart, and picture-matching charts such as the Flash-Card Vision Test for Children (Efron & DuBoff, 1976). Standard procedures for measuring acuity are rarely reliable, however, when used with low-functioning deaf-blind children. In addition, ophthalmological tests furnish little information about visual functioning. While knowledge of ocular pathology is valuable, information about visual functioning is essential.

Daniel Gottlieb (1976), an optometrist, has been successful in helping educators of deaf-blind school-age children determine the visual functioning skills of their students. Gottlieb contends that motor control facilitates visual functioning. In his view, the first step in visual assessment should be to evaluate the child's general movement abilities, e.g., body balance to control motion, followed by the discriminative movement abilities of the eyes, hands, tongue, and lips. Efron and DuBoff (1976) constructed a vision guide that provides information for assessing and improving visual functioning. They feel that an assessment of visual functioning in deaf-blind/severely handicapped individuals should cover these major areas:

1. Sensation—the reception of light or forms by the retina and later the reception of the image by the brain.
2. Visual-motor skills—oculomotor and focusing skills in coordinating one's eyes with other parts of the body.
3. Cognitive/perceptual skills—the learned ability to construct a visual image, to be able to distinguish characteristics, and to give meaning to what one sees.

Visual assessment of deaf-blind children includes but extends far beyond measuring visual acuity. Assessment should include a general evaluation of the child's ability to incorporate visual planning in his or her motor relations with the environment. How the child makes use of his or her vision in the course of normal activities is the information that translates most valuably into educational strategies.

Classroom Assessment Devices

Instruments designed to be administered by classroom teachers for measuring functioning levels of handicapped children often provide more useful information than IQ tests. Traditional tests for this purpose tend to be inappropriate, since they do not take into account the combination of profound sensory, motor, integrative, communicative, and psychological disorders characteristic of children who are deaf-blind (Stillman, 1973).

Some assessment tools have been developed specifically for the deaf-blind population (Callier Azusa Scales), while others have been borrowed from other disciplines. These tools may cover behavioral (e.g., self-confidence and impulse control) and/or curricular (e.g., language and daily living skills) areas. Table 1 lists some of the most frequently used assessment devices.

ETIOLOGY

Several diseases and conditions can have a dramatic effect on both vision and hearing. The Office of Demographic Studies at Gallaudet College, Washington

Table 1. Some classroom assessment devices

	Test	Age	Behaviors assessed	Type	Measurement obtained	Population
1.	Balthazar Scales of Adaptive Behavior	Birth through independence	Section I: self-care, e.g., eating, dressing, and toileting Section II: social adaptation	Formal	Adaptive behavior	Moderately, mildly retarded, and severely profoundly handicapped persons
2.	Behavior Characteristics Progression (BCP)	Birth through independence	59 behavioral strands, e.g., health, dressing, toileting, language, impulse control, and self-confidence	Informal	Developmental age	Multihandicapped persons
3.	Brigance Inventory of Early Development	Birth–7 years	Psychomotor, self-help, speech & language, general knowledge, language comprehension, and early academic skills	Formal	Developmental age	Infants and children developmentally below 7 years
4.	Callier Azusa Scale	Birth–9 years	Motor, perceptual, and language development, as well as daily living and socialization skills	Informal	Developmental age	Deaf-blind, multihandicapped, and severely profoundly handicapped persons
5.	Central Wisconsin Colony and Training School's Education Assessment Device	Preschool to school age	Self-care and language development skills	Informal	Functional level	Severely mentally retarded, cerebral palsied, deaf-blind, multihandicapped hearing impaired, and visually impaired persons

(*continued*)

Table 1. (*continued*)

	Test	Age	Behaviors assessed	Type	Measurement obtained	Population
6.	Research Forms of Bayley Scales of Motor Development	Birth–30 months	A. Mental Scale, e.g., sensory perceptual skills; discrimination B. Motor Scale, e.g., body control and coordination C. Behavior Record, e.g., child's attitudes; child's interests	Formal	Developmental level	Cerebral palsied and other neurologically impaired infants
7.	Denver Developmental Screening Test	Birth–36 months	Personal-social, fine-motor and gross-motor skills, adaptive, and language skills	Formal	Developmental age	Normal infants and preschoolers
8.	Developmental Activities Screening Inventory (DASI)	6–60 months	Cognitive and fine- and gross-motor skills	Formal	Developmental age	Deaf-blind and low-functioning students
9.	Developmental Programming for Infants and Young Children	Birth–36 months	Perceptual fine-motor, cognitive, language, social-emotional, self-care, and gross-motor skills	Formal	Developmental age	Normal and handicapped infants
10.	Developmental Sprial	Birth–5 years	Fine- and gross-motor, self-help, language, and socialization skills	Informal	Developmental age	Multihandicapped children
11.	Koontz Child Developmental Programs (includes curriculum)	Birth–48 months	Gross- and fine-motor, social, and language skills	Formal	Developmental age	Multihandicapped, visually impaired, and hearing impaired children

12.	Learning Accomplishment Profile (LAP)	Birth–33 months	Fine- and gross-motor, social, self-help, cognitive, and language skills	Formal	Developmental age	Handicapped children
13.	A Manual for the Assessment of a Deaf-Blind Multihandicapped Child	(No age given)	Personal, self-help, social development, gross- and fine-motor, language, and cognitive development skills	Informal	Functional level	Deaf-blind children
14.	The Murdoch Center C & Y Program Library	Preschool through school ages	Self-help, residential, gross- and fine-motor, preacademic, and social skills	Formal	Developmental age and functional level	Severely disabled and developmentally disabled children
15.	Pennsylvania Training Model	Birth–5 years	Sensory development, activities of daily living, communication, perceptual cognitive, and social interaction skills	Informal	Developmental age	Normal and handicapped children
16.	The Portage Project Checklist (includes curriculum)	Birth–5 years	Cognitive, self-help, motor, language, and socialization skills	Informal	Developmental age	Multihandicapped, physically handicapped, and visually impaired children
17.	Southern California Sensory Integration Tests	4–10 years	Space visualization, figure/ground, perception in space, design copy, imitation of postures, motor accuracy, kinesthesia, manual form perception, finger identification, graphesthesia, localization of tactile stimuli, double tactile perception, crossing midline of body, bilateral motor coordination, right/left discrimination, standing balance (eyes open) and standing balance (eyes closed)	Formal	Functional level	Children with perceptual motor problems and sensory integrative dysfunctions

(continued)

Table 1. (continued)

	Test	Age	Behaviors assessed	Type	Measurement obtained	Population
18.	The Assessment Inventory for Severely Handicapped Children (TARC)	Adolescence to adulthood	Self-help, motor, communication, and social skills	Formal	Developmental age	Severely handicapped adolescents and adults
19.	Uzgiris and Hunt's Ordinal Scales of Psychological Development	Birth–2 years	Scale I: development of visual pursuit and object permanence Scale II: development of means for obtaining desired environmental events Scale III: development of imitations—vocal and gestural Scale IV: development of operational causality Scale V: construction of object relations in space Scale VI: development of schemes for relating to objects	Formal	Cognitive functional skills	Severely handicapped infants

D.C., obtained the data shown in Table 2 on the causes of hearing loss among children in programs for deaf students for the academic year 1977–78. Maternal rubella, heredity, and meningitis continue to be the leading known etiologies of deaf-blindness in the present school-age population. Deaf-blindness rarely occurs in isolation, since congenital etiologies are usually organismically devastating enough to cause other handicaps. For example, expectant mothers infected with rubella (German measles), especially during the first few months of pregnancy, are at risk for bearing infants who are afflicted with deafness, congenital heart disease, cataracts, and/or gross mental retardation.

A study of 46 deaf children with congenital rubella conducted at the Developmental Evaluation Clinic of the Children's Hospital Medical Center in Boston in 1968 reported evidence of mental retardation, behavioral anomalies, visual handicaps, neurological abnormalities, limitations in motor skills, congenital heart disease, small stature, and receptive language problems (Guldager, 1969). Vernon (1977) found that rubella babies are at high risk for: premature births, below-average intelligence, low academic achievement, poor communication skills, motor disabilities, and brain damage. Campbell (1961) stated that the greatest consequence of rubella is deafness. Cooper, Ziring, Ockerse, Fedun, Kiely, and Krugman (1969) reported on the frequency of major deficits among 376 children born of mothers infected with rubella. Of the 376 cases, 229 cases exhibited multiple handicaps, including various combinations of heart disease, deafness, visual impairment, and mental retardation. All 229 individuals had both vision and hearing deficits, and 70% of the 229 were mentally retarded.

Table 2. Etiologies of hearing loss reported for school-age, hearing-impaired children for the 1977–1978 academic year*

Etiology	Relative frequency (%)
Maternal rubella	17.1
Trauma at birth	2.1
Pregnancy complications	2.8
Heredity	8.8
Prematurity	3.8
Rh incompatibility	2.0
Meningitis	6.2
High fever	2.7
Mumps	0.4
Infections	2.2
Measles	1.3
Otitis media	1.8
Trauma after birth	0.7
Other (at birth)	59.1
Other (after birth)	4.9
Cause not determined	26.7
Data not available	3.7

Source: Office of Demographic Studies, Gallaudet College, Washington, D.C.
*Several etiologies may be listed for a single individual.

Of those with mental retardation, half were in the moderate to severe range. Stein, Palmer, and Weinberg (1980) noted that two-thirds of the deaf-blind students in their study were middle-trainable (moderate) or below; over one-sixth were upper-trainable (high moderate), and the rest could not be classified. Rubella has created perhaps the largest, most seriously involved and difficult to educate group of deaf-blind children.

The following is a composite of characteristics of deaf-blind individuals, based on a review of the literature:

Deafness
Visual impairments/retinopathy/cataracts
Cardiac conditions
Emotional disturbance
Aphasia
Mental retardation
Autistic-like behaviors
Self-stimulation
Motor problems/orthopaedic problems, cerebral palsy
Prematurity
Epilepsy/seizures
Dwarfism or petite stature
Microencephaly
Cowlick (turned up tuft of hair)
Soft teeth enamel

Cerebral palsy can be classified as both an etiologically significant factor in deaf-blindness as well as a frequently accompanying handicapping condition in deaf-blind persons. Actually, it is the result of brain damage or maldevelopment occurring *in utero* or in earliest childhood and is the name of a group of conditions all of which involve impairment of motor coordination. Although loss of motor control, posture, and balance are most obvious, associated sensory and perceptual disturbance are not rare (Bobath & Bobath, 1972). Some problems linked with cerebral palsy that may correlate with a child's communication abilities are:

1. High-frequency loss and auditory agnosia
2. Strabismus, isotropia, homonymous mianopsia, or cataracts (if the etiology is rubella)
3. Loss or decrease in stereognosis (ability to discriminate objects by touch), two-point discrimination, vibration sense, and pain and temperature
4. Defects in articulatory apparatus (cleft palate or overbite)
5. Rhythm disorders and aphasia
6. Mental retardation (40%–70%)
7. Perceptual problems
8. Seizure disorders (Brown & Rutger, 1975).

Children with cerebral palsy present unique educational problems in that they may be incapable of using braille, manual communication, or speech.

Bacterial infections, which are frequent causes of deafness, usually reach the inner ear through the endolymphatic and perilymphatic connections between the inner ear and the cranial cavity. When the meninges or coverings of the brain and spinal cord are affected, the infection is known as meningitis. If the infection reaches the inner ear, it may damage the organ of Corti, the auditory nerve, and most or all of the other delicate auditory structures. Acute vision loss may also occur as a result of destruction of the optic nerve or occipital lobe. During the 1920s and 1930s, meningitis was the most common cause of childhood deafness and a frequent contributor to visual defect. Today, however, preventive innoculation has reduced its incidence considerably.

Peripheral or central dysacusis and blindness also may be caused by erythroblastosis fetalis. This pathology occurs as a result of blood protein incompatibility between a mother who is Rh negative and a fetus who is Rh positive. When the foreign protein crosses the placental barrier, the mother's system develops antibodies which, in turn, cause anemia, lack of oxygen to the blood stream, or miscarriage. Rh children frequently have multiple involvements, among which are cerebral palsy and mental retardation (Masland, Sarason, & Gladwin, 1958).

CLASSIFICATION SYSTEMS

Hearing Classifications

Decibels (dB) are units of measure used to describe the acoustic power of sound and the amount of hearing loss. Zero decibels is generally considered the least audible sound that a normal hearing person can hear. A person is considered to have normal hearing when he or she has no more than a 20-dB loss in the speech range. As a person loses more decibels of hearing acuity, his or her loss has greater implications for language development and, consequently, educational intervention. Hearing loss can be divided into five broad classifications according to degree of loss of sensitivity to hearing, as follows:

1. Mild loss (Class 1)—a loss of hearing ability in which the least audible sound that can be heard in the speech range is between 20 dB and 40 dB. A person with this type of loss usually can understand conversation under normal conditions with minimal difficulty, particularly if he or she has the use of a hearing aid. Such a person's speech may have slight errors in articulation.
2. Moderate loss (Class 2)—a loss of hearing ability in which the least audible sound that can be heard in the speech range is between 41 dB and 55 dB. A person with this type of loss needs assistance in discriminating between various speech sounds. Such a person's speech may have numerous articulation errors.

3. Moderate/severe loss (Class 3)—a loss of hearing ability in which the least audible sound that can he heard in the speech range is between 56 dB and 70 dB. A person with this type of loss can hear little of normal conversation without amplification. Such a person's speech may have numerous errors in articulation and be characterized by significant voice production problems.
4. Severe loss (Class 4)—a loss of hearing ability in which the least audible sound that can be heard in the speech range is between 71 dB and 90 dB. A person with this type of loss cannot hear normal conversation and needs amplification to hear environmental sounds. Such a person's speech is likely to be unintelligible.
5. Profound loss (Class 5)—a loss of hearing ability in which the least audible sound that can be heard in the speech range is equal to or worse than 91 dB. A person with this type of loss can hear environmental sounds only with amplification. Such a person's speech is likely to be unintelligible or non-existent (Davis & Silverman, 1970).

An audiogram is a means of graphically describing hearing sensitivity level. The vertical axis measures loudness in decibels. Usually the 0 dB level (or −10) is at the top of the chart, and the 110 dB level is at the bottom. The greater a person's loss, the lower geographically on the audiogram his or her hearing level will be charted. Frequency or pitch, measured in hertz (Hz), appears along the horizontal axis. Low, bass sounds are found on the left of the axis while high, treble sounds are on the right. The numbers usually range from 125 Hz to 8,000 Hz, with the speech frequencies occurring in the 250 Hz to 2,000 Hz range. Figure 1 shows the approximate appearance of an audiogram for normal persons and for persons with each class of hearing loss.

It is important to point out that a person's ability to function with each type of hearing loss is highly individual and is dependent also upon such factors as intelligence, use of amplification, age of auditory and speech intervention, and presence of other handicapping conditions. Usually, the greater the hearing loss, the greater the difficulty a person will experience learning language.

Visual Classifications

Visual impairment is measured by acuity (how clearly one sees) and the degree of visual field. Normal vision is described as 20/20, which means that a person is able to see clearly an object at 20 feet without corrective lenses. A person with an acuity level described as 20/40 sees an object at 20 feet as clearly as a person with normal vision can see it at 40 feet. The visual field is the hemispherical range to which a person with normal eyesight has access. A legally blind person is one whose visual field does not exceed 20/200 in the better eye after correction, or one who has a limited central visual field of no greater than 20° (Van Etten et al., 1980). A low vision person may have light perception, the ability to tell light from darkness, as well as form perception, the ability to distinguish people or things by their form (Winter, 1977). Rarely does one encounter a totally blind person with no residual vision.

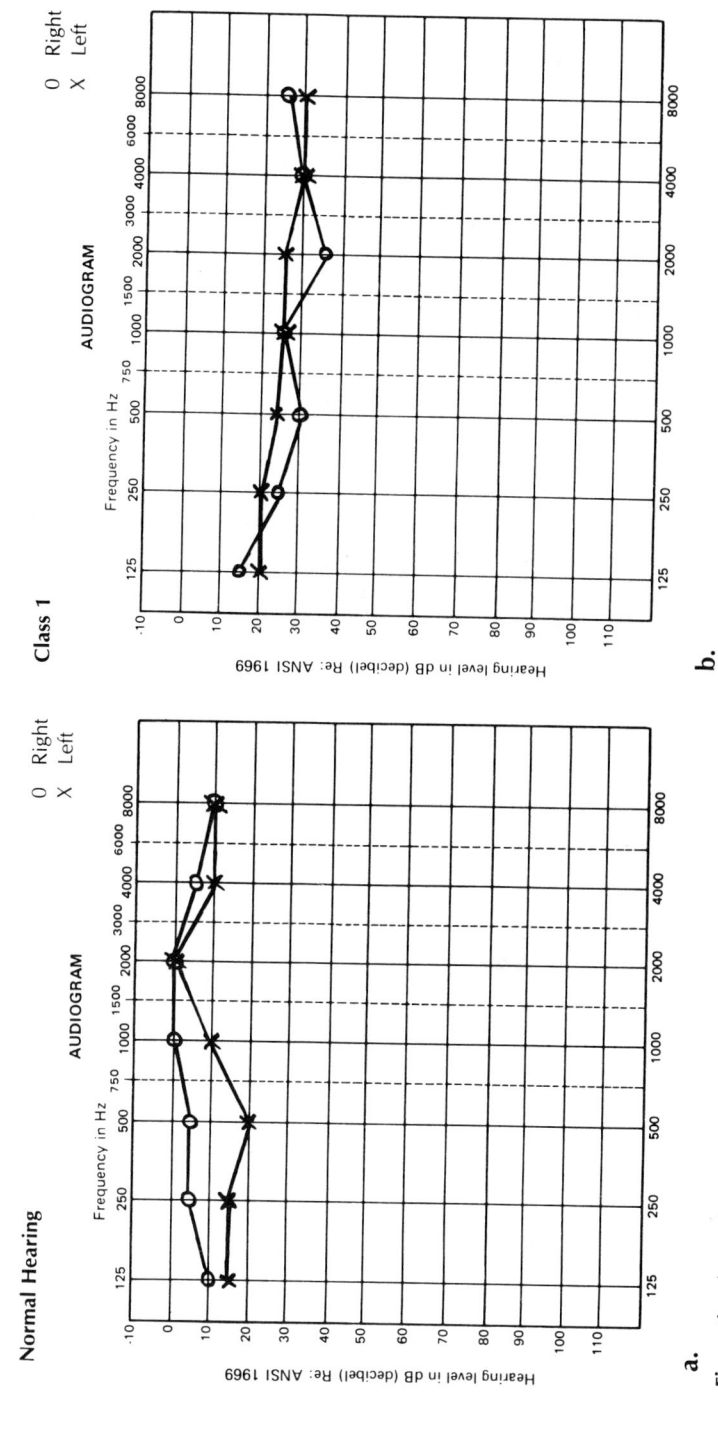

Figure 1. Approximate appearance of audiogram for: a) normal hearing, and b) mild bilateral hearing loss (Class 1).

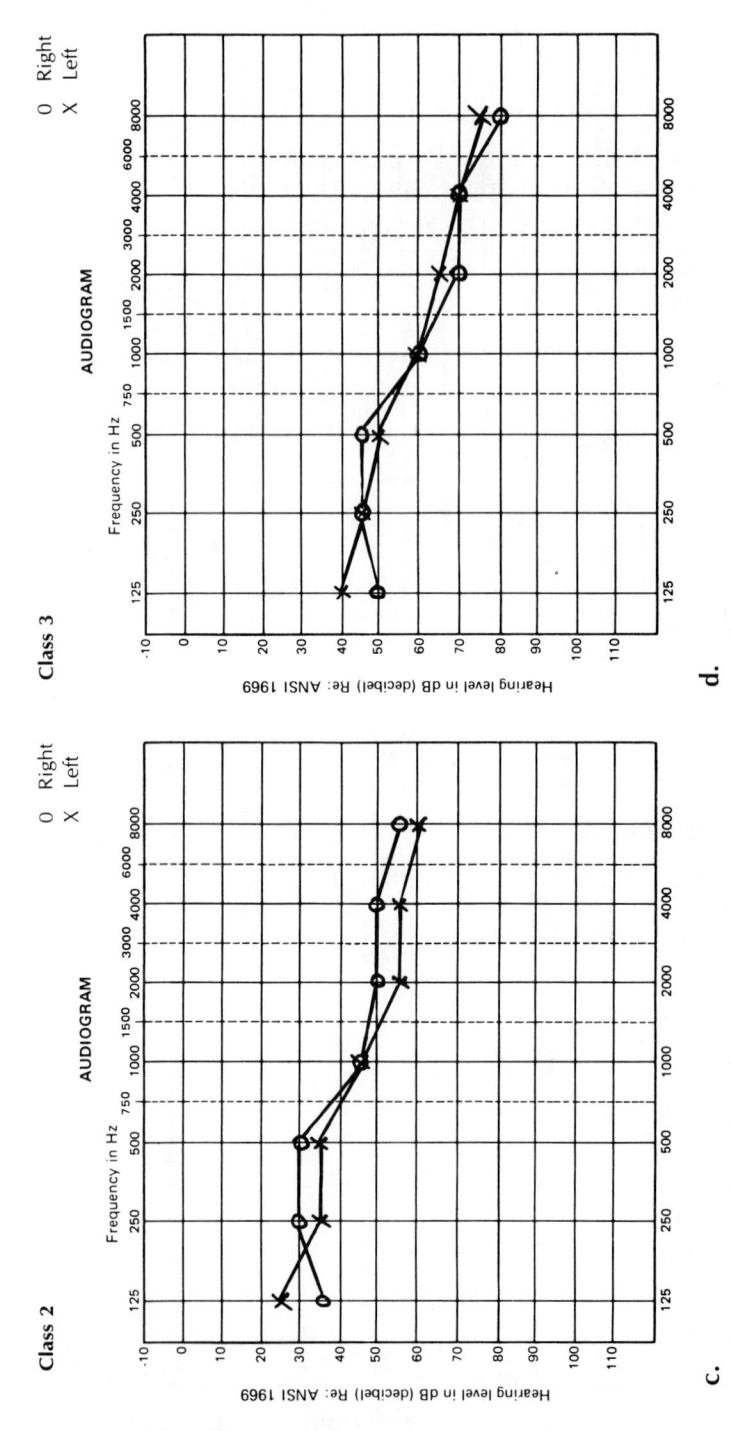

Figure 1 *(continued).* Approximate appearance of audiogram for: c) moderate bilateral hearing loss (Class 2), and d) moderately severe bilateral hearing loss (Class 3).

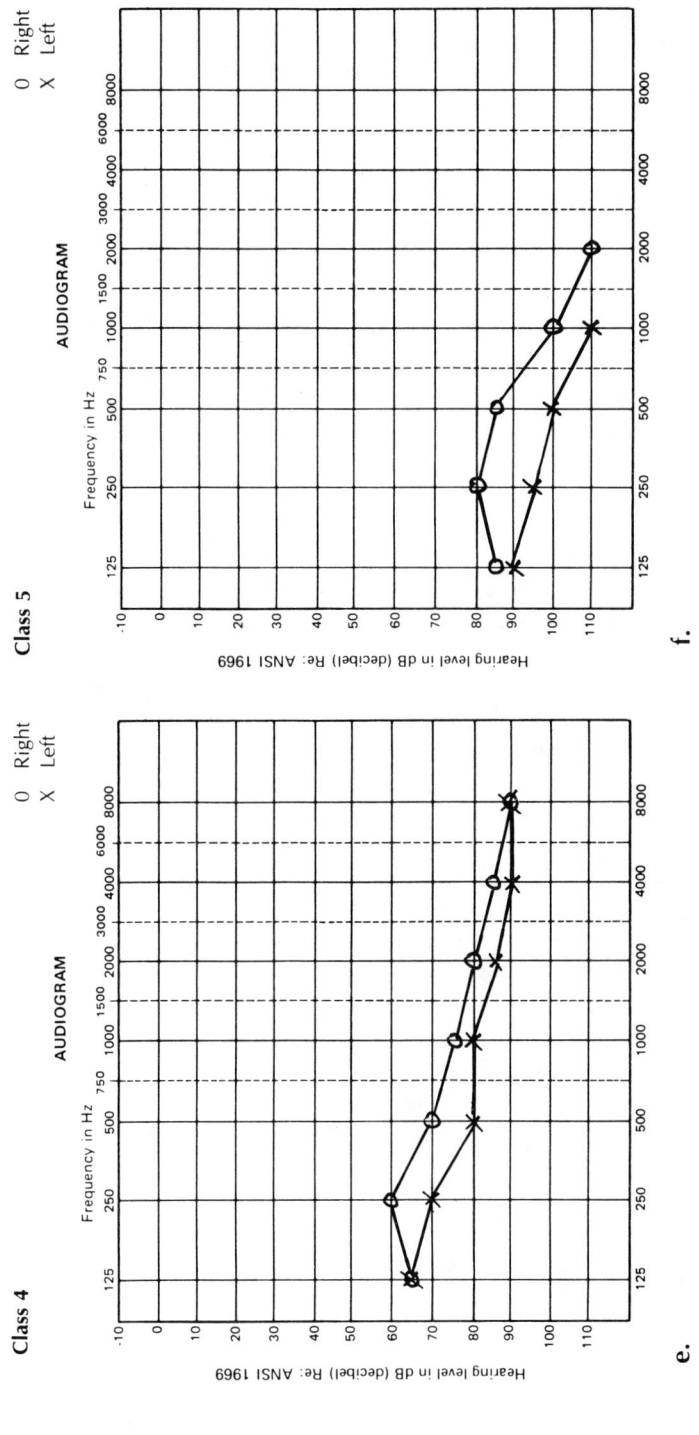

Figure 1 (continued). Approximate appearance of audiogram for: e) severe bilateral hearing loss, (Class 4), and f) profound bilateral hearing loss (Class 5).

Educational Classifications

Educational groupings are ways of representing general functioning ability, which is largely dependent upon the severity of the sensory impairments and the number of other handicaps that appear with these sensory impairments. Educationally, deaf-blind children can be divided into five groups (Stewart, 1981). Stewart outlined the following groups to be used in establishing program needs in correlation with functioning level:

1. Deaf-blind children with mild sensory impairments who can function in a regular school, if the classroom teacher is provided with adequate consultant services. These children can maintain normal academic achievement and compete with nonhandicapped peers. Speech is generally the preferred mode of communication. Such children may require the ancillary services of a speech pathologist, audiologist, low-vision specialist, and/or orientation and mobility trainer. They are able to carry out recreation and daily living activities with minor adaptations and counseling. Their job potential lies within the range of competitive employment.

2. Deaf-blind children with moderate sensory impairments who have enough remaining vision or hearing to learn through techniques devised for deaf persons or blind persons, respectively. These children have abilities similar to those of the first group and usually can participate in activities with hearing impaired or visually impaired individuals with whom they are educationally placed.

3. Deaf-blind children with moderate to severe sensory impairments who require educational techniques provided in a special deaf-blind department. These children can acquire rudimentary to sophisticated gestures and signs that may lead to the development of effective communication. Academic achievement may go as high as the sixth grade level and include reading and writing skills. This group has potential for independence in functional living skills and orientation and mobility. The future holds possibilities for day activity centers, sheltered workshops, and competitive employment. Recreation activities for these children may include swimming, roller skating, hiking, biking, and a variety of games (Smith, 1974).

4. Deaf-blind children who are either too young or too immature for formal education, and, therefore, require a program of developmental and stimulation training. These children can learn rudimentary communication, often in approximated form. They require supervision and assistance in the execution of daily living skills. Orientation and mobility skills are beyond their abilities at this time, and they are more appropriately served by occupational and physical therapists. The older children in this category may be able to learn simple household chores but will always require custodial care. Appropriate social behavior is barely existent, and functioning is marred by bizarre mannerisms.

5. Deaf-blind children who have been exposed to the special methods of training or education devised for deaf-blind children but have failed to shows significant progress. These children may be able to develop minimal social, communicative, and self-help skills but have not demonstrated academic growth. Often the presence of bizarre mannerisms precludes their demonstrating the potential one would expect. They will always require a sheltered environment and are unlikely to attain any form of employment.

SYMPTOMATOLOGY

Deaf-blindness creates physical and behavioral anomalies that are peculiar to this population and to the multiply handicapped population in general. Comprehension of the different types of hearing and vision impairments is enhanced by an understanding of the anatomy and function of the ear and the eye.

The Ear

The ear (see Figure 2) has three sections: 1) external ear and canal, 2) middle ear, and 3) inner ear.

The primary importance of the external ear, the pinna or auricle, is to collect sound waves. The ear canal is irregular in shape and differs from person to person (Davis & Silverman, 1970); it is only 2.5 cm in length and runs from the outer ear to the eardrum (tympanic membrane). The canal secretes a wax that inhibits the entrance of dust, insects, or other foreign objects into the canal.

The middle ear begins at the eardrum and contains three tiny bones (ossicles) named the malleus (hammer), incus (anvil), and the stapes (stirrup). Their main

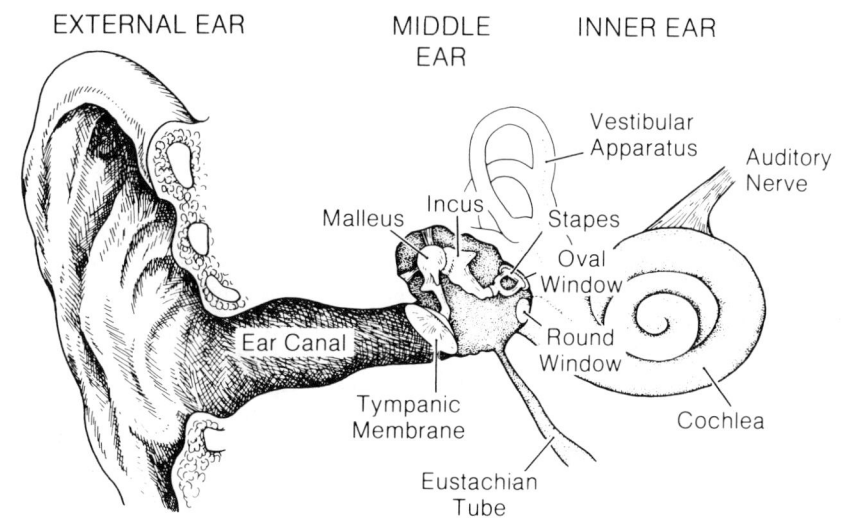

Figure 2. Diagram of the human ear. (Reprinted by permission from Batshaw & Perret, 1981.)

function is to transmit sound vibrations originating at the eardrum to the inner ear. The middle ear opens directly into the air cells of the temporal bone at the oval window, which is the opening to the inner ear. The footplate of the stapes is set in the oval window. The Eustachian tube opens into the anterior wall of the inner ear through the round window about midway between its floor and roof (Davis & Silverman, 1970). The Eustachian tube connects the middle ear with the back of the nasal cavity. The tube helps to equalize air pressure inside and outside the eardrum.

The inner ear is a series of channels in the temporal bone called the labyrinth. The central channel (vestibule) joins the snail-like cochlea, the sense organ for hearing, and the three semicircular canals, the sense organ for equilibrium control. The canal inside the cochlea is divided into the upper (vestibular) and lower (tympanic) galleries. These galleries are divided by the fibrous basilar membrane. On this membrane sits a membranous tube, the organ of Corti, which contains the sensory cells (hair cells) that set off nerve impulses. The nerve impulses are transmitted through nerve fibers that join in the central core of the cochlea to form the auditory nerve. The auditory nerve carries the information to the brain.

The Eye

The eye (see Figure 3) is divided into three major sections: the outer eye, the middle layer, and the interior wall. The outer part of the eye includes: the eyelids, the conjunctiva, the cornea, and the sclera. The eyelids, which are elastic skin folds, function to protect the eye from injury and to preserve clear vision by keeping the cornea clean and lubricated through blinking. The conjunctiva, the outermost part of the eye, is a mucous membrane that covers the front part of the eye and acts as a protective barrier for the cornea. The iris and the pupil are covered by a transparent coating, which is tough and rigid, called the cornea. The cornea focuses and transmits light into the interior eye. If the surface of the cornea does not remain smooth and moist, it becomes easily abraded, and clear vision is impaired. Excess fluid in the cornea is removed by the endothelial cells located in the back of the cornea. All parts of the eye are held stable by the tough, fibrous, opaque sclera, the "white" of the eye.

The middle layer contains the choroid, the iris, and the ciliary body. The choroid, composed of spongy mesh matter, nourishes the outer half of the retina by allowing nerve fibers and blood vessels to pass through it. If the retina moves out of position, it can no longer receive nourishment from the choroid, and vision is lost. The iris is a muscle membrane that surrounds the pupil. It is commonly known as the colored part of the eye. The size of the pupil is adjusted by the iris to regulate the amount of light that goes to the interior part of the eye; the opening is enlarged to let in more light in dark environments and contracts in bright lights. The ciliary body is a specialized structure with two functions: it reduces tension on the crystalline lens, which is fastened to ciliary muscles by ligaments, and produces aqueous humor, a clear, watery fluid that bathes and feeds the lens. The

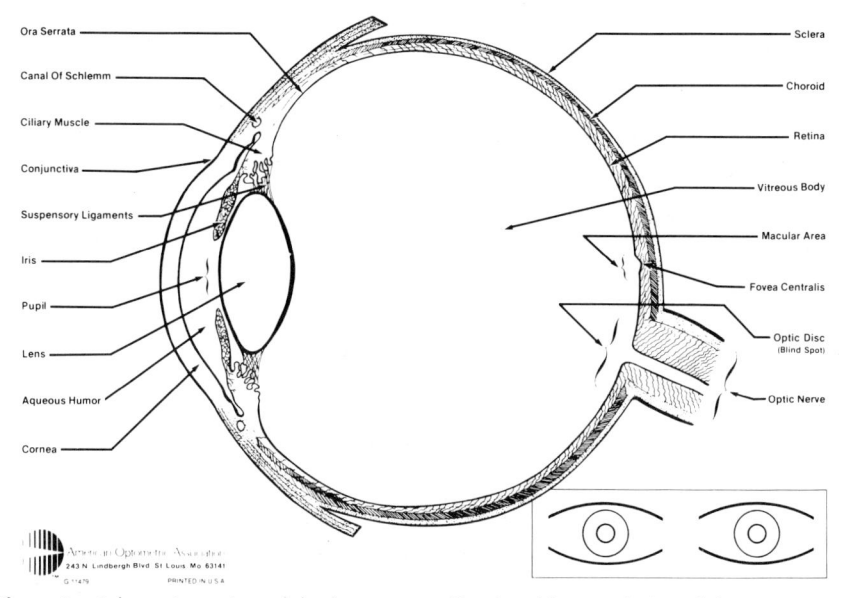

Figure 3. Schematic section of the human eye. (Reprinted by permission of the American Optometric Association, St. Louis.)

crystalline lens is located directly posterior to the aqueous humor and is a thick, gelatin mass of fibers that is capsule-shaped and elastic in nature. Its main function is to focus light on the retina. The lens must remain transparent in order to clearly transmit and focus on the retina.

The retina comprises the inner layer of the eye. It is composed of nerves and fibers that interpret light into nerve impulses that are then transmitted along the optic nerve.

Causes of Hearing Impairments

Auditory impairments may result from three possible conditions: poor conduction of sound to the sense organ, abnormality of the sense organ or its nerve, and impairments that result from injury to or failure of functioning in the central nervous system (Davis & Silverman, 1970). *Conductive hearing loss* is a term normally given to any physical impairment in the conduction of sound to the cochlea. It is frequently associated with reduction in mobility of the middle ear ossicular chain and can result in up to a 70 dB loss. Middle-ear infections, which often plague young children, can create hearing loss, particularly if they are serious and chronic. *Sensorineural loss* describes any disorder resulting from destruction to the cochlea and/or central auditory connections. Most congenital etiologies create a sensorineural loss.

Auditory agnosia is the result of aberrant operation of the central nervous system (Davis & Silverman, 1970), in which the nerve impulses initiated in the ear by sound waves reach the brain, but they are not consciously heard. Other terms used to describe auditory agnosia are central auditory imperception, sensory aphasia, receptive aphasia, and word deafness.

Causes of Vision Impairments

Etiology of vision loss is somewhat more difficult to determine, as it is a result of a condition of the eye, which in turn, is a result of a pathological factor. For example, the etiology may be maternal rubella, but the resulting condition of the eye will be congenital cataracts. In many surveys that investigate etiology of vision loss, these two levels of etiology are confused. Also, many etiologies of vision loss affect the quality of sight differentially. Cataracts, for instance, cloud vision, while a refractive error may directly reduce acuity.

Following is a brief description of some of the frequently-diagnosed conditions causing visual impairment:

Retrolental fibroplasia A bilateral disease characterized by abnormality of the retinal vessels, which can occur in premature infants in whom the immature retina was exposed to high postnatal incubator oxygen concentrations. Associated problems include myopia, glaucoma, retinal detachment, and mental retardation (Berkow & Talbott, 1977).

Retinitis pigmentosa A slowly progressive, bilateral tapetoretinal degeneration. A hereditary pattern is often difficult to establish with this condition, but in most cases (90%), it appears to be autosomal recessive. It may also be autosomal dominant (9%) or, infrequently, X-linked. The retinal rods are affected most, producing defective night vision, which may become symptomatic in early childhood. A midperipheral scotoma (a blind gap in the visual field) gradually widens so that central vision frequently is reduced by middle age and may lead to blindness (Berkow & Talbott, 1977). A particular cause of deaf-blindness, Usher's syndrome, shows up as congenital deafness and retinitis pigmentosa, which develops in the teens or 20s.

Retinal detachment A separation of the sensory and pigment layers of the retina as a result of injury or disease. Detachment is partial at first but becomes complete, in the absence of medical attention, due to seepage of fluid from the large vitreous cavity into the space between the two layers of the retina. The person first experiences flashes of light, then the sensation of a curtain moving across the eye, progressively clouding vision, and, finally, blindness (Clark & Cumley, 1973).

Optic atrophy Atrophy of the optic nerve, which has a direct proportional effect on the degree of vision loss.

Cataract Developmental or degenerative opacity of the lens. Developmental cataract occurs congenitally or during early life from nutritional, inflammatory, hereditary metabolic, or toxic causes (e.g., maternal rubella early in pregnancy). The cardinal symptom is a progressive, painless loss of vision. The degree of loss depends on the location and extent of opacity (Berkow & Talbott, 1977).

Glaucoma A disorder caused by an inability to eliminate at an adequate rate the fluid that is produced by the ciliary body of the eye. The blood supply to the optic nerve is hampered by intraocular pressure, resulting in irreversible damage (Clark & Cumley, 1973).

Toxic amblyopia A reduction in visual acuity believed to be due to a toxic reaction in the orbital portion of the optic nerve (Berkow & Talbott, 1977).

Strabismus The deviation of one eye inward or outward due to imbalance of the muscles of the eyeball. Paralytic (nonconcomitant) strabismus results from paralysis of one or more ocular muscles and may be caused by a specific oculomotor nerve lesion. It is characterized by limitation of eye motion and increasing diplopia (double vision) in fields of action of the paralyzed muscles. Diplopia is not present if the paralysis is congenital, since the vision in the deviated eye is suppressed. Nonparalytic (concomitant) strabismus usually results from unequal ocular muscle tone (Berkow & Talbott, 1977).

Nystagmus Rhythmic oscillation of the eyes in a horizontal, vertical, or rotary direction. Pendular nystagmus (undulatory or oscillating nystagmus) is seen when vision is poor from birth or early age. The eyes move back and forth with roughly the same velocity in both directions. Jerk nystagmus is more common and is characterized by a slow drift, usually away from the direction of gaze, followed by a quick jerk or recovery (Berkow & Talbott, 1977).

Errors of refraction Any condition causing focusing difficulties. Hyperopia (farsightedness) is a refractive error in which the point of focus lies behind the retina, either because the eyeball axis is too short or because the refractive power of the eye is too weak. In myopia (nearsightedness) the image is focused in front of the retina, either because the axis of the eye is too long or the refractive power of the eye is too strong. In astigmatism the refraction is unequal in the different meridians of the eyeball (Berkow & Talbott, 1977).

Behavioral Patterns

Behavioral aberrations are, perhaps, some of the most distinguishing features of deaf-blind children as a group. Deaf-blind children almost without exception engage in some form of self-stimulation (Moersch, 1977). Although every human being indulges in ritualistic and self-stimulatory behaviors, the intensity and single-mindedness with which these are pursued by many deaf-blind children are sufficient to preclude or limit contact with others. Self-preoccupation to this degree is very much akin to the egocentric period in Piaget's schema. During this most primitive and presymbolic stage of development, children view the world as an extension of themselves and manipulatable according to their desires. Their greatest concern is to please and satisfy their sensory pathways.

Robbins and Steinquist (1967) have categorized deaf-blind children according to whether they initiate protosymbolic behavior (pointing, smiling, or gesturing) or indulge in autistic-like (self-stimulatory) behaviors. These authors maintain that speech and language training is inappropriate for children who demonstrate no protosymbolic communication and that, consequently, an alternate educational treatment plan is required. Rothschild (1962) also characterized deaf-blind children as tending to withdraw from human contact and exhibiting a less consistent and intensive drive to be part of what is happening around them. He considered such children to be less successful candidates for educational achievement than severely mentally retarded children.

The reasons why deaf-blind children engage in self-stimulatory behaviors are speculative. Some behaviors appear to be attempts to accelerate the rate of sensory input into severely limited channels, so as to approximate normalcy in intensity or diversity. The behaviors could be the response to the brain's efforts to analyze the environment when normal neurological pathways have been damaged. When the environment is already limited by the absence of sight and sound, self-stimulation could be viewed as a creative alternative to boredom.

Self-stimulatory behaviors can be divided into four categories: 1) stereotypic, 2) self-abusive, 3) autoerotic, and 4) ritualistic-perseverative (Groves, 1975). Stereotypic behaviors might be thought of, in this case, as directly resulting from visual and auditory limitations. These are sometimes called "deafisms" and "blindisms." Deafisms are habitual behaviors designed to render auditory or vibratory/acoustic feedback, such as teeth-grinding and closing the external auditory meatus with the pinna while making repetitive sounds. Blindisms are behaviors involving ocular stimulation such as eye-gouging and light-filtering. Addiction to light is the most prominent behavioral anomaly of deaf-blind children (Thomas, 1970). According to Moersch (1977):

> They [deaf-blind children] assume extreme postures in order to locate a light source. The addiction to light is joined by various self-stimulatory activities, many of which are related to light. Anyone who has watched deaf-blind children is well aware of the lengths these children will go to find sources of light and of the practice of rapidly moving their hand, fingers or an object across the open eye, sometimes referred to as flipping (p. 426).

Self-abusive behavior is common among low functioning deaf-blind children and is chiefly manifested in head-banging. Autoerotic or masturbatory stimulation can occur by any overt or covert means. Repetitious behaviors that appear to have no other mission than ritualistic comfort are called ritualistic-perseverative. "Pill-rolling," a circular activity of the forefinger and thumb, and the twirling of objects are examples of ritualistic-perseverative behaviors.

In addition to self-stimulation, two other characteristics that frequently occur together—hyperactivity and distractibility—are common to deaf-blind children.

Such children are unable to attend to a task and, therefore, to communication for any extended time period: They tend to "expend" this inattention in rapid, sometimes frenzied and usually meaningless motor activity. Minor environmental disturbances can become the center of attention to children who are distractible.

PREVENTION AND TREATMENT PROGRAMS

Prevention

As stated earlier, several diseases and conditions—among them, maternal rubella, heredity disorders, and meningitis/encephalitis—have a dramatic effect on both vision and hearing. The only preventive measure for maternal rubella at present is the rubella vaccine. This vaccine contains a small percent of the rubella virus. After an injection of the vaccine, the body develops antibodies that can be used later to fight off any rubella infection. Because the last rubella epidemic to sweep the United States was in 1963–65, some parents have become negligent about obtaining the rubella vaccine for their preschoolers. This negligence has brought about a recent outbreak of rubella in isolated areas of the United States. Health and welfare agencies are still encouraging parents to have their children inoculated against rubella. The rubella virus has been known to germinate in the bodies of rubella syndrome children long after birth and to continue causing damage to their hearing and vision. At present, no known cure is available to arrest such damage.

Organizations such as the March of Dimes are actively engaged in research seeking cures for congenital birth defects. Several prenatal precautions are now recommended. These include: 1) decreased caffeine intake, 2) decreased aspirin and other over-the-counter drug consumption, 3) deletion of alcohol intake, 4) balanced intake of the four food groups, and 5) increased daily exercise habits.

Treatment

Treatment of deaf-blindness has both medical and educational components. Certain types of medical care can prevent deterioration of hearing and vision, while educational intervention can allay some of the functional inabilities caused by the dual impairments.

Hearing As previously discussed, hearing loss may be conductive or sensorineural in nature. Conductive losses may occur in the outer or middle ear. Most outer ear losses are the result of wax buildup occluding the external auditory meatus. Daily hygiene usually prevents such an occurrence, but, if wax accumulates excessively, a physician may need to remove the plug through such techniques as irrigation. Most middle-ear losses are due to infections that cause fluid buildup and impede the movement of the ossicles. Prescribed antibiotics and, in extreme cases, insertion of silicone tubing can relieve middle-ear infections. Otosclerosis, the growth of a calcium deposit around the edge of the stapes and oval window, can impede the movement of the ossicles. Treatment may necessitate surgical removal of the stapes and replacement with a plastic replica.

Inner-ear damage usually is characterized as sensorineural. Sensorineural loss is caused by destruction of the auditory nerve or the cochlea. Recently, surgeons have been able to remove the cochlea and replace it with an implant. Because the sounds generated through use of this device are abnormal in quality, its effectiveness is highly contested. Severely mentally retarded deaf-blind children are normally not candidates for this type of procedure because of their limited ability to cognitively interpret the input and because of the cost involved.

Treatment of hearing loss often includes use of amplification devices, selected and calibrated to suit a person's particular loss. Behind-the-ear aids and body aids are the two most popular forms of amplification for people with sensorineural losses.

Vision A few conditions of the eye are treatable with antibiotics and surgery. Cataracts, often associated with rubella and other prenatal viruses, can be treated by removal of the cataract itself or the lens of the eye. Surgical removal is achieved through suction of the cataract by a microscopic-sized needle. If the cataract does not cover the entire lens, laser surgery is employed to arrest further growth. Timing of cataract surgery is crucial, since attempting to remove an immature cataract will result in its spreading.

Antibiotics are used to treat inflammations or infections of the eye, including chorioretinitis, conjunctivitis, heratitis, and retinitis. Glaucoma can be treated through medication or laser therapy.

Several conditions of the eye, such as myopia and hyperopia, are adjustable through use of corrective lenses and low-vision aids. Basically, refractive errors are adjusted by providing the necessary accommodation through the curve of the lens. Weak eye muscles or muscles that do not operate in harmony are sometimes treated by patching the good eye and allowing the defective muscle to strengthen or self-correct. Low-vision aids can be magnifying lenses, telescopic lenses, or closed-circuit televisions with magnifying lenses. These aids may be used simultaneously with an individual's corrective lenses.

Role of Teachers and Specialists Prior to the early 1970s, classroom teachers were responsible for all programmatic aspects of deaf-blind students' education. The areas a teacher was expected to cover included: 1) speech/language training, 2) orientation and mobility, 3) physical management and therapy, 4) training in preacademic and academic skills, 5) auditory and visual training, and 6) behavior management training.

Today's educators of deaf-blind children and youth are not necessarily responsible for providing all of the previously mentioned services. Most school districts now employ specialists to assist the classroom teacher. Initially, however, these specialists were not trained to provide services to deaf-blind individuals; thus, specialists were not necessarily knowledgeable about or committed to this population, and inappropriate programmatic suggestions were not uncommon.

Currently, more specialists are trained to handle low-incidence populations and are able to provide the classroom teacher with useful hints and suggestions. Specialists who may provide services to deaf-blind individuals include: 1) behavior specialists, 2) physical/occupational therapists, 3) speech/language therapists, and 4) orientation/mobility specialists.

The amount of time and the level of services provided by these specialists depends on several factors: 1) age of the deaf-blind client, 2) severity of the sensory impairment, 3) severity of the deaf/blind client's mental retardation, and 4) the case load of the specialist. Some specialists never work with low-functioning deaf-blind individuals who have deviant behaviors. The prevailing attitude of such specialists is that these low-functioning individuals do not benefit appreciably from such services, and, given specialists' heavy case loads, it is difficult to justify spending time with persons for whom the expected benefit is so meager.

Behavior Specialist The standard educational resource person who deals with deviant behaviors and provides or directs behavior therapies is the behavior specialist (psychologist, psychiatrist, or behavior modification specialist). Such a specialist develops procedures to discourage maladaptive behaviors and encourage desirable behaviors.

Because of the sensory deprivation caused by their hearing and visual deficits, deaf-blind children often exhibit behavior that indicates lower brain stem (reticular formation) functioning. This behavior often resembles that exhibited by autistic individuals; i.e., it is self-stimulatory in nature, and, as already outlined, can be self-abusive, stereotypic, autoerotic, or ritualistic-perseverative.

Because of the similarity between the behaviors of deaf-blind children and those of autistic children, educators of deaf-blind children have employed instructional techniques found beneficial in working with autistic children. For example, in intrusion therapy, the trainer physically invades the space in which the child is self-stimulating and gradually introduces him- or herself into the activity. In another approach, called play therapy, play activities are structured to allow the child to express emotions and work through problems. Training of desirable habits usually is achieved through operant conditioning. In extreme instances, treatment may also focus on aversive therapy, which utilizes a form of punishment such as restraint or shock. Such treatment cannot be administered, however, until written permission is obtained from the parents or guardians.

Several theories hypothesize that it would be impossible to totally strip a deaf-blind individual of all self-stimulating behavior, because stimulation techniques appear to be a way of providing input to the brain stem, and without such stimulation the human organism would not develop cognitively. Some educators believe, however, that if sensory stimulation is provided along with intrusion therapy, the deaf-blind individual no longer needs to self-stimulate. Controversy continues over the correct methods to use in order to decrease self-stimulatory behaviors in deaf-blind individuals.

Physical/Occupational Therapist Developmentally delayed infants do not acquire motor skills at appropriate ages. The delay in motor skills arises from several factors. Some of these infants evidence high muscle tone (hypertonia) as a result of cerebral palsy or other similar conditions, while others demonstrate low muscle tone (hypotonia). These muscle dysfunctions, along with the sensory deficits of deaf-blindness, increase the probability of delayed fine and gross motor development.

Assistance from an occupational and/or physical therapist is required to adequately construct an effective motor program. Motor programs may include feeding, muscle relaxation, and normalization techniques, and the development of prehension (fine-motor) skills. Motor programs are rarely terminated with the emergence of walking behavior. Often children who are deaf-blind require additional movement therapy programs to assist them in obtaining the prerequisite skills of language development.

Speech/Language Therapist Low functioning deaf-blind children rarely develop oral communication skills. As a result, the language specialist must select an alternative mode of communication for the deaf-blind individual. The mode selected may be sign language and/or communication via symbols (rebus, Blissymbols and/or pictures). (See pages 307 and 308 for examples.)

When an occupational therapist is not available, the speech pathologist may also be required to develop feeding programs for children who have difficulty in controlling the fine-motor muscles needed for eating, or for children who have developed abnormal eating behaviors that inhibit the proper ingestion of food.

Orientation/Mobility Specialist The orientation/mobility specialist's main role is to provide students with the skills needed to travel in the classroom, school, and/or community with as little assistance as possible, using the techniques employed by blind individuals (e.g., cane travel, walking with a sighted guide, or walking independently using one's arms as protective barriers against sharp edges, half-opened doors, and other environmental hazards).

The mobility goals for deaf-blind individuals depend on several factors: 1) the potential for understanding the process of independent travel, 2) the severity of the visual and hearing deficits, and 3) the severity of the individual's mental handicap.

Because it is unlikely that low-functioning deaf-blind individuals will be able to travel unsupervised in the community, primary objectives in mobility training for such persons may be to sit, stand, or move their bodies through space when given verbal and/or physical directions. Some of these low-functioning children can learn to move about in the classroom environment independently with the assistance of coded rope guides that feature textures that the student has learned to associate with a particular activity.

EDUCATIONAL PROGRAMS AND SERVICES

Historically, deaf-blind children have been housed in two different kinds of facilities: those for blind individuals and those for mentally retarded individuals.

As stated at the beginning of this chapter, educational services were restricted to the intellectually elite, and children were typically placed with their visually-impaired peers in residential schools. Because of a lack of educational services and knowledge of how to instructionally program for deaf-blind children, many other deaf-blind persons were institutionalized in facilities for mentally retarded individuals.

As mentioned earlier, the bulge in the deaf-blind population created by the rubella epidemic of 1963–1965 prompted the expansion of services through the establishment in 1967 of Regional Centers for Services to Deaf-Blind Children and Youths. Originally, 10 regional centers were created throughout the country, with the number eventually increased to the current 16: 8 single-state centers and 8 multi-state centers. Although the number of centers has changed, the concept remains the same.

At present, due to the cutbacks in federal support to education, the nature of and responsibility for state and federal services to deaf-blind individuals is undergoing further modifications.

Listed below are regional centers, teacher training programs, and a sampling of exceptional instructional programs for deaf-blind individuals. Further information can be obtained by directly contacting the centers and programs listed.

Regional Centers for Services to Deaf-Blind Children and Youths

Multi-State Centers

New England Region:
Allen Sanderson, Coordinator
c/o Perkins School for the Blind
175 N. Beacon St.
Watertown, MA 02172
(Connecticut, Maine, Massachusetts, New Hampshire, Rhode Island, Vermont)

Mid-Atlantic Region:
Khogendra Das, Coordinator
c/o New York Institute for Education of the Blind
999 Pelham Pkwy.
Bronx, NY 10469
(Delaware, New Jersey, New York, Puerto Rico, Virgin Islands)

Southeast Region:
John Crosby, Coordinator
c/o Alabama Institute for the Deaf-Blind
Box 698
Talladega, AL 35160
(Alabama, Florida, Georgia, Kentucky, Mississippi, Tennessee)

Midwest Region:
George Monk, Coordinator
c/o Michigan Department of Education
Davenport Bldg., 5th fl.
Ottawa & Capitol Sts.
Lansing, MI 48933
(Indiana, Michigan, Minnesota, Wisconsin)

South Central Region:
Jack English, Coordinator
c/o South Central Regional Deaf-Blind Center
2930 Turtle Creek Plaza,
Dallas, TX 75204
(Arkansas, Iowa, Louisiana, Missouri, Oklahoma)

Mountain Plains Region:
Dennis Hanley, Coordinator
c/o 165 Cook St.
Denver, CO 80203
(Idaho, Kansas, Montana, Nebraska, New Mexico, North Dakota, South Dakota, Utah, Wyoming)

South Atlantic Region:
Jeff Garrett, Coordinator
c/o North Carolina Department of Public
  Instruction
Bunn-Hatch Bldg.
317 Hillsboro St.
Raleigh, NC 27611
(District of Columbia, Maryland, North
Carolina, South Carolina, Virginia,
West Virginia)

Southwest Region:
William Blea, Coordinator
c/o California Department
  of Education
721 Capitol Mall
Sacramento, CA 96814
(Arizona, California, Guam, Hawaii,
  Nevada, Trust Territories)

Single-State Centers

Alaska:
Roy Anderson, Coordinator
Alaska State Center for
  Deaf-Blind Children
111 Dowling Rd.
Anchorage, AK 9950

Colorado:
Marilyn Hanley, Coordinator
Colorado Department
  of Education
State Office Building
201 E. Colfax
Denver, CO 80203

Illinois:
Gail Lee, Coordinator
Illinois Office of Education
100 N. 1st St.
Springfield, IL 62777

Ohio:
Phyllis Yeager, Coordinator
Ohio Department of Education,
  Division of Special Education
933 High St.
Worthington, OH 43085

Oregon:
Maureen Otos, Coordinator
University of Oregon,
Health Sciences Child
  Development Center,
Rm. 1250, 707 Gaines Rd.
Portland, OR 97210

Pennsylvania:
Eleanor Long, Coordinator
Pennsylvania Department of Education
P.O. Box 911
Harrisburg, PA 17126

Texas:
Kenneth Crow, Coordinator
Texas Education Agency
201 E. 11th St.
Austin, TX 78701

Washington:
Mick Moore, Coordinator
Educational School District 121
1401 S. 200th St.
Seattle, WA 98148

Teacher Training Programs

California:
San Francisco State University
Special Education Department
  Deaf-Blind Program
1600 Hollway
San Francisco, CA 94132
Director: Philip Hatlen, Ed.D.

Massachusetts:
Boston College
Special Education &
  Rehabilitation Department
Deaf-Blind Progam, McGuinn Hall
Chestnut Hill, MA 02167
Director: Sherrill Butterfield, Ph.D.

Maryland:
Western Maryland College
Graduate Department
Westminster, MD 21157
Director: David Bowlesby, Ed.D.

Michigan:
Michigan State University
Elementary & Special
 Education Department
222 Erickson Hall
East Lansing, MI 48824

New York:
Teachers College,
 Columbia University
Department of Special Education/
 Sensory Impaired
525 W. 120th St.
New York, NY 10027
Director: Robert Bowers, Ed.D.

Ohio:
The Ohio State University
Faculty for Exceptional Children
 Low-Incidence Handicapped
1945 N. High St.
Columbus, OH 43210
Director: (Vacant at time of publication)

Oregon:
Portland State University
Special Education Department
P.O. Box 751,
Portland, OR 97207
Director: Sheldon Maron, Ph.D.

Tennessee:
Vanderbilt University
George Peabody College of Teachers
 Special Education Department
P.O. Box 328
Nashville, TN 37203
Director: S.C. Ashcroft, Ed.D.

Educational Programs Serving Deaf-Blind Students

Day and Residential Programs

1. Perkins School for the Blind, 175 N. Beacon Street, Watertown, MA 02172
2. Michigan School for the Blind, 715 W. Willow Street, Lansing, MI 48913
3. Colorado School for the Deaf and Blind, Kiowa and Institute Streets, Colorado Springs, CO 80903
4. Illinois School for the Visually Impaired, 658 State Street, Jacksonville, IL 62650
5. Minnesota Braille and Sight Saving School, P.O. Box 68, Faribault, MN 55021

Prevocational/Vocational Services

1. Chicago Light House for the Blind, 1850 W. Roosevelt, Chicago, IL 60608
2. Oak Hill School, 120 Holcomb Street, Hartford, CT 06112
3. Perkins School for the Blind, 175 N. Beacon Street, Watertown, MA 02172
4. Dixon Development Center, 2660 N. Brinton, Dixon, IL 61021

Infant Programs

1. Chicago Light House for the Blind, 1850 W. Roosevelt, Chicago, IL 60608
2. Michael Reese Medical Center/David T. Siegel Institute for Communicative Disorders, 3033 S. Cottage Grove, Chicago, IL 60616

Adult Services

1. Helen Keller National Center for Deaf-Blind Youths and Adults, 111 Middle Neck Road, Sands Point, Long Island, NY 11050 (The Helen Keller National Center provides: orientation and mobility training, communication training, daily living programs, sensory aids, and vocational placement [Salmon & Spar, 1977–78]).

Levels of Educational Programming

Educational programming for deaf-blind children may be divided into six levels representing a hierarchy of progressive instruction for educational growth:

1. Early childhood and infant programming
   a. Instruction is provided on a one-to-one basis.
   b. Infant stimulation techniques are employed.
   c. Instruction is provided involving cognitive development, language development, motor development, and feeding skills.
2. Readiness programming
   a. Movement programming (e.g., obstacle courses and coactive movement) is used.
   b. Cognitive concepts (matching, sorting, sequencing, and discrimination) are developed.
   c. Auditory training is initiated.
   d. Prelinguistic skills (e.g., understanding of routines, expressing needs through tugging and pointing) are encouraged.
3. Primary level
   a. Preacademic skills are continued.
   b. Primary academic skills are established.
4. Intermediate level
   a. Communication is given major emphasis.
   b. Academic skills are continued.
5. Advanced level (prevocational)
   a. Emphasis is placed on future independent living, social etiquette, money management skills, and prevocational skills needed for employment or for participation in sheltered workshop programs.
6. Job training (vocational)
   a. Vocational training usually is provided in conjunction with the school program.
   b. The Division of Vocational Rehabilitation (DVR), Department of Health and Human Services (HHS), provides help in placing deaf-blind individuals in workshops and in providing community work experiences.

Various types of instruction and training are employed to correct specific deficits caused by the dual sensory loss of deaf-blindness. The sophistication of training is largely dependent upon the level at which the child is functioning. The sections following describe these types of instruction and training.

Auditory Training

An auditory training program is developed in accordance with the educational prognosis of each child. Auditory training for low-functioning children is usually not pursued with the aim of helping them to acquire speech but rather to assist them in integrating sensory stimuli and to make them aware of warning sounds in the environment (e.g., train sounds signal danger). Although speech acquisition normally is not expected of low-functioning deaf-blind children, it certainly is not automatically excluded.

Development of auditory sensitivity at a very young age is crucial for the deaf-blind low-functioning child. In order to maximize hearing potential and shape auditory responsiveness, early identification of hearing loss and amplification of sound are important. Often environmental sounds are heard, but the deaf-blind child is unable to visually attach meaning to these sounds. After years or months of not receiving reinforcement in the form of a coupled visual image and/or social praise for his or her auditory attentiveness, the deaf-blind child may cease responding to sound. This is known clinically as "nonfunctional hearing."

Auditory training should take place both formally and informally. Formal auditory training begins with the development of sound awareness. Some type of overt reaction to sound is sought. For example, does the child blink his or her eyes, change his or her breathing pattern or motor movements, or increase his or her sucking responses? The awareness of sound is critical in establishing higher levels of auditory functioning. Activities designed to increase awareness of sound can be paired with gross-motor activities (e.g., encouraging a child to make rhythmic movements every time a drum is beaten).

Teaching of gross discrimination of sounds begins following the establishment of consistent responses to individual sound. The child is taught to recognize differences among gross sounds before he or she is instructed in speech sounds discrimination. Upon mastering these skills, the child is taught to respond differently to various sound stimuli.

Localization of sounds is the ability to discriminate the direction of a sound source. Ability to localize is physically manifested by such responses as turning the head and/or body in the direction of an auditory stimulus. Limited visual ability makes development of localization skills more difficult. Training of localization skills is most successful when sound is paired with a visual or tactile stimulus. Gradually this prompt is faded by moving the visual stimulus outside of the child's central visual field.

Those auditory skills developed during formal auditory training sessions are then used to stimulate auditory awareness of environmental sounds. When a loud unrehearsed noise occurs, awareness of the sound is reinforced by tapping the child's ear and saying, "Did you hear that?" If the child appears not to have heard the sound, when possible, the sound is recreated. Again, the teacher taps the child's ear after the sound has been presented.

Besides being knowledgeable in techniques of auditory training, teachers of deaf-blind children must be familiar with the operation of hearing aids and auditory training units (e.g., Phonic Ear). They should also be able to read and interpret audiograms and translate these interpretations into educational programmatic guidelines. The classroom physical design must also be considered. Care should be taken to eliminate as much extraneous noise in the classroom as possible (e.g., echoes and street noises). For example, flooring materials that are good sound conductors should be used.

Visual Training

Because visual functioning affects most areas of development (e.g., motor, cognition, and social), vision training should be incorporated into all areas of the instructional program. Variance in visual functioning among deaf-blind individuals necessitates the use of different educational remediation techniques according to the degree of visual functioning. These techniques may include use of large print books and materials, employment of low-vision devices (e.g., magnifiers), and incorporation of low-vision and visual-perceptual training in instruction. When any visual training activities are performed, light sources and quality should be considered. The teacher must be mindful of both general room lighting and illumination of specific work areas. Winter (1977) suggested several general guidelines for determining level of illumination.

1. Low illumination should be used for those with albinism, aniridia, corneal opacities, macular degeneration, and photophobia.
2. High illumination should be used for those with glaucoma, optic atrophy, high myopia, and aphakia.

In addition, many low-functioning deaf-blind children engage in self-stimulatory behaviors involving light input. They may poke their eyes, wave their fingers rapidly in front of their eyes, or assume extreme postures to get near to light sources. In such an event, care should be taken to filter strong lights and occasionally provide clothing modifications, such as visors, to reduce distractions.

Orientation and mobility training may be required to increase a deaf-blind child's ability to efficiently move about in the environment. Historically, however, these services have not been given to severely mentally retarded deaf-blind children because of these individuals' limited ability to understand the techniques commonly taught.

Before initiating vision training for a deaf-blind child, several questions should be considered:

1. What is the cause of the visual impairment?
2. Is any special treatment required? If so, what is the general nature of the treatment?
3. Is the visual impairment likely to get worse, better, or stay the same?
4. What restrictions, if any, should be placed on the child's activities?
5. What lighting conditions are best?
6. What is the prognosis?
7. What is the child's visual acuity? If not available, what is the doctor's opinion of the child's visual acuity?

Components of Visual Training Visual training may be broken down into a hierarchy of three skill levels: sensation, visual motor functioning, and visual perception. Each of these levels is explained below.

Sensation (Response to Light) For low-functioning deaf-blind children, techniques should be employed to help them become aware of and respond to light. Light stimuli should include various intensities and colors, as well as blinking light (Van Etten et al., 1980). During this sensation period visual fixation develops, with near-object acuity acquired before distant-object acuity (Efron & Duboff, 1976).

Visual Motor Skills The development of visual motor behavior begins with visual tracking skills. The child's favorite objects, color, and peripheral vision are key factors in determining the appropriate materials for visual tracking. Convergence training, the next step in the development of visual motor skills, consists of increasing the child's ability to visually follow an object as it moves toward and away from the body. Accommodation skills emerge after the development of convergence behavior. Accommodation enables the child to see objects at various distances. Eye contact behavior occurs simultaneously with accommodation skills. The development of eye contact behavior requires working within the child's area of usable vision and providing light as a reward for appropriate behavior. Eye-hand coordination activities include the acquisition of skills enabling the child to visually fixate on an object while manipulating it. The teacher's role is to encourage reaching and grasping behavior within the child's range of vision.

Visual Perception Skills Perceptual skills cannot be taught until mastery of visual motor skills is attained. Visual perception skills enable the child to obtain meaning from what he or she sees. Visual perception training begins with the development of perceptual accuracy, i.e., the child's ability to discriminate not only gross differences but also details of an object. Gradually, the child is given less and less time to make discriminations; rate discrimination, as this process is known, is a method of facilitating rapid perception (Efron & DuBoff, 1976). The ability to move the parts of one's body parts in space from left to right is related to visual directionality and can be established through imitative games and movement programs. Directionality is also related to cognitive and language development, in that it fosters organized thinking and reading skills through understanding of left-to-right progression.

Figure perception is often a weak area for low-functioning deaf-blind children. It is important to provide materials that will not create figure-ground confusion or cause problems in distinguishing an object from its environment. Presenting a child with materials that limit his or her choices, and adapting visual stimuli, are techniques that will help decrease figure-ground confusion (Gates, 1981). Visual memory skills are also difficult for the low-functioning deaf-blind student to acquire. Visual memory refers to the ability to recall what has been seen. For low-functioning children, object permanence skills signify the beginning of memory development.

It is imperative that educators serving children with visual deficits obtain professional visual assessments and perform informal classroom assessments before implementing a visual training program. Placement within the training continuum should not occur until a child's functional ability is established. In addition, as stated previously, visual skills can have an impact on other pre-academic performance levels (Muniz, 1980). If a child cannot visually track an object from left-to-right, an activity that requires crossing the midline, then he or she should not be expected to perform a cognitive task such as matching, in which crossing the midline is required.

Communication Training

Oral Communication Oral communication is rarely expected of low-functioning deaf-blind children. As previously mentioned, significant loss of hearing precludes clear access to oral communication, and diminished mental capacity reduces ability to interpret this limited aural input. Consequently, oral communication training is usually confined to two goals: During infancy and early childhood oral response is elicited as a precursor of imitative behavior; in other words, an infant first learns to verbally copy an adult before mimicking motor behavior. In later life, the child's awareness of his or her own oral production as well as that of others is encouraged in order to improve alertness to the environment and to regulate undesirable, self-stimulatory verbalizations.

Manual Communication Before any type of manual communication can be initiated, attending behavior must be established. Low-functioning deaf-blind children typically lack eye contact and other forms of attending behavior. Often, exercises for increasing eye contact are coupled with initial formal communication training.

Once minimal attending behavior is obtained, motoric imitation is sought. In general, manual signing methods require manual signing skills. However, at times imitative skills can be reinforced so strenuously that they surpass a child's ability to associate a sign with the concept it represents. The danger this creates is that the child begins to demonstrate echopraxic behavior, i.e., repetition of signs with no connected meaning.

The Haight Method (R. Haight, personal communication, 1975) provides an alternative to teaching signs through imitation. This method requires that the initial sign taught must be a highly motivating one, e.g., a preferred toy or a favorite food. The beginning steps require the teacher to obtain eye contact (if possible) by placing the highly motivating object in the student's central visual field. Once eye contact is established, the sign is shaped by manually forming the child's hand according to the sign desired. The student is not given the opportunity to imitate the teacher. The child is then verbally and tactually reinforced by the teacher. These procedures are designed in the behaviorist drill fashion, i.e., every appropriate response is reinforced, and inappropriate responses are not accepted.

Communication Boards A "communication board" is a term used to describe any teaching and/or communicative device composed of displays of textures, objects, symbols, pictures, or words that enables nonvocal, expressively disabled, and severely physically limited people to convey information. Communication boards vary in size, overall layout, type of symbols, and type of response required (Stremel-Campbell, 1977). The use of communication boards with the deaf-blind population is relatively new. Normally, the alternative method of communication for deaf-blind children is some type of sign system. Communication boards for deaf-blind children are usually chosen when reasonable communicative gains are not made with a sign system.

Vanderheiden and Grilley (1975) stated that there are three ways for a child to indicate (select) his or her wants or needs using a communication board. They are as follows:

1. Direct selection—responding by pointing directly at the symbol, using a body part, eye gaze, or a head pointer (a helmet-type device that by the movement of the head indicates the objects selected either through an attached pointer or light beam).
2. Scanning—responding by arresting the movement of a person manually scanning or using a traveling pointer, a light, or an electronic device to scan a sequential display of possible selections. At that point the selection is printed or noted by the person receiving the communication. The scan resumes once this has been accomplished.
3. Encoding—responding by matching a series of numbers with the coded associated words or symbols. The child usually indicates the code using a number wheel, and the associated symbols or words are on a display chart.

Representations of concepts can be devised according to a continuum from concrete to abstract. Selection of the level of representative items for the communication board should be made according to the child's conceptual abilities. The following are possible types of communication boards, listed in order of complexity.

1. Texture boards. These are often used with severely mentally retarded deaf-blind children who have little or no concept of representation. Textures are used to give cues for desired activities such as eating, sleeping, and toileting. The purpose is to establish a habitual response rather than an associated image.
2. Object boards. These are concrete objects associated with physical needs, daily activities, or frequently used objects. For instance, a spoon indicates a desire to eat. Individual objects may be the same size or scaled in size to the one they represent.
3. Picture boards. The pictures used on these boards depict single nouns, verbs, and adjectives. The pictures used can be of varying conceptual difficulty ranging from photographs (most concrete) to colored pictures, to black and white pictures, to line drawings (most abstract) (Stremel-Campbell, 1977).

4. Symbol boards. These are printed representations of nouns, verbs, and adjectives that employ some degree of abstraction. The boards may be pictographic, idiographic, logographic, positional, or arbitrary in nature. The two most popular symbol systems are Blissymbolics and rebus. Most communication specialists do not agree as to which is the more difficult.
   a. Blissymbols. These symbols can be pictographic, ideographic, or arbitrary. Some symbols are a combination of other symbols (see Figure 4).
   b. Rebus symbols. These symbols can be concrete (picture drawings that directly resemble the object), relational (position in space relates the concept), and abstract (no apparent relation to the concept or words they represent) (see Figure 5).
5. Communication boards. These boards, which use printed words, appear to be the most abstract and difficult of all symbol boards. If words are employed, the concepts they represent should be highly motivational to the child.

Movement Programs

Movement programs have been used to establish a variety of skills and concepts in low-functioning deaf-blind children. Two of the most often used programs include *movement theory* and *motor circuits,* developed by J. Van Dijk of the Netherlands. Van Dijk has outlined a number of benefits that may be derived from using his movement programs (L. DeLeuw, personal communication, 1973). These benefits include:

1. Development of anticipation of movement and spatial relations
2. Improved sequential memory
3. Development of attachment relationships and awareness of self from others
4. Attachment of meaning to things and events outside of the child
5. Development of imitation skills
6. Awareness of the limitations of the child's own body

Movement Theory Most educators who use Van Dijk's approach begin with his movement theory. *Coactive movement,* a well-known term in deaf-blind education, is actually one of the six stages of Van Dijk's movement theory. Van Dijk believes that learning stems from the child's early movement patterns; these patterns are developmental and sequential and are necessary precursors of cognitive learning. Van Dijk advocates the following instructional sequence in order to facilitate motor learning:

1. *Resonance.* The teacher imitates the child's movements. For example, if the child is rocking, the teacher rocks with the child. Nurturance and affection are important components of this stage. The purpose of this activity is to demonstrate to the child that his or her movement affects the environment.
2. *Coactive movement.* At this stage the teacher imitates movements such as scooting, crawling, or rolling, and the child performs these alongside the

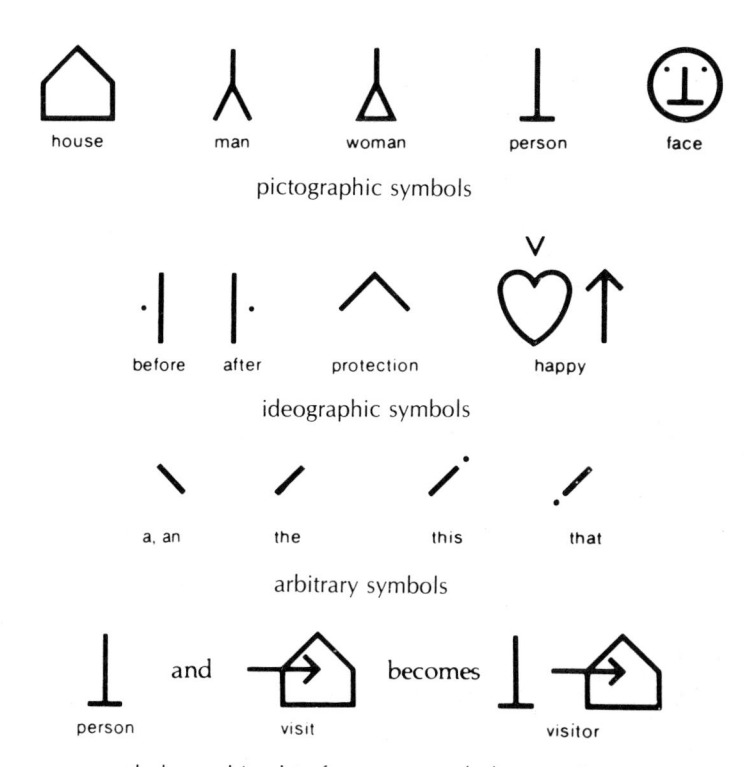

Figure 4. Examples of Blissymbolics. (Blissymbolics used herein derived from the symbols described in the work *Semantography,* original copyright C.K. Bliss 1949. Blissymbolics Communication Institute, Toronto, exclusive licensee, 1982.)

teacher. Movements are performed first at "near distance" and later at "far distance" between the teacher and student. These movements always follow a sequence, so that the child develops a sense of rapport and anticipation.
3. *Nonrepresentational reference.* During this stage the concept of imagery is developed. For example, the teacher points to body parts, and the child imitates the teacher's actions. Other activities include pantomiming, such as using cups and saucers to serve imaginary tea.
4. *Imitation.* At this stage the child is encouraged to imitate at close range, and then, gradually, the distance between the student and the person or object he or she is imitating is increased. Imitative skills are learned in a skill hierarchy:
   a. Person-to-person
   b. Person-to-doll and Person-to-stick figure
   c. Imitation of a picture
      1) Personal space—the child imitates a picture in which there is only one figure (e.g., a child standing with his or her right arm up and left arm down).

The box is under the table.

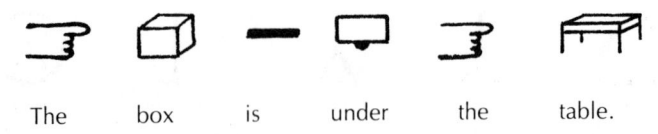

Figure 5. Examples of rebus symbols.

      2) Object space—the child imitates a figure with reference to other objects in a picture (e.g., a child sitting on a chair with a ball in his or her hand).
  d. Picture-to-picture
  e. Imitation of hand and finger positions
5. *Natural gestures.* The child creates gestures for objects or events that are natural extensions of the motor movements he or she employs during related experience (e.g., if a child interacts with a ball by bouncing it, his or her natural gesture becomes the motion of bouncing with his or her hands).
6. *Naming.* During this stage a formal language system is developed. The teacher assists the child in attaching signs to objects and experiences.

Because movement theory creates an attachment relationship between the teacher and student, other educators, such as those working with autistic children, are finding the theory beneficial. Educators of severely mentally retarded children also have begun to use movement theory because it is highly structured and sequential. However, educators who do not subscribe to the idea that movement development is necessary to cognitive functioning, or who are solely interested in improving motor ability, may prefer to use motor circuits.

Motor Circuits Motor circuits are simple to establish and may be used effectively without applying intricate techniques. Motor circuits are obstacle courses designed to teach spatial awareness (up, down, left, and right) and sequential memory. Circuits usually consist of obstacles made from a variety of equipment, furniture, and, in some cases, people. Equipment might include, for example, vestibular boards, climbing stairs, rocking boats, swinging tires, and jungle gyms.

The goal in using a motor circuit is to encourage the child to move independently from one obstacle to the next. Initially, the teacher uses only three or four pieces of equipment. After the child has learned the sequence of events and proceeds through the course with little or no assistance from the teacher, new equipment is added to the obstacle course. Circuits can be designed for non-ambulatory as well as ambulatory children. Choice of equipment should be geared to the child's handicapping conditions.

For low-functioning deaf-blind children, movement theory can greatly assist in teaching awareness of self, attachment relationships, imitation, and sequential memory. For those students who already have established imitation skills but still are having problems in developing formal communication, motor circuits can be helpful.

Prevocational/Vocational Training

The large population of deaf-blind children resulting from the rubella epidemic of 1963–1965 is nearing graduation from educational programs, necessitating the establishment of realistic and relevant prevocational and vocational preparation programs (Lockett, 1978). Effective prevocational training for severely mentally retarded deaf-blind individuals should be provided according to the continuum concept. This concept emphasizes movement from the educational setting to an appropriate community-based vocational program. The continuum concept contains three primary components:

1. Identification of long-term vocational goals
2. An intermediate vocational environment to assist the individual in adjusting to a new vocational setting
3. Identification of the skill areas needed for deaf-blind individuals to experience success in a community-based environment (Lockett & Rudolph, 1981).

The skills required for success in a community environment can be broken down according to age categories at which they should ideally develop: 1) primary (5–10 years old), 2) adolescent (11–17 years old), and 3) adulthood (18–21 years old). Lockett and Rudolph (1981) matched skills, age group, and levels of mental retardation as a model of a prevocational continuum. Table 3 is an adaptation of Lockett and Rudolph's material, outlining the training that should occur within each age category. Definitions of some specific training areas follow:

1. Self-care—activities that pertain to personal care (e.g., toileting, dressing, and feeding)
2. Daily living—activities that pertain to daily routine (e.g., shopping, doing laundry, and managing money)

Table 3. Age categories and training areas for prevocational/vocational training

Training area:	5–10 years old	11–17 years old	18–21 years old
	Self-care skills	Daily living skills	Community living
	Language	Language	Leisure/recreation
	Developmental motor skills	Developmental motor skills	Simulated work settings
			Experience in work activity
	Sensory training	Mobility	Center and sheltered workshop
	Socialization	Sensory training	
		Simulated work settings	

Adapted from Lockett and Rudolph (1981).

3. Work activity—sheltered work environment that emphasizes gainful activity (not production)
4. Sheltered workshop—sheltered work environment characterized by subcontract work and a piece/rate salary schedule
5. Simulated work experience—work experience created by modeling an actual work environment and actual work demands
6. Community living skills—skills necessary to function in a community living environment

Classroom Prevocational Training Educators of severely mentally retarded deaf-blind children have incorporated into their classroom activities techniques used by vocational rehabilitation counselors. These techniques are assembly line type tasks that require sequencing, left-right orientation, on-task behaviors, high rate productivity, completion of piecework, and self-correction. Highly structured and intricate task analysis, using techniques such as those of Marc Gold (see Chapter 2), often is employed to teach the steps necessary to execute a single work-related behavior skill. Current trends emphasize the development of generalizable skills rather than specific steps associated with a single task.

Severely mentally retarded deaf-blind individuals often do not succeed in a sheltered employment situation because they lack basic skills required to function in a work setting. Lockett and Rudolph (1981) contend that prevocational training should be conducted outside the classroom in real or simulated work settings. This training should be scheduled every day at the same time and place, in order to impart in students a sense of routine. Training sites should be modeled after actual community facilities to ease transition, and the work should be geared to the students' levels.

Severely mentally retarded deaf-blind individuals also have difficulty adjusting to the endurance required in workshop settings. These students have usually been conditioned to attend to vocational activities only for 15 to 20 minutes at a time, because the duration of classroom activities is normally limited to the students' attention span. To increase students' vocational success, instructors have developed a two-step procedure for use with deaf-blind persons in sheltered workshops and in community placement (Lockett & Rudolph, 1981). The strategy includes evaluation and development of the continuum of services previously discussed.

Evaluation The vocational evaluation of severely mentally retarded deaf-blind persons in the past has not been successfully pursued by all DVR counselors. Failure to perform appropriate evaluations has resulted in the misplacement, and often the nonplacement, of severely mentally retarded deaf-blind persons in sheltered workshops and/or in the community. State vocational rehabilitation counselors also do not have the training to work effectively with the severely mentally retarded deaf-blind rubella group.

One major problem in the evaluation process has been the type of assessment devices used to collect evaluation data. Some of the common devices employed have been standardized vocational and/or psychological tests. These tests have not been appropriate because of such factors as problems in communicating instructions and because no deaf-blind norms have been established.

Because of the lack of appropriate assessment devices to meet the needs of this population, vocational rehabilitation counselors and educators recently developed a checklist to evaluate vocational potential and to identify skills needed for vocational success (Lockett, 1977). The assessment tool has multiple functions, including serving as: 1) an aid to facilitate the planning of long-range goals and short-term objectives, 2) an assessment device to determine current vocational functioning level, and 3) a guide for developing classroom activities. Educators have found this tool to be easy to use, time-saving, and helpful in identifying skills needed at each level of the vocational continuum.

Vocational Issues Efforts to establish appropriate types of community workshop placement for severely mentally retarded deaf-blind individuals are just beginning. Unfortunately, in many instances, inappropriate placements are made and deaf-blind clients are assigned to well-meaning workshop supervisors who are untrained to work with and unable to communicate with this handicapped group; failure, thus, inevitably results.

In the past, some efforts were made by educators to establish workshops specifically for severely mentally retarded deaf-blind individuals (Lockett & Rudolph, 1981). These efforts were sparked by prior unsuccessful attempts to place such individuals in workshops designed for other populations. The idea, however, proved somewhat idealistic. For one thing, finding funds to create workshops for such a small speciality group was extremely difficult. As a result, deaf-blind people often continued to be placed in activity centers and sheltered workshops that were ill-equipped to accommodate them.

There is still much to be done in the area of establishing appropriate prevocational skills for severely mentally retarded deaf-blind adults. Further research efforts are necessary to ascertain the success of existing techniques and to provide suggestions for formulating new and effective prevocational/vocational activities.

SUMMARY

Although the definition of deaf-blindness has been firmly established by federal legislation, controversy continues over its interpretation. Some people favor a medical interpretation in which inclusion is predicated upon actual physical disability. Others contend that the functional use a person derives from his or her sensory channels should be the determining factor. Varying interpretations of the definition have resulted in differences in the types of children admitted to programs for deaf-blind children.

Many medical and educational professionals agree, nevertheless, on the problems and issues that must be addressed. Because most etiologies of low-functioning deaf-blind children are congenital, the need for prenatal care is a major concern. Advances in medical technology and knowledge have resulted in better fetal monitoring and even surgery *in utero*. Medical advancement, however, is a double-edged sword, because more infants who are severely physically defective or immature are now surviving. Some of these babies later become candidates for deaf-blind programs.

Evaluation of hearing, vision, and other physical attributes of severely mentally retarded deaf-blind children continues to be difficult because these children do not provide feedback to the examiner. In addition, vision and hearing aids often are not tolerated well because many deaf-blind children do not understand or appreciate their purpose or because the aids interfere with self-stimulatory habits.

In recent years, provision of educational services to deaf-blind children has greatly improved due to the passage of state and federal legislation that guarantees appropriate programming to handicapped children regardless of the nature or degree of their impairment. Such enactments have not only resulted in instructional services for deaf-blind children, but have also guaranteed necessary supportive services, such as occupational/physical therapy, speech/language therapy, and behavioral therapy. In addition, instructional strategies have received considerable attention, particularly in the areas of cognition, motor development, and communication. Although there has been some success reported with programs such as those incorporating Van Dijk's movement theory, little formal research has been done to justify their use, to determine the kinds of children with whom these programs should be used, and the circumstances under which they are applicable.

Factors such as the current reduced state of the economy, funding cutbacks, shifts in responsibility for the education of deaf-blind children, and modifications in mission and structure of the Regional Centers for Services to Deaf-Blind Children and Youths are clouding the educational outlook for the deaf-blind population. At this time, a reorganization of efforts and a reassessment of directions is essential. Professionals in deaf-blind education and rehabilitation now face the challenge of preserving services that were once abundantly funded but that are now operating under new auspices and with fewer financial resources. At the same time, research must continue in the areas of developing and refining instructional techniques to meet the complex needs of severely mentally retarded deaf-blind children and youth.

REFERENCES

Ayers, J. *Southern California Sensory Integration Test*. Los Angeles, CA: Western Psychological Services, 1980.

Balthazar, E. E. *Balthazar Scales of Adaptive Behavior II: Scales of Social Adaption*. Palo Alto, CA: Consulting Psychologists Press, 1973.

Balthazar, E. E. *Balthazar Scales of Adaptive Behavior for Profoundly and Severely Mentally Retarded I: Scales of Functional Independence.* Palo Alto, CA: Consulting Psychologists Press, 1976.

Barraga, N. A programmatic approach to visual learning and utilization of low vision. In: J. S. Horsley & W. J. Smith (eds.), *New techniques for working with deaf-blind children: Workshop proceedings, October 4, 5, 6, 1972.* Denver: Colorado Department of Education, 1973.

Batshaw, M. L., & Perret, Y.M. *Children with handicaps: A medical primer.* Baltimore: Paul H. Brookes Publishing Co., 1981.

Bayley, N. *Bayley Scales of Infant Development.* New York: Psychological Corp., 1969.

Behavioral Characteristics Progression (BCP). Palo Alto, CA: Vort Corporation, 1973.

Berkow, R., & Talbott, J. H. (eds.). *The Merck manual* (13th ed.). Rahway, NJ: Merck Sharp & Dohme Research Laboratories, Division of Merck & Co., 1977.

Bobath, B., & Bobath, K. Cerebral palsy. In: P. H. Pearson & C. E. Williams (eds.), *Physical therapy services in the developmental disabilities.* Springfield, IL: Charles C Thomas, 1972.

Brigance, A. *Inventory of Early Development.* Woburn, MA: Curriculum Associates, 1978.

Brown, M. L., & Rutger, S. Cerebral palsy, motor development and leisure activities. In: B Franklin (ed.), *Inservice training for teachers and aides of deaf-blind children.* Sacramento, CA: California State Department of Education, 1975.

Busch, R., Geyer, S., Lemmond, M., & Losoncy, M. *Developmental spiral.* Paper presented at the 58th Annual International Convention of The Council for Exceptional Children, Philadelphia, April, 1980.

Campbell, M. Place of maternal rubella in the etiology of congenital heart disease. *British Medical Journal,* 1961, *1,* 691–696.

Cattell, P. *Cattell Infant Intelligence Scale.* New York: Psychological Corp., 1960.

Cherry, J. Rubella: Past, present, and future. *Volta Review,* 1974, *76,* 8.

Chess, S., Korn, S., & Fernandez, P. *Psychiatric disorders of children with congenital rubella.* New York: Brunner/Mazel, 1971.

Clark, R. L., & Cumley, R. W. (eds.). *The book of health* (3rd ed.). New York: Van Nostrand Reinhold Co. 1973.

Collins, M., & Rudolph, J. (eds.). *A Manual for the assessment of a deaf-blind multiply handicapped child.* Lansing, MI: Midwest Regional Center for Services to Deaf-Blind Children, Spring, 1977.

Collaborative Research. *Color Research Forms of Bayley Scales of Motor Development.* Bethesda, MD: Collaborative Research, Perinatal Research Branch, 1961.

Cooper, L. Z., Ziring, P. R., Ockerse, A. B., Fedun, B. A., Kiely, B., & Krugman, S. Rubella: Clinical manifestations and management. In: Proceedings of the International Conference of Rubella Immunization. *American Journal of Diseases of Children,* 1969, *118,* 18–29.

Cox, B. P., & Lloyd, L. L. Audiologic considerations. In: L. L. Lloyd (ed.), *Communication assessment and intervention strategies.* Baltimore: University Park Press, 1976.

Davis, H., & Silverman, S. R. (eds.). *Hearing and deafness* (3rd ed.), New York: Holt, Rinehart & Winston, 1970.

Dubose, R. F., & Langley, M. B. *The Developmental Activities Screening Inventory.* Boston: Teaching Resources, 1977.

Education of the Handicapped Act, Public Law 91-230 (April 13, 1970), 84 Stat.121.

Efron, M., & DuBoff, B. *A vision guide for teachers of deaf-blind children.* Raleigh, NC: South Atlantic Regional Center for Services to Deaf-Blind Children, 1976.

Federal Register, 1975, *40,* 45 CFR, p. 9.

Frankenburg, W., Dodds, J., Fandal, A., Kazuk, E., & Cohrs, M. *Denver Developmental Screening Test.* Denver: University of Colorado Medical Center, 1975.

Gates, C. Vision assessment and stimulation for deaf-blind. *Viewpoints in Teaching and Learning: Journal of the School of Education* (Indiana University), 1981, *57*, 43–53.

Gottlieb, D. *Visual screening and assessment of low functioning children*. Paper presented at workshop sponsored by the Illinois Office of Education and The David T. Siegel Institute, Springfield, IL, May, 1976.

Gregg, N. Congenital cataract following German measles in the mother. *Transactions of the Opthalmological Society of Australia*, 1941, *3*, 35–46.

Griffin, P., & Sandord, A. *Learning accomplishment profile for infants*. Chapel Hill, NC: Chapel Hill Training Outreach Project, 1975.

Griffing, B. Defining the multihandicapped deaf population. *Viewpoints in Teaching and Learning: Journal of the School of Education* (Indiana University), 1981, *57*, 3–6.

Groves, C. A typical development in deaf-blind children. In: B. Franklin (ed.), *Proceedings of the inservice training program for teachers and aides of deaf-blind children, summer 1975*. Sacramento: California State Department of Education, 1975.

Guldager, L. The deaf-blind: Their education and their needs. *Exceptional Children*, 1969, *36*(3), 203–206.

Hammer, E. K. A time to think: Future needs of deaf-blind persons. In: C. E. Sherrick (ed.), *1980 is now*. Los Angeles: John Tracy Clinic, 1974.

Helen Keller National Center for Deaf-Blind Youths and Adults. Sands Point, NY: Helen Keller National Center for Deaf-Blind Youths and Adults, undated pamphlet.

Hiskey, M.S. *Hiskey-Nebraska Test of Learning Aptitude*. Lincoln: University of Nebraska Press, 1966.

Jensema, C. K. *Methods of communication used by and with deaf-blind children and youths in classroom settings*. Unpublished doctoral dissertation, Gallaudet College, Washington, D.C., 1980.

Kennedy, A. Language awareness and the deaf-blind child. *Teaching Exceptional Children*, Winter 1974, 99–102.

Kramer, L., & Rosenfeld, J. Speech and communication techniques with adult deaf-blind. *Journal of Rehabilitation of the Deaf*, 1975, *8*, 27–34.

Koontz, C. *Koontz Child Developmental Programs*. Los Angeles: Western Psychological Services, 1974.

Leiter, R.G., & Arthur, G. *Leiter International Performance Scale and Arthur Adaptation*. Chicago: C.H. Stoelting Co., 1955.

Lenneberg, E. Prerequisites for language acquisition. *Proceedings of the International Conference in Oral Education of the Deaf, Vol. II*. Washington, D.C.: Alexander Graham Bell Association of the Deaf, 1967.

Lockett, T. (ed.). *An education/training guide to pre-vocational skills for deaf-blind persons*. Lansing, MI: Midwest Regional Center for Services to Deaf-Blind Children, 1977.

Lockett, T. (ed.) *An educational/training guide to pre-vocational skills for deaf-blind persons* (2nd ed.). Lansing, MI: Midwest Regional Center for Services to Blind Children, 1978.

Lockett, T., & Rudolph, J. Deaf-blind children with maternal rubella: Implications for adult services. *American Annals of the Deaf*, 1980, *125*, 1000–1006.

Lockett, T., & Rudolph, J. Prevocational programming for deaf-blind/profoundly handicapped. *Viewpoints in Teaching and Learning: Journal of the School of Education* (Indiana University), 1981, *57*, 33–42.

Masland, R., Sarason, S., & Gladwin, T. *Mental subnormality, biological, psychological and cultural factors*. New York: Basic Books, 1958.

Maxfield, K.E., & Bucholz, S. *Maxfield-Bucholz Scale of Social Maturity for Use with Preschool Blind Children*. New York: American Foundation for the Blind, Inc., 1958.

Moersch, M. S. Training deaf-blind. *The American Journal of Occupational Therapy*, 1977, *3*(7), 425–431.

Muniz, J. The development of specific visual skills in low functioning non-verbal children who are hearing impaired as well as visually impaired. *Education of the Visually Handicapped*, 1980, *12*, 79–82.

Newburg, S., Green, M., & Frant, R. *Central Wisconsin's Colony & Training School's Education Assessment Device*. Madison, 1975.

Perkins School for the Blind. *Children of the silent night* (newsletter). Watertown, MA: Perkins School for the Blind, October, 1980.

Robbins, N., & Steinquist, G. *The deaf-blind "rubella" child*. Watertown, MA: Perkins School for the Blind, 1967.

Rothschild, J. Deaf-blindness. In: J. F. Garrett & E. S. Levine (eds.), *Psychological practices with the physically disabled*. New York: Columbia University Press, 1962.

Sailor, W., & Mix, B. J. *The TARC assessment system*. Lawrence, KS: H & H Enterprises, 1975.

Salmon, P. J., & Spar, H. *The National Center for Deaf-Blind Youth and Adults. Yearbook of Special Education* (New York), 1977-78, *3*, 413–422.

Schofer, D. S., & Moersch, M. S. (eds.). *Developmental Programming for Infants and Young Children: Early Intervention Profile*. Ann Arbor: The University of Michigan Press, 1978.

Shearer, D., Billingsley, J., Frohman, A., Hilliard, J., Johnson, F., & Shearer, M. *Portage Project Checklist*. Portage, WI: Cooperative Educational Service Agency No. 12, 1972.

Silverman, H., McNaughton, S., & Kates, B. *Handbook of Blissymbolics for instructors, users, parents, and administrators*. Toronto: Blissymbolics Communication Institute, 1979.

Smith, B. F. Potentials of rubella deaf-blind children. In: C. E. Sherrick (ed.), *1980 is now*. Los Angeles: John Tracy Clinic, 1974.

Somerton, M. E., & Turner, K. D. *Pennsylvania Training Model: Individual guide*. Harrisburg, PA: Pennsylvania Department of Education, 1975.

Stein L., Palmer, L., & Weinberg, B. *Characteristics of a young deaf-blind population: The Siegel Report No. 18*. Chicago: The David T. Siegel Institute, 1980.

Stewart, J. *The deaf-blind: Their nature and needs*. Paper presented for course requirement. Coppin State College, Baltimore, 1981.

Stillman, R. *Measuring progress in deaf-blind children*. Paper presented at the 46th biennial meeting of the Convention of American Instructors of the Deaf, Indianapolis, IN, 1973.

Stillman, R. D. *Assessment of deaf-blind children: The Callier Azusa Scale*. Reston, VA: The Council for Exceptional Children, 1974.

Stremel-Campbell, K. Decisions concerning oral and non-oral program placement and where do we go from here. In: B. Bjorling (ed.), *Language and communication*. Lansing, MI: Midwest Regional Center for Services to Deaf-Blind Children, May, 1977.

Terman, L.M., & Merrill, M.A. *Stanford-Binet Intelligence Scale* (3rd ed.). Boston: Houghton-Mifflin, 1973.

The New York Association for the Blind. *A Flash-Card Vision Test for Children*. New York: The New York Association for the Blind, 1966.

Thomas, E. D. Medical aspects of deaf-blind children: A five year diary. In: *Behavior modification for deaf-blind children*. Dallas: Callier Hearing & Speech Center, 1970.

Uzgiris, I., & Hunt, J. *Assessment in infancy: Ordinal Scales of Psychological Development*. Urbana, IL: University of Illinois Press, 1975.

Vanderheiden, D., & Vanderheiden, G. Basic considerations in the development of communicative and interactive skills for non-vocal severely handicapped children. In: E. Sontag (ed.), *Educational programming for the severely and profoundly handicapped*. Reston, VA: Division of Mental Retardation, The Council for Exceptional Children, 1977.

Vanderheiden, G., & Grilley, K. *Non-vocal communication techniques and aids for the severely physically handicapped*. Baltimore: University Park Press, 1975.

Van Etten, G., Arkell, C., & Van Etten, C. (eds.). *The severely and profoundly handicapped: Programs, methods, and materials*. St. Louis: C. V. Mosby Co., 1980.

Vernon, McC. *Multiply handicapped deaf children: A study of the significance and cause of the problem*. Unpublished doctoral dissertation, Claremont Graduate School and University Center, Claremont, CA, 1966.

Vernon, McC. Characteristics associated with post-rubella deaf children: Psychological, educational, and physical. *Volta Review*, 1977, *69*, 176–185.

Vernon, McC., & Alles, B. Psychological evaluation of multihandicapped deaf and hard-of-hearing youths. *Directions*, December 1982, (2), 12–18.

Wechsler, D. *Wechsler Intelligence Scale for Children—Revised*. New York: Psychological Corp., 1974.

Wheeler, A., Miller, R., Duke, J., Salisbury, E., Merritt, V., & Horton, B. *Murdoch Center C & Y Program Library*. Butner, NC: Murdoch Center, 1980.

Winter, J. The visually impaired child in the classroom. In: B. Bjorling (ed.), *Language and communication*. Lansing, MI: Midwest Regional Center for Services to Deaf-Blind Children, May, 1977.

Zuromski, E. S., Smith, N. F., & Brown, R. *A simple electromechanical response device for multihandicapped infants*. Paper presented at the Annual Conference of The American Psychological Association, San Francisco, 1977.

SUGGESTED READINGS

Banta, E. Siblings of deaf-blind children. *American Annals of the Deaf*, 1979, *81*, 363–365.

Barraga, N. *Increased visual behavior in low vision children*. New York: American Foundation for the Blind, 1967.

Bjorling, B. *There was only one Helen Keller*. Lansing, MI: Midwest Regional Center for Services to Deaf-Blind Children, 1980.

Curtis, C. (ed.). *A prelanguage curriculum guide for the multihandicapped*. Denver: Mountain Plains Regional Center for Services to Deaf-Blind Children, 1978.

Eisenberg, R. B. *Auditory competence in early life*. Baltimore: University Park Press, 1976.

English, P. *Prevocational services for deaf-blind children and youth: Innovative and experimental happenings in deaf-blind education*. Raleigh, NC: North Carolina State Department of Public Instruction, 1974.

Ficociello, C. *Vision stimuli for low functioning deaf-blind rubella children*. Dallas: South Central Regional Center for Services to Deaf-Blind Children, 1974.

Ficociello, C. *A Manual of Visual Assessment Kit,* Dallas: South Central Regional Center for Services to Deaf-Blind Children, 1975.

Fieber, N. Cognitive skills. In: N. Haring (ed.), *Developing effective individual education programs for severely handicapped children and youth*. Washington, D.C.: Thomas Buffington, 1977.

Guldager, L. The Oak Hill model for severely handicapped persons. *Viewpoints in Teaching and Learning: Journal of the School of Education*, 1981, *57*, 26–32.

Hicks, W. Communication variables associated with hearing impaired/vision impaired persons: A pilot study. *American Annals of the Deaf*, 1980, *124*, 419–422.

Jensema, C. K. Report on communication method usage by teachers of the deaf-blind children. *American Annals of the Deaf,* 1981, *126,* 8–10.

Kahn, J. V. Relationship of Piaget's sensorimotor period to language acquisition of profoundly retarded children. *American Journal of Mental Deficiency,* 1975, *79,* 640–643.

Klein, C. Coping patterns of parents of deaf-blind children. *American Annals of the Deaf,* 1977, *122,* 310–312.

Klein, C. Profile of deaf-blind children within various types of educational facilities. *American Annals of the Deaf.* 1980, *125,* 896–900.

Lowell, E. *Play it by ear.* Los Angeles: John Tracy Clinic, 1970.

Myklebust, H. R. *The psychology of deafness.* New York: Grune & Stratton, 1960.

Orlansky, M. Appropriate educational services for deaf-blind students. *Education of the Visually Handicapped,* 1980, *12,* 122–128.

Pollack, D. *Educational audiology for the limited hearing infant.* Springfield, IL: Charles C Thomas, 1980.

Yarnall, G. D., & Dodgison, B. Identifying effective reinforcers for a multiply handicapped student. *Education of the Visually Handicapped,* 1980, *12,* 11–20.

DISCUSSION QUESTIONS

1. Describe and define characteristics of deaf-blind individuals.
2. What are the levels of hearing deficits?
3. What are the visual characteristics of deaf-blind individuals?
4. What are some key medical factors that concern educators of deaf-blind students?
5. What are the auditory characteristics of deaf-blind persons?
6. What are some communication techniques used with low-functioning deaf-blind individuals?
7. What are the objectives of movement programs? How do motor circuits differ from movement theory?
8. What are the current trends in providing prevocational training to deaf-blind individuals?
9. What are the similarities between severely emotionally disturbed, severely mentally retarded, and deaf-blind persons?

Index

AAMD, *see* American Association on Mental Deficiency
AAP, *see* American Academy of Pediatrics
Abortions, 22, 128, 244
Abuse of children, physical, 196
Academic skills, 14, 27, 52–54, 203
Accidents as causes of handicaps, 139–142
Acoustic signals, 231
Acquisition of language, delayed, 228
Acquisition of skills, 203–204
Acting-out, 172
Adaptive behavior scales, 14, 21, 174, 272, 275
Adaptive Behavior Scales, 174
Adaptive behaviors, 13–14, 16, 18, 21, 198, 200, 272, 275
Adjustment problems, situational, 162
Adler, Alfred, 176
Adults
  aphasic, 219, 232–233
  mentally ill, 188
  schizophrenic, 156
Age of onset, 157, 188, 193–194
Age-appropriate skills, 30, 51, 53, 59, 158
Aggressive behavior, 64, 172, 174, 200–201
  of emotionally disturbed children, 158, 162, 192, 200
Agnosia, 253–254

Aides, classroom, 8
Aids
  hearing, 9, 294, 301
  optical, 138, 294
Albert Einstein Scale of Sensorimotor Intelligence, 166
Alienation, personal-social, 159
Allergies, 93, 178
AMC, *see* Arthrogryposis
American Academy of Pediatrics (AAP), 9, 179
American Association for the Education of the Severely/Profoundly Handicapped, 87
American Association on Mental Deficiency (AAMD), 13
  Adaptive Behavior Scale, 14
  definitions, 16–17
  Manual on Terminology and Classification in Mental Retardation, 20
American Psychiatric Association, 188, 194
Amniocentesis, 22, 128
Amplification of sound, 282, 294
Amputation, 140–141
Amyoplasia congenita, *see* Arthrogryposis
Anomie, 185
Antibiotics, 294
Aphasia, 6, 254, 280
  in adults, 219, 232–233
  childhood, 155, 166, 218, 243–244
  developmental, 218–219

319

Aphasia—*continued*
    receptive, 254, 290
    sensory, 290
Applying Behavior Procedures with Children and Youth, 201
Apraxia, 253–254
Art therapy, 202
Arthritis, juvenile rheumatoid (JRA), 134, 137–138
Arthrogryposis (amyoplasia congenita), 98–99
Articular rigidities, congenital, 98
Articulation
    disorders of, 193, 221, 223, 230, 233, 252, 255
    rules of, 231
    tests of, 223
Articulatory gestures, 248
Articulatory placement, 238
Artificial limbs, 141
ASIEP, *see* Autism Screening Instrument for Educational Planning
Assessment
    of baseline behaviors, 172
    nonverbal, 90
    program, 96
    of skills, 32–33, 38–39
Assessment instruments, 12, 21, 174, 274–279
The Assessment Inventory for Severely Handicapped Children (TARC), 278
    see also Tests
Association for Retarded Citizens, 8
The Association for the Severely Handicapped (TASH), 12, 87
Athetosis, 4
Attention skills, 33–34
Audiograms, 282–285, 301–302
Audiometry, 273
Auditorially-visually impaired students, 269–312
Auditory agnosia, 254, 280, 289–290
Auditory intervention, 282
Auditory memory, 226, 239, 259
Auditory processes, 233, 238–239, 247–248, 259, 290, 301

Auditory stimuli, 224, 233, 256, 273
Auditory tests, 219, 247
Auditory training, 300–301
Autism, infantile, 2, 155–156, 163, 189–190
Autism Behavior Checklist, 171
Autism Screening Instrument for Educational Planning (ASIEP), 171–172
Autistic children, 155, 161, 165, 170–174, 295

Balthazar Scales of Adaptive Behavior, 14, 272, 275
Basic skills, 87
Bayley Scales of Infant Development, 170, 272, 276
BCP, *see* Behavior Characteristics Progression
BEH, *see* Bureau of Education for the Handicapped
Behavior
    adaptive, 13–14, 16, 18, 21, 198, 200, 272, 275
    age-appropriate, 158
    aggressive, 64, 158, 162, 172, 174, 192, 200, 201
    bizarre, 162, 174, 192, 286–287
    deviant, 154, 157, 159, 162, 173, 184
    disruptive, 36, 38, 58, 64, 227
    excessive, 198, 200
    imitative, 40–42, 44, 54, 57–58, 171, 304, 306, 308
    impulsive, 196
    maladaptive, 14, 28, 158, 172, 174, 180
    observable, 186–187
    operant, 181
    ritualistic, 192
    self-injurious, 3, 8, 59, 62–64, 97, 163, 172, 190, 192, 292
    self-stimulatory, 3, 59–62, 65, 173, 192, 291–292, 295, 302
    target, 86
Behavior assessment, 167, 170, 172
Behavior Characteristics Progression (BCP), 275

Index   321

Behavior management, 9, 28, 31, 62, 97, 118, 180, 205
Behavior modification, 180, 203–204, 295
Behavior observation audiometry, 273
The Behavior Rating Instrument for Autistic and Other Atypical Children, 171
Behavior Rating of Pupils Section of a Process for In-School Screening of Emotionally Handicapped Children, 170
Behavior rating scales, 167, 170–172
Behavior reinforcement, 60–64
Behavior scales, adaptive, 14, 21, 174, 272, 275
Behavior therapy, 180, 197–199, 201, 204, 312
Behavioral approaches to classification, 186
Behavioral theory of emotionally disturbed children, 175, 180–182
Behaviorally disordered children, 154, 159, 162
Bell, Terrence, 161
Benhaven School Community for Autistic and Neurologically Impaired Individuals, 205
Bilirubin levels, high, 166
Biological theory of causes of emotionally disturbed children, 177
Birth defects, congenital, 293
Birth trauma, 116
Bizarre behavior, 162, 174, 192, 286–287
Bladder control, 193
Blind, Library for the, 136
Blind children, 4–5, 272
Blindness
  Rh negative factor as a cause of, 279, 281
  see Deaf-blind children
Blissymbols, 306–307
Block Design Test, 228
Blood disorders, 127–131
BOA, see Behavior observation audiometry

Body concepts, 171, 174
Bowel control, 193
Brace, Milwaukee, 136–137
Braille, 281, 299
Brain damage, 17, 19–20, 141, 163, 224, 226, 279
  caused by disease, 179–180
Brain dysfunction, minimal (MBD), 179 188, 229–230
Bridgeman, Laura, 270
Brigance Inventory of Early Development, 275
The Bristol Social Adjustment Guides, 170
Bureau of Education for the Handicapped (BEH), 160, 270–271
Burks Behavior Rating Scale, 167

CA, see Chronological age
Cain-Levine Social Competency Scale, 14
Callier Azusa Scales, 274–275
Cardiac disorders, 93, 123, 125–127, 279
Cardiovascular disorders, 103
Care facilities, 8, 28, 30, 56, 88
Carrow Elicited Language Inventory, 236–237
CARS, see The Childhood Rating Scale
Case histories, 167–170
Case managers, 91, 95
CAT, see Children's Appercention Test
CAT, see Computerized axial tomography
Cataracts, 280, 290, 294
Cattell Infant Intelligence Scale, 272
CELF, see Clinical Evaluation of Language Functions, 240
Central nervous system dysfunction, 156, 177, 221, 243–244
Central Wisconsin Colony and Training School's Education Assessment Device, 275
Cerebral hemisphere, 228
Cerebral palsy, 3–4, 104–111, 134, 280–281, 296

Index

CETA, see Comprehensive Employment Training Act
Chaining, 34, 47–48
Chicago Light House for the Blind, 299
Child abuse, 196
Child-Find, 167, 272
Child study teams (CSTs), 92
Child-therapist relationship, 255
Childhood aphasia, 218, 243–244
Childhood dysphasia, 221–222, 224–227, 231, 246, 260
Childhood psychosis, 154, 157, 161, 163, 165, 172, 189, 202–203
The Childhood Rating Scale (CARS), 174
Childhood schizophrenia, 156, 161, 163–164, 174–175, 177, 189–191, 197
Children's Apperception Test, 174
The Children's Guild, Inc., 204–205
Children's Hospital Medical Center, 91
Chromosomal disorders, 19
Chronic renal disease, 121–124
Chronological age (CA), 223, 235
The Class Picture, 170
A Class Play, 170
Classification systems
 of emotional disabilities, 156–157, 163, 186–191
 of hearing disorders, 281–282
 of language impairments, 245–246
 of mental retardation, 20–21
Classifications, 2–3, 6, 12–13, 15, 17, 19
Classroom assessment tools, 274–279
Classroom organization, 9, 164
Classroom prevocational training, 310
Classrooms, 95, 163, 204
Cleft palate, 221, 280
Clinical Evaluation of Language Functions (CELF), 236, 240–241
Clustering, 54
Cognitive development, 5, 14, 53, 95–96, 220, 233, 312
Cognitive impairments, 15, 223, 227–228

Cognitive learning of emotionally disturbed children, 159
Colorado School for the Deaf and Blind, 299
Communication, 174, 312
 nonverbal, 42–45, 90
Communication boards, 304–305
Communication disturbances, 155, 171, 193
Communication skills, 14, 21, 32, 39–44, 88, 159, 279, 287
 development of, 255
 oral, 296, 304
 teaching of, 39–41, 45–46, 90, 304–306
 see also Language skills; Speech development
Community living skills, 14, 27–28, 30, 33, 35, 46, 48–49, 53, 309–310
Community placement, 8, 27–30, 39, 49, 62, 310
Community services, 26–27, 96
Community values, 183
Comprehension skills for spoken language, 246
Comprehensive Behavior Checklist, 14
Comprehensive Employment Training Act, 37
Computerized axial tomography (CAT), 142
Conditioning, 182, 199
Congenital birth defects, 98–104, 224, 290, 293
Congenital rubella, 180, 279
Congenitally aphasic children, 243, 254
Convulsions, see Seizures
Cora plana, 131–132
Correction procedures, 34
Counseling
 family, 205
 genetic, 119–120, 128, 130, 195
 by physicians, 90–91
 rehabilitation, 31, 310–311
Counselors' ratings of children, 170
Court cases, 25–26, 29, 50
Crisis intervention, 202

Criterion-referenced tests, 166–167, 172
Cruickshank, William M., 6
Cues, 48, 52, 54, 194
Cultural transmission, 185–186
Curriculum development, 51, 53
Cystic fibrosis, 118–120

Daily living skills, 3, 15, 27, 46–47, 49, 51, 111, 171, 286, 309
  see also Self-care skills; Self-help skills
Dance therapy, 202
DASI, *see* Developmental Activities Screening Inventory
Deaf-blind children, 269–312
  definition of, 271
  educational services for, 270–272, 296, 299–300
  imitation skills of, 306–308
  schools for, 271, 296–297
  sensory training of, 286, 309
  sequential memory of, 308
  simulated work settings of, 309–310
  social development of, 260, 308–309
Deaf-blind persons, characteristics of, 280, 292–293
Deaf-blindness, causes of, 279, 281
Deaf students, 4–5, 166, 222, 251, 254, 290
  see also Hearing loss
Deaths, neonatal, 244
Deconditioning, 199
Deinstitutionalization, 7–8, 26–30, 46, 86, 91
Denver Developmental Screening Test, 276
Department of Health and Human Services (HHS), 300
Department of Psychiatry at the University of California, 173
Depression, 57, 158, 160, 172, 179, 197
Detroit Test of Learning Aptitude, 236, 241
Development
  cognitive, 95–96
  physical, 14
  of skills, 27, 203
  of speech and language, 233–234, 243
Development therapy programs, 203
Developmental Activities Screening Inventory (DASI), 276
Developmental aphasia, 218–219
Developmental classrooms, 95
Developmental disabilities, 15, 157, 161, 163, 188–189, 218
The Developmental Disabilities Assistance and Bill of Rights Act of 1975 (PL 94-103), 15
Developmental evaluation, 166, 170, 272
Developmental Evaluation Clinic of the Children's Hospital Medical Center, 279
Developmental pediatricians, 91
Developmental period, 14–15
Developmental Programming for Infants and Young Children, 276
Developmental rates of autistic children, 173
Developmental Sentence Scoring (DSS), 235–236
Developmental spiral, 276
Developmentally delayed infants, 296
The Devereux Elementary Behavior Rating Scale, 170
Deviant behaviors, 154, 157, 159, 162, 173, 184
  see also Bizarre behavior; Disruptive behaviors; Maladaptive behavior
Diagnosis, 9, 13, 17, 88, 102, 104, 123, 157
  of autism, 171, 173–174
  of dysphasia, 222
  of emotional disturbance, 166–167, 175
Diagnostic and Statistical Manual of Mental Disorders classification system (DSM-III), 156–157, 188–189
Differential reinforcement, 36, 60
  of incompatible behaviors (DRI), 60–64
  of other behaviors (DRO), 60–64
Disabilities, pregnancy-related, 18–20,

Disabilities—*continued*
  100, 107–108, 120, 126,
  243–244, 279
Discrimination
  of importance of tasks, 34
  of sounds, 233
Dislocation of the hip, *see* Dysplasia
Disruptive behaviors, 36, 38, 58, 64, 227
Division of Vocational Rehabilitation
  (DVR), 300
Dixon Development Center, 299
Domestic skills, 14, 53
Down's syndrome, 195
Dressing skills, 7, 46 47, 51
DRI, *see* Differential reinforcement of
  incompatible behaviors
DRO, *see* Differential reinforcement of
  other behaviors
Drug therapy, 110, 113–115, 120, 126
Drug treatment, psychoactive, 179,
  196–197
Drugs, *see* Medications
DSM-III, *see* Diagnostic and Statistical
  Manual of Mental Disorders
  classification system
DSS, *see* Developmental Sentence Scoring
Duration counting, 172
DVR, *see* Division of Vocational
  Rehabilitation
Dyslalia, 221
Dyslexic children, 229–230
Dysphasia, 221–222, 224–228, 230–234,
  242, 246, 260
  developmental, 217–260
  identification of, 218, 222–242
Dysplasia, congenital, 101–102

Ear, anatomy of the, 287–288
The Early Detection Inventory, 167
The Early School Personality
  Questionnaire, 167
Eating disorders, 188
Eating skills, 46, 48, 51, 109, 296
Echolalia, 173
Ecological theory of emotional
  disturbance, 175, 182–184

Education for All Handicapped Children
  Act (PL 94-142), 6–7, 12, 26, 86,
  89, 90, 92, 154–155, 160–161,
  163, 167, 270
Education programs
  books that concentrate on, 256–258
  for deaf-blind students, 270–272, 296,
    299–300
  individualized, 51–53, 86, 88–89, 91,
    93, 95, 127, 202, 255
Educational performance of emotionally
  disturbed children, 159–160
Educational placement, 163
Educational programming, 8–9, 155, 194
  see also Instructional programming
Educational services, 49–50, 93, 256–258
EEGs, *see* Electroencephalograms
Electroencephalograms (EEGs), 110,
  174, 191, 243, 273
Elementary and Secondary Education
  Assistance Programs, 160
Ellis, Albert, 176
Emotional disturbance
  causes of, 175–186
  definitions of, 154–162
  theories of, 175–180, 182–184
Emotionally disturbed children
  case study of, 191–192
  educational performance of, 159–160
  identification of, 165–170, 175
  intervention programs for, 159, 163,
    180, 182, 184, 187
  parents of, 162
  social-emotional development of,
    158–159, 162, 171
Emotionally disturbed people, 16, 87,
  153–206, 222–223
  labeling of, 155, 161, 166, 173, 183,
    188
  traditional treatment of, 175
Emotional-social development, 4,
  158–159, 162, 174
Employment
  competitive, 27, 32, 37–38
  sheltered, 28, 33, 35, 37–38, 96, 118,
    309–311
Encephalitis, postnatal, 180

Environment, interaction with the, 183–184, 187–188
Environmental-behavioral maladaption, 159
Environmental deprivation, 19
Environments
 home, 95, 173
 learning, 7, 94–95
 least restrictive, 7–8, 25, 29, 90, 93, 163
EPEC, *see* Evaluation and Prescription for Exceptional Children
Epilepsy, 111–115
Equipment, specialized, 8–9, 86, 89, 90, 93, 111, 118, 140
Errors of refraction, 291
Evaluation, 88–89, 93, 95, 97, 166, 185
 see also Assessment; Tests
Evaluation and Prescription for Exceptional Children (EPEC), 173
Excessive behavior, 198, 200
Expressive language, 222–223, 245–246
Expressive language age (LAE), 223
Expressive speech, 171, 174, 203
Extinction, 62–63, 200
Eye, anatomy of the, 288–289

Fading, 41
Family counseling, 205
Family environments, 95, 173
Fatal illnesses, 118–125
Federal laws, 161
Feedback to students, 34
Feeding skills, 296
Femoral capital epiphysis, slipped, 132–133
Figure perception, 303
Flash-Card Vision Test for Children, 273
The Fletcher Time-by-Count Test of Diadochokinetic Syllable Rate, 236, 238
Flooding, 199
Food preparation skills, 48
Foster homes, 8
Frequency counting, 172

Freudian interpretation of emotional development, 176
FSM, *see* Functional Sequencing Model
Functional analysis, 198
Functional Sequencing Model, 53–54
Functional skills, 171
Functionalism, 185–186

GAP classification system, *see* Group for the Advancement of Psychiatry classification system
Generalization of skills, 37–38, 41–42, 45–46, 53–55, 58, 203
Genetic counseling, 119–120, 128, 130, 195
Genetic impairments, 17, 19, 22, 194
Genetic research, 177
Gesell Development Schedule, 166
Glasser, William, 176
Glaucoma, 291
Goldman-Fristoe Test of Articulation, 236–237
Grooming skills, 7, 46–47
Group care homes, 8, 30, 56, 88
Group for the Advancement of Psychiatry (GAP) classification system, 157
Group training, 52

Haight Method of manual communication, 304
Halfway houses, 8, 28
Health care facilities, 88
Health impaired, 16, 87–88
Hearing aids, 9, 294, 301
Hearing disorders, classification systems of, 281–282
Hearing impaired persons, 271–272
Hearing loss, 104, 166, 222–223, 284–285, 289, 294
 causes of, 289–290
 treatment of, 293–294
Hearing testing, 222, 235, 247, 273–274, 301
Heart defects, 93, 123, 125–127, 279

Helen Keller National Center for
    Deaf-Blind Youths and Adults,
    271, 299–300
Hemophilia, 127–129
Hereditary causes of disabilities, 166,
    279
HEW, see U.S. Department of Health,
    Education, and Welfare
HHS, see Department of Health and
    Human Services
Hierarchy of language, 248, 251–252,
    260
Hip disorders, 101–102, 132–133
Hiskey-Nebraska Test of Learning
    Aptitude, 272
Home-bound employment, 118
Home-bound instruction, 136, 138
Home environments, 173
Homonymous mianopsia, 280
Hydrocephaly, 124
Hyperactivity, 193, 202, 227, 257,
    292–293
Hyperkinetic behavior, 196–197
Hypoactivity, 193, 202

ICFs, see Intermediate care facilities
Identification
    of dysphasic children, 222
    of emotional disorders, 165–166
    of mentally retarded children, 12, 17
    of skills, 311
IEPs, see Individualized education
    programs
Illinois School for the Visually Impaired,
    299
Illinois Test of Psycholinguistic Abilities
    (ITPA), 228, 236, 239–240, 254,
    257
Imitative behavior, 40–42, 44, 54,
    57–58, 171, 304, 306, 308
Impulse control, testing for, 174
Impulsive behaviors, 196
Inappropriate behavior, see Deviant
    behaviors
Independence, social, 14–15

Individualized education programs (IEPs),
    86, 88–89, 91, 93, 95, 127, 255
Individualized instruction, 51–53, 86,
    88–89, 91, 93, 95, 127, 202, 255,
    262
Infantile autism, 2, 155–156, 163,
    189–190
Infection as a cause of disabilities, 166,
    293
Institutionalization, 23–26, 28, 297
Institutions, 12, 24, 36, 50, 59
Instructional materials for speech and
    language development, 258
Instructional programming, 54, 164
    see also Educational programming
Integration between the handicapped and
    nonhandicapped, 96–97
Intellectual functioning, 13–14, 18,
    196–197
    in autistic children, 179
    depressed, 159, 167
Intelligence quotients (IQ), 13–14,
    16–18, 21, 27, 31, 45, 50, 56,
    228
Intelligence tests, 13–14, 17–18, 32, 227,
    272
Interdisciplinary approaches to
    educational services for the
    handicapped, 6–7, 88–89, 97, 101
Interdisciplinary teams, 31, 171
Intermediate care facilities (ICFs), 88
Interpersonal relationships, 157–158,
    160–162
Intersound interval (ISI), 225–226
Interval recording, 172
Intervention, 196, 202, 282
Intervention programs
    behavioral, 197–199
    for emotionally disturbed children,
        159, 163, 180, 182, 184, 187
Interviews, 31, 33, 201
IQ, see Intelligence quotients
ISI, see Intersound interval
Isotropia, 280
Itard, J.M.G., 1
ITPA, see Illinois Test of
    Psycholinguistic Abilities

Johns Hopkins Hospital, 2
Joint Commission on Mental Health of
    Children, 156
JRA, *see* Juvenile rheumatoid arthritis
Judevine Center, 203
Jung's Word Association Test, 174
Juvenile rheumatoid arthritis (JRA), 134,
    137–138

Kanner, Leo, 155
Keller, Helen, 1, 270
Kidney dysfunction, 121–124
Klinefelter's syndrome, 195
Koontz Child Developmental Programs,
    276
Kyphosis, 136–137

LA, *see* Language age
Labeling, *see* Classifications
Labeling of emotionally disturbed
    students, 155, 161, 166, 173,
    183–188
LAE, *see* Expressive language age
Language
  expressive, 15, 40–41, 44, 222–223,
    245–246
  hierarchy of, 248, 251–252, 260
  phonological aspects of, 240, 245,
    249–250, 253–254, 257
  receptive, 15, 40–44, 171, 203, 245,
    254, 290
  semantics of, 240, 245
  sign, 3, 42–45
  syntax of, 233, 240, 245, 249–250
Language age (LA), 223, 235–236
Language assessment tests, standardized,
    219
Language development, 233, 243, 245
  of aphasic children, 155
  of autistic children, 155, 171
  of dysphasic children, 232–234
  in psychotic children, 202–203
  publishing companies that concentrate
    on, 258–259

The Language Development Program,
    204
Language disorders, 4–6, 161, 173–174,
    218, 223, 225, 228, 232–234
Language impaired students, 5–6,
    217–260
Language skills, 15, 27, 39–44, 53, 220
Language structure, 248
Language therapy, 6–7, 295–296, 312
Language Training Lattice, 256
LAP, *see* Learning Accomplishment
    Profile
LAR, *see* Receptive language age
The League School for the Seriously
    Disturbed, 205
Learning Accomplishment Profile (LAP),
    277
*Learning and Behavior Characteristics of
    Exceptional Children and Youth,*
    201
Learning disabled, 222
Learning environments, 7, 94–95
Learning rates, 52, 171
Least restrictive environments, 8, 25, 29,
    90, 93, 163
Left-handedness, 244
Legg-Calvé-Perthes disease, 131–132
Leisure skills, 53, 58–59, 309
Leiter International Performance Scale
    and Arthur adaptation, 272
Library for the Blind, 136
Life-space interviews, 201
Linguistic and articulation rules, 231–233
Linwood Children's Center, 202
Living with Children, 201
Localization of sounds, 301
Lung disease, 118–119

Mainstreaming, 7–8, 30, 163
Maintenance of skills, 28, 55
Maladaptive behavior, 14, 28, 158, 172,
    174, 180
  see also Bizarre behavior; Deviant
    behaviors; Disruptive behaviors
Maladjustment, emotional, 4
Management, self, 201

Managers, case, 91, 95
Manual communication, 304
    see also Nonverbal communication;
        Sign language
A Manual for the Assessment of a
    Deaf-Blind Multihandicapped
    Child, 277
MAP, see Mental performance age
March of Dimes, 293
Maslow, Abraham, 176
Match-Sort-Assembly (MSA), 37
Matching, 37, 174
Maxfield-Bucholz Scale of Social
    Maturity for Use with Preschool
    Blind Children, 272
MBD, see Minimal brain dysfunction
Mean length of utterance, 234
Medical classifications, 2, 6
Medical needs of handicapped people,
    93, 196
Medications, 60, 93, 110, 294
    see also Drugs
Memory, 179, 240
    auditory, 226, 239, 259
    of deaf-blind children, 308
    short-term, 232-233, 259
    visual, 244, 303
Memory skills, 54, 156, 247, 303
Meningitis as a cause of deaf blindness,
    279, 281
Meningocele, 99
Meningomyelocele, 99-100
Mental health centers, 28, 88
Mental illness, adult, 188
Mental performance age (MAP), 223
Mentally retarded, 12-13, 17, 222-223
Michael Reese Medical Center, 299
Michigan School for the Blind, 299
Milieu therapy, 201-202, 295
Milwaukee brace, 136-137
Minimal brain dysfunction (MBD), 179,
    188, 229-230
Minnesota Braille and Sight Saving
    School, 299
The Minnesota Sociometric Status Test,
    170
Mobility skills, 3, 15, 27, 286, 309
Mobility specialists, 295-296, 302

Modeling, 34, 52, 57-58
Money usage, 46, 49
Mother-child interactions, 156
Mother's behavioral ratings, 170
Motivation, self, 260
Motor control, visual functioning
    facilitated by, 274
Motor development, 21, 53, 57, 109,
    296, 303, 312
Motor function, impaired, 105, 110-111,
    280
Motor skills, 4, 51, 174, 279, 296, 303,
    309
Movement programs, 306-308
MSA, see Match-Sort-Assembly
Multihandicapped persons, 4-5, 16, 87,
    104, 279, 287
    hearing impaired, 272
The Murdoch Center C and Y Program
    Library, 277
Muscular dystrophy, 98, 120-121, 134
Music therapy, 202
Mutism, elective, 4, 193

National Institute for Neurological and
    Communicative Disorders and
    Stroke, 161
National Society for Children and Adults
    with Autism, 156, 160-161, 189,
    206
Neurodevelopmental therapy, 109
Neurofibromatosis, 134, 222
Neurological disorders, 104-118, 167,
    227, 245-246
Neurologists, 91, 171
Neuropsychiatric Institute (NPI), 173,
    203-204
Neuropsychopharmacologic theory of
    emotional disturbance, 179
Newborns, 166
Nonhandicapped peers, 7-8, 26, 58, 96,
    163
Nonverbal communication, 42-45, 90, 225
    see also Manual communication; Sign
        language
Normalization, 7, 26, 30, 86
Norm-referenced tests, 166

Noun phrase (NP), 221, 248–249, 251
NP, *see* Noun phrase
NPI, *see* Neuropsychiatric Institute
Nutrition, 19, 22, 100, 123
Nystagmus, 291

Oak Hill School, 299
Object fixation, 192
Objectives, educational, 8–9
Observable behaviors, 186–187
Observation, direct, 170–173
Obsessive-compulsive behaviors, 192
Occupational skills, 14, 28
Occupational therapy, 7, 90–91, 108–109, 138, 141, 286, 312
Office of Special Education (OSE), 91
Ohio State University's Nisonger Center, 92
On-the-job training, 27
One-to-one instruction, 51–53, 86, 88–89, 91, 93, 95, 127, 202, 255, 262
Operant behavior techniques, 181, 199, 204, 255–256
Optic atrophy, 290
Optical aids, 136, 294
Oral apraxia, 254
Oral communication skills, 222, 247, 296, 304
Ordinal Scales of Psychological Development, 166
Organic theory of emotional disturbance, 175, 177–180
Orientation skills, 286, 295–296, 302
Orthopaedically impaired, 87, 98–104, 115–116, 131–138
Orthotics, 141
OSE, *see* Office of Special Education
Osteogenesis imperfecta, 103–104
Other health impaired, autism as classified under, 155, 161
Otitis media, recurrent, 222, 279
Otosclerosis, 293–294
Overcorrection, 34, 48, 60–61, 63–64

PACG, *see* Prevocational Assessment and Curriculum Guide

Parental involvement, 94, 155, 180, 196, 203–205
Parents of disabled children, 162, 170–171
Pathologists, 296
  speech-language (SLPs), 218–219, 235–236, 242, 255–256, 258–260
PBS, *see* Psychiatric Behavior Scale
Peabody Picture Vocabulary Test (PPVT), 246, 254
Peabody Picture Vocabulary Test–Revised, 236, 238
Pediatricians, 91–92
Peer behavior rating scales, 170
Peers, nonhandicapped, 7–8, 26, 58, 96, 163, 200–201
Pennsylvania Training Model, 277
Perceptual abilities of dysphasic children, 228, 230
Performance tests, 228
Perkins School for the Blind, 270, 299
Personality assessment instruments, 174
Personal-social alienation, 159
Phenylketonuria (PKU), 180, 195
Phonemes, 231, 232
Phonic Ear, 301
Phonological aspects of language, 237, 240, 245–246, 249–250, 253–254, 257
Photo Articulation Test, 232
Physical environmental theories on causes of emotional disturbances, 14, 178, 182–183
Physical impairments, 271
Physical therapy, 90–91, 108, 138, 141, 286, 295–296, 312
Physicians, 90–92
Picture Arrangement task, 228
PKU, *see* Phenylketonuria
PL 91-230, 160, 270
PL 94-103, 15
PL 94-112, 15
PL 94-142, *see* Education for All Handicapped Children Act
PL 95-602, 15
Placement
  community, 27–30, 39, 49, 62, 310
  educational, 38, 64, 163
Play therapy, 201, 273, 295

Playing, 57–58, 61, 155, 229
Pneumoencephalograms, 243
Polio, 134
The Portage Project Checklist, 277
Pregnancy, precautions during, 293–294
Pregnancy-related disabilities, 18–20, 100, 107–108, 120, 126, 243–244, 279
Prelanguage vocalization, 219–220
Preschool children, 174, 272, 293
Prevention programs, 22, 94, 194–202, 255–256, 293
Prevocational Assessment and Curriculum Guide (PACG), 33
Prevocational training, 205, 309–311
Probes, 53
Program assessment, 96
Programming
  educational, 8–9, 155, 194
  instructional, 54, 164
Prompting procedures, 34, 37–38, 40, 42, 47–49, 52, 54, 57–58, 199, 256
Prosthetic devices, 93, 141
Psychiatric Behavior Scale (PBS), 174
Psychiatric disturbances in parents, 196
Psychiatrists, 90–91, 154, 156, 170, 175, 295
Psychodynamic approaches to classification, 188, 201
Psychoeducational theory of emotional disturbance, 175–177
Psycholinguistic age, 240
Psychological tests, 31, 311
Psychologists, 91, 154, 156–157, 170, 175–176, 295
Psychomotor learning of emotionally disturbed children, 159
Psychosis
  childhood, 154, 157, 161, 163, 165, 172, 189, 202–203
  symbiotic, 156, 163, 189–191
Psychosocial development of emotionally disturbed children, 159, 171
Punishment, 60, 62, 181–182, 204
Pupil-teacher contacts, 173

Quay-Peterson Behavior Problem Checklist, 167

Radiation therapy, 125
Rapid-eye movement (REM), 197
Ravens Progressive Matrices Test, 228
REA, *see* Right-ear advantage, 244
Reading, development of, 233
Rebus symbols, 306, 308
Receptive language age (LAR), 223
Receptive language problems, 254, 279, 290
Recreation of deaf-blind children, 309
The Referral Form Checklist of Problem Behaviors, 167
Regional Centers for Services to Deaf-Blind Children and Youths, 297–299, 312
Rehabilitation, 15, 31, 310–311
Rehabilitation Act of 1973 (PL 94-112), 15
Rehabilitation Comprehensive Services and Developmental Disabilities Amendments of 1978 (PL 95-602), 15
Rehearsal of skills, 54, 58
Reimbursement for services, 88
Reinforcement, 34–36, 40–42, 47–48, 57, 59, 62–64, 181–182, 256
  differential, 36, 60–62, 64
  positive, 36, 199–200, 204
Reliability of tests, 18
REM, *see* Rapid-eye movement
Renal disease, chronic, 121–124
Repetition of Sentence Test, 247
Representational development, 229
Residential schools, 202–203, 271, 297
Respondent learning based interventions, 199
Response cost, 200
Retinal damage, 290
Rh negative factor as a cause of blindness, 279, 281
Rheumatoid arthritis, juvenile (JRA), 134, 137–138
Right-ear advantage (REA), 244

Right handedness, 243
Ritualistic behaviors, 192
Rogers, Carl, 176
Rorschach Inkblot Test, 174
Rosenzweig Picture-Frustration Test, 174
Rubella, 180, 279–280, 290, 294
Rubella epidemics, 270–272, 293, 297, 311
Rule breakers, 184–186
Rutland Center, 203

Schizophrenia, 156
   childhood, 156, 161, 163–164, 174–175, 177, 189–191, 197
   twin studies of, 177, 195
School phobia, 197
Schools for deaf-blind children, private, 271
Scoliosis, 133–136
Screening, 17, 92–93
   of autistic children, 170–172
   of dysphasic children, 222–242
   of emotionally disturbed children, 165–170, 175
   for hearing loss, 222
   of high risk infants, 166–167
Screening Test for Developmental Apraxia, 254
Screening tests, 167, 170, 254
Segregation of students, 23
Seizures, 93, 105, 110–114, 280
Self-care skills, 7, 14–15, 46–47, 51, 53, 87, 90, 109, 296, 309
Self-contained classrooms, 163, 204
Self-control, 157, 172, 199
Self-direction, 14–15, 36, 201, 260
Self-esteem of disabled children, 159, 162, 172, 260
Self-help skills, 14, 21, 25, 28, 46–49, 51, 53–54, 88, 287
   see also Daily living skills; Self-care skills
Self-injurious behaviors (SIB), 3, 8, 59, 62–64, 97, 163, 172, 190, 192, 292

Self-protection skills, 21
Self-ratings of children, 170
Self-stimulatory behaviors, 3, 59–65, 173, 192, 291–292, 295, 302, 304
Semantics of language, 233–234, 237, 240, 245, 259
Sensorimotor skill development, 14, 53, 309
Sensorineural hearing loss, 289, 294
Sensory aphasia, 290
Sensory impairments of deaf-blind children, 6, 163, 286
Sensory stimuli, 173, 190, 253, 303
SEP, see Special Education Programs
Sequence of developmental skills, 203
Sequencing, auditory, 225, 238–239, 245, 247
Sequential memory of deaf-blind children, 306, 308
Shaping, 32, 47–48, 199
Sheltered employment, 33, 35, 118
Sheltered workshops, 28, 37–38, 96, 309–311
SIB, see Self-injurious behaviors
Sickle cell anemia, 129–131, 195
Sign language, 3, 42–45
   see also Manual communication; Nonverbal communication
Signals, acoustic, 231
Skill assessment, 32–33, 38–39
Skill development, 14, 27, 53, 203–204
Skill generalization, 37–38, 41–42, 45–46, 53–55, 58, 203
Skill identification, 311
Skill maintenance, 28, 55
Skill rehearsal, 54, 58
Skills
   academic, 14, 27, 52–54, 203
   age-appropriate, 30, 51, 53, 59
   attention, 33–34
   communication, 14, 21, 32, 39–44, 88, 159, 255, 279, 287
   community living, 14, 27–28, 30, 33, 35, 46, 48–49, 53, 309–310
   daily living, 3, 15, 27, 46–47, 49, 51, 111, 171, 286, 309
   imitation, 306–308

Skills—*continued*
  language, 15, 27, 39–41, 44, 53, 220, 246
  leisure, 53, 58–59
  memory, 54, 156, 247, 303
  motor, 4, 51, 174, 279, 296, 303, 309
  self-care, 7, 14–15, 46–47, 51, 53, 87, 90, 109, 296, 309
  self-help, 14, 21, 25, 28, 46–49, 51, 53–54, 88, 287
  social, 14, 21, 28, 53–59, 88, 287
  visual-motor, 274, 286, 303
Skinner, B.F., 181–182
SLPs, *see* Speech-language pathologists
Snellen Chart, 273
Social control, 185–187
Social interaction, 94, 171, 193, 203
Social maladjustment, 154–155, 158, 161, 165, 170
Social skills, 14, 21, 28, 53–59, 88, 287
Socialization, 5, 14, 25, 174, 309
Sociological theory of emotional disturbance, 175, 184–188
Sociometric procedures, 170
Sound
  amplification of, 282, 294
    see also Hearing aids
  development of, 225, 233, 238, 247
  discrimination of, 233, 248, 301
Southern California Sensory Integration Tests, 277
Spasticity, 105–106, 110
Spatial awareness, 308
Special Education Programs (SEP), 270
Specialized equipment, 8–9, 86, 89–90, 93, 111, 118, 140
Speech development, 171, 173–174, 220, 225, 231, 233, 243
  publishing companies that concentrate on, 258–259
  in psychotic children, 202–203
Speech disorders, 105, 111, 173, 222, 230
Speech intervention, 282
Speech therapy, 6–7, 21, 90–91, 109, 312
Speech-language pathologists (SLPs), 218–219, 235–236, 242, 255–256, 258–260

Speech/language therapists, 295–296
Spina bifida, 99–101, 134
Spinal cord injuries, 115–118, 133–136
Standardized tests, 12, 21, 219, 227, 311
Stanford-Binet Intelligence Scale, 13, 17–18, 272
State laws, 161
Still's disease, 137–138
Stimulant drugs, 196
Stimuli, sensory, 173, 181, 190, 224, 233, 253, 273
Strabismus, 280, 291
Stress, reaction to, 174
Sullivan, Anne, 1
Surgery
  as a means to return hearing, 294
  as treatment, 93, 99, 101–103, 108, 110, 116, 124–128, 132–133, 135–136, 141
  to remove cataracts, 294
  in utero, 312
Symbiotic psychosis, 156, 163, 189–191
Symbol boards, 306
Symbolic play, 229
Syntax of language, 231–233, 237, 240, 245, 249–250

TACL, *see* Test for Auditory Comprehension of Language
TARC, *see* The Assessment Inventory for Severely Handicapped Children
Target behaviors, 86
TASH, *see* The Association for the Severely Handicapped
Task analysis, 34–35, 37–38, 46–47, 95, 97
TAT, *see* Thematic Apperception Test
Tay-Sachs disease, 195
TEACCH, *see* The Treatment and Education of Autistic and Related Communications Handicapped Children Program
Teacher-parent interactions, 203
Teacher-pupil contacts, 173, 200
Teacher-rating scales of behavior, 167, 170
Teacher training programs, 297

Telephone skills, 27, 46, 49
Templin-Darley Test of Articulation, 223
TES, see Treatment emergent symptoms
Test for Auditory Comprehension of Language (TALC), 236, 254
The Test of Language Development, 236, 242
Test reliability, 18
Test scores, 234
Test validity, 18, 172
Tests
    auditory, 222, 235, 247, 273–274, 301
    coding, 228
    for impulse control, 174
    intelligence, 13–14, 17–18, 32, 227, 272
    language, 223, 225, 235–238, 242, 246
    performance, 228
    for preschool blind children, 272
    for preschool children, 174
    psychological, 31, 311
    vision, 273–274
    vocational, 31–33, 311
Thematic Apperception Test (TAT), 174
Therapeutic intervention programs, 163, 182
Therapists, 9, 204, 255–256
Therapy, 93, 203
    behavior, 180, 198–199, 201, 204, 295
    drug, 110, 113–115, 120, 126
    hearing, 6–7
    language, 6–7, 295–296, 312
    milieu, 201–202, 295
    neurodevelopmental, 109
    occupational, 7, 90–91, 108–109, 138, 141, 286, 295–296, 312
    parental, 155
    physical, 90–91, 108, 138, 141, 286, 295–296, 312
    radiation, 125
    speech, 6–7, 21, 90–91, 109, 295–296, 312
    vitamin, 179, 197
Time sampling, 172
Timeout, 36, 47–48, 60–64, 200
Title XIX reimbursement, 88
Toilet training, 3, 9, 46–47

Token economy, 200
TOLD, see The Test of Language Development
Toxic amblyopia, 291
Tracking, visual, 303
Training, 52, 196, 297, 303
    communication, 39, 41, 45–46, 90, 304–306
    mobility, 3, 15, 27, 286, 295–296, 309
    toilet, 3, 9, 46–47
    visual-perceptual, 302–304
    vocational, 33–38, 46, 205, 300, 309–311
Tranquilizers, 197
Transdisciplinary approaches, 88–89, 92
Transfer of students, 29
Transformational rules of language, 249–251, 253, 260
Transportation skills, 46, 49
Treatment
    of chronic renal diseases, 123
    of congenital defects, 98–99, 101–104
    of cystic fibrosis, 119–120
    of hearing loss, 293
    of heart defects, 126
    of muscular dystrophy, 121
    of neurological disorders, 108–109, 111, 114–115, 117–118
    surgery as, see Surgery as treatment
    of tumors, 125
The Treatment and Education of Autistic and Related Communications Handicapped Children Program (TEACCH), 204
Treatment emergent symptoms (TES), 197
Treatment programs, 65, 194–202, 255–256, 293–294
Tuberous sclerosis, 180
Tumbling E Chart, 273
Tumors, 124–125
Twins, research on, 177–178, 254

University affiliated facilities (UAFs), 88
U.S. Department of Health, Education, and Welfare (HEW), 160

Uzgiris and Hunt's Ordinal Scales of Psychological Development, 278

Validity of tests, 18, 172
VARS, *see* Vocational Adaptation Rating Scale
Verb phrase (VP), 221, 248–251
Verbal development, 25, 227, 304
  see also Language development; Speech development
Victor, the wild boy of Aveyron, 1, 156
Vineland Social Maturity Scale, 14, 174, 272
Viruses, prenatal, 294
Vision impairments, 105, 107, 110, 229, 244, 269–312
  causes of, 279, 281, 290
Vision testing, 273–274
Visual acuity, 167, 273
Visual discrimination, 52
Visual-motor skills, 274, 303
Visual stimuli with auditory stimuli, 256, 272
Visual training, 302–304
Visually-reinforced audiometry, 273
Vitamins, 178–179, 194, 197
Vocalization, 162, 171, 219–220
Vocational Adaptation Rating Scale (VARS), 38
Vocational rehabilitation, 15, 31, 310–311
Vocational responsibilities, 14
Vocational skills, 30, 33, 35, 38, 53

Vocational tests, 31–33, 311
Vocational training, 31, 33–38, 46, 205, 300, 309–311
VP, *see* Verb phrase

Waisman Center on Mental Retardation and Human Development, 36
Walker Problem Behavior Identification Checklist, 167
Wechsler Intelligence Scale for Children (WISC), 222, 272
Wechsler Preschool and Primary Scale of Intelligence (WPPSI), 222
Wepman Auditory Discrimination Test, 247
Werry and Quay Observational Procedure, 172–173
Wheelchairs, 3, 9, 111
Wide Range Achievement Test (WRAT), 32
WISC, *see* Wechsler Intelligence Scale for Children
Wolpe, Joseph, 182
Word Association Test, Jung's, 174
Word comprehension, 247
Word deafness, 290
Word finding, language functions in, 240
Work settings of deaf-blind children, simulated, 309–310
WPPSI, *see* Wechsler Preschool and Primary Scale of Intelligence
WRAT, *see* Wide Range Achievement Test

DISCHARGED
JUL 17 1989
DISCHARGED 1985
APR DISCH 1990

7 1986
DISCHARGED

MAR 19 1985

DISCHARGED
OCT 28 1986

FEB 27 1987

DISCHARGED
MAR 12 1987

FEB 23 1989